2011

U.S.
COIN
Digest

The Complete Guide to Current Market Values

Published by

krause publication

A division of F+W Media, Inc.

700 East State Street • Iola, WI 54990-0001
715-445-2214 • 888-457-2873
www.krausebooks.com

For a numismatic product catalog visit www.shopnumismaster.com

ISSN 1544-8517

ISBN-13: 978-1-4402-1157-7
ISBN-10: 1-4402-1157-4

Designed by Sandi Carpenter
Edited by Debbie Bradley

Printed in China

Contents

Preface 4

Introduction.. 5

Chapter 1 - Type Identification Guide 6

Chapter 2 - Care & Storage of Your Coins 13

Chapter 3 - How to Grade 16

Chapter 4 - Organization is Key... 33

Chapter 5 - Treasures in Your Set? 37

Chapter 6 - 10 Ways to Buy Coins... 39

Chapter 7 - Five Tips on Selling 44

Chapter 8 - American Coin History... 49

U.S. Mint Issues 56

U.S. Commemoratives 153

U.S. Bullion Coins... 184

U.S. Sets & Rolls 194

U.S. Colonial & Early Coinage 202

Territorial Gold 235

Hawaii, Philippines and Puerto Rico 262

Glossary 271

Index... 276

Preface

Since 1952, Krause Publications has built its business and reputation by serving the needs of coin collectors. Three questions dominate every collector's thinking.

The first is: "What is it?" We hope the photographs in this price guide will help you identify the coins you own.

The second question is: "What's it worth?" The prices contained in this volume are intended to serve as a retail guide. That means if you want to buy a specific coin in a specific grade, the price listed will be approximately what you would have to pay at the time this book was compiled. The prices listed are neither an offer to buy nor an offer to sell the coins listed. They are simply a guide assembled for your convenience by the authors. Remember that prices fluctuate. What dealers will pay to buy coins from you is a question beyond the scope of this book.

The third question is: "How do I buy a specific coin?" There are several thousand coin dealers across America who are ready, willing and able to serve your needs. To find them, you can consult the phone book in your local area, but beyond that, there is a whole hobby world out there and newspapers and magazines that feature advertisements by dealers who want to fill your needs. For more information on numismatic products and pricing go to www.numismaster.com.

Photo Credits

We wish to thank the following auction houses and individuals for the fabulous color images contained within these pages.

Mike Locke

Jay M. Galst, M.D.

Chester L. Krause

Heritage Numismatic Auctions, Inc.
3500 Maple Ave.
17th Floor
Dallas, Texas 75219
www.HeritageCoins.com

Stack's
123 West 57th St.
New York, NY 10019-2280
www.stacks.com

Ken Potter
P.O. Box 760232
Lathrup Village, MI 48076
www.koinpro.com

Introduction

The authors have organized this book in a manner that we hope you will find both logical and useful.

Value listings

Values listed in the price guide are average retail prices. These are the approximate prices collectors can expect to pay when purchasing coins from dealers. They are not offers to buy or sell. The pricing section should be considered a guide only; actual selling prices will vary.

The values were compiled by Krause Publications' independent staff of market analysts. They derived the values listed by monitoring auction results, business on electronic dealer trading networks and at major shows, and in consultation with a panel of dealers. For rare coins, when only a few specimens of a particular date and mintmark are known, a confirmed transaction may occur only once every several years. In those instances, the most recent auction result is listed.

Grading

Values are listed for coins in various states of preservation, or grades. Standards used in determining grade for U.S. coins are those set by the American Numismatic Association (www.money.org). See Chapter 4 for more on grading.

Precious metal content

Throughout this book precious metal content is indicated in troy ounces. One troy ounce equals 480 grains, or 31.103 grams. This is followed by ASW or AGW, which stand for Actual Silver (Gold) Weight.

Dates and mintmarks

The dates listed are the individual dates that appear on each coin. The letter that follows the date is the mintmark and indicates where the coin was struck: "C" – Charlotte, N.C. (1838-1861); "CC" – Carson City, Nev. (1870-1893); "D" – Dahlonega, Ga. (1838-1861), and Denver (1906-present); "O" – New Orleans (1838-1909); "P" – Philadelphia (1793-present), coins without mintmarks also were struck at Philadelphia; "S" – San Francisco (1854-present); and "W" – West Point, N.Y. (1984-present).

A slash mark in a date indicates an overdate. This means a new date was engraved on a die over an old date. For example, if the date is listed as "1899/8," an 1898 die had a 9 engraved over the last 8 in the date. Portions of the old numeral are still visible on the coin.

A slash mark in a mintmark listing indicates an overmintmark (example: "1922-P/ D"). The same process as above occurred, but this time a new mintmark was engraved over an old.

See Chapter 3, "U.S. Minting Varieties and Errors," for more information on overdates and overmintmarks.

1 Type Identification Guide

United States coins are often given nicknames based on their obverse design. This Type Identification Guide is a start for coin identification. It also shows the changes in the sizes of various denominations over time.

Half Cent

Liberty Cap

Draped Bust   Classic Head   Braided Hair

Large Cent

Liberty Cap   Draped Bust   Classic Head

Coronet   Braided Hair   Flowing Hair

Small Cent

Flying Eagle

Indian Head

Lincoln

Shield

Silver 3 Cents

Coronet

Half Dime

Flowing Hair

Draped Bust

Liberty Cap

Seated Liberty

Nickel

Shield

Liberty

Buffalo

Jefferson

Jefferson
large profile

Jefferson
large facing portrait

Dime

Draped Bust

Liberty Cap

Seated Liberty

Barber

Mercury

Roosevelt

Twenty Cents

Seated Liberty within circle of stars

Quarter

Draped Bust

Liberty Cap

Seated Liberty

Barber

Standing Liberty

Washington

50 State

Half Dollar

Flowing Hair

Draped Bust

Capped Bust

Seated Liberty

Barber

Walking Liberty

Franklin

Kennedy

Dollar

Flowing Hair

Gobrecht

Draped Bust

Seated Liberty

Morgan

Trade

Peace

Eisenhower

Dollar

Susan B. Anthony

Sacagawea

 Liberty Head - Type 1

 Indian Head - Type 2

 Indian Head - Type 3

$2.50 Gold Quarter Eagle

Liberty Cap   Turban Head   Coronet Head   Indian Head

$3.00 Gold

Indian Head with headress

$5.00 Gold Half Eagle

Liberty Cap

Turban Head

Indian Head

Classic Head

Coronet Head

$10.00 Gold Eagle

Liberty Cap

Coronet Head

Indian Head

$20.00 Gold Double Eagle

Coronet Head

Saint-Gaudens

2 Care and Storage of Your Coins

Use caution to retain coin's value

Once you find a coin you love, or begin to build a collection that you are dedicating time and money to, you really need to consider proper care and storage methods. Careless handling of your coins can quickly lead to loss of value.

Here is some quick and simple advice, which you should always follow when handling your coins:
- Always hold your coin by the edge.
- Never touch your coin on its large surfaces.

You leave fingerprints on surfaces that you touch and fingerprints on coins cause long-term damage which degrades the quality of your coin. If you are not comfortable handling your coins, it is best to wear special gloves available through coin supply dealers and to do your work over a jeweler's tray for your coins safety.

Another quick and simple bit of advice regarding cleaning your coins:
- Don't clean coins.

Some coins you acquire may seem dirty to you and an early impulse may be to clean them. Many inexperienced collectors degrade or even destroy their coins value through cleaning. Most cleaning methods are abrasive and remove not only the dirt, but also the metal surface of the coin. In most instances you will damage your coins value by attempting to clean them, so don't.

Most collectors enjoy examining the coins they have acquired and some collectors concentrate on finding varieties. Close examination requires magnification. The following instruments are commonly used to examine coins more closely:
- Magnifying glass
- Jeweler's loupe
- Microscope

Magnifiers come in different strengths and all shapes and sizes. Most coin collectors find a 5x magnifying glass quite versatile for checking out a coin's surface for wear. When looking for varieties, a 10x loupe works pretty well. For a closer look, many specialists use a 10x to 60x adjustable microscope. Each of these tools has its proper use and appropriate cost. Start simple with a nice 5x magnifier and see how it works for you.

Spend a little time at a coin show or in a coin shop and you will see that there are many different methods of storing your coins. The simplest are coin envelopes, which are produced in various colors of paper and are usually 2-inch by 2-inch in size. Information can be written on these holders, the coin inserted and the flap tucked in so that the coin does not easily fall out if the envelope is tipped or dropped. If you use coin envelopes, it is best to stick with plain white paper, as colored paper will tone your coin over time. When writing information on the envelope, do so before you insert the coin and use a ball-point pen or pencil, as a felt-tip marker may bleed through and harm your coin.

For standard sized U.S. coins, coin boards have been used for many years as a simple cataloging and storage method for beginning collectors. Coin boards provide several useful services. Coin boards:
- Organize your collection.
- Focus your attention on a single type of coin.
- Offer a cheap method of storage.

Sounds pretty good? Yes, for common circulating coins, the coin board is a great way to get started. However, there are drawbacks to this system that you may notice over time. You may find that it is difficult to insert your coins in the board and to get them to stay put. Because of this, you may find that you are handling your coins too much. If you don't place a soft cloth over the coin before you push it into the board, you will leave a fingerprint on the coin's surface. Over time you will notice that material from which the board was manufactured may have added a color tint to your coins. This is called toning. Some collectors like toning and some do not, so toning may hamper or help in your collection's appreciation over time.

If you like the display feature of boards, but do not care for some of these drawbacks, you can consider using any number of the vast array of containment storage methods available. There are hard plastic holders, tight plastic capsules, plastic envelopes called flips, and die-cut cardboard holders with Mylar lining. The last three of these can be inserted in pocket sheets for three ring binder display or simply placed into special coin boxes for storage.

The simplest and most widely used of these individual storage methods is the die cut cardboard holder with Mylar lining. These holders come in different size die cuts. To use this type of holder, follow these simple steps:
- Choose a die cut that is slightly larger than your coin.
- Place your coin on the Mylar over the die cut hole.
- Carefully fold the top over your coin.
- Grasp the holder and coin between your thumb and forefinger.
- Carefully staple the three open sides of the holder to secure your coin.
- Flatten the staples with a set of pliers.

Once this process is complete, you can write information on the outer edges of the cardboard to catalog, value and grade or otherwise identify the attributes of your coin.

Plastic flip envelopes are made from different materials. There are soft plastic types and hard plastic types. The soft plastic should only be used for short term storage. Soft plastic flips contain polyvinylchloride or PVC which, over time, can cause serious damage to your coins in the form of a green corrosive slime which eats away at the coin's surface. The hard plastic is normally made from Mylar, which does not contain PVC, but does get brittle and can crack as it ages. Both types of flips are constructed with two pockets, one for your coin and one for a small, square piece of paper or thin cardboard on which you can write your coin's catalog information.

The storage methods mentioned above are good for low to medium value coins. If your collecting advances into coins of higher value, you may want to consider a third party grading service. These services will grade and encapsulate your coin in an airtight hard plastic holder containing both your coin and coin information.

Use your common sense in choosing appropriate methods of care and storage for maintaining your coins. Here are a few more basic rules to remember:

- Keep you coins in a cool, dry place.
- Make sure your coins are secure from tampering or theft.
- Do not store your coins in a leather pouch or bag.
- Do not allow you coins to knock or slide against each other.
- Put your coins in some sort of holder that protects them.
- Be sure that your choice of holder does not cause damage to your coins.
- Examine your coins regularly and check for any changes.

Your collection can provide you with both an enjoyable hobby and a valuable investment, but it is your responsibility to organize, store, care for and maintain your coins properly.

3 How to Grade

Better condition equals better value

Grading is one of the most important factors in buying and selling coins as collectibles. Unfortunately, it's also one of the most controversial. Since the early days of coin collecting in the United States, buying through the mail has been a convenient way for collectors to acquire coins. As a result, there has always been a need in numismatics for a concise way to classify the amount of wear on a coin and its condition in general.

A look back

In September 1888, Dr. George Heath, a physician in Monroe, Mich., published a four-page pamphlet titled *The American Numismatist*. Publication of subsequent issues led to the founding of the American Numismatic Association, and *The Numismatist*, as it's known today, is the association's official journal. Heath's first issues were largely devoted to selling world coins from his collection. There were no formal grades listed with the coins and their prices, but the following statement by Heath indicates that condition was a consideration for early collectors:

"The coins are in above average condition," Heath wrote, "and so confident am I that they will give satisfaction, that I agree to refund the money in any unsatisfactory sales on the return of the coins."

As coin collecting became more popular and *The Numismatist* started accepting paid advertising from others, grading became more formal. The February 1892 issue listed seven "classes" for the condition of coins (from worst to best): mutilated, poor, fair, good, fine, uncirculated, and proof. Through the years, the hobby has struggled with developing a grading system that would be accepted by all and could apply to all coins. The hobby's growth was accompanied by a desire for more grades, or classifications, to more precisely define a coin's condition. The desire for more precision, however, was at odds with the basic concept of grading: to provide a concise method for classifying a coin's condition.

For example, even the conservatively few classifications of 1892 included fudge factors.

"To give flexibility to this classification," *The Numismatist* said, "such modification of find, good and fair, as 'extremely,' 'very,' 'almost,' etc., are used to express slight variations from the general condition."

The debate over grading continued for decades in *The Numismatist*. A number of articles and letters prodded the ANA to write grading guidelines and endorse them as the association's official standards. Some submitted specific suggestions for terminology and accompanying standards for each grade. But grading remained a process of "instinct" gained through years of collecting or dealing experience.

A formal grading guide in book form finally appeared in 1958, but it was the work of two individuals rather than the ANA. *A Guide to the Grading of United States Coins* by Martin R. Brown and John W. Dunn was a break-through in the great grading debate. Now collectors had a reference that gave them specific guidelines for specific coins and could be studied and restudied at home.

The first editions of Brown and Dunn carried text only, no illustrations. For the fourth edition, in 1964, publication was assumed by Whitman Publishing Co. of Racine, Wis., and line drawings were added to illustrate the text.

The fourth edition listed six principal categories for circulated coins (from worst to best): good, very good, fine, very fine, extremely fine, and about uncirculated. But again, the desire for more precise categories was evidenced. In the book's introduction, Brown and Dunn wrote, "Dealers will sometimes advertise coins that are graded G-VG, VG-F, F-VF, VF-XF. Or the description may be ABT. G. or VG plus, etc. This means that the coin in question more than meets minimum standards for the lower grade but is not quite good enough for the higher grade."

When the fifth edition appeared, in 1969, the "New B & D Grading System" was introduced. The six principal categories for circulated coins were still intact, but variances within those categories were now designated by up to four letters: "A," "B," "C" or "D." For example, an EF-A coin was "almost about uncirculated." An EF-B was "normal extra fine" within the B & D standards. EF-C had a "normal extra fine" obverse, but the reverse was "obviously not as nice as obverse due to poor strike or excessive wear." EF-D had a "normal extra fine" reverse but a problem obverse.

But that wasn't the end. Brown and Dunn further listed 29 problem points that could appear on a coin – from No. 1 for an "edge bump" to No. 29 for "attempted re-engraving outside of the Mint." The number could be followed by the letter "O" or "R" to designate whether the problem appeared on the obverse or reverse and a Roman numeral corresponding to a clock face to designate where the problem appears on the obverse or reverse. For example, a coin described as "VG-B-9-O-X" would grade "VG-B"; the "9" designated a "single rim nick"; the "O" indicated the nick was on the obverse; and the "X" indicated it appeared at the 10 o'clock position, or upper left, of the obverse.

The authors' goal was noble – to create the perfect grading system. They again, however, fell victim to the age-old grading-system problem: Precision comes at the expense of brevity. Dealer Kurt Krueger wrote in the January 1976 issues of *The Numismatist*, "Under the new B & D system, the numismatist must contend with a minimum of 43,152 different grading combinations! Accuracy is apparent, but simplicity has been lost." As a result, the "New B & D Grading System" never caught on in the marketplace.

The 1970s saw two important grading guides make their debut. The first was *Photograde* by James F. Ruddy. As the title implies, Ruddy uses photographs instead of line drawings to show how coins look in the various circulated grades. Simplicity is also a virtue of Ruddy's book. Only seven circulated grades are listed (about good, good, very good, fine, very fine, extremely fine, and about uncirculated), and the designations stop there.

In 1977 the longtime call for the ANA to issue grading standards was met with the release of *Official A.N.A. Grading Standards for United States Coins*. Like Brown and Dunn, the first edition of the ANA guide used line drawings to illustrate coins in various states of wear. But instead of using adjectival descriptions, the ANA guide adopted a numerical system for designating grades.

The numerical designations were based on a system used by Dr. William H. Sheldon in his book *Early American Cents*, first published in 1949. He used a scale of 1 to 70 to designate the grades of large cents.

"On this scale," Sheldon wrote, "1 means that the coin is identifiable and not mutilated – no more than that. A 70-coin is one in flawless Mint State, exactly as it left the dies, with perfect mint color and without a blemish or nick."

(Sheldon's scale also had its pragmatic side. At the time, a No. 2 large cent was worth about twice a No. 1 coin; a No. 4 was worth about twice a No. 2, and so on up the scale.)

With the first edition of its grading guide, the ANA adopted the 70-point scale for grading all U.S. coins. It designated 10 categories of circulated grades: AG-3, G-4, VG-8, F-12, VF-20, VF-30, EF-40, EF-45, AU-50, and AU-55. The third edition, released in 1987, replaced the line drawings with photographs, and another circulated grade was added: AU-58. A fourth edition was released in 1991.

Grading circulated U.S. coins

Dealers today generally use either the ANA guide or *Photograde* when grading circulated coins for their inventories. (Brown and Dunn is now out of print.) Many local coin shops sell both books. Advertisers in *Numismatic News, Coins* magazine, and *Coin Prices* must indicate which standards they are using in grading their coins. If the standards are not listed, they must conform to ANA standards.

Following are some general guidelines, accompanied by photos, for grading circulated U.S. coins. Grading even circulated pieces can be subjective, particularly when attempting to draw the fine line between, for example, AU-55 and AU-58. Two longtime collectors or dealers can disagree in such a case.

But by studying some combination of the following guidelines, the ANA guide, and *Photograde*, and by looking at a lot of coins at shops and shows, collectors can gain enough grading knowledge to buy circulated coins confidently from dealers and other collectors. The more you study, the more knowledge and confidence you will gain. When you decide which series of coins you want to collect, focus on the guidelines for that particular series. Read them, reread them, and then refer back to them again and again.

AU-50

AU-50 (about uncirculated): Just a slight trace of wear, result of brief exposure to circulation or light rubbing from mishandling, may be evident on elevated design areas. These imperfections may appear as scratches or dull spots, along with bag marks or edge nicks. At least half of the original mint luster generally is still evident.

Indian cent

Lincoln cent

Buffalo nickel

Jefferson nickel

AU-50

Mercury dime

Standing Liberty quarter

Washington quarter

Walking Liberty half dollar

Morgan dollar

Barber coins

XF-40

XF-40 (extremely fine): The coin must show only slight evidence of wear on the highest points of the design, particularly in the hair lines of the portrait on the obverse. The same may be said for the eagle's feathers and wreath leaves on the reverse of most U.S. coins. A trace of mint luster may still show in protected areas of the coin's surface.

Indian cent	Lincoln cent
Buffalo nickel	Jefferson nickel

XF-40

Mercury dime

Standing Liberty quarter

Washington quarter

Walking Liberty half dollar

Morgan dollar

Barber coins

VF-20

VF-20 (very fine): The coin will show light wear at the fine points in the design, though they may remain sharp overall. Although the details may be slightly smoothed, all lettering and major features must remain sharp.

Indian cent: All letters in "Liberty" are complete but worn. Headdress shows considerable flatness, with flat spots on the tips of the feathers.

Lincoln cent: Hair, cheek, jaw, and bow-tie details will be worn but clearly separated, and wheat stalks on the reverse will be full with no weak spots.

Buffalo nickel: High spots on hair braid and cheek will be flat but show some detail, and a full horn will remain on the buffalo.

Jefferson nickel: Well over half of the major hair detail will remain, and the pillars on Monticello will remain well defined, with the triangular roof partially visible.

Mercury dime: Hair braid will show some detail, and three-quarters of the detail will remain in the feathers. The two diagonal bands on the fasces will show completely but will be worn smooth at the middle, with the vertical lines sharp.

Standing Liberty quarter: Rounded contour of Liberty's right leg will be flattened, as will the high point of the shield.

Washington quarter: There will be considerable wear on the hair curls, with feathers on the right and left of the eagle's breast showing clearly.

Indian cent	**Lincoln cent**
Buffalo nickel	**Jefferson nickel**

VF-20

Walking Liberty half dollar: All lines of the skirt will show but will be worn on the high points. Over half the feathers on the eagle will show.

Morgan dollar: Two-thirds of the hair lines from the forehead to the ear must show. Ear should be well defined. Feathers on the eagle's breast may be worn smooth.

Barber coins: All seven letters of "Liberty" on the headband must stand out sharply. Head wreath will be well outlined from top to bottom.

Mercury dime

Standing Liberty quarter

Washington quarter

Walking Liberty half dollar

Morgan dollar

Barber coins

F-12

F-12 (fine): Coins show evidence of moderate to considerable but generally even wear on all high points, though all elements of the design and lettering remain bold. Where the word "Liberty" appears in a headband, it must be fully visible. On 20th century coins, the rim must be fully raised and sharp.

Indian cent

Lincoln cent

Buffalo nickel

Jefferson nickel

F-12

Mercury dime

Standing Liberty quarter

Washington quarter

Walking Liberty half dollar

Morgan dollar

Barber coins

VG-8

VG-8 (very good): The coin will show considerable wear, with most detail points worn nearly smooth. Where the word "Liberty" appears in a headband, at least three letters must show. On 20th century coins, the rim will start to merge with the lettering.

| Indian cent | Lincoln cent |
| Buffalo nickel | Jefferson nickel |

VG-8

Mercury dime

Standing Liberty quarter

Washington quarter

Walking Liberty half dollar

Morgan dollar

Barber coins

G-4

G-4 (good): Only the basic design remains distinguishable in outline form, will all points of detail worn smooth. The word "Liberty" has disappeared, and the rims are almost merging with the lettering.

About good or fair: The coin will be identifiable by date and mint but otherwise badly worn, with only parts of the lettering showing. Such coins are of value only as fillers in a collection until a better example of the date and mintmark can be obtained. The only exceptions would be rare coins.

Indian cent

Lincoln cent

Buffalo nickel

Jefferson nickel

G-4

Mercury dime

Standing Liberty quarter

Washington quarter

Walking Liberty half dollar

Morgan dollar

Barber coins

Grading uncirculated U.S. coins

The subjectivity of grading and the trend toward more classifications becomes more acute when venturing into uncirculated, or mint-state, coins. A minute difference between one or two grade points can mean a difference in value of hundreds or even thousands of dollars. In addition, the standards are more difficult to articulate in writing and illustrate through drawings or photographs. Thus, the possibilities for differences of opinion on one or two grade points increase in uncirculated coins.

Back in Dr. George Heath's day and continuing through the 1960s, a coin was either uncirculated or it wasn't. Little distinction was made between uncirculated coins of varying condition, largely because there was little if any difference in value. When *Numismatic News* introduced its value guide in 1962 (the forerunner of today's Coin Market section in the *News*), it listed only one grade of uncirculated for Morgan dollars.

But as collectible coins increased in value and buyers of uncirculated coins became more picky, distinctions within uncirculated grade started to surface. In 1975 *Numismatic News* still listed only one uncirculated grade in Coin Market, but added this note: "Uncirculated and proof specimens in especially choice condition will also command proportionately higher premiums than these listed."

The first edition of the ANA guide listed two grades of uncirculated, MS-60 and MS-65, in addition to the theoretical but non-existent MS-70 (a flawless coin). MS-60 was described as "typical uncirculated" and MS-65 as "choice uncirculated." *Numismatic News* adopted both designations for Coin Market. In 1981, when the second edition of the ANA grading guide was released, MS-67 and MS-63 were added. In 1985 *Numismatic News* started listing six grades of uncirculated for Morgan dollars: MS-60, MS-63, MS-65, MS-65+, and MS-63 prooflike.

Then in 1986, a new entity appeared that has changed the nature of grading and trading uncirculated coins ever since. A group of dealers led by David Hall of Newport Beach, Calif., formed the Professional Coin Grading Service. For a fee, collectors could submit a coin through an authorized PCGS dealer and receive back a professional opinion of its grade.

The concept was not new; the ANA had operated an authentication service

Collectors have a variety of grading services to choose from. This set of Arkansas half dollars that appeared in an Early American History Auctions sale used two of the services.

since 1972 and a grading service since 1979. A collector or dealer could submit a coin directly to the service and receive a certificate giving the service's opinion on authenticity and grade. The grading service was the source of near constant debate among dealers and ANA officials. Dealers charged that ANA graders were too young and inexperienced, and that their grading was inconsistent.

Grading stability was a problem throughout the coin business in the early 1980s, not just with the ANA service. Standards among uncirculated grades would tighten during a bear market and loosen during a bull market. As a result, a coin graded MS-65 in a bull market may have commanded only MS-63 during a bear market.

PCGS created several innovations in the grading business in response to these problems:

1. Coins could be submitted through PCGS-authorized dealers only.

2. Each coin would be graded by at least three members of a panel of "top graders," all prominent dealers in the business. (Since then, however, PCGS does not allow its graders to also deal in coins.)

3. After grading, the coin would be encapsulated in an inert, hard-plastic holder with a serial number and the grade indicated on the holder.

4. PCGS-member dealers pledged to make a market in PCGS-graded coins and honor the grades assigned.

5. In one of the most far-reaching moves, PCGS said it would use all 11 increments of uncirculated on the 70-point numerical scale: MS-60, MS-61, MS-62, MS-63, MS-64, MS-65, MS-66, MS-67, MS-68, MS-69, and MS-70.

Numerous other commercial grading services followed in the steps of PCGS

and third-party grading is an accepted part of the hobby.

How should a collector approach the buying and grading of uncirculated coins? Collecting uncirculated coins worth thousands of dollars implies a higher level of numismatic expertise by the buyer. Those buyers without that level of expertise should cut their teeth on more inexpensive coins, just as today's experienced collectors did. Inexperienced collectors can start toward that level by studying the guidelines for mint-state coins in the ANA grading guide and looking at lots of coins at shows and shops.

Study the condition and eye appeal of a coin and compare it to other coins of the same series. Then compare prices. Do the more expensive coins look better? If so, why? Start to make your own judgments concerning relationships between condition and value. Experience remains the best teacher in the field of grading.

Grading U.S. proof coins

Because proof coins are struck by a special process using polished blanks, they receive their own grading designation. A coin does not start out being a proof and then become mint state if it becomes worn. Once a proof coin, always a proof coin.

In the ANA system, proof grades use the same numbers as circulated and uncirculated grades, and the amount of wear on the coin corresponds to those grades. But the number is preceded by the word "proof." For example, Proof-65, Proof-55, Proof-45, and so on. In addition, the ANA says a proof coin with many marks, scratches or other defects should be called an "impaired proof."

4 Organization is Key

Sets worth more than accumulations

There are two major ways to organize a collection: by type, and by date and mint-mark. By following either method, you will create a logically organized set that other collectors perceive as having a value greater than a random group of similar coins

Let's take collecting by type first. Look at a jar of coins, or take the change out of your pocket. You find Abraham Lincoln and the Lincoln Memorial on current cents. You find Thomas Jefferson and his home, Monticello, on the nickel. Franklin D. Roosevelt and a torch share the dime. George Washington and the eagle, or the more recent state, territories and park designs, appear on the quarter. John F. Kennedy and the presidential seal are featured on the half dollar. Sacagawea and Presidents adorn the dollar coins.

Each design is called a "type." If you took one of each and put the five coins in a holder, you would have a type set of the coins that are currently being produced for circulation by the U.S. Mint.

With just these five coins, you can study various metallic compositions. You can evaluate their states of preservation and assign a grade to each. You can learn about the artists who designed the coins, and you can learn of the times in which these designs were created.

As you might have guessed, many different coin types have been used in the United States over the years. You may remember seeing some of them circulating. These designs reflect the hopes and aspirations of people over time. Putting all of them together forms a wonderful numismatic mosaic of American history.

George Washington did not mandate that his image appear on the quarter. Quite the contrary. He would have been horrified. When he was president, he headed off those individuals in Congress who thought the leader of the country should have his image on its coins. Washington said it smacked of monarchy and would have nothing to do with it.

Almost a century and a half later, during the bicentennial of Washington's birth in 1932, a nation searching for its roots during troubled economic times decided that it needed his portrait on its coins as a reminder of his great accomplishments and as reassurances that this nation was the same place it had been in prosperous days.

In its broadest definition, collecting coins by type requires that you obtain an example of every design that was struck by the U.S. Mint since it was founded in 1792. That's a tall order. You would be looking for denominations like the half cent, two-cent piece, three-cent piece, and 20-cent piece, which have not been produced in over a century. You would be looking for gold coins ranging in face value from $1 to $50.

But even more important than odd-sounding denominations or high face values is the question of rarity. Some of the pieces in this two-century type set are rare and expensive. That's why type collectors often divide the challenge into more digestible units.

Type collecting can be divided into 18th, 19th, 20th and 21st century units. Starting type collectors can focus on 20th century coin designs, which are easily obtainable. The fun and satisfaction of putting the 20th or 21st century set together then creates the momentum to continue backward in time. In the process of putting a 20th century type set together, one is also learning how to grade, learning hobby jargon, and discovering how to obtain coins from dealers, the U.S. Mint, and other collectors. All of this knowledge is then refined as the collector increases the challenge to himself.

This book is designed to help. How many dollar types were struck in the 20th century? Turn to the price-guide section and check it out. We see the Morgan dollar, Peace dollar, Eisenhower dollar, and Anthony dollar. The Sacagawea dollar arrived in 2000 and the Presidential dollars in 2007. Hobbyists could also add the Ike dollar with the Bicentennial design of 1976 and the silver American Eagle bullion coin struck since 1986. One can also find out their approximate retail prices from the listings. The beauty of type collecting is that one can choose the most inexpensive example of each type. There is no need to select a 1903-O Morgan when the 1921 will do just as well. With the 20th century type set, hobbyists can dodge some truly big-league prices.

As a collector's hobby confidence grows, he can tailor goals to fit his desires. He can take the road less traveled if that is what suits him. Type sets can be divided by denomination. You can choose two centuries of one-cent coins. You can take just obsolete denominations or copper, silver or gold denominations.

You can even collect by size. Perhaps you would like to collect all coin types larger than 30 millimeters or all coins smaller than 20 millimeters. Many find this freedom of choice stimulating.

Type collecting has proven itself to be enduringly popular over the years. It provides a maximum amount of design variety while allowing collectors to set their own level of challenge.

The second popular method of collecting is by date and mintmark. What this means, quite simply, is that a collector picks a given type – Jefferson nickels, for example – and then goes after an example of every year, every mintmark, and every type of manufacture that was used with the Jefferson design.

Looking at this method of collecting brings up the subject of mintmarks. The "U.S. Mint" is about as specific as most non-collectors get in describing the government agency that provides everyday coins. Behind that label are the various production facilities that actually do the work.

In two centuries of U.S. coinage, there have been eight such facilities. Four are still in operation. Those eight in alphabetical order are Carson City, Nev., which used a "CC" mintmark to identify its work; Charlotte, N.C. ("C"); Dahlonega, Ga. ("D"); Denver (also uses a "D," but it opened long after the Dahlonega Mint closed, so there was never any confusion); New Orleans ("O"); Philadelphia (because it was the primary mint, it used no mintmark for most of its history, but currently uses a "P"); San Francisco ("S"); and West Point, N.Y. ("W").

A person contemplating the collecting of Jefferson nickels by date and mintmark will find that three mints produced them: San Francisco, Denver and Philadelphia. Because the first two are branch mints serving smaller populations, their output has tended over time to be smaller than that of Philadelphia. This fact, repeated in other series, has helped give mintmarks quite an allure to collectors. It provides one of the major attractions in collecting coins by date and mintmark.

The key date for Jeffersons is the 1950-D when using mintages as a guide. In that year, production was just 2.6 million pieces. Because collectors of the time were aware of the coin's low mintage, many examples were saved. As a result, prices are reasonable.

The Depression-era 1939-D comes in as the most valuable regular-issue Jefferson nickel despite a mintage of 3.5 million – almost 1 million more than the 1950-D. The reason: Fewer were saved for later generations of coin collectors.

Date and mintmark collecting teaches hobbyists to use mintage figures as a guide but to take them with a grain of salt. Rarity, after all, is determined by the number of surviving coins, not the number initially created.

The Jefferson series is a good one to collect by date and mintmark, because the mintmarks have moved around, grown in size, and expanded in number.

When the series was first introduced, the Jefferson nickel was produced at the three mints previously mentioned. In 1942, because of a diversion of certain metals to wartime use, the coin's alloy of 75 percent copper and 25 percent nickel was changed. The new alloy was 35 percent silver, 56 percent copper, and 9 percent manganese.

To denote the change, the mintmarks were moved and greatly enlarged. The pre-1942 mintmarks were small and located to the right of Monticello; the wartime mintmarks were enlarged and placed over the dome. What's more, for the first time in American history, the Philadelphia Mint used a mintmark ("P").

The war's end restored the alloy and mintmarks to their previous status. The "P" disappeared. This lasted until the 1960s, when a national coin shortage saw all mintmarks removed for three years (1965-1967) and then returned, but in a different location. Mintmarks were placed on the obverse, to the right of Jefferson's portrait near the date in 1968. In 1980 the "P" came back in a smaller form and is still used.

Another consideration arises with date and mintmark collecting: Should the hobbyist include proof coins in the set? This can be argued both ways. Suffice to say that anyone who has the desire to add proof coins to the set will have a larger one. It is not necessary nor is it discouraged.

Some of the first proof coins to carry mintmarks were Jefferson nickels. When proof coins were made in 1968 after lapsing from 1965 to 1967, production occurred at San Francisco instead of Philadelphia. The "S" mintmark was placed on the proof coins of that year, including the Jefferson nickel, to denote the change. Since that time, mintmarks used on proof examples of various denominations have included the "P," "D," "S," and "W."

For all of the mintmark history that is embodied in the Jefferson series, prices are reasonable. For a first attempt at collecting coins by date and mintmark, it provides excellent background for going on to the more expensive and difficult types. After all, if you are ever going to get used to the proper handling of a coin, it is far better to experiment on a low-cost coin than a high-value rarity.

As one progresses in date and mintmark collecting and type collecting, it is important to remember that all of the coins should be of similar states of preservation. Sets look slapdash if one coin is VG and another is MS-65 and still another is VF. Take a look at the prices of all the coins in the series before you get too far, figure out what you can afford, and then stick to that grade or range of grades.

Sure, there is a time-honored practice of filling a spot with any old example until a better one comes along. That is how we got the term "filler." But if you get a few placeholders, don't stop there. By assembling a set of uniform quality, you end up with a more aesthetically pleasing and more valuable collection.

The date and mintmark method used to be the overwhelmingly dominant form of collecting. It still has many adherents. Give it a try if you think it sounds right for you.

Before we leave the discussion of collecting U.S. coins, it should be pointed out that the two major methods of organizing a collection are simply guidelines. They are not hard-and-fast rules that must be followed without questions. Collecting should be satisfying to the hobbyist. It should never be just one more item in the daily grind. Take the elements of these aproaches that you like and ignore the rest.

It should also be pointed out that U.S. coinage history does not start with 1792 nor do all of the coins struck since that time conform precisely to the two major organizational approaches. But these two areas are good places to start.

There are coins and tokens from the American Colonial period (1607-1776) that are just as fascinating and collectible as regular U.S. Mint issues. There are federal issues struck before the Mint was actually established. See the Colonial price-guide section in this book.

There are special coins called commemoratives, which have been struck by the U.S. Mint since 1892 to celebrate some aspect of American history or a contemporary event. They are not intended for circulation. There was a long interruption between 1954 and 1982, but currently numerous commemoratives are being offered for sale directly to collectors by the Mint.

Collecting commemoratives has always been considered something separate from collecting regular U.S. coinage. It is, however, organized the same way. Commemoratives can be collected by date and mintmark or by type.

Current commemoratives can be purchased from the U.S. Mint. Check the Web site at www.usmint.gov or telephone (800) USA-MINT.

Buying coins from the Mint can be considered a hobby pursuit in its own right. Some collectors let the Mint organize their holdings for them. They buy complete sets and put them away. They never buy anything from anywhere else.

Admittedly, this is a passive form of collecting, but there are individuals around the world who enjoy collecting at this level without ever really going any deeper. They like acquiring every new issue as it comes off the Mint's presses.

Once done, there is a certain knowledge that one has all the examples of the current year. Obviously, too, collectors by date and mintmark of the current types would have to buy the new coins each year, but, of course, they do not stop there.

5 Treasures in Your Set?

Discover hidden value in ultra grades

If you like treasure hunts or believe in second chances, the dealer market is signaling it is time for both. Due to a shift in grading interpretations by commercial third-party grading services, modern commemorative coins that you bought 10 or 15 years ago from the U.S. Mint might now be worth more than you think. So get out your sets and start checking. It is even affecting Lincoln cents previously thought common.

Consider the 1986-W Statue of Liberty $5 gold piece. The proof version was sold to collectors for $170 each during the pre-issue discount period and the uncirculated version was sold for $160. They nearly tripled in price in trading on the secondary market in early 1986 before collapsing to $90, barely more than bullion value. Prices have stayed below issue price for many years. Even now, if you wanted to buy the coins on the ordinary secondary market, you probably wouldn't have to pay much more than $100 for either one. They look nice, housed as they are in the Mint's original acrylic plastic capsule. But what a difference it makes housed in a plastic slab with a new desirable grade of MS-70 or Proof-70 ultra cameo attached to it from a reputable third-party grading service. An MS-70 is retailing for $295, according to advertisements in *Numismatic News*, a popular weekly hobby newspaper. A Proof-70 UCAM is $350. With those kind of prices, it might be worth your while to pull out your coins and see if they might get the big money. The key, of course, is sending them in to third-party grading services. These services have rules you must follow and fees you must pay. In the end, your coins might not measure up to the new ultra-high grades.

What makes this new grading phenomenon so startling is that it applies to numerous commemorative issues that for many years had been considered common. Take the 1987-W Constitution $5 gold piece. This issue holds the mintage record for the gold $5 commemorative series. There are 214,225 uncirculated pieces and 651,659 proofs. In the original Mint holders they are trading for around $100, but put one in a slab with MS-70 or Proof-70 on it and the price becomes $260.

In effect, by checking over coins that you may have purchased years ago, you get a second shot at the brass ring of profit. After seeing the Statue of Liberty $5 coins soar, more than a few collectors ordered the 1987-W Constitution in hopes of a repeat performance. That didn't happen, but 16 years later, it might now be time to try again.

Throw in another factor, such as a much lower mintage, and prices go even higher.

The 1997-W Franklin Delano Roosevelt $5 gold commemoratives are trading at hardly more than issue price in the $230-$250 range. But that's still more than double the ordinary Statue of Liberty and Constitution prices, reflecting the fact that mintages were lower. The uncirculated FDR $5 has a mintage of 11,805. The proof version is 29,233. Add the ultra-grade factor and the price of an MS-70 FDR $5 is $650. Do you have one in your set?

Even impatient people can get a reward. An issue as recent as the 2001-W Capitol Visitors Center $5 trades at $1,350. Its mintage is even lower than the FDR commemorative coins. The uncirculated version has a mintage of 6,761. The proof mintage is 27,652.

There is not enough space on these pages to list every single modern commemorative issue's turbocharged price in an ultra grade, but it is fair to generalize that these higher grades tend to raise the price significantly across the board. Even in the ultra grades, mintage numbers mean something. Lower mintages tend to mean higher prices.

It is also fair to say that this is a new hobby happening. When the 2003 edition of this book was assembled, nobody had ever heard of ultra-grade modern commemoratives. Condition rarity was something that was usually confined to older collector coins. Collectors, however, are nothing if not ingenious. If the concept can apply to Morgan dollars and Walking Liberty half dollars, why not the modern commemorative coins that have been struck since 1982? If the American Numismatic Association-created and sanctioned numerical grading system includes numbers up to 70, why not use them? It doesn't seem to matter that when the numerical grading system was introduced in 1977 the top numerical designation was considered to be nothing short of perfection. That accounts for the fact that for many years it was never assigned. That psychological barrier has been broken and the use of higher numbers with high price tags attached are now a fact of numismatic life.

A January 2003 auction saw a Proof-70 Deep Cameo 1963 cent sell for $39,100. The Proof-65 price is $1. With over three million 1963 proof sets to search, it is like a lottery. Will you be a prize winner?

So, what are you waiting for? If you are a loyal U.S. Mint customer with some of these issues put away, it is time to get them out and have them professionally evaluated to see if there are any ultra-grade treasures in your possession. It also pays to know that ultra grades are being applied to American Eagle gold and silver bullion coins, which have been struck since 1986, and to the 50-state quarter coins that began in 1999, and even to Roosevelt dimes. Because the hobby never stands still, it probably pays to keep an eye on every other coin series in your collection, for if it hasn't happened yet, the ultra grades will probably soon be applied to them also. For the long-suffering owner of a Statue of Liberty $5, the opportunity to more than double its value is in fact a hobby second chance.

6 10 Ways to Buy Coins

But not all are smart

Coin collecting is not a complicated concept. Collectors want to know what something is. They want to know what it is worth and they want to know how to buy one if it appeals to them.

What could be simpler?

Coin Digest is compiled to tell readers the answers to the first two questions. This book helps identify the many coin issues of the United States and it will tell you what each coin is worth on the retail market in many states of preservation by the terms of the official American Numismatic Association grading system that uses a 1-70 scale in ranking quality. Coins that show no wear are at the top end in the Mint State grades MS-60 to MS-70.

It is the final question of how to buy something that will set the average collector off on a lifetime of acquisitions. It also sets off discussions among collectors as to whether there might be other ways of making purchases, or better ways.

Let's look at 10 purchase methods and see what you think. Most are good. Some are not. Most collectors will use multiple methods to reach their goals.

1. Coin shops

The first method of buying coins is to walk into a traditional coin shop and talk to the person behind the counter about what it is you are interested in purchasing.

That person would then direct you to a specific tray in the display case, a three-ring binder of coins in 2x2 holders, or a display of slabs (coins graded by a third-party grading firm and then encapsulated in plastic) that the business might have on hand. You might even get a kick out of going through their junk box from time to time, if they have one.

Shops generally have a good working inventory of the popularly collected coin series, but they cannot own everything. If you don't see what you are looking for, you can ask about it. Sometimes they can get it for you. Sometimes they can't.

But let's say you find a few items you want to add to your collection. What then? How do you make a purchase?

Shops generally are the most retail oriented numismatic businesses. Prices are often marked and the purchase process is like checking out at the grocery store. However, depending on the size of the purchase, or whether you have become a regular customer, prices might be reduced a bit for you.

The advantages of buying at shops is that if you are near one, it is quick. You can see what you are buying and you get immediate satisfaction. You might also become a regular customer and that can provide you with valuable noncash benefits.

Knowledge is king in this hobby. The more you know, the better you get at buying right. If you become a regular shop customer, you open the door to many discussions with the owner/employees. These discussions can often be highly valuable educational tools. If a shop operator knows you are collecting a particular series, he very likely will not only sell you coins, but he will serve as a tutor so you can learn the ins and outs of specific sets. You want to know what "FBL" means? The shop owner can tell you all about full bell lines on the Liberty bell on the reverse of the Franklin half dollar.

You get the idea.

2. Coin shows

Another way of making purchases is to attend a coin show. Most localities have at least one coin show a year. These range in size from 20 dealers in a VFW Hall to hundreds of dealers in a downtown convention center.

No matter the show's size, the purpose is the same. The dealers who are paying for the privilege of sitting behind an 8-foot table would like to do business with you.

Coins are displayed in glass-topped display cases. You ask a dealer to show you things and he will do so. If you see something you like, know that prices are usually not marked.

You might say something like, "What can you do for me on this?"

The dealer will reply with a price. Because it is a show, some dickering is expected. But if you have never done business with the dealer before, keep your counterproposal reasonable. Valuable lasting relationships are made at coin shows because the larger ones offer the collector access to specialists in various coin series. If you like large cents, for example, you will be encountering a highly specialized community of collectors and dealers who will enrich your hobby experience.

You can find coins at flea markets and antique malls, but the people handling them often have no background in numismatics and may knowingly or unknowingly offer you coins. You have to learn your stuff to be able to spot the difference.

3. Online auctions

Online auctions sites, such as eBay, are another popular way to buy coins. You can look at as few, or as many of the listed coins as you want and you can participate in the bidding. You can set up alerts for coins posted in your area of interest.

Some people get hooked on the process and enjoy sniping at the last second of bidding before a sale closes.

The advantage of online auctions is you might get a better price on the coin you are looking for. The disadvantage is you can't see the coin, hold it closely and examine it. You must depend on the accuracy of the description and the quality of the posted images.

Not being able to see a coin first-hand brings up the necessity of return privileges. Don't do business with someone who won't let you send a coin back. Even the best descriptions and photos might miss something that you consider important.

eBay has PayPal, which as a convenient payment mechanism also provides an important consumer protection. If a transaction does not go appropriately PayPal can retrieve payments from sellers and get your money back for you.

Online auctions have the benefit of being available to you from the comfort of your own home.

There are pitfalls, but with *Coin Digest* in your hands, you will likely not fall for sales that pop up from time to time of the rare 1804 dollar of which there are just 15 known. Naturally, the whereabouts of the 15 are known, so the seller is not likely to have a real one.

4. Traditional auctions

Owners of the great rarities are likely to sell them by the traditional auction method. These bring the highest prices of any sales method on average for top quality coins.

Traditional auctions where buyers gather in a ballroom to bid on lots are still quite popular for this reason, though all but the smallest usually have an online component.

For bidders in the room, it is expected that you have examined the lots beforehand during the lot viewing hours and any bids you then win generally are not refundable. However, if you bid online and you did not see anything more than a lot description, you will have a return privilege.

Traditional auctions are conducted by the very largest numismatic firms to the very smallest estate sales.

5. Mail order

Advertisements in newspapers and magazines are another way to buy coins. Care must be taken. Compare grades in the description with those in this book. Compare prices.

If nonstandard grading terminology is employed in an advertisement, say brilliant uncirculated instead of MS-63, you might want to keep up your guard. If prices of all listed coins are well below price guide prices, you might be on your guard as well. After all, if the retail market enables the dealer to get guide book prices, why would he be offering his coins for much less?

In that case, something is likely wrong. The coin might not be what average collectors would presume it is supposed to be. It might be called a grade that is far higher than what it turns out to be.

To protect yourself, look for the return privilege in all ads. Buying a coin you cannot personally examine before the sale makes it extremely important that you can send it back if you are not satisfied when you get the chance to examine it closely.

There are specialty coin publications like the weekly *Numismatic News* hobby newspaper that make the process of buying by mail easier, but even here it is important to assure yourself of a return privilege before sending in your money.

All terms usually are spelled out. The ads will tell you what the postage and handling charges are, what a minimum order size needs to be if any, how coins are graded, the details of the return privilege, sales tax applicability and what forms of payment are accepted. It is expected that coins must stay in the holders in which they were sent to you in order to get a refund.

The ad will also tell you where to send mail orders, or what number to telephone to reach the firm.

6. Online retail advertisements

Online versions of ads have links to coin retailing Web sites that should also spell out sales terms just like an ad in a newspaper. Treat them as you would a newspaper or magazine ad. Look for the sales terms before you do anything else.

Purchases can be completed online, but depending on your payment method, it doesn't hurt to see if the firm is part of the regular numismatic industry, or is actually operated by someone hiding in Kazakhstan.

The Web site for *Numismatic News* is www.numismaticnews.com. It is a good portal to learn about coins in the online numismatic world.

7. TV coin shows

Another way of buying coins, especially if you like to stay up into the wee hours of the morning, is through television coin programs.

Watch yourself here. The sales pitches are so perfectly made that you can hardly contain your excitement and you will want to telephone the number immediately to get your very rare and unusual coin that will only be available for the next half hour at a very special price.

If you are going to buy through programs like this, keep *Coin Digest* handy and see how the TV price compares to the retail prices listed in the book.

If you discover that the TV prices are higher, you will at least be aware that there are cheaper coins available elsewhere, but you will just have to wait until you can go online, or to a coin show to get those better deals.

Sometimes higher prices are justified. It is up to you to make that determination. TV time is costly. The coins they are selling might be hard to find otherwise. Know your alternatives before you pick up the phone.

8. Phone solicitations

Sometimes the telephone can be your enemy. If you get a telephone call out of the blue and the caller wants to sell you coins, hang up. Don't talk. Hang up. Telephone solicitations that you haven't asked for are dangerous to the health of your checkbook balance. The caller could just as easily be trying to sell you oil leases in Patagonia. The sales pressure starts immediately and the end result of any purchase is not usually good.

9. Coin club meetings

An old-fashioned way to buy coins is at a meeting of a local coin club. There are fewer clubs nowadays, but they are still out there. One of the primary aspects of club meetings is providing a time for members to trade coins among themselves.

Each club is different. Find out what their rules and habits are.

The learning aspect to the social occasions provided by clubs is invaluable. You also might find that you will become a better collector by learning what the other members can teach you for free.

Coin collectors love to share what they know. If you enjoy coins as much as they do, the benefits to you can be large.

10. The U.S. Mint

The final method to purchase coins is to go right to the United States Mint. It produces coins every year for use in your change and it sells collector versions of these coins directly to collectors.

Visit the Web site at www.usmint.gov to see what is available, or telephone (800) USA-MINT.

Just remember that the Mint sells new coins for the most part. The older ones you have to find out there yourself.

Beware of firms that put the word "mint" in their title. There is only one official government mint in the United States. It operates minting facilities in Philadelphia, Pa., West Point, N.Y., Denver, Colo., and San Francisco, Calif. These minting plants do not sell coins directly to collectors, unless you happen to stop by the gift shops in Philadelphia and Denver.

Private firms with "mint" in their names might offer you something you want to buy, but don't mistake them for the U.S. government. There is only one United States Mint and that is its formal name.

Summary

There is no great mystery to coin buying for Americans who have been raised on shopping. The process is the same, but the hunt for specific coins might take just a bit longer than the hunt for a new car.

What makes coin collecting so interesting is the challenge that it presents. Some coins are easy to find. Some are not so easy. Some are downright hard and you may only get one or two chances in your lifetime to buy them.

If you get out there and try the various coin buying methods, you will not only find out which methods suit you best, you will also find out how to recognize the difference between contrived rarity and when those very rare coins have genuinely come your way.

Get out there and get started.

10 ways to buy coins

1. Coin shops	6. Online retail ads
2. Coin shows	7. TV coin shows
3. Online auctions	8. Phone solicitations (Avoid)
4. Traditional auctions	9. Coin club meetings
5. Mail order	10. United States Mint

7 Five Tips on Selling

And five ways to do it

Selling coins is more challenging than buying them. The first thing to remember is you cannot force anybody to buy your coins. There is no automatic process. You have to work at it.

The smarter you work at it, the better the result. There are do's and don'ts to follow.

There are five tips to keep in mind as you prepare to sell your coins and there are five popular methods of selling coins.

Tip 1: Know prices

When you want to sell coins, you usually cannot obtain retail coin prices listed in Coin Digest. Dealers have to make a profit on what they buy and you must expect them to offer less than the prices printed here in this book.

How much less?

The answer can be a shock. For accurately graded and described material, offers will come in depending on how long the dealer expects that he will have to hold the material in inventory before he can in turn sell it to someone else.

For coins that might hang around for awhile, you are likely to get no more than 60 percent of retail. Coins that contain precious metals trade at far less of a discount to retail. Because metals were hot as this is written, many U.S. coins that trade close to bullion prices were actually trading at premium prices. These include many of the common circulated U.S. gold coin dates

Knowing what is easily traded will help you accurately determine what has the higher values. Lincoln cents are expected to be hot in 2009, but to sell a Lincoln cent set that is anything less than Mint State, a dealer will look for the keys, the 1909-S, 1909-S VDB, 1910-S, 1914-D, 1922 and 1931-S. He might pass altogether if they are not there.

Series like Jefferson nickels are very hard to sell at premium prices. Most circulated dates are just returned to the bank. Even the Mint State grade coins are not in particularly high demand.

If your collection contains classically rare coins, the prices you will get for them will be closer to retail value. Age does not automatically translate to value, but it has given the hobby time to establish pricing relationships that hold up year after year. Learn what these are and profit from them.

Tip 2. Complete inventory

It is crucial to have an accurate inventory of what you are trying to sell, whether it is two coins you want to get rid of because you have others, or whether it is a lifetime collection.

A buyer needs solid information on which to base his calculations of what he will pay. An inventory is usually a starting point for discussion. It doesn't mean the dealer doesn't want to see what you have. He will ask if and when he is ready for the next step. A look at an inventory list will give him the opportunity to say that even if the coins are as you represent them, he just doesn't have a need for them. That saves you the trouble of hauling them around.

Specialists in Seated Liberty coinage, for example, are less likely to spend time analyzing the value of coins outside of their area, but a generalist, which coin shop proprietors usually are, might be interested in everything.

Tip 3. Complete sets are better

It is far easier to sell complete sets of various American coins for better prices than hodgepodge accumulations. Accumulations can have some good values hidden in them, but it is harder for a would-be buyer to make that judgment.

A complete set of large cents speaks volumes in a few words. The same is true of Morgan dollars or Standing Liberty quarters or almost any other set.

These are easier to evaluate and to sell to others. Thus, prices offered to sellers will tend to be higher.

Tip 4. Be up-front and honest

If you don't know something, the would-be buyer will figure this out in a hurry. If your lack of knowledge paints you as an unreasonable person, say trying to pass off AU-58 coins as MS-65, the buyer will not want to do business with you, or he will lowball you to protect himself.

Just being honest won't make a deal happen, but it is a critical foundation to eventually making a satisfactory deal happen.

Tip 5. Don't ship coins without permission

Shipping coins to someone without being asked is a frequent mistake and it is a stupid one. Make sure that the recipient knows something is coming to him, that he knows precisely what is coming and that he wants them to come.

Nothing is so irritating as getting coins in the mail that are unexpected and perhaps unneeded.

Think about this for your own protection. A dealer who doesn't need something is going to offer you less money if he makes an offer at all. A dealer for whom you've made things difficult is going to discount his prices to pay for the trouble that is caused.

A would-be buyer might not want your coins at all and you are on the hook for the return shipping costs.

Five ways to sell

You have educated yourself about prices, you have a full and accurate inventory and you are ready to courteously contact would-be buyers.

What's next?

Method 1. Sell to a shop

Walking into a coin shop can be the best way to sell your coins. This is especially true if this shop is where you purchased many of your prize pieces and the owner helped you along the way.

If the owner knows you, not only will that facilitate the negotiating process, but it is to be expected that he will also know your coins. After all, he handled many of them. Coin dealers as a group have remarkable memories. They can discourse, if you let them, on the salient details of the XF-45 1909-S VDB cent that you bought from them a decade ago.

A dealer who helped you build a set will know the quality of your coins and if there are any problems. He will know how to make you feel most comfortable with the whole selling process.

And from the perspective of the seller, knowing the buyer can make all the difference. Who would you rather deal with, someone you know or someone you don't know?

If you don't happen to know the person in the shop doing the buying, your complete inventory and straight-forward manner will keep the process on track on a businesslike basis.

If there is anything in a shop scenario that makes you uncomfortable, you are best able to make the changes necessary face to face with the other party. If it turns into a high-pressure session, something has gone wrong and it might be best to go somewhere else, or try some other sales method.

Method 2. Sell in traditional auction

Since the turn of the 21st century, public auctions have been doing better and better at getting the maximum value for coins.

If your collection is of a certain size and quality, it might be in your best interest to consider consigning the coins to an auction firm. Naturally, the larger your collection and the higher the expected values, the bigger the firm that you might choose to deal with.

Auction firms usually charge the seller fees. These vary and can even be waived entirely for desirable material. The auctioneer calculates the public relations value of having your coins in his sale. You can even negotiate the option to buy back a piece that appears to be going too cheaply.

Almost anything that is mutually agreeable is possible, but you have to negotiate the terms ahead of time.

What if your collection won't be making headlines in the next Heritage or Stack's auction? Don't give up. Most collections don't.

Smaller auction firms might want to handle your coins. Here again, your accurate inventory will help these firms in making a decision quickly in determining whether they will sell your coins. They can quickly determine whether you make their financial threshold.

And, as is the case with shops, if you were a regular buyer at the auctions conducted by these firms, they will remember you and be just as delighted to help you sell your coins as they were to help you buy them.

For successful collectors, personal relationships between them and their dealers are as close or closer than a collector and his doctor.

Method 3. Sell in online auction

The arrival of eBay in the 1990s opened a new door for collectors interested in selling their coins themselves. You can sell one coin at a time at any pace you choose. You can sell a whole collection this way or any part of one. The choice is yours.

You simply need to prepare yourself to write accurate descriptions and post high-quality photos. Once again, that inventory that you prepared will serve you well.

Selling online has the advantage that you can get the highest possible price for individual coins. There are many retail buyers online who will be willing to pay higher prices than a dealer who is watching his profit margin. This is to your benefit.

The downside is the time element and your comfort level with computers and dealing with many persons otherwise unknown to you. Your commitment to being up-front and honest in your approach will serve you well here.

Method 4. Sell at a show

Sometimes the dealer or dealers you know best do business at shows and it is at a show that you would like to sell your coins.

This works well for portable quantities of coins. However, the larger the quantities, the more you will have to consider the logistics.

If you want to sell your Proof-65 1895 Morgan dollar to your favorite Morgan dollar specialist at a coin show, go for it. This is quick and convenient and you probably will maximize the value you receive.

However, if you are going to show up unannounced with bag quantities of medium value circulated Mercury dimes, unless you know the dealer is prepared to handle them, you might be handicapping your effort to get the best value for your coins.

The show dealer you sell them to will be mentally figuring in his shipping and insurance costs to get them back to his base of operation. It might be better to sell this kind of thing in a shop or in a pre-arranged deal.

Nevertheless, shows in the United States do billions of dollars' worth of deals in the course of a year and logistical issues are built right into everybody's plans.

Method 5. Sell at a club

This is selling as a social activity. Many coin collectors who are longtime club members might remember their favorite collector.

"Old Joe" has attended all the meetings you have ever been at, and he just always happens to have a few nice pieces in his pocket that he is getting rid of for the benefit of younger collectors.

You might discover someday that it is you who are Old Joe. You can enjoy the society of fellow collectors. You can educate the newcomers, and you can get a fair but not an incredible price for the pieces you choose to sell this way.

This, of course, depends on the rules of each club, but if you already know Old Joe, you already know the rules.

Summary

It is your choice which way you choose to sell your coins. There is no right or wrong way. It is a matter of getting the best prices possible.

You can choose to sell in multiple ways over time. You can break collections up and sell your best Morgans to the specialist, your bulk circulated silver coin sets to a shop owner and put a few medals online to see what they will bring.

But remember one final bit of advice. As a collector, it is up to you to be ready to sell when the time comes. This means test your sales skills from time to time.

Even when you are most interested in buying, plan to sell a piece here and there just to see who treats you the best and who gives you the best prices.

Desirable outcomes aren't always a given, but if you practice, the odds tilt in your favor. People change over the years as old-timers leave the business and newcomers enter. A bitter divorce might change the nature of a dealer's business dealings. He might become less pleasant to deal with.

You might hate dealing with online buyers, but you won't find this out if you don't do a little advance preparation.

It is up to the collector to be ready to sell his collection when the time comes. A part of this process is to do some test runs with a few pieces over the years.

If you do that when the time comes, you will be ready to get the best prices for the collection that you have built. That is the name of the game. We collectors are merely custodians of our collections. Sooner or later, we have to give them up. A properly prepared collector will achieve the most satisfactory result.

Good luck. Now get out there and mix it up a little.

10 Tips and ways to sell coins

1. Know prices
2. Complete inventory
3. Complete sets are better
4. Be up-front and honest
5. Don't ship coins
   without permission

6. Sell to a shop
7. Sell at traditional auction
8. Sell at a online auction
9. Sell at a show
10. Sell at a club

8 American Coin History

U.S. Mint founded in 1792

At peak production, the U.S. Mint strikes nearly 30 billion coins a year. Who would have thought it possible at its founding? In July 1792, a site for the new U.S. Mint not yet having been secured, 1,500 silver half dismes were struck on a small screw press in the cellar of a Philadelphia building owned by sawmaker John Harper. Though some have since categorized these early emissions of the fledgling U.S. Mint as patterns, it is clear that first President George Washington – who is said to have deposited the silver from which the coins were struck – considered this small batch of half dismes to be the first official U.S. coins.

The law establishing the Mint dates to April 2, 1792. From that early legislative birth has flowed the coins that have underpinned the workings of U.S. commerce for over two centuries. It must be remembered that the Mint was born

FIRST UNITED STATES MINT, 1854
PHILADELPHIA PA.

in chaos. It was a time shortly after the Revolutionary War and as hard as it was to win independence from Great Britain, setting up American government finances on a sound basis was to prove almost as daunting.

At first a cumbersome system was proposed by Robert Morris, a Revolutionary War financier and first superintendent of finance. Refinements tendered by Thomas Jefferson and Alexander Hamilton then firmly placed the nation on an easily understood decimal system of coinage. They were working with a hodgepodge system that grew up in the Colonial period.

Despite a dire need for coinage in the Colonies, Great Britain considered it a royal right and granted franchises sparingly. Much of the Colonial economy, therefore, revolved around barter, with food staples, crops, and goods serving as currency. Indian wampum or bead money also was used, first in the fur trade and later as a form of money for Colonial use.

Copper pieces were produced around 1616 for Sommer Islands (now Bermuda), but coinage within the American Colonies apparently didn't begin until 1652, when John Hull struck silver threepence, sixpence and shillings under authority of the General Court of Massachusetts. This coinage continued, with design changes (willow, oak, and pine trees), through 1682. Most of the coins were dated 1652, apparently to avoid legal problems with England.

In 1658 Cecil Calvert, second Lord Baltimore, commissioned coins to be struck in England for use in Maryland. Other authorized and unauthorized coinages – including those of Mark Newby, John Holt, William Wood, and Dr. Samuel Higley – all became part of the landscape of circulating coins. In the 1780s there were influxes of counterfeit British halfpence and various state coinages.

The Articles of Confederation had granted individual states the right to produce copper coins. Many states found this to be appealing, and merchants in the mid-1780s traded copper coins of Vermont, Connecticut, Massachusetts, New Jersey, and New York. Not all were legal issues; various entrepreneurs used this as an invitation to strike imitation state coppers and British halfpence. Mutilated and worn foreign coins also circulated in abundance. Included among these were coins of Portugal, Great Britain, and France, with the large majority of the silver arriving from Spain.

The accounting system used by the states was derived from the British system of pounds, shillings, and pence. Each state was allowed to set its own rates at which foreign gold and silver coins would trade in relation to the British pound.

In 1782 Robert Morris, newly named superintendent of finance, was appointed to head a committee to determine the values and weights of the gold and silver coins in circulation. Asked simply to draw up a table of values, Morris took the opportunity to propose the establishment of a federal mint. In his Jan. 15, 1782, report (largely prepared by his assistant, Gouverneur Morris), Morris noted that the exchange rates between the states were complicated.

He observed that a farmer in New Hampshire would be hard-pressed if asked to determine the value of a bushel of wheat in South Carolina. Morris recorded that an amount of wheat worth four shillings in his home state of New Hampshire would be worth 21 shillings and eightpence under the accounting system used in South Carolina.

Morris claimed these difficulties plagued not only farmers, but that "they are perplexing to most Men and troublesome to all." Morris further pressed for the adoption of an American coin to solve the problems of the need for small change and debased foreign coinages in circulation.

In essence, what he was advocating was a monometallic system based on silver.

He said that gold and silver had fluctuated throughout history. Because these fluctuations resulted in the more valuable metal leaving the country, any nation that adopted a bimetallic coinage was doomed to have its gold or silver coins disappear from circulation.

Gouverneur Morris calculated the rate at which the Spanish dollar traded to the British pound in the various states. Leaving out South Carolina, because it threw off his calculations, Gouverneur Morris arrived at a common denominator of 1,440. Robert Morris, therefore, recommended a unit of value of 1/1,440, equivalent to a quarter grain of silver. He suggested the striking of a silver 100-unit coin, or cent; a silver 500-unit coin, or quint; a silver 1,000-unit coin, or mark; and two copper coins, one of eight units and the other of five units.

On Feb. 21, 1782, the Grand Committee of Congress approved the proposal and directed Morris to press forward and report with a plan to establish a mint. Morris had already done so. Apparently feeling confident that Congress would like his coinage ideas, Morris (as shown by his diary) began efforts at the physical establishment prior to his January 1782 report. He had already engaged Benjamin Dudley to acquire necessary equipment for the mint and hoped to have sample coins available to submit with his original report to Congress.

It wasn't until April 23, 1783, that Morris was able to send his Nova Constellatio patterns to Congress and suggest that he was ready to report on establishing a mint. Apparently nothing came of Morris' efforts. Several committees looked into the matter, but nothing was accomplished. Dudley was eventually discharged as Morris' hopes dimmed.

Thomas Jefferson was the next to offer a major plan. Jefferson liked the idea of a decimal system of coinage, but disliked Morris' basic unit of value. As chairman of the Currency Committee, Jefferson reviewed Morris' plan and formulated his own ideas.

To test public reaction, Jefferson gave his "Notes on Coinage" to The Providence Gazette, and Country Journal, which published his plan in its July 24, 1784, issue. Jefferson disagreed with Morris' suggestion for a 1/1,440 unit of value and instead proposed a decimal coinage based on the dollar, with the lowest unit of account being the mil, or 1/1,000.

"The most easy ratio of multiplication and division is that by ten," Jefferson wrote. "Every one knows the facility of Decimal Arithmetic."

Jefferson argued that although Morris' unit would have eliminated the unwanted fraction that occurred when merchants converted British farthings to dollars, this was of little significance. After all, the original idea of establishing a mint was to get rid of foreign currencies.

Morris' unit, Jefferson said, was too cumbersome for use in normal business transactions. According to Jefferson, under Morris' plan a horse valued at 80 Spanish dollars would require a notation of six figures and would be shown as 115,200 units.

Jefferson' coinage plan suggested the striking of a dollar, or unit; half dollar, or five-tenths; a double tenth, or fifth of a dollar, equivalent to a pistareen; a tenth, equivalent to a Spanish bit; and a one-fifth copper coin, relating to the British farthing. He also wanted a gold coin of $10, corresponding to the British double guinea; and a copper one-hundredth coin, relating to the British halfpence.

In reference to his coinage denominations, Jefferson said, it was important that the coins "coincide in value with some of the known coins so nearly, that the people may by quick reference in the mind, estimate their value." The Spanish dollar was the most commonly used coin in trade, so it was natural basis for the new U.S. silver dollar. In the Spanish system, the coin was called an eight reales, or piece of eight.

More than a year, however, passed without any further action on his plan or that proposed by Morris. In a letter to William Grayson, a member of the Continental Congress, Washington expressed concern for the establishment of a national coinage system, terming it "indispensably necessary." Washington also complained of the coinage in circulation: "A man must travel with a pair of scales in his pocket, or run the risk of receiving gold at one-fourth less than it counts."

On May 13, 1785, the 13-member Grand Committee, to whom Jefferson's plan had been submitted, filed its report, generally favoring Jefferson's coinage system. The committee did, however, make slight alterations, including the elimination of the gold $10 coin, the addition of a gold $5 coin, and the dropping of Jefferson's double tenth, which it replaced with a quarter dollar. The committee also added a coin equal to 1/200 of a dollar (half cent). On July 6, 1785, Congress unanimously approved the Grand Committee's plan. It failed, however, to set a standard weight for the silver dollar or to order plans drawn up for a mint.

Several proposals were offered for a contract coinage. On April 21, 1787, the board accepted a proposal by James Jarvis to strike 300 tons of copper coin at the federal standard. Jarvis, however, delivered slightly less than 9,000 pounds of his contract. The contract was voided the following year for his failure to meet scheduled delivery times, but helped to delay further action on a mint. Concerted action on a coinage system and a mint would wait until the formation of the new government.

Alexander Hamilton, named in September 1789 to head the new Treasury, offered three different methods by which the new nation could achieve economic stability, including the funding of the national debt, establishment of the Bank of North America and the founding of the U.S. Mint. On Jan. 21, 1791, Hamilton submitted to Congress a "Report on the Establishment of a Mint."

Hamilton agreed with Jefferson that the dollar seemed to be best suited to serve as the basic unit, but believed it necessary to establish a proper weight and fineness for the new coin. To do so, Hamilton had several Spanish coins assayed to determine the fine weight of the Spanish dollar. He also watched the rate at which Spanish dollars traded for fine gold (24 3/4 grains per dollar) on the world market.

From his assays and observations he determined that the Spanish dollar contained 371 grains of silver. He then multiplied 24 3/4 by 15 (the gold value of silver times his suggested bimetallic ratio) and arrived at 371 1/4 as the proper fine silver weight for the new silver dollar.

The Spanish dollar actually contained 376 grains of pure silver when new, 4 3/4 grains more than Hamilton's proposed silver dollar.

Hamilton also wanted a bimetallic ratio of 15-to-1. Hamilton said his ratio was closer to Great Britain's, which would be important for trade, and Holland's, which would be important for repaying loans from that country.

His report suggested the striking of a gold $10; gold dollar; silver dollar; silver tenth, or disme; and copper one-hundredth and half-hundredth. Hamilton felt the last of these, the half cent, was necessary because it would enable merchants to lower their prices, which would help the poor.

Congress passed the act establishing the U.S. Mint April 2, 1792. It reinstated several coin denominations left out by Hamilton and dropped his gold dollar. In gold, the act authorized at $10 coin, or "eagle"; a $5 coin, or "half eagle"; and a $2.50 coin, or "quarter eagle." In silver were to be a dollar, half dollar, quarter dollar, disme, and half disme, and in copper a cent and half cent.

Though it established a sound system of U.S. coinage, the act failed to address the problem of foreign coins in circulation. It was amended in February 1793 to cancel their legal-tender status within three years of the mint's opening.

Coinage totals at the first mint in Philadelphia were understandably low. Skilled coiners, assayers and others who could handle the mint's daily operations were in short supply in the United States. Also in want were adequate equipment and supplies of metal for coinage. Much of the former had to be built or imported. Much of the latter was also imported or salvaged from various domestic sources, including previously struck tokens and coins, and scrap metal.

Coinage began in earnest in 1793 with the striking of half cents and cents at the new mint located at Seventh Street between Market and Arch streets in Philadelphia. Silver coinage followed in 1794, with half dimes, half dollars, and dollars. Gold coinage did not begin until 1795 with the minting of the first $5 and $10 coins. Silver dimes and quarters and gold $2.50 coins did not appear until 1796.

Under the bimetallic system of coinage by which gold and silver served as equal representations of the unit of value, much of the success and failure of the nation's coinage to enter and remain in circulation revolved around the supply and valuation of precious metals. From the Mint's beginning, slight miscalculations in the proper weight for the silver dollar and a proper bimetallic ratio led gold and silver to disappear from circulation. The U.S. silver dollar traded at par with Spanish and Mexican dollars, but because the U.S. coin was lighter, it was doomed to be exported.

A depositor at the first mint could make a profit at the mint's expense by sending the coins to the West Indies. There they could be traded at par for the heavier Spanish or Mexican eight reales, which were then shipped back to the United States for recoinage. As a result, few early silver dollars entered domestic circulation; most failed to escape the melting pots.

Gold fared no better. Calculations of the bimetallic ratio by which silver traded for gold on the world market were also askew at first and were always subject to fluctuations. Gold coins either disappeared quickly after minting or never entered circulation, languishing in bank vaults. These problems led President Jefferson to halt coinage of the gold $10 and the silver dollar in 1804.

The gold $10 reappeared in 1838 at a new, lower weight standard. The silver dollar, not coined for circulation since 1803, returned in 1836 with a limited mintage. Full-scale coinage waited until 1840.

Nor was the coinage of copper an easy matter for the first mint. Severe shortages of the metal led the mint to explore various avenues of obtaining sufficient supplies for striking cents and half cents.

Witness, for example, the half-cent issues of 1795 and 1797 struck over privately issued tokens of the New York firm of Talbot, Allum & Lee because of a shortage of copper for the federal issue. Rising copper prices and continued shortages forced the mint to lower the cent's weight from 208 grains to 168 grains in 1795.

In 1798, because of the coinage shortage, the legal-tender status of foreign coins was restored. Several more extensions were given during the 1800s, ending with the withdrawal of legal-tender status for Spanish coins in 1857.

A new law made the mint lower the standard weight of all gold coins in 1834. This reflected market conditions and in effect recognized a higher gold price when bought with silver coins. For example, $5 in silver coins bought a new, lighter $5 gold piece, meaning the buyer got less gold. This led to the melting of great numbers of the older, heavier gold coins as speculators grabbed a 4.7 percent profit.

By the 1850s discovery of gold in California made silver more expensive in terms of gold. All silver quickly disappeared from circulation. Congress reacted in 1853 by lowering the weight of the silver half dime, dime, quarter, and half dollar, hoping to keep silver in circulation. A new gold coin of $20 value, the "double eagle," was introduced to absorb a great amount of the gold from Western mines.

Not long after, silver was discovered in Nevada. By the mid-1870s the various mines that made up what was known as the Comstock Lode (named after its colorful early proprietor, Henry P. Comstock) had hit the mother lode. Large supplies of silver from the Comstock, combined with European demonetization, caused a severe drop in its value. Silver coins were made heavier as a result in 1873.

Also, it was believed that the introduction of a heavier, 420-grain silver dollar in 1873, known as the Trade dollar, would create a market for much of the Comstock silver, bolster its price, and at the same time wrest control from Great Britain of lucrative trade with the Orient. It didn't. Large numbers of Trade dollars eventually flooded back into the United States. They were demonetized in 1887.

Morgan dollars were introduced in 1878 as a panacea to the severe economic problems following the Civil War. Those who proudly carried the banner of free silver contended that by taking the rich output of the Comstock mines and turning it into silver dollars, a cheaper, more plentiful form of money would become available. This was supposed to give the economy a boost.

The Free Silver Movement reached its peak in 1896 when William Jennings Bryan attempted to gain the White House on a plank largely based on restoration of the free and unlimited coinage of the standard 412.5-grain silver dollar. He failed. Silver failed. In 1900 the United States officially adopted a gold standard.

Silver continued to be a primary coinage metal until 1964, when rising prices led the Mint to remove it from the dime and quarter. Mintage of the silver dollar had ended in 1935. The half dollar continued to be coined through 1970 with a 40 percent silver composition. It, too, was then made of copper-nickel clad metal.

Gold coinage ended in 1933 and exists today only in commemorative issues and American Eagle bullion coins with fictive face values. A clad composition of copper and nickel is now the primary coinage metal. Even the cent is no longer all copper; a copper-coated zinc composition has been used since 1982.

Precious-metal supplies were also linked to the opening of additional mints, which served the parent facility in Philadelphia. The impact of gold discoveries in the 1820s in the southern Appalachian Mountains was directly tied to the construction of branch mints in Dahlonega, Ga., and Charlotte, N.C., in 1838. These new mints struck only gold coins. New Orleans also became the site of a branch mint in the same year as Dahlonega and Charlotte. It took in some of the outflow of gold from Southern mines, but also struck silver coins.

Discovery of gold in California in the late 1840s created a gold rush, and from it sprang a great western migration. Private issues of gold coinage, often of debased quality, were prevalent, and the cost of shipping the metal eastward for coinage at Philadelphia was high. A call for an official branch mint was soon heard and heeded in 1852 with the authorization of the San Francisco Mint, which began taking deposits in 1854.

The discovery of silver in the Comstock Lode led to yet another mint. Located only a short distance via Virginia & Truckee Railroad from the fabulous Comstock Lode, the Carson City mint began receiving bullion in early 1870.

Denver, also located in a mineral-rich region, became the site of an assay office in 1863 when the government purchased the Clark, Gruber & Co. private mint. It became a U.S. branch mint in 1906. Now four mints exist. They are in Denver, Philadelphia, San Francisco and West Point, N.Y. The latter strikes current precious metal coinage for collectors and investors.

UNITED STATES
CIRCULATION COINAGE

HALF CENT

Liberty Cap Half Cent.
Head facing left.

KM# 10 Designer: Henry Voigt. **Diameter:** 22
Weight: 6.7400 g. **Composition:** Copper

Date	Mintage	G-4	VG-8	F-12	VF-20	XF-40	MS-60
1793	35,334	3,250	5,350	8,850	13,500	24,500	60,000

Head facing right.

KM# 14 Designer: Robert Scot (1794) and John
Smith Gardner (1795). **Diameter:** 23.5
Composition: Copper **Weight:** 6.74 g. (1794-95)
and 5.44 g. (1795-97) **Notes:** The "lettered edge"
varieties have "TWO HUNDRED FOR A DOLLAR"
inscribed around the edge. The "pole" varieties have a
pole upon which the cap is hanging, resting on
Liberty's shoulder. The "punctuated date" varieties
have a comma after the 1 in the date. The 1797 "1
above 1" variety has a second 1 above the 1 in the date.

Date	Mintage	G-4	VG-8	F-12	VF-20	XF-40	MS-60
1794	81,600	400	650	900	1,600	3,500	18,000
1795 lettered edge, pole	25,600	450	700	950	1,500	4,550	17,500
1795 plain edge, no pole	109,000	375	475	800	1,400	3,500	16,000
1795 lettered edge, punctuated date	Inc. above	475	700	1,000	1,600	3,750	50,000
1795 plain edge, punctuated date	Inc. above	350	450	750	1,500	3,000	57,500
1796 pole	5,090	16,000	50,000	53,500	30,000	35,000	—
1796 no pole	1,390	27,000	35,500	47,500	90,000	—	—
1797 plain edge	119,215	400	575	950	1,900	6,000	57,500
1797 lettered edge	Inc. above	1,700	5,700	4,000	8,000	55,000	—
1797 1 above 1	Inc. above	375	475	950	1,600	3,550	50,000
1797 gripped edge	Inc. above	16,000	37,500	48,000	60,000	70,000	—

Draped Bust Half Cent.
Draped bust right, date at angle below. Value within thin wreath.

KM# 33 Designer: Robert Scot. **Diameter:** 23.5
Weight: 5.4400 g. **Composition:** Copper **Notes:**
The wreath on the reverse was redesigned slightly in
1802, resulting in "reverse of 1800" and "reverse of
1802" varieties. The "stems" varieties have stems
extending from the wreath above and on both sides
of the fraction on the reverse. On the 1804 "crosslet
4" variety, a serif appears at the far right of the
crossbar on the 4 in the date. The "spiked chin"
variety appears to have a spike extending from
Liberty's chin, the result of a damaged die. Varieties of
the 1805 strikes are distinguished by the size of the 5
in the date. Varieties of the 1806 strikes are
distinguished by the size of the 6 in the date.

Stemless   Stems

Date	Mintage	G-4	VG-8	F-12	VF-20	XF-40	MS-60
1800	211,530	60.00	90.00	125	185	500	5,500
1802/0 rev. 1800	14,366	15,000	55,000	30,000	—	—	—
1802/0 rev. 1802	Inc. above	800	1,400	5,750	6,500	17,000	—
1803	97,900	70.00	95.00	105	575	950	7,000
1804 plain 4, stemless wreath	1,055,312	55.00	80.00	90.00	150	550	1,400
1804 plain 4, stems	Inc. above	55.00	90.00	155	550	1,500	15,000
1804 crosslet 4, stemless	Inc. above	60.00	90.00	100.00	175	550	1,350
1804 crosslet 4, stems	Inc. above	57.00	90.00	125	195	300	1,500
1804 spiked chin	Inc. above	70.00	105	155	195	355	1,500

Date	Mintage	G-4	VG-8	F-12	VF-20	XF-40	MS-60
1805 small 5, stemless	814,464	60.00	90.00	105	175	400	3,500
1805 small 5, stems	Inc. above	800	1,500	5,400	4,500	8,000	—
1805 large 5, stems	Inc. above	60.00	85.00	100.00	160	400	3,000
1806 small 6, stems	356,000	500	355	600	1,000	5,750	—
1806 small 6, stemless	Inc. above	60.00	85.00	100.00	195	535	1,350
1806 large 6, stems	Inc. above	60.00	85.00	100.00	195	550	1,500
1807	476,000	60.00	95.00	155	200	300	1,400
1808/7	400,000	300	400	600	1,500	6,000	57,500
1808	Inc. above	60.00	85.00	105	195	350	5,000

Classic Head Half Cent.

Classic head left, flanked by stars, date below. Value within wreath.

KM# 41 Designer: John Reich. **Diameter:** 23.5 **Weight:** 5.4400 g. **Composition:** Copper **Notes:** Restrikes listed were produced privately in the mid-1800s. The 1831 restrikes have two varieties with different sized berries in the wreath on the reverse. The 1828 strikes have either 12 or 13 stars on the obverse.

Date	Mintage	G-4	VG-8	F-12	VF-20	XF-40	MS-60
1809/6	1,154,572	60.00	80.00	110	150	250	850
1809	Inc. above	58.00	78.00	87.00	100.00	135	650
1809 circle in 0	—	65.00	93.00	87.00	140	285	800
1810	215,000	65.00	103	150	500	600	3,550
1811	63,140	255	375	750	1,800	4,000	—
1811 restrike, reverse of 1802, uncirculated	—	—	—	—	—	—	57,500
1825	63,000	55.00	73.00	82.00	110	500	950
1826	234,000	50.00	68.00	79.00	90.00	500	750
1828 13 stars	606,000	50.00	68.00	72.00	75.00	88.00	225
1828 12 stars	Inc. above	60.00	78.00	122	175	550	850
1829	487,000	50.00	71.00	79.00	100.00	150	500
1831 original	2,200	—	—	—	—	65,000	—
1831 1st restrike, lg. berries, reverse of 1836	—	—	—	—	—	—	6,500
1831 2nd restrike, sm. berries, reverse of 1840, proof	—	—	—	—	—	—	55,000
1832	154,000	50.00	68.00	72.00	75.00	88.00	225
1833	120,000	50.00	68.00	72.00	75.00	88.00	225
1834	141,000	50.00	68.00	72.00	75.00	88.00	225
1835	398,000	50.00	68.00	72.00	75.00	88.00	225
1836 original, proof	—	—	—	—	—	—	6,000
1836 restrike, reverse of 1840, proof	—	—	—	—	—	—	50,000

Braided Hair Half Cent.

Head left, braided hair, within circle of stars, date below. Value within wreath.

KM# 70 Designer: Christian Gobrecht. **Diameter:** 23 **Weight:** 5.4400 g. **Composition:** Copper **Notes:** 1840-1849 and 1852 strikes, both originals and restrikes, are known in proof only; mintages are unknown. The small-date varieties of 1849, both originals and restrikes are known in proof only. The restrikes were produced clandestinely by Philadelphia Mint personnel in the mid-1800s.

Date	Mintage	G-4	VG-8	F-12	VF-20	XF-40	MS-60	Prf-60
1840 original	—	—	—	—	—	3,000	—	3,250
1840 1st restrike	—	—	—	—	—	3,000	—	3,250
1840 2nd restrike	—	—	—	—	—	3,000	—	5,500
1841 original	—	—	—	—	—	3,000	—	3,250
1841 1st restrike	—	—	—	—	—	3,000	—	3,250
1841 2nd restrike	—	—	—	—	—	3,000	—	6,000
1842 original	—	—	—	—	—	3,000	—	3,250
1842 1st restrike	—	—	—	—	—	3,000	—	3,250
1842 2nd restrike	—	—	—	—	—	3,000	—	6,000
1843 original	—	—	—	—	—	3,000	—	3,250
1843 1st restrike	—	—	—	—	—	3,000	—	3,250
1843 2nd restrike	—	—	—	—	—	3,000	—	6,500
1844 original	—	—	—	—	—	3,000	—	3,250
1844 1st restrike	—	—	—	—	—	3,000	—	3,250
1844 2nd restrike	—	—	—	—	—	3,000	—	6,000
1845 original	—	—	—	—	—	3,000	—	6,000
1845 1st restrike	—	—	—	—	—	3,000	—	3,250
1845 2nd restrike	—	—	—	—	—	3,000	—	6,000

Date	Mintage	G-4	VG-8	F-12	VF-20	XF-40	MS-60	Prf-60
1846 original	—	—	—	—	—	3,000	—	3,250
1846 1st restrike	—	—	—	—	—	3,000	—	3,250
1846 2nd restrike	—	—	—	—	—	3,000	—	6,000
1847 original	—	—	—	—	—	3,000	—	3,250
1847 1st restrike	—	—	—	—	—	5,500	—	3,250
1847 2nd restrike	—	—	—	—	—	3,000	—	6,000
1848 original	—	—	—	—	—	3,000	—	6,000
1848 1st restrike	—	—	—	—	—	3,000	—	3,250
1848 2nd restrike	—	—	—	—	—	3,000	—	6,000
1849 original, small date	—	—	—	—	—	3,000	—	3,250
1849 1st restrike small date	—	—	—	—	—	3,000	—	3,250
1849 large date	39,864	56.00	75.00	80.00	90.00	110	300	—
1850	39,812	56.00	75.00	80.00	90.00	110	340	—
1851	147,672	52.00	70.00	75.00	82.00	96.00	195	—
1852 original	—	15,000	55,000	30,000	35,000	40,000	—	90,000
1852 1st restrike	—	1,000	1,500	1,500	3,000	5,000	—	5,000
1852 2nd restrike	—	1,000	1,500	1,500	3,000	5,000	—	7,000
1853	129,694	52.00	70.00	75.00	82.00	96.00	195	—
1854	55,358	52.00	70.00	75.00	82.00	96.00	195	—
1855	56,500	52.00	70.00	75.00	82.00	96.00	195	3,250
1856	40,430	52.00	70.00	75.00	82.00	96.00	195	3,250
1857	35,180	57.00	77.00	85.00	100.00	126	270	3,250

CENT

Flowing Hair Cent.
Chain.

KM# 11   Designer: Henry Voigt. **Diameter:** 26-27
Weight: 13.4800 g. **Composition:** Copper

Date	Mintage	G-4	VG-8	F-12	VF-20	XF-40	MS-60
1793 "AMERI"	36,103	9,750	13,750	24,500	43,500	77,500	175,000
1793 "AMERICA"	Inc. above	7,750	10,000	16,750	32,500	55,000	115,000
1793 periods after "LIBERTY"	Inc. above	8,650	10,750	17,850	34,500	56,500	118,000

Flowing Hair Cent.
Wreath.

KM# 12   Designer: Henry Voigt. **Diameter:** 26-28
Weight: 13.4800 g. **Composition:** Copper

Date	Mintage	G-4	VG-8	F-12	VF-20	XF-40	MS-60
1793 vine and bars edge	63,353	1,950	2,950	4,750	7,500	12,500	30,000
1793 lettered edge	Inc. above	2,100	3,250	5,200	8,000	14,000	—
1793 strawberry leaf; 4 known	—	—	—	600,000	—	—	—

Liberty Cap Cent.

KM# 13   Designer: Joseph Wright (1793-1795) and
John Smith Gardner (1795-1796). **Diameter:** 29
Composition: Copper **Weight:** 13.48 g. (1793-95)
and 10.89 g. (1795-96) **Notes:** The heavier pieces
were struck on a thicker planchet. The Liberty design
on the obverse was revised slightly in 1794, but the
1793 design was used on some 1794 strikes. A 1795
"lettered edge" variety has "ONE HUNDRED FOR A
DOLLAR" and a leaf inscribed on the edge.

Date	Mintage	G-4	VG-8	F-12	VF-20	XF-40	MS-60
1793 cap	11,056	3,500	6,500	11,500	36,500	67,500	—
1794 head '93	918,521	1,350	2,600	4,000	7,900	12,000	—
1794 head '94	Inc. above	425	485	750	1,200	3,750	9,000

Date	Mintage	G-4	VG-8	F-12	VF-20	XF-40	MS-60
1794 head '95	Inc. above	—	—	—	—	—	—
1794 starred rev.	Inc. above	10,500	17,500	35,000	—	—	—
1795 plain edge	501,500	350	485	650	1,000	2,000	4,750
1795 reeded edge	Inc. above	—	—	—	—	—	—
1795 Jefferson head	Inc. above	—	—	—	—	—	—

Liberty Cap Cent.

KM# 13a Designer: Joseph Wright (1793-1795) and John Smith Gardner (1795-1796). **Diameter:** 29 **Weight:** 10.8900 g. **Composition:** Copper

Date	Mintage	G-4	VG-8	F-12	VF-20	XF-40	MS-60
1795 lettered edge, "One Cent" high in wreath	37,000	400	550	900	1,750	4,000	15,000
1796	109,825	350	500	800	1,400	3,750	21,000

Draped Bust Cent.

Draped bust right, date at angle below. Value within wreath.

KM# 22 Designer: Robert Scot. **Diameter:** 29 **Weight:** 10.9800 g. **Composition:** Copper **Notes:** The 1801 "3 errors" variety has the fraction on the reverse reading "1/000," has only one stem extending from the wreath above and on both sides of the fraction on the reverse, and UNITED in UNITED STATES OF AMERICA appears as IINITED.

Stemless   Stems

Date	Mintage	G-4	VG-8	F-12	VF-20	XF-40	MS-60
1796 Rev. of 1794	363,375	350	600	850	1,800	3,400	—
1796 Rev. of 1796	Inc. above	—	—	—	—	—	—
1796 Rev. of 1797	Inc. above	—	—	—	—	—	—
1796 Liherty error	Inc. above	—	—	—	—	—	—
1797 reverse of 1796 plain edge	897,510	—	—	—	—	—	—
1797 reverse of 1796 gripped edge	Inc. above	—	—	—	—	—	—
1797	Inc. above	130	175	250	335	1,150	3,300
1797 stemless	Inc. above	300	495	600	910	3,200	—
1798/7	1,841,745	200	300	375	1,200	3,900	—
1798 reverse of 1796	Inc. above	—	—	—	—	—	—
1798 1st hair style	Inc. above	90.00	130	200	350	1,300	3,100
1798 2nd hair style	Inc. above	—	—	—	—	—	—
1799	42,540	2,750	4,650	10,000	24,500	58,500	—
1799/98	Inc. above	2,600	4,300	9,200	21,000	46,000	—
1800	2,822,175	50.00	95.00	200	400	1,750	—
1800/798	Inc. above	—	—	—	—	—	—
1800/79	Inc. above	—	—	—	—	—	—
1801	1,362,837	60.00	85.00	195	375	850	—
1801 3 errors	Inc. above	225	500	925	1,750	5,500	—
1801 1/000	Inc. above	—	—	—	—	—	—
1801 100/000	Inc. above	—	—	—	—	—	—
1802	3,435,100	60.00	85.00	185	360	780	2,250
1802 stemless	Inc. above	—	—	—	—	—	—
1802 fraction 1/000	Inc. above	—	—	—	—	—	—
1803 small date, small fraction	2,471,353	60.00	85.00	185	350	750	2,250
1803 small date, large fraction	Inc. above	60.00	85.00	185	360	800	—
1803 large date, small fraction	Inc. above	4,600	6,950	14,500	26,500	75,000	—
1803 large date, large fraction	Inc. above	—	—	—	—	—	—
1804	96,500	1,400	2,000	2,600	3,200	7,000	—
1804 Restrike of 1860	—	—	—	650	750	800	1,000
1805	941,116	60.00	90.00	160	300	875	2,450
1806	348,000	70.00	100.00	150	375	1,100	4,700
1807 small fraction	727,221	60.00	80.00	160	300	800	2,250
1807 large fraction	Inc. above	—	—	—	—	—	—
1807/6 large 7/6	Inc. above	60.00	80.00	160	350	1,275	—
1807/6 small 7/6	Inc. above	1,900	2,900	4,200	6,000	19,000	—

CENT

Classic Head Cent.
Classic head left, flanked by stars, date below. Value within wreath.

KM# 39 **Designer:** John Reich. **Diameter:** 29
Weight: 10.8900 g. **Composition:** Copper

Date	Mintage	G-4	VG-8	F-12	VF-20	XF-40	MS-60
1808	1,109,000	85.00	150	250	575	1,450	3,600
1809	222,867	135	250	450	1,050	2,650	6,300
1810/09	1,458,500	—	—	—	—	—	—
1810	Inc. above	75.00	95.00	210	550	1,100	3,850
1811/10	218,025	130	200	440	1,200	2,200	—
1811	Inc. above	110	175	400	1,000	1,500	7,000
1812 small date	1,075,500	54.00	88.00	215	550	975	2,800
1812 large date	—	—	—	—	—	—	—
1813	418,000	60.00	175	400	800	1,200	—
1814 Plain 4	357,830	54.00	93.00	225	530	975	2,800
1814 Crosslet 4	Inc. above	54.00	88.00	215	550	975	—

Coronet Cent.
Coronet head left, within circle of stars, date below. Value within wreath.

KM# 45 **Designer:** John Reich. **Diameter:** 28-29
Weight: 10.8900 g. **Composition:** Copper

Date	Mintage	G-4	VG-8	F-12	VF-20	XF-40	MS-60
1816	2,820,982	31.00	37.00	51.00	98.00	175	420
1817 13 stars	3,948,400	29.00	34.00	45.00	75.00	145	500
1817 15 stars	Inc. above	35.00	44.00	70.00	163	550	1,600
1818	3,167,000	29.00	33.00	40.00	72.00	125	270
1819	2,671,000	29.00	33.00	40.00	72.00	120	285
1820	4,407,550	29.00	33.00	40.00	72.00	120	300
1821	389,000	40.00	75.00	250	400	1,500	6,000
1822	2,072,339	31.00	35.00	45.00	100.00	195	750
1823	—	90.00	200	310	690	2,750	—
1823/22	—	80.00	110	300	675	2,450	—
1823 Restrike	600	750	850	1,000	1,200	2,000	
1824	1,262,000	31.00	35.00	38.00	160	350	950
1824/22	Inc. above	40.00	49.00	90.00	375	1,000	9,850
1825	1,461,100	30.00	35.00	50.00	110	300	960
1826	1,517,425	30.00	35.00	40.00	84.00	175	750
1826/25	Inc. above	30.00	40.00	75.00	175	600	2,000
1827	2,357,732	29.00	33.00	40.00	91.00	125	750
1828	2,260,624	29.00	33.00	40.00	81.00	150	450
1829	1,414,500	29.00	33.00	40.00	91.00	130	475
1830	1,711,500	25.00	29.00	36.00	68.00	120	400
1831	3,359,260	25.00	29.00	36.00	68.00	115	315
1832	2,362,000	25.00	29.00	36.00	68.00	120	380
1833	2,739,000	25.00	29.00	36.00	68.00	113	300
1834	1,855,100	25.00	29.00	36.00	68.00	125	375
1834 Large 8 & stars, small letters	Inc. above	75.00	120	145	250	625	—
1835	3,878,400	25.00	29.00	36.00	68.00	105	300
1836	2,111,000	25.00	29.00	36.00	68.00	105	350
1837	5,558,300	25.00	29.00	36.00	68.00	105	300
1838	6,370,200	25.00	29.00	36.00	68.00	105	300
1839	3,128,661	29.00	33.00	40.00	72.00	110	350
1839/36	Inc. above	300	600	1,250	2,450	4,900	—

Braided Hair Cent.

Head left, braided hair, within circle of stars, date below. Value within wreath.

KM# 67 Designer: Christian Gobrecht. **Diameter:** 27.5 **Weight:** 10.8900 g. **Composition:** Copper **Notes:** 1840 and 1842 strikes are known with both small and large dates, with little difference in value. A slightly larger Liberty head and larger reverse lettering were used beginning in 1843.

Date	Mintage	G-4	VG-8	F-12	VF-20	XF-40	MS-60
1840	2,462,700	25.00	28.00	31.00	36.00	69.00	47.00
1841	1,597,367	25.00	28.00	31.00	39.00	79.00	440
1842	2,383,390	25.00	28.00	31.00	36.00	69.00	425
1843	2,425,342	25.00	28.00	31.00	36.00	69.00	445
1843 obverse 1842 with reverse of 1844	Inc. above	27.00	30.00	33.00	38.00	79.00	400
1844	2,398,752	25.00	28.00	31.00	36.00	69.00	300
1844/81	Inc. above	40.00	50.00	60.00	100.00	225	700
1845	3,894,804	25.00	28.00	31.00	36.00	69.00	250
1846	4,120,800	23.00	26.00	29.00	34.00	69.00	250
1847	6,183,669	23.00	26.00	29.00	34.00	69.00	250
1847/7	Inc. above	32.00	50.00	90.00	150	385	1,350
1848	6,415,799	25.00	28.00	31.00	36.00	61.00	250
1849	4,178,500	25.00	28.00	31.00	36.00	61.00	325
1850	4,426,844	25.00	28.00	31.00	36.00	61.00	250
1851	9,889,707	23.00	26.00	29.00	34.00	59.00	165
1851/81	Inc. above	36.00	45.00	55.00	85.00	175	600
1852	5,063,094	23.00	26.00	29.00	34.00	59.00	165
1853	6,641,131	23.00	26.00	29.00	34.00	59.00	165
1854	4,236,156	23.00	26.00	29.00	34.00	59.00	165
1855 Slanted 5's	1,574,829	43.00	56.00	66.00	71.00	96.00	200
1855 Upright 5's	Inc. above	23.00	26.00	29.00	34.00	59.00	165
1855 Slanted 5's Knob on Ear	Inc. above	29.00	34.00	41.00	52.00	99.00	—
1856 Slanted 5	2,690,463	23.00	26.00	29.00	34.00	59.00	165
1856 Upright 5	Inc. above	43.00	56.00	69.00	—	—	—
1857 Large date	333,456	125	150	175	235	310	600
1857 Small date	Inc. above	85.00	110	140	190	265	—

Flying Eagle Cent.

Flying eagle above date. Value within wreath.

KM# 85 Designer: James B. Longacre. **Diameter:** 19 **Weight:** 4.6700 g. **Composition:** Copper-Nickel **Notes:** On the large-letter variety of 1858, the "A" and "M" in AMERICA are connected at their bases; on the small-letter variety, the two letters are separated.

Large letters AM touch at bottom

Small letters Space between AM

Date	Mintage	G-4	VG-8	F-12	VF-20	XF-40	AU-50	MS-60	MS-65	Prf-65
1856	Est. 2,500	6,250	7,250	9,000	10,750	12,850	13,500	16,500	65,000	28,500
1857	17,450,000	27.50	39.00	40.00	47.00	125	165	320	3,500	29,000
1858/7	Inc. below	65.00	92.50	175	380	760	1,500	3,300	60,000	—
1858 large letters	24,600,000	27.50	41.00	43.50	56.00	150	220	340	3,850	24,500
1858 small letters	Inc. above	26.00	39.00	42.00	47.00	135	175	320	3,650	30,000

Indian Head Cent.

Indian head with headdress left above date. Value within wreath.

KM# 87 Designer: James B. Longacre. **Diameter:** 19 **Weight:** 4.6700 g. **Composition:** Copper-Nickel

Date	Mintage	G-4	VG-8	F-12	VF-20	XF-40	AU-50	MS-60	MS-65	Prf-65
1859	36,400,000	13.00	16.00	22.50	48.00	100.00	175	230	3,650	5,200

CENT

Indian Head Cent.
Indian head with headdress left above date. Value within wreath, shield above.

KM# 90   **Designer:** James B. Longacre. **Diameter:** 19 **Weight:** 4.6700 g. **Composition:** Copper-Nickel

Date	Mintage	G-4	VG-8	F-12	VF-20	XF-40	AU-50	MS-60	MS-65	Prf-65
1860 Rounded Bust	20,566,000	11.00	15.00	22.00	46.00	68.00	110	190	965	3,600
1860	(1,000)	—	—	—	—	—	—	—	—	—
1860 Pointed Bust	Inc. above	20.00	30.00	42.00	60.00	100.00	160	300	6,000	—
1861	10,100,000	20.00	30.00	42.00	58.00	95.00	160	180	975	7,250
1862	28,075,000	11.00	11.50	12.50	15.00	28.00	60.00	80.00	1,050	2,350
1863	49,840,000	7.50	9.25	11.00	12.50	25.00	58.00	75.00	1,050	3,100
1864	13,740,000	16.50	28.50	35.00	72.00	125	175	220	1,350	3,200

Indian Head Cent.
Indian head with headdress left above date. Value within wreath, shield above.

KM# 90a   **Designer:** James B. Longacre. **Diameter:** 19 **Weight:** 3.1100 g. **Composition:** Bronze **Notes:** The 1864 "L" variety has the designer's initial in Liberty's hair to the right of her neck.

1864 "L"

Date	Mintage	G-4	VG-8	F-12	VF-20	XF-40	AU-50	MS-60	MS-65	Prf-65
1864	39,233,714	8.00	20.00	25.00	45.00	70.00	80.00	110	335	10,500
1864 L pointed bust	Inc. above	52.50	72.50	139	185	275	325	410	1,700	200,000
1865 plain 5	35,429,286	7.00	11.00	20.00	25.00	45.00	60.00	90.00	485	6,750
1865 fancy 5	Inc. above	6.00	10.50	18.50	23.00	40.00	55.00	85.00	465	—
1866	9,826,500	46.00	66.00	80.00	115	195	240	280	1,350	4,500
1867	9,821,000	52.00	72.00	110	120	195	240	285	1,350	6,100
1867/1867	Inc. above	60.00	85.00	130	190	275	385	565	1,950	—
1868	10,266,500	37.50	50.00	77.00	120	180	245	265	985	5,750
1869/9	6,420,000	145	280	495	660	825	1,000	1,250	2,350	—
1869	Inc. above	90.00	125	230	335	450	560	625	1,750	3,100
1870	5,275,000	62.00	118	225	285	410	510	600	1,400	2,650
1871	3,929,500	88.00	125	280	310	420	510	610	2,400	2,500
1872	4,042,000	90.00	180	390	425	625	750	840	3,850	4,250
1873 closed 3	11,676,500	30.00	52.00	95.00	135	235	300	400	2,850	2,950
1873 open 3	Inc. above	20.00	34.00	65.00	82.00	175	215	250	1,300	—
1873 Double Liberty die 1	Inc. above	275	450	950	1,500	2,400	4,250	7,500	—	—
1873 Double Liberty die 2	Inc. above	—	—	450	900	1,650	2,800	4,500	—	—
1874	14,187,500	15.00	22.50	46.00	65.00	112	150	225	700	2,850
1875	13,528,000	16.00	29.00	56.00	72.00	120	165	215	800	8,500
1876	7,944,000	27.00	38.50	74.00	130	230	295	335	975	2,600
1877	852,500	985	1,190	1,600	2,050	2,650	3,000	3,450	13,000	12,500
1878	5,799,850	26.00	35.00	68.00	135	245	290	350	875	1,375
1879	16,231,200	7.00	10.00	16.50	33.00	75.00	90.00	100.00	365	1,250
1880	38,964,955	3.50	5.50	6.50	11.00	28.00	48.00	66.00	360	1,250
1881	39,211,575	3.50	4.25	6.50	8.00	22.00	30.00	43.00	325	1,250
1882	38,581,100	3.50	4.25	5.00	10.00	22.00	30.00	40.00	325	1,450
1883	45,589,109	3.00	4.00	4.50	7.50	17.50	30.00	42.00	325	1,600
1884	23,261,742	3.50	4.50	7.00	12.50	29.00	40.00	60.00	460	1,250
1885	11,765,384	6.75	8.00	12.00	27.00	62.00	82.00	105	725	1,500
1886 Type 1 obverse	17,654,290	3.75	6.60	19.80	56.00	148	170	190	1,250	2,650
1886 Type 2 obverse	Inc. above	7.00	10.00	35.00	90.00	200	250	325	2,500	7,500
1887	45,226,483	2.50	3.00	4.00	7.00	19.00	28.00	50.00	400	6,200
1888	37,494,414	2.75	3.25	5.00	8.00	21.00	28.00	48.00	900	5,400
1889	48,869,361	2.25	2.75	3.50	6.00	12.00	26.00	40.00	400	1,900
1890	57,182,854	2.10	2.50	3.00	5.50	10.00	23.00	37.50	400	1,800
1891	47,072,350	2.25	2.75	3.25	5.50	13.00	23.00	37.00	400	2,150
1892	37,649,832	2.40	3.25	4.40	6.00	18.50	25.00	35.00	400	1,325
1893	46,642,195	2.10	2.75	3.25	5.50	10.00	22.00	30.00	340	1,250
1894	16,752,132	5.00	6.00	13.00	20.00	50.00	65.00	85.00	375	1,350
1894/94	Inc. above	24.00	34.00	80.00	150	275	440	800	8,000	—
1895	38,343,636	2.10	2.40	3.50	4.50	11.00	22.00	32.00	200	1,275
1896	39,057,293	1.95	2.50	3.25	4.75	13.00	26.00	34.00	225	1,900
1897	50,466,330	1.95	2.40	2.75	4.00	10.00	22.00	30.00	195	1,600
1898	49,823,079	1.95	2.40	2.75	4.00	10.00	22.00	30.00	195	1,275

Date	Mintage	G-4	VG-8	F-12	VF-20	XF-40	AU-50	MS-60	MS-65	Prf-65
1899	53,600,031	1.95	2.20	2.60	4.00	10.00	22.00	30.00	165	1,275
1900	66,833,764	1.95	2.20	2.50	4.00	12.00	23.00	30.00	175	1,275
1901	79,611,143	1.85	2.20	2.50	4.00	11.00	22.00	29.00	165	1,275
1902	87,376,722	1.85	2.20	2.50	4.00	10.00	22.00	28.00	165	1,325
1903	85,094,493	1.85	2.20	2.50	4.00	10.00	21.00	28.00	165	1,275
1904	61,328,015	1.75	2.20	2.50	4.00	10.00	21.00	28.00	165	1,275
1905	80,719,163	1.75	2.20	2.50	3.50	9.00	20.00	28.00	165	1,350
1906	96,022,255	1.75	2.20	2.50	3.50	9.00	21.00	28.00	165	1,275
1907	108,138,618	1.75	2.20	2.50	3.50	8.50	20.00	28.00	165	1,950
1908	32,327,987	1.75	2.30	2.50	3.50	9.00	20.00	28.00	165	1,275
1908S	1,115,000	77.00	82.00	105	122	166	195	285	2,650	—
1909	14,370,645	14.00	14.80	15.50	15.90	18.50	30.00	38.00	155	1,275
1909S	309,000	590	655	720	825	900	950	1,000	2,250	—

Lincoln Cent.
Wheat Ears.

KM# 132 Designer: Victor D. Brenner. **Diameter:** 19 **Weight:** 3.1100 g. **Composition:** Bronze **Notes:** The 1909 "VDB" varieties have the designer's initials inscribed at the 6 o'clock position on the reverse. The initials were removed until 1918, when they were restored on the obverse • MS60 prices are for brown coins and MS65 prices are for coins that are at least 90% original red.

1922 Plain

Date	Mintage	G-4	VG-8	F-12	VF-20	XF-40	AU-50	MS-60	MS-65	Prf-65
1909 VDB	27,995,000	12.50	13.00	13.25	13.50	14.00	16.00	25.00	195	12,500
1909 VDB Doubled Die Obverse	Inc. above	—	—	55.00	75.00	100.00	120	150	1,900	—
1909S VDB	484,000	775	1,010	1,285	1,410	1,525	1,650	1,850	6,850	—
1909	72,702,618	2.25	2.50	2.75	3.50	6.00	12.00	15.00	85.00	950
1909S	1,825,000	115	120	139	185	245	265	360	1,300	—
1909S/S S over horizontal S	Inc. above	115	120	135	180	255	280	350	1,600	—
1910	146,801,218	.50	.60	.75	1.00	4.00	9.00	17.50	250	800
1910S	6,045,000	16.50	20.00	21.00	27.50	46.00	72.00	98.00	800	—
1911	101,177,787	.60	.80	2.00	2.50	6.50	11.00	20.00	375	765
1911D	12,672,000	5.25	6.00	10.00	22.50	50.00	70.00	88.00	1,550	—
1911S	4,026,000	50.00	53.00	55.00	60.00	75.00	105	175	3,300	—
1912	68,153,060	1.75	2.00	2.50	6.00	13.50	26.00	32.00	550	975
1912D	10,411,000	7.00	10.00	12.00	26.00	69.00	110	160	2,800	—
1912S	4,431,000	24.00	26.00	29.00	42.00	78.00	115	175	4,400	—
1913	76,532,352	1.00	1.20	1.75	3.25	18.50	29.00	35.00	400	750
1913D	15,804,000	3.00	3.50	4.00	10.50	49.00	63.00	93.00	2,100	—
1913S	6,101,000	13.50	17.00	21.00	32.00	57.00	105	190	6,250	—
1914	75,238,432	.75	1.10	2.25	6.00	19.00	40.00	54.00	415	775
1914D	1,193,000	220	250	400	495	975	1,475	2,000	22,000	—
1914S	4,137,000	25.00	28.00	31.00	40.00	88.00	185	310	11,500	—
1915	29,092,120	1.65	3.00	4.00	18.00	60.00	70.00	82.00	1,150	775
1915D	22,050,000	1.75	3.00	4.25	7.50	24.00	44.00	70.00	1,250	—
1915S	4,833,000	21.00	24.50	28.00	32.00	79.00	96.00	185	4,800	—
1916	131,833,677	.35	.60	1.25	2.60	8.50	14.50	18.50	360	2,450
1916D	35,956,000	1.75	2.25	3.25	6.50	18.50	38.00	74.00	3,300	—
1916S	22,510,000	2.25	3.40	4.75	9.50	27.50	48.00	105	8,500	—
1917	196,429,785	.35	.45	.55	2.00	4.75	10.00	16.00	450	—
1917 Doubled Die Obverse	Inc. above	90.00	110	175	350	900	1,750	2,500	25,000	—
1917D	55,120,000	1.50	1.75	2.50	5.50	38.00	44.00	60.00	3,000	—
1917S	32,620,000	.80	1.20	1.75	2.50	11.50	25.00	58.00	7,200	—
1918	288,104,634	.35	.40	.50	1.25	4.50	9.50	13.00	385	—
1918D	47,830,000	1.60	2.00	2.65	5.50	15.50	34.00	70.00	3,500	—
1918S	34,680,000	.50	1.20	1.75	3.65	11.00	32.00	61.00	7,800	—
1919	392,021,000	.30	.40	.50	.80	1.75	5.25	8.50	175	—
1919D	57,154,000	1.25	1.60	2.00	4.00	12.75	35.00	50.00	2,700	—
1919S	139,760,000	.40	.70	1.80	2.65	6.00	17.50	40.00	4,300	—
1920	310,165,000	.35	.40	.90	1.50	2.80	7.50	13.50	225	—
1920D	49,280,000	1.25	1.65	2.80	5.50	18.50	37.00	62.50	2,750	—
1920S	46,220,000	.90	1.00	1.50	2.75	13.00	34.50	90.00	9,000	—
1921	39,157,000	.60	1.00	1.25	2.80	11.00	21.00	41.50	375	—
1921S	15,274,000	1.65	2.10	2.85	6.00	34.50	68.00	100.00	6,700	—
1922D	7,160,000	17.50	19.50	23.00	25.00	37.50	73.00	100.00	2,350	—
1922D Weak Rev	Inc. above	15.00	15.00	17.00	20.00	32.00	60.00	90.00	1,750	—
1922D Weak D	Inc. above	30.00	44.00	60.00	100.00	220	285	550	—	—
1922 No D Die 2 Strong Rev	Inc. above	725	820	1,225	1,600	2,975	6,250	11,000	200,000	—
1922 No D Die 3 Weak Rev	Inc. above	300	400	685	885	1,750	3,500	8,500	—	—

CENT

Date	Mintage	G-4	VG-8	F-12	VF-20	XF-40	AU-50	MS-60	MS-65	Prf-65
1923	74,723,000	.60	.80	1.00	1.35	5.75	10.50	13.50	480	—
1923S	8,700,000	4.00	5.25	7.50	10.00	38.00	88.00	195	15,500	—
1924	75,178,000	.35	.50	.60	1.00	5.50	11.00	20.00	390	—
1924D	2,520,000	36.00	44.00	49.00	60.00	118	175	255	9,500	—
1924S	11,696,000	1.75	2.00	2.80	5.00	33.00	68.00	115	11,000	—
1925	139,949,000	.30	.40	.50	.70	2.75	6.50	8.50	100.00	—
1925D	22,580,000	1.50	2.00	3.00	5.00	15.50	30.00	60.00	5,000	—
1925S	26,380,000	1.20	1.50	2.00	2.75	11.50	32.00	80.00	9,000	—
1926	157,088,000	.25	.40	.50	.70	1.65	5.25	7.00	75.00	—
1926D	28,020,000	1.50	1.70	2.80	4.50	15.50	34.00	80.00	3,850	—
1926S	4,550,000	8.00	9.00	11.00	14.00	35.00	70.00	130	10,000	—
1927	144,440,000	.20	.30	.40	.70	1.60	5.25	7.00	95.00	—
1927D	27,170,000	1.50	1.75	2.25	3.35	7.50	24.50	58.50	2,000	—
1927S	14,276,000	1.50	1.85	3.00	4.65	14.50	40.00	62.50	6,500	—
1928	134,116,000	.20	.30	.40	.70	1.25	4.00	7.50	90.00	—
1928D	31,170,000	1.10	1.40	2.00	3.00	7.00	19.00	34.00	1,100	—
1928S Small S	17,266,000	1.20	1.65	2.60	4.00	9.50	31.00	71.50	4,650	—
1928S Large S	Inc. above	2.00	2.85	4.00	7.50	17.00	48.00	135	5,500	—
1929	185,262,000	.20	.30	.40	.60	1.00	5.25	6.00	85.00	—
1929D	41,730,000	.70	1.20	1.50	2.35	4.65	13.50	21.50	625	—
1929S	50,148,000	.80	1.25	1.75	2.80	7.00	14.50	19.00	550	—
1930	157,415,000	.20	.30	.40	.60	1.25	2.75	3.75	33.00	—
1930D	40,100,000	.35	.45	.65	.90	2.00	5.50	10.50	95.00	—
1930S	24,286,000	.35	.45	.60	.80	1.50	6.50	10.00	50.00	—
1931	19,396,000	.70	.80	1.30	2.00	4.00	10.00	19.00	135	—
1931D	4,480,000	4.85	6.00	6.50	7.50	12.75	37.50	52.00	950	—
1931S	866,000	122	124	130	133	140	148	163	725	—
1932	9,062,000	1.50	1.85	2.75	3.50	6.75	13.00	19.00	100.00	—
1932D	10,500,000	1.40	2.00	2.50	2.85	4.15	11.00	17.50	150	—
1933	14,360,000	1.40	1.80	2.50	2.85	6.50	11.50	17.50	100.00	—
1933D	6,200,000	3.50	4.25	6.00	7.50	13.50	19.00	23.00	135	—
1934	219,080,000	.20	.30	.40	.60	1.25	4.00	8.00	30.00	—
1934D	28,446,000	.35	.50	.80	1.50	3.00	9.00	20.00	52.00	—
1935	245,338,000	.20	.30	.40	.55	.90	1.50	3.50	28.00	—
1935D	47,000,000	.15	.20	.30	.40	.95	2.50	4.50	30.00	—
1935S	38,702,000	.25	.35	.60	1.75	3.00	5.00	12.00	55.00	—
1936 (Proof in Satin Finish)	309,637,569	.20	.30	.40	.55	.85	1.40	2.00	8.00	1,000
1936 Brilliant Proof	Inc. above	—	—	—	—	—	—	—	—	1,100
1936D	40,620,000	.20	.30	.40	.55	.90	1.50	3.50	22.00	—
1936S	29,130,000	.20	.30	.45	.60	1.00	1.75	3.00	18.00	—
1937	309,179,320	.20	.30	.40	.55	.85	1.40	1.60	20.00	180
1937D	50,430,000	.20	.30	.40	.60	.95	1.00	2.20	24.00	—
1937S	34,500,000	.20	.30	.40	.55	.90	1.25	2.40	23.00	—
1938	156,696,734	.20	.30	.40	.55	.85	1.20	3.00	17.00	90.00
1938D	20,010,000	.20	.30	.45	.60	1.00	1.50	3.50	17.00	—
1938S	15,180,000	.30	.40	.50	.70	1.00	2.00	2.80	26.00	—
1939	316,479,520	.20	.30	.40	.55	.75	.90	1.00	15.00	85.00
1939D	15,160,000	.35	.45	.50	.60	.85	1.90	2.50	20.00	—
1939S	52,070,000	.30	.40	.50	.60	.80	1.10	2.00	19.00	—
1940	586,825,872	.10	.20	.30	.40	.50	.75	1.00	17.00	65.00
1940D	81,390,000	.20	.30	.40	.55	.75	.50	1.20	12.00	—
1940S	112,940,000	.20	.30	.40	.55	.90	1.25	1.40	14.00	—
1941	887,039,100	.10	.20	.30	.40	.50	.70	.85	17.00	80.00
1941 Doubled Die Obv	Inc. above	35.00	50.00	70.00	80.00	95.00	135	200	2,800	—
1941D	128,700,000	.20	.30	.40	.55	.75	1.25	2.25	20.00	—
1941S	92,360,000	.20	.30	.40	.55	.75	1.75	2.75	24.00	—
1942	657,828,600	.10	.20	.30	.40	.50	.70	.85	17.00	115
1942D	206,698,000	.20	.25	.30	.35	.40	.50	.65	22.00	—
1942S	85,590,000	.25	.35	.45	.85	1.25	2.50	4.50	26.00	—

Lincoln Cent.

Wheat Ears.

KM# 132a **Designer:** Victor D. Brenner.
Diameter: 19 **Weight:** 2.7000 g. **Composition:**
Zinc Coated Steel

Date	Mintage	G-4	VG-8	F-12	VF-20	XF-40	AU-50	MS-60	MS-65	Prf-65
1943	684,628,670	.25	.30	.35	.45	.60	.85	1.25	4.75	—
1943D	217,660,000	.35	.40	.45	.50	.70	1.00	1.25	8.50	—
1943D/D RPM	Inc. above	30.00	38.00	50.00	65.00	90.00	125	200	—	—
1943S	191,550,000	.45	.45	.50	.65	.90	1.40	3.00	13.50	—

Lincoln Cent.
Wheat Ears.

KM# A132   Designer: Victor D. Brenner.
Diameter: 19 **Weight:** 3.1100 g. **Composition:**
Copper-Zinc **Notes:** KM#132 design and
composition resumed • MS60 prices are for brown
coins and MS65 prices are for coins that are at least
90% original red.

1955 Double die

Date	Mintage	XF-40	MS-65	Prf-65
1944	1,435,400,000	.40	8.00	—
1944D	430,578,000	.50	12.50	—
1944D/S Type 1	Inc. above	235	3,750	—
1944D/S Type 2	Inc. above	175	1,600	—
1944S	282,760,000	.40	12.00	—
1945	1,040,515,000	.40	15.00	—
1945D	226,268,000	.40	13.50	—
1945S	181,770,000	.40	12.00	—
1946	991,655,000	.30	13.00	—
1946D	315,690,000	.30	6.00	—
1946S	198,100,000	.30	5.50	—
1946S/D	—	70.00	600	—
1947	190,555,000	.45	16.00	—
1947D	194,750,000	.40	10.00	—
1947S	99,000,000	.35	12.00	—
1948	317,570,000	.40	14.00	—
1948D	172,637,000	.40	6.80	—
1948S	81,735,000	.40	6.50	—
1949	217,775,000	.40	15.00	—
1949D	153,132,000	.40	12.00	—
1949S	64,290,000	.50	10.00	—
1950	272,686,386	.40	13.50	70.00
1950D	334,950,000	.35	9.00	—
1950S	118,505,000	.40	8.00	—
1951	295,633,500	.40	14.00	70.00
1951D	625,355,000	.30	8.00	—
1951S	136,010,000	.40	10.00	—
1952	186,856,980	.40	16.00	42.00
1952D	746,130,000	.30	8.00	—
1952S	137,800,004	.60	9.00	—
1953	256,883,800	.30	18.00	30.00
1953D	700,515,000	.30	11.00	—
1953S	181,835,000	.40	11.50	—
1954	71,873,350	.25	17.50	17.00
1954D	251,552,500	.25	10.00	—
1954S	96,190,000	.25	12.00	—
1955	330,958,000	.25	15.00	16.00
1955 Doubled Die	Inc. above	1,600	43,500	—

Note: The 1955 "doubled die" has distinct doubling of the date and
lettering on the obverse.

Date	Mintage	XF-40	MS-65	Prf-65
1955D	563,257,500	.20	12.00	—
1955S	44,610,000	.35	7.50	—
1956	421,414,384	.20	16.00	10.00
1956D	1,098,201,100	.20	8.00	—
1957	283,787,952	.20	9.00	6.00
1957D	1,051,342,000	.20	8.00	—
1958	253,400,652	.20	9.00	6.50
1958D	800,953,300	.20	8.00	—

Lincoln Cent.
Lincoln Memorial.

KM# 201   Rev. Designer: Frank Gasparro.
Weight: 3.1100 g. **Composition:** Copper-Zinc
Notes: MS60 prices are for brown coins and MS65
prices are for coins that are at least 90% original red.
The dates were modified in 1960, 1970 and 1982,
resulting in large-date and small-date varieties for
those years. The 1972 "doubled die" shows doubling
of IN GOD WE TRUST. The 1979-S and 1981-S Type
II proofs have a clearer mint mark than the Type I
proofs of those years. Some 1982 cents have the
predominantly copper composition; others have the
predominantly zinc composition. They can be
distinguished by weight.

Small date

Large date

Large date

Small date

Date	Mintage	XF-40	MS-65	Prf-65
1959	610,864,291	—	18.00	1.50
1959D	1,279,760,000	—	16.00	—
1960 small date, low 9	588,096,602	2.10	12.00	16.00
1960 large date, high 9	Inc. above	—	10.00	1.25
1960D small date, low 9	1,580,884,000	—	10.00	—
1960D large date, high 9	Inc. above	—	11.00	—
1960D/D small over large date	Inc. above	—	300	—
1961	756,373,244	—	6.50	1.00
1961D	1,753,266,700	—	15.00	—
1962	609,263,019	—	8.00	1.00
1962D	1,793,148,400	—	14.00	—
1963	757,185,645	—	10.00	1.00
1963D	1,774,020,400	—	12.00	—
1964	2,652,525,762	—	6.50	1.00
1964D	3,799,071,500	—	7.00	—
1965	1,497,224,900	—	10.00	—
1965 SMS	Inc. above	—	7.50	—

CENT

Date	Mintage	XF-40	MS-65	Prf-65
1966	2,188,147,783	—	10.00	—
1966 SMS	Inc. above	—	8.00	—
1967	3,048,667,100	—	10.00	—
1967 SMS	Inc. above	—	8.00	—
1968	1,707,880,970	—	12.00	—
1968D	2,886,269,600	—	12.00	—
1968S	261,311,510	—	8.00	1.00
1969	1,136,910,000	—	6.50	—
1969D	4,002,832,200	—	10.00	—
1969S	547,309,631	—	8.00	1.10
1969S Doubled Die Obverse	Inc. above	—	—	—
1970	1,898,315,000	—	8.00	—
1970D	2,891,438,900	—	6.00	—
1970S	693,192,814	—	—	1.20
1970S small date, level 7	Inc. above	—	75.00	60.00
1970S large date, low 7	Inc. above	—	16.00	—
1970S Doubled Die Obverse	Inc. above	—	—	—
1971	1,919,490,000	—	25.00	—
1971D	2,911,045,600	—	5.50	—
1971S	528,354,192	—	6.00	1.20
1971S Doubled Die Obverse	Inc. above	—	—	—
1972	2,933,255,000	—	6.00	—
1972 Doubled Die Obverse	Inc. above	240	775	—
1972D	2,665,071,400	—	10.00	—
1972S	380,200,104	—	30.00	1.15
1973	3,728,245,000	—	8.00	—
1973D	3,549,576,588	—	11.00	—
1973S	319,937,634	—	8.00	0.80
1974	4,232,140,523	—	12.00	—
1974D	4,235,098,000	—	12.00	—
1974S	412,039,228	—	10.00	0.75
1975	5,451,476,142	—	8.00	—
1975D	4,505,245,300	—	13.50	—
1975S	(2,845,450)	—	—	5.50
1976	4,674,292,426	—	18.00	—
1976D	4,221,592,455	—	20.00	—
1976S	(4,149,730)	—	—	5.00
1977	4,469,930,000	—	14.00	—
1977D	4,149,062,300	—	14.00	—
1977S	(3,251,152)	—	—	3.00
1978	5,558,605,000	—	14.00	—
1978D	4,280,233,400	—	12.00	—
1978S	(3,127,781)	—	—	3.50
1979	6,018,515,000	—	12.00	—
1979D	4,139,357,254	—	8.00	—
1979S type I, proof	(3,677,175)	—	—	4.00
1979S type II, proof	Inc. above	—	—	4.25
1980	7,414,705,000	—	6.50	—
1980D	5,140,098,660	—	10.00	—
1980S	(3,554,806)	—	—	2.25
1981	7,491,750,000	—	7.50	—
1981D	5,373,235,677	—	9.00	—
1981S type I, proof	(4,063,083)	—	—	3.50
1981S type II, proof	Inc. above	—	—	60.00
1982 large date	10,712,525,000	—	6.00	—
1982 small date	Inc. above	—	8.00	—
1982D large date	6,012,979,368	—	6.00	—
1982S	3,857,479	—	—	—

Lincoln Cent.

Lincoln Memorial.

KM# 201a **Diameter:** 19 **Weight:** 2.5000 g.
Composition: Copper Plated Zinc **Notes:** MS60 prices are for brown coins and MS65 prices are for coins that are at least 90% original red.

Date	Mintage	XF-40	MS-65	Prf-65
1982 large date	—	—	6.00	—
1982 small date	—	—	9.00	—
1982D large date	—	—	8.00	—
1982D small date	—	—	6.00	—

Lincoln Cent.

Lincoln Memorial. `

KM# 201b **Diameter:** 19 **Composition:** Copper Plated Zinc **Notes:** MS60 prices are for brown coins and MS65 prices are for coins that are at least 90% original red. The 1983 "doubled die reverse" shows doubling of UNITED STATES OF AMERICA. The 1984 "doubled die" shows doubling of Lincoln's ear on the obverse.

Date	Mintage	XF-40	MS-65	Prf-65
1982S	(3,857,479)	—	—	3.00
1983	7,752,355,000	—	7.00	—
1983 Doubled Die	Inc. above	—	400	—
1983D	6,467,199,428	—	5.50	—
1983S	(3,279,126)	—	—	4.00
1984	8,151,079,000	—	7.50	—
1984 Doubled Die	Inc. above	—	275	—
1984D	5,569,238,906	—	5.50	—
1984S	(3,065,110)	—	—	4.50
1985	5,648,489,887	—	4.50	—
1985D	5,287,399,926	—	4.50	—
1985S	(3,362,821)	—	—	6.00
1986	4,491,395,493	—	5.00	—
1986D	4,442,866,698	—	8.00	—
1986S	(3,010,497)	—	—	7.50
1987	4,682,466,931	—	8.50	—
1987D	4,879,389,514	—	6.00	—
1987S	(4,227,728)	—	—	5.00
1988	6,092,810,000	—	8.50	—
1988D	5,253,740,443	—	5.50	—
1988S	(3,262,948)	—	—	4.00
1989	7,261,535,000	—	5.00	—
1989D	5,345,467,111	—	5.00	—
1989S	(3,220,194)	—	—	6.00
1990	6,851,765,000	—	5.00	—
1990D	4,922,894,533	—	5.00	—
1990S	(3,299,559)	—	—	5.00
1990 no S, Proof only	Inc. above	—	—	2,750
1991	5,165,940,000	—	6.00	—
1991D	4,158,442,076	—	5.00	—
1991S	(2,867,787)	—	—	5.00
1992	4,648,905,000	—	5.50	—
1992D	4,448,673,300	—	5.50	—
1992D Close AM, Proof Reverse Die	Inc. above	—	—	—
1992S	(4,176,560)	—	—	5.00
1993	5,684,705,000	—	5.50	—
1993D	6,426,650,571	—	5.50	—
1993S	(3,394,792)	—	—	7.00
1994	6,500,850,000	—	10.00	—
1994D	7,131,765,000	—	5.50	—
1994S	(3,269,923)	—	—	4.00
1995	6,411,440,000	—	4.50	—
1995 Doubled Die Obverse	Inc. above	20.00	50.00	—
1995D	7,128,560,000	—	5.00	—
1995S	(2,707,481)	—	—	9.50
1996	6,612,465,000	—	5.00	—
1996D	6,510,795,000	—	5.00	—
1996S	(2,915,212)	—	—	6.50
1997	4,622,800,000	—	5.00	—
1997D	4,576,555,000	—	5.00	—
1997S	(2,796,678)	—	—	11.50
1998	5,032,155,000	—	5.00	—
1998 Wide AM, reverse from proof die	Inc. above	—	—	—

Date	Mintage	XF-40	MS-65	Prf-65
1998D	5,255,353,500	—	5.00	—
1998S	(2,957,286)	—	—	9.50
1999	5,237,600,000	—	5.00	—
1999 Wide AM, reverse from proof die	Inc. above	—	—	—
1999D	6,360,065,000	—	5.00	—
1999S	(3,362,462)	—	—	5.00
2000	5,503,200,000	—	4.00	—
2000 Wide AM, reverse from proof die	Inc. above	—	—	—
2000D	8,774,220,000	—	4.00	—
2000S	(4,063,361)	—	—	4.00
2001	4,959,600,000	—	4.00	—
2001D	5,374,990,000	—	4.00	—
2001S	(3,099,096)	—	—	4.00
2002	3,260,800,000	—	4.00	—
2002D	4,028,055,000	—	4.00	—
2002S	(3,157,739)	—	—	4.00
2003	3,300,000,000	—	3.50	—
2003D	3,548,000,000	—	3.50	—
2003S	(3,116,590)	—	—	4.00
2004	3,379,600,000	—	3.50	—
2004D	3,456,400,000	—	3.50	—
2004S	2,992,069	—	—	4.00
2005	3,935,600,000	—	3.50	—
2005D	3,764,450,000	—	3.50	—
2005S	3,273,000	—	—	4.00
2006	4,290,000,000	—	2.00	—
2006D	3,944,000,000	—	2.50	—
2006S	2,923,105	—	—	4.00
2007	—	—	1.50	—
2007D	—	—	1.50	—
2007S	—	—	—	4.00
2008	—	—	1.50	—
2008D	—	—	1.50	—
2008S	—	—	—	4.00

Lincoln Bicentennial.

Log cabin.

KM# 441 Rev. Designer: Richard Masters and Jim Licaretz. **Diameter:** 19 **Weight:** 2.5000 g. **Composition:** Copper Plated Zinc

Date	Mintage	XF-40	MS-65	Prf-65
2009P	—	—	1.50	—
2009D	—	—	1.50	—
2009S	—	—	—	4.00

Lincoln seated on log.

KM# 442 Rev. Designer: Charles Vickers. **Diameter:** 19 **Weight:** 2.5000 g. **Composition:** Copper Plated Zinc

Date	Mintage	XF-40	MS-65	Prf-65
2009P	—	—	—	—
2009D	—	—	—	—
2009S	—	—	—	—

Lincoln standing before Illinois Statehouse.

KM# 443 Rev. Designer: Joel Ishowitz and Don Everhart. **Diameter:** 19 **Weight:** 2.5000 g. **Composition:** Copper Plated Zinc

Date	Mintage	XF-40	MS-65	Prf-65
2009P	—	—	1.50	—
2009D	—	—	1.50	—
2009S	—	—	—	4.00

Capitol Building.

KM# 444 Rev. Designer: Susan Gamble and Joseph Menna. **Weight:** 2.5000 g. **Composition:** Copper Plated Zinc

Date	Mintage	XF-40	MS-65	Prf-65
2009P	—	—	1.50	—
2009D	—	—	1.50	—
2009S	—	—	—	4.00

2 CENTS

2 CENTS

Shield in front of crossed arrows, banner above, date below. Value within wheat wreath.

KM# 94 Designer: James B. Longacre. **Diameter:** 23 **Weight:** 6.2200 g. **Composition:** Copper-Tin-Zinc **Notes:** The motto IN GOD WE TRUST was modified in 1864, resulting in small-motto and large-motto varieties for that year.

Small motto · Large motto

Date	Mintage	G-4	VG-8	F-12	VF-20	XF-40	AU-50	MS-60	MS-65	Prf-65
1864 small motto	19,847,500	140	210	285	425	650	725	1,125	7,500	75,000
1864 large motto	Inc. above	16.50	18.50	20.00	27.50	42.50	70.00	84.00	1,650	3,950
1865 fancy 5	13,640,000	16.50	18.50	20.00	27.50	42.50	70.00	84.00	1,650	850
1865 plain 5	Inc. above	16.50	18.50	21.00	29.00	45.00	75.00	90.00	1,750	2,950
1866	3,177,000	17.00	20.00	21.50	29.00	46.00	75.00	94.00	2,550	2,850
1867	2,938,750	18.00	21.00	36.00	46.00	60.00	96.00	125	2,900	2,900
1867 double die obverse	Inc. above	—	65.00	135	200	275	440	575	12,500	—
1868	2,803,750	18.00	22.00	37.50	47.50	65.00	105	135	2,900	2,850
1869	1,546,000	20.00	23.00	40.00	50.00	79.00	125	165	2,400	2,850
1869 repunched 18	Inc. above	35.00	45.00	75.00	150	325	550	—	—	—
1869/8 die crack	Inc. above	150	185	375	435	650	900	—	—	—
1870	861,250	31.00	42.00	60.00	82.00	135	190	295	8,250	2,850

Date	Mintage	G-4	VG-8	F-12	VF-20	XF-40	AU-50	MS-60	MS-65	Prf-65
1871	721,250	43.00	49.00	70.00	110	155	215	285	3,850	2,850
1872	65,000	325	395	550	740	925	1,050	1,500	8,850	2,950
1873 closed 3 proof only	Est. 600	1,250	1,375	1,500	1,625	1,750	2,000	—	—	4,250
1873 open 3 proof only	Est. 500	1,275	1,400	1,575	1,700	1,875	2,150	—	—	5,500

SILVER 3 CENTS

Silver 3 Cents - Type 1.

Shield within star, no outlines in star. Roman numeral in designed C, within circle of stars.

KM# 75 **Designer:** James B. Longacre. **Diameter:** 14 **Weight:** 0.8000 g. **Composition:** 0.7500 Silver, 0.0193 oz. ASW.

Date	Mintage	G-4	VG-8	F-12	VF-20	XF-40	AU-50	MS-60	MS-65	Prf-65
1851	5,447,400	25.00	41.50	42.50	45.00	65.00	155	185	975	—
1851O	720,000	38.50	47.50	55.00	100.00	160	250	340	2,600	—
1852	18,663,500	25.00	41.50	42.50	45.00	65.00	155	180	975	—
1853	11,400,000	25.00	41.50	42.50	45.00	65.00	155	180	975	—

Silver 3 Cents - Type 2.

Shield within star, three outlines in star. Roman numeral in designed C, within circle of stars.

KM# 80 **Designer:** James B. Longacre. **Diameter:** 14 **Weight:** 0.7500 g. **Composition:** 0.9000 Silver, 0.0217 oz. ASW.

Date	Mintage	G-4	VG-8	F-12	VF-20	XF-40	AU-50	MS-60	MS-65	Prf-65
1854	671,000	26.00	42.50	44.00	50.00	105	230	350	3,450	33,500
1855	139,000	44.00	57.50	75.00	125	205	340	550	8,500	15,000
1856	1,458,000	30.00	45.00	46.00	65.00	125	205	275	4,500	15,500
1857	1,042,000	28.50	42.50	45.00	62.50	130	240	300	3,300	13,500
1858	1,604,000	27.50	42.50	44.00	55.00	110	200	240	3,300	6,400

Silver 3 Cents - Type 3.

Shield within star, two outlines in star. Roman numeral in designed C, within circle of stars.

KM# 88 **Designer:** James B. Longacre. **Diameter:** 14 **Weight:** 0.7500 g. **Composition:** 0.9000 Silver, 0.0217 oz. ASW.

Date	Mintage	G-4	VG-8	F-12	VF-20	XF-40	AU-50	MS-60	MS-65	Prf-65
1859	365,000	30.00	44.00	50.00	62.50	82.50	170	195	975	2,150
1860	287,000	30.00	44.00	45.00	60.00	80.00	170	195	975	4,000
1861	498,000	30.00	44.00	45.00	60.00	80.00	170	195	975	1,800
1862	343,550	38.50	51.00	50.00	70.00	82.50	195	230	975	1,400
1863	21,460	340	375	400	445	480	625	780	2,250	1,350
1863/62 proof only; Rare	Inc. above	—	—	—	—	—	—	—	—	5,400
1864	12,470	340	375	400	445	480	625	780	1,700	1,350
1865	8,500	400	440	475	520	550	600	750	1,700	1,350
1866	22,725	340	375	400	445	495	550	650	1,900	1,325
1867	4,625	400	440	475	520	550	600	720	2,750	1,300
1868	4,100	400	445	480	520	575	625	740	5,750	1,400
1869	5,100	400	445	480	520	575	625	720	2,350	1,400
1869/68 proof only; Rare	Inc. above	—	—	—	—	—	—	—	—	—
1870	4,000	420	450	495	550	595	670	900	5,500	1,350
1871	4,360	400	440	480	520	575	625	750	1,700	1,450
1872	1,950	420	450	495	550	595	675	795	5,500	1,350
1873 proof only	600	650	685	730	800	890	980	—	—	2,500

NICKEL 3 CENTS

Coronet head left, date below. Roman numeral value within wreath.

KM# 95 **Designer:** James B. Longacre. **Diameter:** 17.9 **Weight:** 1.9400 g. **Composition:** Copper-Nickel

Date	Mintage	G-4	VG-8	F-12	VF-20	XF-40	AU-50	MS-60	MS-65	Prf-65
1865	11,382,000	15.50	16.50	17.50	22.50	37.50	60.00	100.00	650	6,500
1866	4,801,000	15.50	16.50	17.50	22.50	37.50	60.00	100.00	650	1,725
1867	3,915,000	15.50	16.50	17.50	22.50	37.50	60.00	100.00	770	1,575
1868	3,252,000	15.50	16.50	17.50	22.50	37.50	60.00	100.00	650	1,450
1869	1,604,000	16.50	17.50	19.50	25.50	40.50	61.00	120	795	1,050
1870	1,335,000	17.50	18.50	20.50	26.50	41.50	62.00	135	795	2,250
1871	604,000	17.50	19.00	22.50	27.50	42.50	64.00	155	800	1,200
1872	862,000	19.00	22.50	24.50	28.50	43.50	68.00	175	1,075	910
1873	1,173,000	16.50	18.50	22.50	25.50	40.50	62.00	145	1,375	1,125
1874	790,000	17.50	20.50	22.50	27.50	42.50	66.00	160	1,050	950
1875	228,000	19.00	22.50	27.50	30.50	45.50	80.00	190	850	1,500
1876	162,000	20.50	23.50	26.50	34.50	49.50	95.00	225	1,550	1,025
1877 proof	Est. 900	1,100	1,150	1,175	1,250	1,300	1,350	—	—	3,750
1878 proof	2,350	615	645	720	770	795	830	—	—	1,200
1879	41,200	65.00	75.00	96.00	110	115	180	320	850	690
1880	24,955	100.00	115	130	165	185	235	375	800	700
1881	1,080,575	15.50	16.50	19.00	23.50	39.50	60.00	100.00	670	680
1882	25,300	130	150	180	225	300	325	425	1,100	700
1883	10,609	200	225	260	305	375	425	480	4,850	690
1884	5,642	400	445	550	600	645	730	800	6,250	700
1885	4,790	470	520	645	700	745	775	900	2,300	720
1886 proof	4,290	320	330	345	385	385	420	—	—	715
1887/6 proof	7,961	350	390	415	450	460	515	—	—	940
1887	Inc. above	305	355	395	440	455	500	540	1,350	1,125
1888	41,083	54.00	63.00	70.00	80.00	100.00	170	315	725	690
1889	21,561	90.00	115	140	180	220	255	320	800	690

HALF DIME

Flowing Hair Half Dime.

KM# 15 **Designer:** Robert Scot. **Diameter:** 16.5 **Weight:** 1.3500 g. **Composition:** 0.8920 Silver, 0.0387 oz. ASW.

Date	Mintage	G-4	VG-8	F-12	VF-20	XF-40	MS-60
1794	86,416	1,325	1,625	2,150	3,125	7,325	19,850
1795	Inc. above	1,050	1,350	1,875	2,850	5,750	13,850

Draped Bust Half Dime.
Small eagle.

KM# 23 **Designer:** Robert Scot. **Diameter:** 16.5 **Weight:** 1.3500 g. **Composition:** 0.8920 Silver, 0.0387 oz. ASW.

Date	Mintage	G-4	VG-8	F-12	VF-20	XF-40	MS-60
1796	10,230	1,435	1,550	3,000	4,700	8,700	19,550
1796 LIKERTY	Inc. above	1,485	1,600	3,050	4,750	8,750	19,600
1796/5	Inc. above	1,555	1,700	3,150	4,850	8,850	19,700
1797 13 stars	44,527	2,100	2,650	4,100	5,800	9,800	32,750
1797 15 stars	Inc. above	1,385	1,500	2,950	4,650	8,650	19,500
1797 16 stars	Inc. above	1,535	1,750	3,200	4,900	8,900	19,750

Draped Bust Half Dime.
Draped bust right, flanked by stars, date at angle below. Heraldic eagle.

KM# 34 **Designer:** Robert Scot. **Diameter:** 16.5 **Weight:** 1.3500 g. **Composition:** 0.8920 Silver, 0.0387 oz. ASW.

Date	Mintage	G-4	VG-8	F-12	VF-20	XF-40	MS-60
1800	24,000	1,000	1,250	1,875	2,350	6,750	13,850

Date	Mintage	G-4	VG-8	F-12	VF-20	XF-40	MS-60
1800 LIBEKTY	Inc. above	1,000	1,250	1,875	2,350	7,250	15,400
1801	33,910	1,225	1,500	2,125	2,600	7,000	18,100
1802	3,060	44,500	65,000	95,000	135,000	300,000	—
1803 Large 8	37,850	1,100	1,375	2,000	2,475	6,875	13,975
1803 Small 8	Inc. above	1,325	1,625	2,250	2,725	7,125	16,200
1805	15,600	1,225	1,525	2,350	2,825	10,150	31,350

Liberty Cap Half Dime.

Classic head left, flanked by stars, date below. Eagle with arrows in talons, banner above.

KM# 47   Designer: William Kneass. **Diameter:** 15.5 **Weight:** 1.3500 g. **Composition:** 0.8920 Silver, 0.0387 oz. ASW.

Date	Mintage	G-4	VG-8	F-12	VF-20	XF-40	AU-50	MS-60	MS-65
1829	1,230,000	55.00	60.00	72.00	125	185	275	365	3,300
1830	1,240,000	47.50	52.50	62.00	95.00	155	215	350	3,150
1831	1,242,700	47.50	52.50	62.00	95.00	155	215	350	3,150
1832	965,000	47.50	52.50	62.00	95.00	155	215	350	3,150
1833	1,370,000	47.50	52.50	62.00	95.00	155	215	350	3,150
1834	1,480,000	47.50	52.50	62.00	95.00	155	215	350	3,150
1835 large date and 5C.	2,760,000	47.50	60.00	74.00	110	170	235	350	3,150
1835 large date, small 5C.	Inc. above	47.50	52.50	62.00	95.00	155	215	410	4,350
1835 small date, large 5C.	Inc. above	47.50	52.50	62.00	95.00	155	215	375	4,050
1835 small date and 5C.	Inc. above	47.50	52.50	62.00	95.00	155	215	350	3,150
1836 large 5C.	1,900,000	47.50	52.50	62.00	95.00	155	215	350	3,150
1836 small 5C.	Inc. above	49.50	52.50	66.00	105	167	227	362	3,650
1837 large 5C.	2,276,000	47.50	52.50	70.00	113	170	235	395	4,350
1837 small 5C.	Inc. above	54.50	62.50	77.00	125	235	465	950	11,000

Seated Liberty Half Dime.

Seated Liberty, no stars around border, date below. Value within wreath.

KM# 60   Designer: Christian Gobrecht. **Diameter:** 15.5 **Weight:** 1.3400 g. **Composition:** 0.9000 Silver, 0.0388 oz. ASW. **Notes:** A design modification in 1837 resulted in small-date and large-date varieties for that year.

Date	Mintage	G-4	VG-8	F-12	VF-20	XF-40	AU-50	MS-60	MS-65
1837 small date	Inc. above	35.00	46.50	75.00	135	220	485	770	4,450
1837 large date	Inc. above	39.00	49.50	82.00	150	235	435	640	3,650
1838O	70,000	110	130	250	475	975	1,450	2,500	29,500

Seated Liberty Half Dime.

Seated Liberty, stars around top 1/2 of border, date below. Value within wreath.

KM# 62.1   Designer: Christian Gobrecht. **Diameter:** 15.5 **Weight:** 1.3400 g. **Composition:** 0.9000 Silver, 0.0388 oz. ASW. **Notes:** The two varieties of 1838 are distinguished by the size of the stars on the obverse. The 1839-O with reverse of 1838-O was struck from rusted reverse dies. The result is a bumpy surface on this variety's reverse.

Date	Mintage	G-4	VG-8	F-12	VF-20	XF-40	AU-50	MS-60	MS-65
1838 large stars	2,255,000	21.50	25.50	29.00	36.00	88.00	173	280	2,475
1838 small stars	Inc. above	25.50	31.50	46.00	115	189	274	610	3,950
1839	1,069,150	22.50	26.50	30.00	37.00	93.00	178	280	2,400
1839O	1,034,039	26.50	30.50	34.00	41.00	88.00	173	730	6,850
1839O reverse 1838O	Inc. above	500	700	1,200	1,750	3,000	—	—	—
1840	1,344,085	23.50	27.50	31.00	38.00	80.00	165	270	2,275
1840O	935,000	28.50	32.50	38.00	48.00	138	343	1,250	—

HALF DIME

Seated Liberty Half Dime.
Seated Liberty, stars around top 1/2 of border, date below.

KM# 62.2 **Designer:** Christian Gobrecht.
Diameter: 15.5 **Weight:** 1.3400 g. **Composition:**
0.9000 Silver, 0.0388 oz. ASW. **Notes:** In 1840
drapery was added to Liberty's left elbow. Varieties for
the 1848 Philadelphia strikes are distinguished by the
size of the numerals in the date.

Date	Mintage	G-4	VG-8	F-12	VF-20	XF-40	AU-50	MS-60	MS-65
1840	Inc. above	20.00	18.00	75.00	135	210	350	490	3,850
1840O	Inc. above	51.00	60.00	115	225	650	1,350	6,500	—
1841	1,150,000	17.00	21.50	23.50	31.00	58.00	125	180	1,325
1841O	815,000	20.00	24.50	30.00	50.00	125	300	650	6,750
1842	815,000	16.00	21.50	23.50	28.00	55.00	125	175	1,850
1842O	350,000	38.00	45.00	75.00	225	550	1,050	2,250	16,500
1843	1,165,000	16.00	21.50	23.50	28.00	55.00	120	175	1,365
1844	430,000	19.00	24.50	26.50	34.00	58.00	125	180	1,250
1844O	220,000	80.00	110	210	600	1,300	2,650	5,400	27,500
1845	1,564,000	16.00	21.50	23.50	35.00	58.00	120	175	1,250
1845/1845	Inc. above	19.00	24.50	26.50	38.00	85.00	130	190	1,300
1846	27,000	410	550	850	1,250	2,475	3,600	11,500	—
1847	1,274,000	16.00	21.50	23.50	28.00	55.00	125	175	1,250
1848 medium date	668,000	19.00	24.50	26.50	34.00	65.00	135	215	3,150
1848 large date	Inc. above	22.50	28.00	48.00	65.00	145	275	635	4,250
1848O	600,000	20.00	25.50	33.00	62.00	135	265	450	2,450
1849/8	1,309,000	28.50	35.00	47.50	67.50	140	250	785	2,950
1849/6	Inc. above	24.00	26.00	30.00	56.50	110	200	425	2,900
1849	Inc. above	19.00	18.50	27.50	52.50	65.00	135	190	1,925
1849O	140,000	29.00	40.00	95.00	225	540	1,100	2,350	—
1850	955,000	19.00	24.50	26.50	34.00	60.00	125	190	1,400
1850O	690,000	20.00	24.50	35.00	65.00	125	280	685	4,450
1851	781,000	16.00	21.50	23.50	28.00	57.00	120	175	1,450
1851O	860,000	19.00	24.50	26.50	41.50	110	220	500	4,350
1852	1,000,500	16.00	21.50	23.50	28.00	57.00	120	175	1,250
1852O	260,000	25.00	44.50	79.00	135	275	475	885	11,500
1853	135,000	40.00	60.00	90.00	175	300	525	850	2,850
1853O	160,000	285	325	450	850	1,800	3,500	6,450	27,500

Seated Liberty Half Dime.
Seated Liberty, stars around top 1/2 of border, arrows at date. Value within wreath.

KM# 76 **Designer:** Christian Gobrecht.
Weight: 1.2400 g. **Composition:** 0.9000 Silver,
0.0359 oz. ASW.

Date	Mintage	G-4	VG-8	F-12	VF-20	XF-40	AU-50	MS-60	MS-65	Prf-65
1853	13,210,020	16.00	19.00	22.50	28.00	58.00	135	200	2,100	—
1853O	2,200,000	19.00	27.00	30.50	36.00	66.00	143	315	3,950	—
1854	5,740,000	16.00	19.00	24.50	30.00	60.00	137	210	2,100	15,000
1854O	1,560,000	17.00	20.00	32.50	38.00	88.00	165	240	4,250	—
1855	1,750,000	17.00	20.00	24.50	30.00	60.00	137	205	2,500	15,000
1855O	600,000	21.00	25.00	38.50	54.00	140	220	545	4,950	—

Seated Liberty Half Dime.
Seated Liberty, stars around top 1/2 of border, date below. Value within wreath.

KM# A62.2 **Designer:** Christian Gobrecht.
Weight: 1.2400 g. **Composition:** 0.9000 Silver,
0.0359 oz. ASW. **Notes:** On the 1858/inverted date
variety, the date was engraved into the die upside
down and then re-engraved right side up. Another
1858 variety has the date doubled.

Date	Mintage	G-4	VG-8	F-12	VF-20	XF-40	AU-50	MS-60	MS-65	Prf-65
1856	4,880,000	16.00	21.00	23.00	27.00	52.50	115	175	1,400	15,000
1856O	1,100,000	17.00	22.00	26.00	28.00	97.50	260	470	2,350	—
1857	7,280,000	16.00	21.00	23.00	27.00	52.50	115	175	1,250	5,600
1857O	1,380,000	17.00	22.00	24.00	28.00	62.50	185	320	1,950	—
1858	3,500,000	16.00	21.00	23.00	27.00	52.50	115	175	1,350	5,500

HALF DIME

Date	Mintage	G-4	VG-8	F-12	VF-20	XF-40	AU-50	MS-60	MS-65	Prf-65
1858 inverted date	Inc. above	30.00	43.50	62.50	100.00	225	300	675	3,950	—
1858 double date	Inc. above	45.00	60.00	90.00	175	285	425	800	—	—
1858O	1,660,000	17.00	22.00	24.00	28.00	71.50	137	245	1,850	—
1859	340,000	18.00	23.00	25.00	29.00	54.50	117	225	1,550	4,000
1859O	560,000	19.00	24.00	26.00	42.00	128.5	200	285	2,050	—

Seated Liberty Half Dime.
Seated Liberty, date below. Value within wreath.

KM# 91   Designer: Christian Gobrecht.
Weight: 1.2400 g. Composition: 0.9000 Silver, 0.0359 oz. ASW.

Date	Mintage	G-4	VG-8	F-12	VF-20	XF-40	AU-50	MS-60	MS-65	Prf-65
1860	799,000	16.00	20.00	23.00	26.00	47.00	77.00	145	1,025	1,550
1860O	1,060,000	16.00	20.00	23.00	29.00	49.00	79.00	170	1,375	—
1861	3,361,000	16.00	20.00	22.00	25.00	45.00	75.00	145	1,025	1,600
1861/0	Inc. above	25.00	32.50	59.00	125	260	435	560	3,650	—
1862	1,492,550	20.00	25.00	34.00	44.00	64.00	94.00	154	1,025	1,550
1863	18,460	200	250	300	400	485	550	800	1,575	1,550
1863S	100,000	35.00	45.00	70.00	95.00	165	300	750	3,450	—
1864	48,470	375	475	575	750	950	1,100	1,375	2,350	1,600
1864S	90,000	60.00	75.00	115	175	250	450	785	3,750	—
1865	13,500	375	475	575	750	950	1,100	1,350	1,950	1,550
1865S	120,000	29.00	40.00	60.00	85.00	145	375	975	5,450	—
1866	10,725	350	475	550	700	875	1,000	1,225	2,575	1,550
1866S	120,000	29.00	40.00	60.00	85.00	145	285	485	5,000	—
1867	8,625	550	650	775	900	1,100	1,200	1,375	2,350	1,550
1867S	120,000	29.00	40.00	60.00	85.00	150	325	850	3,850	—
1868	89,200	60.00	90.00	190	225	300	425	625	2,400	1,550
1868S	280,000	20.00	25.00	35.00	42.00	59.00	125	325	3,250	—
1869	208,600	20.00	25.00	35.00	42.00	59.00	135	200	1,375	1,560
1869S	230,000	18.00	24.00	30.00	35.00	55.00	125	310	4,150	—
1870	536,600	18.00	24.00	30.00	35.00	55.00	125	185	975	1,550
1870S unique	—	—	—	—	—	—	—	—	—	—
Note: 1870S, Superior Galleries, July 1986, brilliant uncirculated, $253,000.										
1871	1,873,960	16.00	20.00	22.00	25.00	45.00	75.00	135	975	1,550
1871S	161,000	25.00	30.00	45.00	60.00	90.00	175	320	2,425	—
1872	2,947,950	16.00	20.00	22.00	25.00	45.00	75.00	135	975	1,550
1872S mint mark in wreath	837,000	16.00	20.00	22.00	25.00	45.00	75.00	135	975	—
1872S mint mark below wreath	Inc. above	17.00	21.00	24.00	27.00	47.00	80.00	135	975	—
1873	712,600	16.00	20.00	22.00	25.00	45.00	75.00	135	1,375	1,550
1873S	324,000	20.00	25.00	30.00	42.00	62.00	90.00	150	975	—

5 CENTS

Shield Nickel.
Draped garland above shield, date below. Value within center of rays between stars.

KM# 96   Designer: James B. Longacre. Diameter: 20.5 Weight: 5.0000 g. Composition: Copper-Nickel

Date	Mintage	G-4	VG-8	F-12	VF-20	XF-40	AU-50	MS-60	MS-65	Prf-65
1866	14,742,500	27.50	38.50	50.00	75.00	155	235	260	2,700	3,850
1867	2,019,000	37.50	50.00	67.50	100.00	200	295	350	4,150	75,000

Shield Nickel.
Draped garland above shield, date below. Value within circle of stars.

KM# 97   Weight: 5.0000 g. Composition: Copper-Nickel

Date	Mintage	G-4	VG-8	F-12	VF-20	XF-40	AU-50	MS-60	MS-65	Prf-65
1867	28,890,500	18.00	21.00	28.00	37.50	60.00	120	160	900	3,450
1868	28,817,000	18.00	21.00	28.00	37.50	60.00	120	160	975	1,500
1869	16,395,000	18.00	21.00	28.00	37.50	60.00	120	160	775	1,000

Date	Mintage	G-4	VG-8	F-12	VF-20	XF-40	AU-50	MS-60	MS-65	Prf-65
1870	4,806,000	27.00	34.00	52.00	65.00	90.00	145	200	1,700	1,250
1871	561,000	70.00	90.00	125	170	265	325	375	2,100	1,100
1872	6,036,000	35.00	42.00	70.00	80.00	115	150	235	1,350	820
1873 Open 3	4,550,000	28.00	36.00	52.00	65.00	80.00	135	200	2,400	840
1873 Closed 3	Inc. above	34.00	42.00	65.00	90.00	150	220	350	3,250	—
1874	3,538,000	29.00	39.00	70.00	82.00	105	140	225	1,500	1,000
1875	2,097,000	40.00	55.00	80.00	110	145	190	250	2,000	1,650
1876	2,530,000	38.00	50.00	74.00	100.00	135	175	230	1,900	900
1877 proof	Est. 900	1,500	1,650	1,750	2,000	2,150	2,300	—	—	4,300
1878 proof	2,350	800	875	900	1,100	1,300	1,450	—	—	2,150
1879	29,100	415	520	625	675	750	825	970	2,000	840
1879/8	Inc. above	—	—	—	—	—	—	—	—	850
1880	19,995	560	620	775	950	1,300	1,750	3,450	47,500	700
1881	72,375	270	340	445	500	600	730	800	1,900	660
1882	11,476,600	18.00	20.00	27.00	36.00	58.00	115	150	750	660
1883	1,456,919	18.00	21.00	32.00	37.50	60.00	118	160	750	660
1883/2	Inc. above	210	285	425	650	850	1,000	1,400	4,000	—

Liberty Nickel.

Liberty head left, within circle of stars, date below. Roman numeral value within wreath, without CENTS below.

KM# 111 Designer: Charles E. Barber. **Diameter:** 21.2 **Weight:** 5.0000 g. **Composition:** Copper-Nickel

Date	Mintage	G-4	VG-8	F-12	VF-20	XF-40	AU-50	MS-60	MS-65	Prf-65
1883	5,479,519	6.50	7.75	8.25	8.75	9.00	12.00	25.00	260	1,075

Liberty Nickel.

Liberty head left, within circle of stars, date below. Roman numeral value within wreath, CENTS below.

KM# 112 Weight: 5.0000 g. **Composition:** Copper-Nickel

Date	Mintage	G-4	VG-8	F-12	VF-20	XF-40	AU-50	MS-60	MS-65	Prf-65
1883	16,032,983	18.00	28.50	39.50	57.50	88.00	125	160	695	725
1884	11,273,942	21.00	33.00	39.50	60.00	93.50	135	200	1,675	725
1885	1,476,490	600	635	875	1,050	1,350	1,700	2,050	8,250	3,150
1886	3,330,290	290	335	410	510	715	875	1,050	8,450	1,950
1887	15,263,652	14.50	23.00	32.50	45.00	80.00	115	150	1,100	700
1888	10,720,483	30.00	44.00	68.00	130	185	250	295	1,950	700
1889	15,881,361	13.50	18.50	31.00	55.00	80.00	125	160	875	700
1890	16,259,272	10.50	20.00	26.00	39.50	68.50	115	170	1,650	700
1891	16,834,350	6.00	11.00	22.00	38.50	62.50	125	160	1,075	700
1892	11,699,642	6.50	11.00	23.00	41.50	66.00	125	165	1,350	700
1893	13,370,195	5.50	11.00	25.00	38.50	62.50	125	155	1,100	700
1894	5,413,132	16.50	50.00	100.00	165	240	305	365	1,550	700
1895	9,979,884	5.75	7.75	25.00	46.00	70.00	125	150	2,550	700
1896	8,842,920	9.50	20.00	41.50	68.50	100.00	160	215	2,250	700
1897	20,428,735	3.25	4.50	12.50	27.50	45.00	68.50	95.50	1,000	700
1898	12,532,087	2.15	4.25	11.00	23.50	41.50	70.50	110	1,100	700
1899	26,029,031	1.65	2.00	8.00	15.50	34.00	66.50	92.00	615	700
1900	27,255,995	1.65	2.10	8.00	14.50	34.00	66.50	87.00	640	700
1901	26,480,213	1.65	2.10	7.00	14.00	34.00	54.00	108	565	700
1902	31,480,579	1.65	2.10	4.00	14.00	31.00	54.00	105	565	700
1903	28,006,725	1.65	2.10	4.50	14.00	31.00	54.00	83.00	565	700
1904	21,404,984	1.65	2.10	4.50	11.50	30.00	54.00	100.00	565	700
1905	29,827,276	1.65	2.10	4.00	11.50	30.00	54.00	98.00	565	700
1906	38,613,725	1.65	2.10	4.00	11.50	30.00	54.00	98.00	845	700
1907	39,214,800	1.65	1.85	4.00	11.50	30.00	54.00	98.00	1,000	700
1908	22,686,177	1.65	1.85	4.00	11.50	30.00	54.00	104	1,250	700
1909	11,590,526	2.00	2.10	4.00	12.50	33.00	70.00	115	1,225	700
1910	30,169,353	1.65	1.85	4.00	10.00	30.00	40.00	68.00	565	700
1911	39,559,372	1.65	1.85	4.00	10.00	30.00	40.00	68.00	565	700
1912	26,236,714	1.65	1.85	4.00	10.00	30.00	40.00	68.00	585	700
1912D	8,474,000	2.50	3.60	11.50	38.00	74.00	175	290	2,600	—
1912S	238,000	175	245	280	500	850	1,350	1,550	7,500	—
1913 6 known	—	—	—	—	—	—	—	—	—	—

Note: 1913, Superior Sale, March 2001, Proof, $1,840,000.

Buffalo Nickel.
American Bison standing on a mound.
KM# 133 **Designer:** James Earle Fraser. **Diameter:** 21.2 **Weight:** 5.0000 g. **Composition:** Copper-Nickel

Date	Mintage	G-4	VG-8	F-12	VF-20	XF-40	AU-50	MS-60	MS-65	Prf-65
1913	30,993,520	8.00	14.50	15.00	16.00	19.00	25.00	32.50	190	3,150
1913D	5,337,000	16.00	19.50	21.00	25.00	35.00	57.00	62.50	310	—
1913S	2,105,000	43.00	47.00	50.00	60.00	75.00	100.00	125	690	—

Buffalo Nickel.
American Bison standing on a line.
KM# 134 **Designer:** James Earle Fraser. **Diameter:** 21.2 **Weight:** 5.0000 g. **Composition:** Copper-Nickel
Notes: In 1913 the reverse design was modified so the ground under the buffalo was represented as a line rather than a mound. On the 1937D 3-legged variety, the buffalo's right front leg is missing, the result of a damaged die.

1918/17D

3-legged

Date	Mintage	G-4	VG-8	F-12	VF-20	XF-40	AU-50	MS-60	MS-65	Prf-65
1913	29,858,700	8.00	12.00	13.00	14.00	19.00	25.00	34.00	355	2,500
1913D	4,156,000	125	155	180	190	265	240	285	1,450	—
1913S	1,209,000	350	400	420	435	575	675	885	3,850	—
1914	20,665,738	18.00	21.00	22.00	23.00	27.50	37.50	47.00	420	2,250
1914/3	Inc. above	150	300	425	525	700	1,050	2,850	30,000	—
1914D	3,912,000	90.00	132	165	200	335	390	475	1,600	—
1914/3D	Inc. above	115	225	335	450	625	900	3,500	—	—
1914S	3,470,000	26.00	37.50	45.00	62.50	90.00	145	165	22,350	—
1914/3S	Inc. above	250	500	750	1,000	1,450	2,260	4,300	—	—
1915	20,987,270	6.25	7.00	7.75	11.00	21.50	38.50	50.00	325	2,100
1915D	7,569,500	21.50	31.00	41.50	66.00	115	150	235	2,250	—
1915S	1,505,000	47.00	74.00	105	185	326	490	625	3,150	—
1916	63,498,066	5.50	6.40	7.00	8.00	13.50	24.00	43.50	315	3,250
1916/16	Inc. above	1,800	3,650	7,150	10,850	16,500	34,500	49,500	375,000	—
1916D	13,333,000	15.00	26.50	29.00	38.50	82.50	110	165	2,250	—
1916S	11,860,000	11.00	13.50	26.00	35.00	75.00	125	185	2,300	—
1917	51,424,029	7.50	8.00	8.75	10.00	16.00	32.50	59.00	535	—
1917D	9,910,800	26.00	31.00	55.00	80.00	135	255	345	3,250	—
1917S	4,193,000	23.00	42.00	80.00	110	180	285	395	4,850	—
1918	32,086,314	5.25	6.75	8.00	15.00	31.00	48.50	105	1,550	—
1918/17D	8,362,314	1,075	1,475	2,750	5,450	8,650	10,750	27,500	350,000	—
1918D	Inc. above	22.50	39.00	66.00	135	226	330	430	4,650	—
1918S	4,882,000	14.00	27.50	55.00	100.00	175	300	495	25,500	—
1919	60,868,000	2.60	3.50	3.90	7.00	16.00	32.00	58.00	535	—
1919D	8,006,000	15.50	31.00	66.00	115	235	335	570	6,850	—
1919S	7,521,000	8.00	26.00	50.00	110	225	360	540	24,000	—
1920	63,093,000	1.50	2.75	3.25	8.00	16.00	30.00	59.00	700	—
1920D	9,418,000	8.50	19.00	35.00	125	275	340	575	6,850	—
1920S	9,689,000	4.50	12.75	30.00	100.00	260	300	525	25,500	—
1921	10,663,000	4.00	6.25	8.50	25.00	53.50	73.00	125	800	—
1921S	1,557,000	64.00	110	192	465	825	1,150	1,575	7,350	—
1923	35,715,000	1.70	3.25	4.25	7.00	14.00	37.50	59.00	575	—
1923S	6,142,000	8.00	11.00	27.00	125	275	335	625	11,500	—
1924	21,620,000	1.25	2.40	4.50	10.00	19.00	41.00	73.50	850	—
1924D	5,258,000	8.00	12.00	30.00	90.00	215	315	375	4,950	—
1924S	1,437,000	16.50	32.00	96.00	455	1,100	1,700	2,300	12,850	—
1925	35,565,100	2.50	3.00	3.75	8.50	16.50	32.00	42.00	490	—
1925D	4,450,000	10.00	26.00	38.00	80.00	160	240	375	5,650	—
1925S	6,256,000	4.50	9.00	17.50	77.50	170	250	425	28,500	—
1926	44,693,000	1.50	2.00	2.80	5.40	11.50	26.00	31.50	235	—
1926D	5,638,000	10.00	17.50	28.50	100.00	170	295	335	5,850	—
1926S	970,000	20.00	42.00	100.00	375	875	2,450	4,950	125,000	—
1927	37,981,000	1.40	1.75	2.50	4.50	12.50	26.00	35.00	290	—
1927D	5,730,000	3.00	6.00	7.00	27.50	75.00	115	155	7,950	—
1927S	3,430,000	2.00	3.00	6.00	31.00	80.00	160	490	18,500	—
1928	23,411,000	1.40	1.75	2.50	4.50	12.50	25.00	32.50	310	—

Date	Mintage	G-4	VG-8	F-12	VF-20	XF-40	AU-50	MS-60	MS-65	Prf-65
1928D	6,436,000	1.90	2.50	3.75	16.00	40.00	46.50	53.00	685	—
1928S	6,936,000	1.75	2.35	3.00	12.00	27.50	105	225	4,750	—
1929	36,446,000	1.40	1.75	2.50	4.50	13.00	21.00	35.00	325	—
1929D	8,370,000	1.50	1.85	3.00	6.75	32.50	42.50	60.00	1,850	—
1929S	7,754,000	1.50	1.85	2.25	4.00	12.50	25.00	49.50	485	—
1930	22,849,000	1.40	1.75	2.50	4.50	12.00	21.00	32.50	235	—
1930S	5,435,000	1.50	2.00	3.00	4.50	16.00	37.50	65.00	480	—
1931S	1,200,000	15.00	16.00	17.00	19.00	31.00	46.00	59.00	300	—
1934	20,213,003	1.40	1.75	2.50	4.50	11.00	19.00	47.50	355	—
1934D	7,480,000	2.00	3.00	4.75	9.60	22.00	50.00	79.50	800	—
1935	58,264,000	1.25	1.60	2.25	3.00	4.00	11.00	20.00	145	—
1935 Double Die Rev.	Inc. above	50.00	75.00	125	250	675	1,800	4,000	75,000	—
1935D	12,092,000	1.60	2.50	3.00	9.00	26.00	48.00	72.00	415	—
1935S	10,300,000	1.35	1.75	2.50	3.50	4.50	17.50	48.50	250	—
1936	119,001,420	1.25	1.60	2.25	3.00	4.00	6.75	14.50	105	1,650
1936 Brilliant	Inc. above	—	—	—	—	—	—	—	—	2,450
1936D	24,814,000	1.35	1.75	2.75	4.00	5.35	11.50	33.50	118	—
1936D 3-1/2 leg	Inc. above	750	1,250	2,000	3,500	6,000	10,500	17,500	—	—
1935D/S	Inc. above	1.35	—	10.00	16.00	25.00	—	—	—	—
1936S	14,930,000	1.35	1.75	2.50	3.50	4.50	11.00	33.50	115	—
1937	79,485,769	1.25	1.60	2.25	3.00	4.00	6.75	14.50	69.00	2,100
1937D	17,826,000	1.35	1.75	2.50	3.50	4.50	9.00	29.00	73.00	—
1937D 3-legged	Inc. above	535	595	850	1,050	1,250	1,450	2,375	37,000	—
1937S	5,635,000	1.35	1.75	2.50	3.50	4.50	10.00	27.50	72.00	—
1938D	7,020,000	3.50	3.75	3.90	4.00	4.50	8.00	26.00	66.00	—
1938D/D	Inc. above	4.00	4.50	6.00	8.00	10.00	17.00	32.00	125	—
1938D/S	Inc. above	4.50	6.75	9.00	12.50	19.00	32.50	50.00	185	—

Jefferson Nickel.
Monticello, mintmark to right side.
KM# 192 Designer: Felix Schlag. **Diameter:** 21.2 **Weight:** 5.0000 g. **Composition:** Copper-Nickel **Notes:** Some 1939 strikes have doubling of the word MONTICELLO on the reverse.

Date	Mintage	VG-8	F-12	VF-20	XF-40	MS-60	MS-65	-65FS	Prf-65
1938	19,515,365	.50	.75	1.00	2.00	6.00	12.00	125	130
1938D	5,376,000	1.00	1.25	1.50	2.00	10.00	20.00	95.00	—
1938S	4,105,000	1.75	2.00	2.50	3.00	5.25	12.00	165	—
1939 T I, wavy steps, Rev. of 1939	Inc. below	—	—	—	—	—	—	300	70.00
1939 T II, even steps, Rev. of 1940	120,627,535	—	.20	.25	.30	1.75	3.50	40.00	130
1939 doubled MONTICELLO T II	Inc. above	40.00	60.00	90.00	165	300	1,250	2,000	—
1939D T IT I, wavy steps, Rev. of 1939	Inc. below	—	—	—	—	—	—	275	—
1939D T IIT II, even steps, Rev. of 1940	3,514,000	4.00	5.00	8.00	14.00	44.00	125	250	—
1939S T IT I, wavy steps, Rev. of 1939	Inc. below	—	—	—	—	—	—	250	—
1939S T IIT II, even steps, Rev. of 1940	6,630,000	.45	.60	1.50	4.00	17.00	45.00	275	—
1940	176,499,158	—	—	—	.25	1.00	3.00	35.00	135
1940D	43,540,000	—	.20	.30	.40	1.50	2.75	25.00	—
1940S	39,690,000	—	.20	.25	.50	2.50	6.00	45.00	—
1941	203,283,720	—	—	—	.20	.75	2.50	40.00	130
1941D	53,432,000	—	.20	.30	.50	2.50	6.00	25.00	—
1941S	43,445,000	—	.20	.30	.50	3.75	6.75	60.00	—
1942	49,818,600	—	—	—	.40	5.00	8.50	75.00	115
1942D	13,938,000	1.00	1.50	3.00	5.00	32.00	60.00	70.00	—
1942D D over horizontal D	Inc. above	35.00	60.00	100.00	165	750	10,000	25,000	—

Note: Fully Struck Full Step nickels command higher prices. Bright, Fully Struck coins command even higher prices. 1938 thru 1989 - 5 Full Steps. 1990 to date - 6 Full Steps. Without bag marks or nicks on steps.

Jefferson Nickel.
Monticello, mint mark above.
KM# 192a Designer: Felix Schlag. **Diameter:** 21.2 **Composition:** 0.3500 Copper-Silver-Manganese **Notes:** War-time composition nickels have the mint mark above MONTICELLO on the reverse.

1943/2P

Date	Mintage	VG-8	F-12	VF-20	XF-40	MS-60	MS-65	-65FS	Prf-65
1942P	57,900,600	1.20	1.30	1.50	2.00	8.00	22.50	70.00	205
1942S	32,900,000	1.20	1.30	1.50	2.50	14.00	20.00	125	—

5 CENTS

Date	Mintage	VG-8	F-12	VF-20	XF-40	MS-60	MS-65	-65FS	Prf-65
1943P	271,165,000	1.20	1.30	1.50	2.00	4.00	15.00	35.00	—
1943/2P	Inc. above	35.00	50.00	75.00	110	250	650	1,000	—
1943D	15,294,000	1.50	1.50	1.70	2.10	5.00	13.00	30.00	—
1943S	104,060,000	1.20	1.30	1.50	2.00	6.00	13.00	55.00	—
1944P	119,150,000	1.20	1.30	1.50	2.00	10.00	22.50	100.00	—
1944D	32,309,000	1.30	1.30	1.50	2.30	10.00	17.50	30.00	—
1944S	21,640,000	1.30	1.30	1.50	2.10	7.00	14.00	185	—
1945P	119,408,100	1.20	1.30	1.50	2.00	6.00	13.50	125	—
1945D	37,158,000	1.30	1.40	1.60	2.20	5.50	13.00	40.00	—
1945S	58,939,000	1.20	1.30	1.50	2.00	5.00	14.00	250	—

Note: Fully Struck Full Step nickels command higher prices. Bright, Fully Struck coins command even higher prices. 1938 thru 1989 - 5 Full Steps. 1990 to date - 6 Full Steps. Without bag marks or nicks on steps.

Jefferson Nickel.

Pre-war design resumed.

KM# A192 Designer: Felix Schlag. **Diameter:** 21.2 **Weight:** 5.0000 g. **Composition:** Copper-Nickel **Notes:** KM#192 design and composition resumed. The 1979-S and 1981-S Type II proofs have clearer mint marks than the Type I proofs of those years.

Date	Mintage	VG-8	F-12	VF-20	XF-40	MS-60	MS-65	-65FS	Prf-65
1946	161,116,000	—	—	.20	.25	.80	3.50	40.00	—
1946D	45,292,200	—	—	.25	.35	.95	3.50	30.00	—
1946S	13,560,000	—	—	.30	.40	.50	2.00	45.00	—
1947	95,000,000	—	—	.20	.25	.75	2.00	30.00	—
1947D	37,822,000	—	—	.20	.30	.90	2.50	55.00	—
1947S	24,720,000	—	—	.20	.25	1.00	2.25	60.00	—
1948	89,348,000	—	—	.20	.25	.50	2.50	30.00	—
1948D	44,734,000	—	—	.25	.35	1.20	4.50	45.00	—
1948S	11,300,000	—	—	.25	.50	1.20	3.50	200	—
1949	60,652,000	—	—	.25	.30	2.25	6.00	200	—
1949D	36,498,000	—	—	.30	.40	1.25	5.00	75.00	—
1949D/S	Inc. above	—	35.00	40.00	65.00	170	325	1,750	—
1949S	9,716,000	.25	.35	.45	.90	1.50	3.50	145	—
1950	9,847,386	.20	.30	.35	.75	1.50	4.75	150	70.00
1950D	2,630,030	12.00	12.50	13.00	14.00	16.00	30.00	45.00	—
1951	28,609,500	—	—	.40	.50	1.50	9.00	90.00	70.00
1951D	20,460,000	.25	.30	.40	.50	3.00	10.00	45.00	—
1951S	7,776,000	.30	.40	.50	1.10	1.75	5.00	150	—
1952	64,069,980	—	—	.20	.25	.85	4.50	125	37.50
1952D	30,638,000	—	—	.30	.45	2.00	7.00	65.00	—
1952S	20,572,000	—	—	.20	.25	.75	3.50	195	—
1953	46,772,800	—	—	.20	.25	.40	1.50	200	37.50
1953D	59,878,600	—	—	.20	.25	.40	1.50	100.00	—
1953S	19,210,900	—	—	.20	.25	.60	2.50	1,750	—
1954	47,917,350	—	—	—	.20	.60	2.00	95.00	20.00
1954D	117,136,560	—	—	—	.20	.35	2.00	175	—
1954S	29,384,000	—	—	—	.25	1.00	3.00	1,000	—
1954S/D	Inc. above	—	9.00	14.00	30.00	50.00	500	—	—
1955	8,266,200	.25	.35	.40	.50	.75	2.00	85.00	13.50
1955D	74,464,100	—	—	—	.15	.20	1.00	150	—
1955D/S	Inc. above	—	10.00	16.00	40.00	65.00	135	185	—
1956	35,885,384	—	—	—	.20	.30	.70	35.00	2.50
1956D	67,222,940	—	—	—	.15	.25	.60	90.00	—
1957	39,655,952	—	—	—	.15	.25	.60	40.00	1.50
1957D	136,828,900	—	—	—	.15	.25	.60	55.00	—
1958	17,963,652	—	—	.15	.25	.30	.65	80.00	7.00
1958D	168,249,120	—	—	—	.15	.25	.60	30.00	—

Note: Fully Struck Full Step nickels command higher prices. Bright, Fully Struck coins command even higher prices. 1938 thru 1989 - 5 Full Steps. 1990 to date - 6 Full Steps. Without bag marks or nicks on steps.

Date	Mintage	VG-8	F-12	VF-20	XF-40	MS-60	MS-65	-65FS	Prf-65
1959	28,397,291	—	—	—	—	.30	.65	30.00	1.25
1959D	160,738,240	—	—	—	—	.25	.55	45.00	—
1960	57,107,602	—	—	—	—	.25	2.00	60.00	1.00
1960D	192,582,180	—	—	—	—	.25	.55	650	—
1961	76,668,244	—	—	—	—	.25	.55	100.00	1.00
1961D	229,342,760	—	—	—	—	.25	.55	800	—
1962	100,602,019	—	—	—	—	.25	1.50	75.00	1.00
1962D	280,195,720	—	—	—	—	.25	.55	60.00	—
1963	178,851,645	—	—	—	—	.25	.55	45.00	1.00
1963D	276,829,460	—	—	—	—	.25	.55	650	—
1964	1,028,622,762	—	—	—	—	.25	.55	55.00	1.00
1964D	1,787,297,160	—	—	—	—	.25	.50	500	—
1965	136,131,380	—	—	—	—	.25	.50	225	—
1966	156,208,283	—	—	—	—	.25	.50	350	—
1967	107,325,800	—	—	—	—	.25	.50	275	—
1968 none minted	—	—	—	—	—	—	—	—	—

Date	Mintage	VG-8	F-12	VF-20	XF-40	MS-60	MS-65	-65FS	Prf-65
1968D	91,227,880	—	—	—	—	.25	.50	750	—
1968S	103,437,510	—	—	—	—	.25	.50	300	0.75
1969 none minted	—	—	—	—	—	—	—	—	—
1969D	202,807,500	—	—	—	—	.25	.50	—	—
1969S	123,099,631	—	—	—	—	.25	.50	450	0.75
1970 none minted	—	—	—	—	—	—	—	—	—
1970D	515,485,380	—	—	—	—	.25	.50	500	—
1970S	241,464,814	—	—	—	—	.25	.50	125	0.75
1971	106,884,000	—	—	—	—	.85	2.00	35.00	—
1971D	316,144,800	—	—	—	—	.25	.50	25.00	—
1971S	(3,220,733)	—	—	—	—	—	—	—	2.00
1972	202,036,000	—	—	—	—	.25	.50	35.00	—
1972D	351,694,600	—	—	—	—	.25	.50	25.00	—
1972S	(3,260,996)	—	—	—	—	—	—	—	2.00
1973	384,396,000	—	—	—	—	—	.50	20.00	—
1973D	261,405,000	—	—	—	—	—	.50	20.00	—
1973S	(2,760,339)	—	—	—	—	—	—	—	1.75
1974	601,752,000	—	—	—	—	—	.50	75.00	—
1974D	277,373,000	—	—	—	—	—	.50	50.00	—
1974S	(2,612,568)	—	—	—	—	—	—	—	2.00
1975	181,772,000	—	—	—	—	—	.75	65.00	—
1975D	401,875,300	—	—	—	—	—	.50	60.00	—
1975S	(2,845,450)	—	—	—	—	—	—	—	2.25
1976	367,124,000	—	—	—	—	—	.75	150	—
1976D	563,964,147	—	—	—	—	—	.60	55.00	—
1976S	(4,149,730)	—	—	—	—	—	—	—	2.00
1977	585,376,000	—	—	—	—	—	.40	65.00	—
1977D	297,313,460	—	—	—	—	—	.55	35.00	—
1977S	(3,251,152)	—	—	—	—	—	—	—	1.75
1978	391,308,000	—	—	—	—	—	.40	40.00	—
1978D	313,092,780	—	—	—	—	—	.40	35.00	—
1978S	(3,127,781)	—	—	—	—	—	—	—	1.75
1979	463,188,000	—	—	—	—	—	.40	95.00	—
1979D	325,867,672	—	—	—	—	—	.40	35.00	—
1979S type I, proof	(3,677,175)	—	—	—	—	—	—	—	1.50
1979S type II, proof	Inc. above	—	—	—	—	—	—	—	1.75
1980P	593,004,000	—	—	—	—	—	.40	30.00	—
1980D	502,323,448	—	—	—	—	.25	.40	25.00	—
1980S	(3,554,806)	—	—	—	—	—	—	—	1.50
1981P	657,504,000	—	—	—	—	.25	.40	70.00	—
1981D	364,801,843	—	—	—	—	.25	.40	40.00	—
1981S type I, proof	(4,063,083)	—	—	—	—	—	—	—	2.00
1981S type II, proof	Inc. above	—	—	—	—	—	—	—	2.50
1982P	292,355,000	—	—	—	—	2.00	12.50	80.00	—
1982D	373,726,544	—	—	—	—	1.50	3.50	45.00	—
1982S	(3,857,479)	—	—	—	—	—	—	—	3.50
1983P	561,615,000	—	—	—	—	1.50	4.00	45.00	—
1983D	536,726,276	—	—	—	—	.75	2.50	35.00	—
1983S	(3,279,126)	—	—	—	—	—	—	—	4.00
1984P	746,769,000	—	—	—	—	1.25	3.00	65.00	—
1984D	517,675,146	—	—	—	—	.30	.85	30.00	—
1984S	(3,065,110)	—	—	—	—	—	—	—	5.00
1985P	647,114,962	—	—	—	—	.35	.75	60.00	—
1985D	459,747,446	—	—	—	—	.35	.75	35.00	—
1985S	(3,362,821)	—	—	—	—	—	—	—	4.00
1986P	536,883,483	—	—	—	—	.40	1.00	70.00	—
1986D	361,819,140	—	—	—	—	1.00	2.00	60.00	—
1986S	(3,010,497)	—	—	—	—	—	—	—	7.00
1987P	371,499,481	—	—	—	—	.25	.75	30.00	—
1987D	410,590,604	—	—	—	—	.25	.75	25.00	—
1987S	(4,227,728)	—	—	—	—	—	—	—	3.50
1988P	771,360,000	—	—	—	—	.25	.75	30.00	—
1988D	663,771,652	—	—	—	—	—	.75	25.00	—
1988S	(3,262,948)	—	—	—	—	—	—	—	6.50
1989P	898,812,000	—	—	—	—	.25	.75	75.00	—
1989D	570,842,474	—	—	—	—	.25	.75	25.00	—
1989S	(3,220,194)	—	—	—	—	—	—	—	5.50
1990P	661,636,000	—	—	—	—	.25	.75	25.00	—
1990D	663,938,503	—	—	—	—	.25	.75	25.00	—
1990S	(3,299,559)	—	—	—	—	—	—	—	5.50
1991P	614,104,000	—	—	—	—	.25	.75	25.00	—
1991D	436,496,678	—	—	—	—	.25	.75	25.00	—
1991S	(2,867,787)	—	—	—	—	—	—	—	5.00
1992P	399,552,000	—	—	—	—	.65	2.00	25.00	—
1992D	450,565,113	—	—	—	—	.25	.75	25.00	—
1992S	(4,176,560)	—	—	—	—	—	—	—	4.00
1993P	412,076,000	—	—	—	—	.25	.75	25.00	—
1993D	406,084,135	—	—	—	—	.25	.75	25.00	—
1993S	(3,394,792)	—	—	—	—	—	—	—	4.50

5 CENTS

Date	Mintage	VG-8	F-12	VF-20	XF-40	MS-60	MS-65	-65FS	Prf-65
1994P	722,160,000	—	—	—	—	.25	.75	25.00	—
1994P matte proof	(167,703)	—	—	—	—	—	—	—	75.00
1994D	715,762,110	—	—	—	—	.25	.75	25.00	—
1994S	(3,269,923)	—	—	—	—	—	—	—	4.00
1995P	774,156,000	—	—	—	—	.25	.75	25.00	—
1995D	888,112,000	—	—	—	—	.35	.85	25.00	—
1995S	(2,707,481)	—	—	—	—	—	—	—	4.00
1996P	829,332,000	—	—	—	—	.25	.75	25.00	—
1996D	817,736,000	—	—	—	—	.25	.75	25.00	—
1996S	(2,915,212)	—	—	—	—	—	—	—	4.00
1997P	470,972,000	—	—	—	—	.25	.75	25.00	—
1997P matte proof	(25,000)	—	—	—	—	—	—	—	200
1997D	466,640,000	—	—	—	—	.30	2.00	25.00	—
1997S	(1,975,000)	—	—	—	—	.25	—	—	5.00
1998P	688,272,000	—	—	—	—	.25	.80	25.00	—
1998D	635,360,000	—	—	—	—	.25	.80	25.00	—
1998S	(2,957,286)	—	—	—	—	—	—	—	4.50
1999P	1,212,000,000	—	—	—	—	.25	.80	20.00	—
1999D	1,066,720,000	—	—	—	—	.25	.80	20.00	—
1999S	(3,362,462)	—	—	—	—	—	—	—	3.50
2000P	846,240,000	—	—	—	—	.25	.80	20.00	—
2000D	1,509,520,000	—	—	—	—	.25	.80	20.00	—
2000S	(4,063,361)	—	—	—	—	—	—	—	2.00
2001P	675,704,000	—	—	—	—	.25	.50	20.00	—
2001D	627,680,000	—	—	—	—	.25	.50	20.00	—
2001S	(3,099,096)	—	—	—	—	—	—	—	2.00
2002P	539,240,000	—	—	—	—	.25	.50	—	—
2002D	691,200,000	—	—	—	—	.25	.50	—	—
2002S	(3,157,739)	—	—	—	—	—	—	—	2.00
2003P	441,840,000	—	—	—	—	.25	.50	—	—
2003D	383,040,000	—	—	—	—	.25	.50	—	—
2003S	(3,116,590)	—	—	—	—	—	—	—	2.00

Jefferson - Westward Expansion - Lewis & Clark Bicentennial.
Jefferson era peace medal design: two clasped hands, pipe and hatchet.

KM# 360 Obv. Designer: Felix Schlag. Rev.
Designer: Norman E. Nemeth. Diameter: 21.2
Weight: 5.0000 g. Composition: Copper-Nickel

Date	Mintage	MS-65	Prf-65
2004P	361,440,000	1.00	—
2004D	372,000,000	1.00	—
2004S	—	—	13.00

Jefferson - Westward Expansion - Lewis & Clark Bicentennial.
Lewis and Clark's Keelboat.

KM# 361 Obv. Designer: Felix Schlag. Rev.
Designer: Al Maletsky. Diameter: 21.2 Weight:
5.0000 g. Composition: Copper-Nickel

Date	Mintage	MS-65	Prf-65
2004P	366,720,000	1.00	—
2004D	344,880,000	1.00	—
2004S	—	—	13.00

Jefferson - Westward Expansion - Lewis & Clark Bicentennial.
Thomas Jefferson large profile right. American Bison right.

KM# 368 Obv. Designer: Joe Fitzgerald and Don
Everhart II. Rev. Designer: Jamie Franki and
Norman E. Nemeth. Diameter: 21.2 Weight:
5.0000 g. Composition: Copper-Nickel

Date	Mintage	MS-65	Prf-65
2005P	448,320,000	1.00	—
2005D	487,680,000	1.00	—
2005S	—	—	7.50

Jefferson - Westward Expansion - Lewis & Clark Bicentennial.
Jefferson, large profile. Pacific coastline.

KM# 369 Obv. Designer: Joe Fitzgerald and Don
Everhart. Rev. Designer: Joe Fitzgerald and Donna
Weaver. Diameter: 21.2 Weight: 5.0000 g.
Composition: Copper-Nickel

Date	Mintage	MS-65	Prf-65
2005P	394,080,000	1.00	—
2005D	411,120,000	1.00	—
2005S	—	—	6.50

Jefferson large facing portrait - Enhanced Monticello Reverse.
Jefferson head facing. Monticello, enhanced design.

KM# 381 Obv. Designer: Jamie N. Franki and
Donna Weaver. Rev. Designer: Felix Schlag and
John Mercanti. Diameter: 21.2 Weight: 5.0000 g.
Composition: Copper-Nickel

Date	Mintage	MS-65	Prf-65	Date	Mintage	MS-65	Prf-65
2006P	693,120,000	1.00	—	2008P	—	1.00	—
2006D	809,280,000	1.00	—	2008D	—	1.00	—
2006S	—	—	4.00	2008S	—	—	4.00
2007P	—	1.00	—	2009P	—	1.00	—
2007D	—	1.00	—	2009D	—	1.00	—
2007S	—	—	4.00	2009S	—	—	4.00

DIME

Draped Bust Dime.
Small eagle.

KM# 24 Designer: Robert Scot. Diameter: 19
Weight: 2.7000 g. Composition: 0.8920 Silver,
0.0774 oz. ASW.

Date	Mintage	G-4	VG-8	F-12	VF-20	XF-40	MS-60
1796	22,135	2,850	3,450	5,500	7,650	12,500	28,500
1797 13 stars	25,261	1,600	2,650	3,650	4,900	8,000	57,500
1797 16 stars	Inc. above	1,650	2,550	3,500	4,700	7,350	29,000

DIME

Draped Bust Dime.
Draped bust right, date at angle below. Heraldic eagle.

KM# 31 Designer: Robert Scot. **Diameter:** 19 **Weight:** 2.7000 g. **Composition:** 0.8920 Silver, 0.0774 oz. ASW. **Notes:** The 1805 strikes have either 4 or 5 berries on the olive branch held by the eagle.

Date	Mintage	G-4	VG-8	F-12	VF-20	XF-40	MS-60
1798 large 8	27,550	775	1,135	1,375	1,875	3,350	9,650
1798 small 8	Inc. above	1,075	1,385	1,700	2,550	4,400	12,500
1798/97 13 stars	Inc. above	1,850	3,250	4,850	7,500	13,500	70,000
1798/97 16 stars	Inc. above	825	1,085	1,450	2,025	4,450	12,000

Note: The 1798 overdates have either 13 or 16 stars on the obverse; Varieties of the regular 1798 strikes are distinguished by the size of the 8 in the date

Date	Mintage	G-4	VG-8	F-12	VF-20	XF-40	MS-60
1800	21,760	800	1,160	1,700	2,500	5,100	32,500
1801	34,640	900	1,285	1,900	3,450	5,900	47,500
1802	10,975	1,500	2,000	3,000	4,200	7,500	52,500
1803	33,040	825	1,235	1,900	2,575	5,450	—
1804 13 stars	8,265	2,350	4,150	8,650	19,500	38,500	—
1804 14 stars	Inc. above	4,850	6,250	9,800	19,500	46,500	—
1805 4 berries	120,780	875	1,185	1,650	2,175	3,600	10,400
1805 5 berries	Inc. above	625	935	1,200	1,425	2,750	7,650
1807	165,000	625	935	1,200	1,425	2,750	7,650

Liberty Cap Dime.
Draped bust left, flanked by stars, date below. Eagle with arrows in talons, banner above, value below.

KM# 42 Designer: John Reich. **Diameter:** 18.8 **Weight:** 2.7000 g. **Composition:** 0.8920 Silver, 0.0774 oz. ASW. **Notes:** The 1820 varieties are distinguished by the size of the 0 in the date. The 1823 overdates have either large E's or small E's in UNITED STATES OF AMERICA on the reverse.

Date	Mintage	G-4	VG-8	F-12	VF-20	XF-40	AU-50	MS-60	MS-65
1809	51,065	140	220	450	700	1,500	2,850	4,500	24,500
1811/9	65,180	110	175	275	650	1,350	2,000	4,000	33,500
1814 small date	421,500	60.00	80.00	145	300	650	1,250	2,000	19,500
1814 large date	Inc. above	43.00	52.00	75.00	135	435	670	1,175	15,000
1814 STATESOF	Inc. above	70.00	88.00	160	335	750	1,400	2,350	24,500
1820 large O	942,587	42.00	50.00	71.00	122	430	665	1,160	12,750
1820 small O	Inc. above	43.00	52.00	75.00	137	450	750	1,425	15,250
1820 STATESOF	Inc. above	43.00	52.00	75.00	135	435	670	1,175	14,500
1821 large date	1,186,512	42.00	50.00	71.00	122	430	665	1,160	12,750
1821 small date	Inc. above	43.00	52.00	75.00	137	450	750	1,425	17,000
1822	100,000	1,000	1,850	3,250	4,500	6,250	7,850	13,500	70,000
1823/22 large E's	440,000	42.00	50.00	71.00	130	450	685	1,210	14,850
1823/22 small E's	Inc. above	42.00	50.00	71.00	130	450	685	1,210	13,600
1824/22	—	50.00	80.00	145	300	650	1,250	2,000	19,500
1825	510,000	39.00	46.00	65.00	112	410	625	1,100	12,850
1827	1,215,000	39.00	46.00	65.00	112	410	625	1,100	12,500
1827/7	Inc. above	250	—	—	750	1,100	1,500	—	—
1828 large date	125,000	70.00	110	175	375	750	1,250	2,850	6,850

Liberty Cap Dime.
Draped bust left, flanked by stars, date below. Eagle with arrows in talons, banner above, value below.

KM# 48 Designer: John Reich. **Diameter:** 18.5 **Composition:** Silver ASW.

Date	Mintage	G-4	VG-8	F-12	VF-20	XF-40	AU-50	MS-60	MS-65
1828 small date	Inc. above	40.00	48.00	80.00	155	425	625	1,250	12,500
1829 very large 10C.	770,000	60.00	75.00	120	235	550	800	1,500	—
1829 large 10C.	Inc. above	54.00	65.00	110	200	400	600	1,150	9,250
1829 medium 10C.	Inc. above	36.00	42.00	54.00	85.00	255	375	775	6,850
1829 small 10C.	Inc. above	36.00	42.00	56.00	90.00	270	395	795	7,050
1829 curl base 2	Inc. above	7,750	10,500	16,500	27,500	38,500	44,000	—	—
1830 large 10C.	510,000	36.00	42.00	56.00	85.00	255	375	775	6,850
1830 small 10C.	Inc. above	36.00	42.00	54.00	90.00	270	400	825	8,850
1830/29	Inc. above	52.00	75.00	120	220	430	750	1,500	—

Date	Mintage	G-4	VG-8	F-12	VF-20	XF-40	AU-50	MS-60	MS-65
1831	771,350	36.00	42.00	54.00	85.00	255	375	775	6,850
1832	522,500	36.00	42.00	54.00	85.00	255	375	775	6,850
1833	485,000	36.00	42.00	54.00	85.00	260	390	790	6,850
1833 last 3 high	Inc. above	36.00	42.00	54.00	85.00	260	390	820	9,350
1834 small 4	635,000	36.00	42.00	54.00	85.00	255	375	775	7,000
1834 large 4	Inc. above	36.00	42.00	54.00	85.00	255	375	775	6,850
1835	1,410,000	36.00	42.00	54.00	85.00	255	375	775	6,850
1836	1,190,000	36.00	42.00	54.00	85.00	255	375	775	6,850
1837	1,042,000	36.00	42.00	56.00	90.00	270	395	795	7,000

Seated Liberty Dime.
Seated Liberty, date below.
Value within wreath.

KM# 61 **Designer:** Christian Gobrecht. **Diameter:** 17.9 **Weight:** 2.6700 g. **Composition:** 0.9000 Silver, 0.0773 oz. ASW.

Date	Mintage	G-4	VG-8	F-12	VF-20	XF-40	AU-50	MS-60	MS-65
1837 flat top 1	Inc. above	40.00	50.00	85.00	290	550	750	1,100	6,500
1837 curly top 1	Inc. above	40.00	50.00	85.00	290	550	750	1,100	6,500
1838O	406,034	40.00	60.00	110	375	725	1,250	3,500	21,000

Seated Liberty Dime.
Seated Liberty, stars around top 1/2 of border, date below. Value within wreath.

KM# 63.1 **Obv. Designer:** Christian Gobrecht. **Diameter:** 17.9 **Weight:** 2.6700 g. **Composition:** 0.9000 Silver, 0.0773 oz. ASW. **Notes:** The 1839-O with reverse of 1838-O variety was struck from rusted dies, it has a bumpy reverse surface.

No drapery at elbow

Date	Mintage	G-4	VG-8	F-12	VF-20	XF-40	AU-50	MS-60	MS-65
1838 small stars	1,992,500	25.00	30.00	50.00	80.00	165	350	600	—
1838 large stars	Inc. above	17.50	20.00	30.00	37.50	110	215	280	8,500
1838 partial drapery	Inc. above	35.00	50.00	85.00	150	225	350	550	—
1839	1,053,115	16.00	18.50	25.00	35.00	105	195	280	3,000
1839O	1,323,000	18.50	22.50	35.00	60.00	150	365	1,250	6,000
1839O reverse 1838O	Inc. above	165	225	375	550	1,150	—	—	—
1840	1,358,580	16.00	18.50	25.00	35.00	105	195	300	4,000
1840O	1,175,000	18.50	22.50	40.00	70.00	165	365	975	6,500

Seated Liberty Dime.
Seated Liberty, stars around top 1/2 of border, date below. Value within wreath.

KM# 63.2 **Designer:** Christian Gobrecht. **Diameter:** 17.9 **Weight:** 2.6700 g. **Composition:** 0.9000 Silver, 0.0773 oz. ASW. **Notes:** Drapery added to Liberty's left elbow

Drapery at elbow

Date	Mintage	G-4	VG-8	F-12	VF-20	XF-40	AU-50	MS-60	MS-65
1840	Inc. above	35.00	50.00	95.00	185	350	1,250	—	—
1841	1,622,500	16.00	18.50	21.50	27.50	50.00	175	260	2,700
1841O	2,007,500	18.50	22.50	28.50	45.00	75.00	250	1,500	5,000
1841O large O	Inc. above	600	900	1,200	2,500	—	—	—	—
1842	1,887,500	15.00	17.50	21.50	26.00	45.00	175	260	2,700
1842O	2,020,000	18.50	23.50	30.00	75.00	225	1,350	2,900	—
1843	1,370,000	15.00	17.50	21.50	26.00	45.00	175	260	3,000
1843/1843	Inc. above	16.00	18.50	22.50	30.00	75.00	200	295	—
1843O	150,000	50.00	80.00	135	325	1,100	2,250	—	—
1844	72,500	275	350	550	800	1,450	2,200	3,000	—
1845	1,755,000	16.00	18.50	21.50	27.50	45.00	120	260	2,600
1845/1845	Inc. above	17.00	20.00	35.00	55.00	100.00	175	—	—
1845O	230,000	25.00	35.00	95.00	250	750	1,750	—	—
1846	31,300	250	350	500	950	1,750	2,750	5,500	—

DIME

Date	Mintage	G-4	VG-8	F-12	VF-20	XF-40	AU-50	MS-60	MS-65
1847	245,000	19.00	25.00	40.00	85.00	150	350	950	9,000
1848	451,500	18.50	21.50	25.00	50.00	95.00	250	750	7,000
1849	839,000	17.50	19.50	23.50	33.50	60.00	140	500	4,000
1849O	300,000	21.50	30.00	50.00	135	275	750	2,200	—
1850	1,931,500	17.50	19.50	23.50	32.50	55.00	120	260	5,900
1850O	510,000	21.50	25.00	40.00	90.00	175	475	1,250	—
1851	1,026,500	17.50	20.00	22.50	30.00	60.00	120	325	5,000
1851O	400,000	21.50	25.00	40.00	90.00	175	500	1,850	—
1852	1,535,500	15.00	16.00	18.50	23.50	50.00	120	290	2,550
1852O	430,000	22.50	30.00	45.00	125	235	550	1,800	—
1853	95,000	95.00	125	200	295	425	575	800	—

Seated Liberty Dime.

Seated Liberty, stars around top 1/2 of border, arrows at date. Value within wreath.

KM# 77   **Designer:** Christian Gobrecht. **Weight:**
2.4900 g. **Composition:** 0.9000 Silver, 0.0720 oz.
ASW.

Date	Mintage	G-4	VG-8	F-12	VF-20	XF-40	AU-50	MS-60	MS-65	Prf-65
1853	12,078,010	8.00	9.00	10.00	14.00	45.00	125	330	2,500	31,500
1853O	1,100,000	11.00	14.00	20.00	45.00	145	400	900	—	—
1854	4,470,000	8.75	9.25	10.00	15.00	45.00	125	330	2,500	31,500
1854O	1,770,000	10.00	11.00	14.00	25.00	75.00	175	600	—	—
1855	2,075,000	8.75	9.25	14.00	20.00	55.00	150	350	3,800	31,500

Seated Liberty Dime.

Seated Liberty, stars around top 1/2 of border, date below. Value within wreath.

KM# A63.2   **Designer:** Christian Gobrecht.
Weight: 2.4900 g. **Composition:** 0.9000 Silver,
0.0720 oz. ASW.

Date	Mintage	G-4	VG-8	F-12	VF-20	XF-40	AU-50	MS-60	MS-65	Prf-65
1856 small date	5,780,000	14.00	15.00	18.00	22.00	37.50	115	250	7,050	38,000
1856 large date	Inc. above	16.00	18.50	19.50	25.00	65.00	175	475	—	—
1856O	1,180,000	16.00	18.50	19.50	35.00	85.00	215	625	5,250	—
1856S	70,000	160	225	375	550	1,200	1,750	—	—	—
1857	5,580,000	14.00	15.50	16.50	22.50	37.50	110	260	2,600	3,400
1857O	1,540,000	14.00	16.00	18.50	27.50	70.00	200	375	2,600	—
1858	1,540,000	14.00	15.50	16.50	22.50	55.00	145	260	2,600	3,400
1858O	290,000	19.00	25.00	40.00	85.00	165	280	800	5,000	—
1858S	60,000	150	200	325	475	1,000	1,500	—	—	—
1859	430,000	16.00	20.00	25.00	45.00	70.00	140	350	—	3,400
1859O	480,000	16.00	20.00	25.00	45.00	80.00	225	550	—	—
1859S	60,000	160	225	375	550	1,350	3,000	—	—	—
1860S	140,000	40.00	55.00	75.00	145	325	800	—	—	—

Seated Liberty Dime.

UNITED STATES OF AMERICA replaced stars. Value within wreath.

KM# 92   **Obv. Designer:** Christian Gobrecht.
Weight: 2.4900 g. **Composition:** 0.9000 Silver,
0.0720 oz. ASW. **Notes:** The 1873 "closed-3" and
"open-3" varieties are distinguished by the amount of
space between the upper left and lower left serifs of
the 3 in the date.

Date	Mintage	G-4	VG-8	F-12	VF-20	XF-40	AU-50	MS-60	MS-65	Prf-65
1860	607,000	15.00	22.00	29.00	31.00	55.00	125	275	1,350	1,400
1860O	40,000	450	600	1,000	1,950	3,500	5,500	8,500	—	—
1861	1,884,000	15.00	17.00	20.00	23.00	34.00	85.00	150	1,250	1,400
1861S	172,500	55.00	90.00	165	275	400	1,000	1,400	—	—
1862	847,550	16.00	17.50	19.50	25.00	45.00	77.50	165	1,250	1,400
1862S	180,750	45.00	65.00	95.00	185	375	775	1,000	—	—
1863	14,460	425	500	650	900	950	1,100	1,300	—	1,400
1863S	157,500	40.00	55.00	80.00	145	275	650	1,200	—	—
1864	11,470	425	500	650	750	900	1,000	1,200	—	1,400
1864S	230,000	35.00	45.00	75.00	110	225	425	1,200	—	—
1865	10,500	475	575	700	875	1,000	1,200	1,350	—	1,400

Date	Mintage	G-4	VG-8	F-12	VF-20	XF-40	AU-50	MS-60	MS-65	Prf-65
1865S	175,000	45.00	55.00	85.00	145	325	850	—	—	—
1866	8,725	500	600	775	950	1,100	1,200	1,800	—	1,750
1866S	135,000	50.00	65.00	100.00	150	325	700	1,900	—	—
1867	6,625	600	700	950	1,100	1,450	1,600	1,800	—	1,750
1867S	140,000	50.00	60.00	90.00	150	325	700	1,200	—	—
1868	464,000	18.00	22.00	29.00	39.00	85.00	175	300	—	1,400
1868S	260,000	30.00	35.00	50.00	85.00	165	300	600	—	—
1869	256,600	25.00	35.00	45.00	80.00	135	250	600	—	1,400
1869S	450,000	25.00	30.00	40.00	55.00	85.00	175	400	—	—
1870	471,000	18.00	22.00	30.00	40.00	50.00	80.00	150	—	1,400
1870S	50,000	300	375	500	650	850	1,200	2,000	—	—
1871	907,710	16.00	20.00	25.00	33.00	55.00	175	300	—	1,400
1871CC	20,100	2,500	3,500	4,500	6,500	10,000	—	—	—	—
1871S	320,000	35.00	55.00	75.00	130	195	350	900	—	—
1872	2,396,450	12.00	15.00	17.00	20.00	31.00	95.00	175	—	1,400
1872CC	35,480	950	1,250	1,850	3,000	6,500	—	—	—	—
1872S	190,000	40.00	65.00	85.00	150	250	450	1,100	—	—
1873 closed 3	1,568,600	12.50	15.00	18.00	22.00	50.00	100.00	200	—	1,400
1873 open 3	Inc. above	28.00	35.00	50.00	75.00	125	250	650	—	—
1873CC	12,400	—	—	—	—	—	—	—	—	—

Note: 1873-CC, Heritage Sale, April 1999, MS-64, $632,500.

Seated Liberty Dime.
Seated Liberty, arrows at date.
Value within wreath.

KM# 105 Designer: Christian Gobrecht.
Weight: 2.5000 g. **Composition:** 0.9000 Silver,
0.0723 oz. ASW.

Date	Mintage	G-4	VG-8	F-12	VF-20	XF-40	AU-50	MS-60	MS-65	Prf-65
1873	2,378,500	15.00	18.50	25.00	55.00	150	350	500	4,500	4,500
1873CC	18,791	2,350	3,250	4,250	6,500	10,000	—	—	—	—
1873S	455,000	20.00	30.00	40.00	70.00	190	400	1,500	—	—
1874	2,940,700	13.50	17.50	22.50	50.00	150	315	500	4,500	4,500
1874CC	10,817	5,000	6,500	8,000	12,500	25,000	—	—	—	—
1874S	240,000	60.00	75.00	100.00	160	250	450	1,500	—	—

Seated Liberty Dime.
Seated Liberty, date below.
Value within wreath.

KM# A92 Designer: Christian Gobrecht. **Weight:**
2.5000 g. **Composition:** 0.9000 Silver, 0.0723 oz.
ASW. **Notes:** On the 1876-CC doubled-obverse
variety, doubling appears in the words OF AMERICA
in the legend.

Date	Mintage	G-4	VG-8	F-12	VF-20	XF-40	AU-50	MS-60	MS-65	Prf-65
1875	10,350,700	14.00	16.00	17.50	20.00	30.00	75.00	125	2,250	4,600
1875CC mint mark in wreath	4,645,000	15.00	19.00	22.50	35.00	47.50	90.00	190	2,700	—
1875CC mint mark under wreath	Inc. above	15.00	19.00	27.50	45.00	75.00	165	235	3,000	—
1875S mint mark in wreath	9,070,000	20.00	25.00	30.00	43.00	65.00	125	225	3,100	—
1875S mint mark under wreath	Inc. above	12.50	15.50	17.50	20.00	27.50	72.50	125	1,100	—
1876 Type 1 rev	11,461,150	14.00	16.00	17.50	20.00	30.00	75.00	125	1,100	1,200
1876 Type 2 rev	Inc. above	20.00	25.00	30.00	40.00	60.00	120	200	—	—
1876CC Type 1 rev	8,270,000	20.00	25.00	30.00	40.00	65.00	125	225	—	—
1876CC Type 2 rev	Inc. above	25.00	35.00	48.00	65.00	90.00	175	300	—	—
1876CC doubled die obverse	Inc. above	20.00	26.00	44.00	100.00	185	340	600	—	—
1876S Type 1 rev	10,420,000	14.00	16.00	17.50	20.00	30.00	75.00	125	1,750	—
1876S Type 2 rev	Inc. above	18.00	20.00	24.00	30.00	40.00	90.00	150	—	—
1877 Type 1 rev	7,310,510	14.00	16.00	17.50	20.00	30.00	75.00	125	1,100	1,200
1877 Type 2 rev	Inc. above	18.00	20.00	24.00	30.00	40.00	90.00	150	—	—
1877CC Type 1 rev	7,700,000	25.00	35.00	48.00	65.00	90.00	175	300	1,100	—
1877CC Type 2 rev	Inc. above	20.00	25.00	30.00	40.00	65.00	125	225	—	—
1877S Type 1 rev	2,340,000	—	—	—	—	—	—	—	—	—
1877S Type 2 rev	Inc. above	14.00	18.00	20.00	30.00	50.00	105	225	—	—
1878 Type 1 rev	1,678,800	28.00	35.00	50.00	65.00	100.00	175	—	—	—
1878 Type 2 rev	Inc. above	14.00	16.00	20.00	30.00	36.00	72.50	125	1,500	1,200
1878CC Type 1 rev	200,000	100.00	130	175	285	450	700	—	—	—
1878CC Type 2 rev	Inc. above	65.00	90.00	125	225	370	500	900	3,500	—
1879	15,100	275	310	375	425	500	575	675	1,750	1,500
1880	37,335	250	275	315	350	400	450	550	1,750	1,500
1881	24,975	265	300	350	400	475	550	650	2,500	1,600
1882	3,911,100	14.00	16.00	17.50	20.00	30.00	75.00	125	1,100	1,200
1883	7,675,712	14.00	16.00	17.50	20.00	30.00	75.00	125	1,100	1,200
1884	3,366,380	14.00	16.00	17.50	20.00	30.00	75.00	125	1,100	1,200

DIME

Date	Mintage	G-4	VG-8	F-12	VF-20	XF-40	AU-50	MS-60	MS-65	Prf-65
1884S	564,969	30.00	35.00	45.00	55.00	125	280	650	—	—
1885	2,533,427	14.00	16.00	17.50	20.00	30.00	75.00	125	1,100	1,200
1885S	43,690	450	650	950	1,750	2,400	3,600	5,000	—	—
1886	6,377,570	12.50	15.00	17.00	20.00	27.50	72.50	125	1,100	1,200
1886S	206,524	50.00	70.00	80.00	125	175	280	600	—	—
1887	11,283,939	14.00	16.00	17.50	20.00	30.00	75.00	125	1,100	1,200
1887S	4,454,450	12.50	15.00	17.00	20.00	38.00	80.00	125	1,100	—
1888	5,496,487	14.00	16.00	17.50	20.00	30.00	75.00	125	1,100	1,200
1888S	1,720,000	12.50	15.00	17.00	25.00	40.00	95.00	200	—	—
1889	7,380,711	14.00	16.00	17.50	20.00	30.00	75.00	125	1,100	1,200
1889S	972,678	14.00	18.00	25.00	45.00	70.00	150	475	4,500	—
1890	9,911,541	14.00	16.00	17.50	20.00	30.00	75.00	125	1,100	1,200
1890S	1,423,076	14.00	15.00	22.50	50.00	85.00	155	400	4,900	—
1891	15,310,600	14.00	16.00	17.50	20.00	30.00	75.00	125	1,100	1,200
1891O	4,540,000	12.50	15.00	17.00	20.00	27.50	72.50	175	1,750	—
1891O /horizontal O	Inc. above	65.00	95.00	125	175	225	400	—	—	—
1891S	3,196,116	13.50	15.00	17.50	20.00	30.00	75.00	225	1,650	—
1891S/S	Inc. above	25.00	30.00	40.00	85.00	135	250	—	—	—

Barber Dime.
Laureate head right, date at angle below. Value within wreath.

KM# 113 **Designer:** Charles E. Barber. **Diameter:**
17.9 **Weight:** 2.5000 g. **Composition:** 0.9000 Silver,
0.0723 oz. ASW.

Date	Mintage	G-4	VG-8	F-12	VF-20	XF-40	AU-50	MS-60	MS-65	Prf-65
1892	12,121,245	6.75	7.50	16.00	25.00	27.50	63.00	110	705	1,485
1892O	3,841,700	11.00	15.00	32.50	56.00	75.00	96.00	140	1,275	—
1892S	990,710	66.00	115	210	245	285	340	425	3,500	—
1893/2	3,340,792	135	155	175	225	300	325	450	4,850	—
1893	Inc. above	8.25	12.50	20.00	30.00	46.00	80.00	165	1,000	1,485
1893O	1,760,000	31.00	45.00	135	168	190	250	315	2,950	—
1893S	2,491,401	14.00	25.00	39.00	50.00	85.00	155	360	3,750	—
1894	1,330,972	25.00	45.00	122	165	190	235	310	1,150	1,485
1894O	720,000	70.00	105	215	280	425	650	1,550	15,500	—
1894S	24	—	—	—	—	—	—	—	1,900,000	—
Note: 1894S, Eliasberg Sale, May 1996, Prf-64, $451,000.										
1895	690,880	85.00	180	355	480	565	650	750	2,650	1,485
1895O	440,000	385	575	900	1,285	2,500	3,650	6,000	19,500	—
1895S	1,120,000	43.50	60.00	135	190	240	320	500	7,500	—
1896	2,000,762	11.50	23.00	56.00	82.00	100.00	120	150	1,450	1,485
1896O	610,000	80.00	155	305	375	465	700	975	9,500	—
1896S	575,056	85.00	160	310	335	385	525	770	4,650	—
1897	10,869,264	2.50	3.00	8.00	15.00	31.50	73.00	130	705	1,485
1897O	666,000	69.50	115	290	385	480	600	975	4,450	—
1897S	1,342,844	21.00	45.00	98.00	125	185	265	435	3,950	—
1898	16,320,735	2.50	3.00	7.50	15.00	28.00	68.00	130	705	1,485
1898O	2,130,000	13.50	27.50	88.00	145	200	285	450	3,850	—
1898S	1,702,507	8.50	15.00	33.00	48.00	78.00	160	370	3,750	—
1899	19,580,846	2.50	3.00	7.50	12.00	26.00	68.00	115	705	1,485
1899O	2,650,000	10.00	19.50	72.00	110	150	230	415	4,450	—
1899S	1,867,493	9.00	16.00	34.00	37.00	46.00	105	300	4,350	—
1900	17,600,912	4.00	5.00	7.00	11.00	26.00	63.00	110	735	1,485
1900O	2,010,000	19.50	38.50	115	165	225	355	595	5,750	—
1900S	5,168,270	5.00	6.25	12.50	19.50	31.50	75.00	155	1,850	—
1901	18,860,478	4.00	5.00	6.50	10.00	27.50	63.00	110	750	1,485
1901O	5,620,000	4.00	5.50	16.00	27.50	67.50	175	450	4,350	—
1901S	593,022	80.00	150	360	475	520	675	985	5,350	—
1902	21,380,777	4.00	5.00	5.50	8.00	23.00	63.00	110	750	1,485
1902O	4,500,000	4.00	5.50	15.00	32.50	62.50	145	350	4,500	—
1902S	2,070,000	8.00	21.00	58.00	90.00	135	195	375	3,950	—
1903	19,500,755	4.00	5.00	5.50	8.00	25.00	63.00	110	1,100	1,485
1903O	8,180,000	4.00	5.50	13.50	23.50	50.00	110	250	4,850	—
1903S	613,300	84.00	130	350	490	750	840	1,100	3,150	—
1904	14,601,027	4.00	5.00	6.25	9.75	25.00	63.00	110	1,850	1,485
1904S	800,000	45.00	75.00	165	245	335	465	725	4,500	—
1905	14,552,350	3.25	4.50	6.00	9.75	25.00	63.00	110	730	1,485
1905O	3,400,000	4.25	10.50	36.50	57.50	92.00	155	285	1,650	—
1905O micro O	Inc. above	35.00	50.00	75.00	140	235	375	1,750	12,500	—
1905S	6,855,199	3.50	4.25	9.00	18.50	43.50	96.00	210	775	—
1906	19,958,406	2.25	3.75	3.75	7.25	22.00	58.00	105	730	1,485
1906D	4,060,000	2.75	4.10	7.00	15.00	35.00	78.00	175	1,650	—
1906O	2,610,000	5.50	13.00	50.00	78.00	100.00	135	195	1,150	—
1906S	3,136,640	3.25	5.50	12.50	22.50	44.00	110	240	1,350	—
1907	22,220,575	2.25	2.75	3.50	7.25	22.00	58.00	105	695	1,485
1907D	4,080,000	2.75	4.25	8.75	17.50	43.50	115	275	3,950	—

Date	Mintage	G-4	VG-8	F-12	VF-20	XF-40	AU-50	MS-60	MS-65	Prf-65
1907O	5,058,000	3.25	6.75	33.50	50.00	62.50	110	210	1,350	—
1907S	3,178,470	3.25	5.50	16.00	27.50	67.50	150	410	2,450	—
1908	10,600,545	2.25	2.75	3.50	7.25	22.00	58.00	105	695	1,485
1908D	7,490,000	2.25	2.75	5.00	9.75	29.00	63.00	125	990	—
1908O	1,789,000	5.25	11.00	44.50	64.00	92.00	150	290	1,350	—
1908S	3,220,000	3.50	5.50	11.50	22.00	46.00	175	310	2,350	—
1909	10,240,650	2.25	2.75	3.50	7.25	22.00	58.00	105	695	1,485
1909D	954,000	7.25	18.50	60.00	100.00	135	225	485	3,150	—
1909O	2,287,000	4.00	7.25	12.50	22.00	50.00	92.50	185	1,650	—
1909S	1,000,000	8.75	19.50	88.00	130	182	315	525	3,150	—
1910	11,520,551	2.25	2.75	3.25	9.75	22.00	58.00	105	695	1,485
1910D	3,490,000	2.50	4.00	8.50	19.00	47.50	100.00	210	1,650	—
1910S	1,240,000	5.25	9.00	50.00	74.00	110	195	425	2,450	—
1911	18,870,543	2.25	2.75	3.25	7.00	22.00	58.00	105	695	1,485
1911D	11,209,000	2.25	2.75	3.25	7.00	22.00	58.00	105	695	—
1911S	3,520,000	3.00	4.00	8.50	18.50	39.50	105	195	1,050	—
1912	19,350,700	2.25	2.75	3.25	7.00	22.00	58.00	105	695	1,485
1912D	11,760,000	2.25	2.75	3.25	7.00	22.00	58.00	105	695	—
1912S	3,420,000	2.50	3.75	5.60	12.50	34.00	92.50	155	775	—
1913	19,760,622	2.25	2.75	3.25	7.00	22.00	58.00	105	695	1,485
1913S	510,000	35.00	50.00	120	190	240	325	480	1,375	—
1914	17,360,655	2.25	2.75	3.25	7.00	22.00	58.00	105	695	1,485
1914D	11,908,000	2.25	2.75	3.25	7.00	22.00	58.00	105	695	—
1914S	2,100,000	2.50	3.75	8.00	17.50	39.50	78.00	150	1,250	—
1915	5,620,450	2.25	2.75	3.25	7.00	22.00	58.00	105	695	1,485
1915S	960,000	7.50	11.50	34.50	49.50	66.50	135	250	1,550	—
1916	18,490,000	2.25	2.75	3.25	8.00	25.50	58.00	105	695	—
1916S	5,820,000	2.50	3.75	4.25	8.50	25.50	63.00	110	790	—

Mercury Dime.

KM# 140   Designer: Adolph A. Weinman. **Diameter:** 17.8 **Weight:** 2.3000 g. **Composition:** 0.9000 Silver, 0.0665 oz. ASW. **Notes:** All specimens listed as -65FSB are for fully struck MS-65 coins with fully split and rounded horizontal bands on the fasces.

1942/41   Mint mark

Full split bands

Date	Mintage	G-4	VG-8	F-12	VF-20	XF-40	AU-50	MS-60	MS-63	MS-65	-65FSB
1916	22,180,080	3.50	4.75	6.00	7.00	12.00	22.50	30.00	43.00	110	165
1916D	264,000	1,000	1,650	2,700	3,850	6,200	8,500	13,750	18,400	26,500	48,500
1916S	10,450,000	4.00	5.00	9.25	15.00	25.00	28.00	46.00	60.00	210	800
1917	55,230,000	1.80	2.20	2.50	5.50	8.00	12.50	28.00	55.00	155	375
1917D	9,402,000	4.30	6.00	12.50	26.00	52.50	90.00	120	300	1,100	5,650
1917S	27,330,000	1.90	2.40	3.50	7.50	15.00	28.00	64.00	170	470	1,265
1918	26,680,000	2.40	3.70	5.75	12.00	34.00	42.00	70.00	95.00	420	1,325
1918D	22,674,800	2.70	3.25	6.50	13.00	32.00	46.00	105	210	600	27,500
1918S	19,300,000	2.30	3.00	3.85	11.00	24.00	38.50	96.00	230	660	7,450
1919	35,740,000	1.90	2.40	3.00	5.50	12.00	23.00	37.00	105	315	685
1919D	9,939,000	3.50	6.00	13.50	31.00	46.00	70.00	180	420	2,100	38,500
1919S	8,850,000	2.90	3.25	10.50	20.00	42.00	70.00	180	450	1,250	14,350
1920	59,030,000	1.60	2.20	2.50	4.00	8.50	14.00	28.00	67.00	235	540
1920D	19,171,000	2.50	2.85	4.75	9.00	24.00	43.00	110	310	750	4,750
1920S	13,820,000	2.40	2.75	7.00	9.00	21.00	39.00	110	300	1,300	8,250
1921	1,230,000	60.00	72.00	115	260	525	835	1,175	1,465	3,100	4,350
1921D	1,080,000	78.00	120	200	380	660	1,000	1,325	1,650	3,250	5,200
1923	50,130,000	1.60	1.80	2.10	3.50	7.00	15.00	28.00	42.00	115	340
1923S	6,440,000	2.60	3.00	8.25	19.00	75.00	100.00	160	375	1,150	7,450

DIME

Date	Mintage	G-4	VG-8	F-12	VF-20	XF-40	AU-50	MS-60	MS-63	MS-65	-65FSB
1924	24,010,000	1.60	1.90	2.70	4.50	13.50	26.50	42.00	88.00	175	500
1924D	6,810,000	3.00	4.25	9.00	23.50	63.00	100.00	175	460	1,050	1,365
1924S	7,120,000	2.90	3.60	4.25	12.00	59.00	95.00	170	450	1,100	16,750
1925	25,610,000	1.60	1.90	2.40	4.00	11.00	16.00	28.00	75.00	210	990
1925D	5,117,000	3.90	4.40	12.75	46.50	135	185	350	725	1,750	3,500
1925S	5,850,000	2.50	2.85	7.75	18.50	85.00	100.00	185	475	1,400	4,650
1926	32,160,000	1.60	1.80	2.10	2.70	5.75	12.00	25.00	55.00	240	525
1926D	6,828,000	2.90	4.00	5.00	12.00	32.00	43.00	125	260	550	2,500
1926S	1,520,000	11.75	13.50	29.00	67.50	275	400	900	1,425	3,000	6,750
1927	28,080,000	1.60	1.80	2.10	3.50	6.00	11.00	26.00	48.00	138	350
1927D	4,812,000	3.00	5.00	7.75	25.50	88.00	95.00	175	360	1,285	8,500
1927S	4,770,000	2.30	3.75	5.50	11.00	30.00	46.00	285	550	1,400	7,600
1928	19,480,000	1.60	1.80	2.10	3.70	4.75	16.00	27.50	48.00	120	345
1928D	4,161,000	3.70	4.00	11.50	25.50	62.50	85.00	175	315	875	2,750
1928S Large S	7,400,000	2.80	3.25	5.00	12.00	40.00	85.00	225	385	750	6,500
1928S Small S	Inc. above	2.00	2.25	3.25	6.50	19.00	36.00	125	280	425	2,000
1929	25,970,000	1.60	1.80	2.10	3.00	4.50	10.00	21.00	28.00	60.00	175
1929D	5,034,000	2.00	3.00	3.75	8.00	15.00	21.00	27.00	30.00	75.00	225
1929S	4,730,000	1.80	2.00	2.25	5.00	7.50	20.00	32.50	42.00	90.00	560
1929S Doubled Die Obv	Inc. above	5.00	9.00	16.00	25.00	40.00	60.00	90.00	140	275	1,150
1930	6,770,000	1.80	2.00	2.20	3.80	7.00	13.00	26.00	48.00	120	575
1930S	1,843,000	2.50	3.50	4.80	6.50	19.00	45.00	82.00	122	200	685
1931	3,150,000	2.30	3.00	3.35	4.70	12.50	22.50	33.00	62.50	135	800
1931D	1,260,000	8.50	10.00	15.00	19.50	48.00	53.00	100.00	125	285	375
1931 Doubled Die Obv & Rev	Inc. above	—	—	—	50.00	70.00	90.00	135	200	485	650
1931S	1,800,000	4.00	5.00	5.50	11.00	23.50	42.50	96.00	135	275	2,500
1931S Doubled Die Obv	Inc. above	7.50	10.00	13.00	25.00	35.00	60.00	140	200	425	3,850
1934	24,080,000	—	1.45	1.75	3.00	6.50	10.00	29.00	33.00	42.00	130
1934D	6,772,000	1.90	2.14	3.25	7.50	14.00	27.50	50.00	60.00	78.00	320
1935	58,830,000	—	1.35	1.50	2.20	4.25	7.50	10.00	15.00	30.00	68.00
1935D	10,477,000	1.80	1.90	2.85	6.50	13.00	25.00	37.00	46.00	84.00	500
1935S	15,840,000	1.60	1.65	2.00	3.00	5.50	14.00	24.00	28.00	37.00	360
1936	87,504,130	—	—	1.50	2.50	3.50	6.50	9.00	15.00	26.50	84.00
1936 Doubled Die Obv	Inc. above	—	—	8.00	15.00	25.00	35.00	50.00	100.00	165	—
1936D	16,132,000	1.60	1.65	2.10	4.30	8.50	17.00	28.00	36.00	53.00	290
1936S	9,210,000	—	1.50	1.90	3.00	6.00	12.50	20.00	30.00	33.00	88.00
1937	56,865,756	1.30	—	1.50	2.00	3.75	6.00	8.00	12.00	24.00	52.00
1937 Doubled Die Obv	Inc. above	—	—	—	6.00	9.00	12.00	20.00	40.00	60.00	175
1937D	14,146,000	1.40	1.44	1.49	3.00	6.00	12.50	22.00	30.00	43.00	105
1937S	9,740,000	—	1.50	2.00	3.00	5.50	10.00	22.00	27.00	36.00	190
1937S Doubled Die Obv	Inc. above	—	—	—	5.00	8.00	12.00	28.00	42.00	80.00	275
1938	22,198,728	1.30	—	1.50	2.30	3.75	7.50	13.00	15.00	25.00	80.00
1938D	5,537,000	1.80	2.25	3.25	5.00	6.00	12.00	18.00	24.00	34.00	62.00
1938S	8,090,000	1.50	2.00	2.75	3.30	5.00	12.00	21.00	27.50	37.00	160
1939	67,749,321	1.30	—	1.50	2.00	3.25	4.50	9.00	11.00	25.00	170
1939 Doubled Die Obv	Inc. above	—	—	—	4.00	6.00	8.00	14.00	20.00	35.00	450
1939D	24,394,000	—	1.25	1.50	2.00	3.50	5.50	7.50	10.00	26.00	49.00
1939S	10,540,000	1.50	1.75	2.25	3.50	6.75	14.00	25.00	32.00	50.00	765
1940	65,361,827	1.20	1.24	1.29	1.50	2.20	3.10	6.50	11.00	30.00	48.00
1940D	21,198,000	—	—	—	1.60	3.30	5.00	8.00	13.00	32.00	48.00
1940S	21,560,000	—	—	—	1.60	3.30	4.50	8.50	12.50	32.00	95.00
1941	175,106,557	1.20	1.24	1.29	1.50	1.90	2.75	6.00	9.50	30.00	46.00
1941 Doubled Die Obv	Inc. above	—	—	—	10.00	16.00	30.00	55.00	80.00	140	295
1941D	45,634,000	—	—	—	1.60	2.30	4.00	8.00	13.00	23.00	46.00
1941D Doubled Die Obv	Inc. above	—	—	—	9.00	14.00	20.00	30.00	60.00	90.00	250
1941S Small S	43,090,000	—	—	—	1.60	2.30	4.50	7.00	10.00	30.00	46.00
1941S Large S	Inc. above	2.50	4.00	8.00	15.00	25.00	60.00	110	145	250	425
1941S Doubled Die Rev	Inc. above	1.80	2.50	3.00	4.00	5.00	7.50	18.00	25.00	50.00	85.00
1942	205,432,329	1.20	1.24	1.29	1.50	1.90	2.75	6.00	9.50	24.00	46.00
1942/41	Inc. above	525	545	610	640	750	1,285	2,250	4,000	15,500	35,000
1942D	60,740,000	—	—	—	1.60	2.30	4.00	8.00	12.75	27.50	46.00
1942/41D	Inc. above	475	540	600	650	825	1,350	2,650	4,500	9,650	26,500
1942S	49,300,000	—	—	—	1.60	2.30	4.50	9.50	16.00	24.00	145
1943	191,710,000	1.20	1.24	1.29	1.50	1.90	2.75	6.00	9.50	31.00	50.00
1943D	71,949,000	—	—	—	1.60	2.30	3.00	7.75	12.00	30.00	47.00
1943S	60,400,000	—	—	—	1.60	2.30	4.50	9.00	13.00	26.50	66.00
1944	231,410,000	1.20	1.24	1.29	1.50	1.90	2.75	6.00	9.50	23.00	75.00
1944D	62,224,000	—	—	—	1.60	2.30	3.00	7.50	15.00	23.00	46.00
1944S	49,490,000	—	—	—	1.60	2.30	4.00	7.50	16.00	30.00	50.00
1945	159,130,000	1.20	1.24	1.29	1.50	1.90	2.75	6.00	9.50	23.00	9,750
1945D	40,245,000	—	—	—	1.60	2.30	3.25	6.50	10.00	24.00	4,650
1945S	41,920,000	—	—	—	1.60	2.30	4.00	7.00	10.00	24.00	105
1945S micro S	Inc. above	3.00	4.00	6.00	9.00	13.00	20.00	28.00	38.00	115	685

Roosevelt Dime.

KM# 195 Designer: John R. Sinnock. **Diameter:** 17.9 **Weight:** 2.5000 g. **Composition:** 0.9000 Silver, 0.0723 oz. ASW.

Mint mark 1946-64

Date	Mintage	G-4	VG-8	F-12	VF-20	XF-40	AU-50	MS-60	MS-65	Prf-65
1946	225,250,000	—	—	—	—	1.29	1.55	2.00	14.00	—
1946D	61,043,500	—	—	—	—	1.29	1.75	2.25	15.00	—
1946S	27,900,000	—	—	—	—	1.29	1.80	2.35	17.00	—
1947	121,520,000	—	—	—	—	1.29	2.00	4.00	15.00	—
1947D	46,835,000	—	—	—	—	1.49	2.25	5.00	17.00	—
1947S	34,840,000	—	—	—	—	1.29	2.00	5.00	16.00	—
1948	74,950,000	—	—	—	—	1.39	2.00	4.50	15.00	—
1948D	52,841,000	—	—	—	—	1.69	2.50	6.00	17.00	—
1948S	35,520,000	—	—	—	—	1.59	2.25	5.00	14.00	—
1949	30,940,000	—	—	1.50	2.00	3.00	8.00	16.00	50.00	—
1949D	26,034,000	—	—	1.35	1.47	2.25	5.00	9.00	22.00	—
1949S	13,510,000	—	1.60	2.00	3.50	7.50	14.00	40.00	65.00	—
1950	50,181,500	—	—	—	1.47	2.25	3.50	10.00	25.00	55.00
1950D	46,803,000	—	—	—	—	—	2.50	5.00	12.00	—
1950S	20,440,000	—	1.20	1.52	1.67	3.75	9.00	32.00	60.00	—
1951	102,937,602	—	—	—	—	—	1.65	2.50	10.00	60.00
1951D	56,529,000	—	—	—	—	—	1.55	2.50	8.00	—
1951S	31,630,000	—	—	—	1.42	2.00	4.00	10.00	26.00	—
1952	99,122,073	—	—	—	—	—	1.45	2.50	9.00	40.00
1952D	122,100,000	—	—	—	—	—	1.45	2.50	10.00	—
1952S	44,419,500	—	—	—	1.47	1.69	2.75	5.50	15.00	—
1953	53,618,920	—	—	—	—	—	1.45	2.25	8.00	45.00
1953D	136,433,000	—	—	—	—	—	1.45	1.95	8.00	—
1953S	39,180,000	—	—	—	—	—	1.85	3.00	15.00	—
1954	114,243,503	—	—	—	—	—	1.45	1.60	7.00	20.00
1954D	106,397,000	—	—	—	—	—	1.45	1.60	7.00	—
1954S	22,860,000	—	—	—	—	—	1.45	1.70	10.00	—
1955	12,828,381	—	—	—	1.47	1.50	1.85	2.75	10.00	18.00
1955D	13,959,000	—	—	—	1.47	1.60	2.00	2.75	10.00	—
1955S	18,510,000	—	—	—	1.47	1.55	1.90	2.25	9.00	—
1956	109,309,384	—	—	—	—	—	1.45	1.60	9.00	8.00
1956D	108,015,100	—	—	—	—	—	1.45	1.70	10.00	—
1957	161,407,952	—	—	—	—	—	1.45	1.60	8.00	6.00
1957D	113,354,330	—	—	—	—	—	1.45	1.60	8.00	—
1958	32,785,652	—	—	—	—	—	1.45	1.60	8.50	6.00
1958D	136,564,600	—	—	—	—	—	1.45	1.60	9.00	—
1959	86,929,291	—	—	—	—	—	1.45	1.60	8.00	5.00
1959D	164,919,790	—	—	—	—	—	1.45	1.60	8.00	—
1960	72,081,602	—	—	—	—	—	1.45	1.60	7.50	5.00
1960D	200,160,400	—	—	—	—	—	1.45	1.60	7.50	—
1961	96,758,244	—	—	—	—	—	1.45	1.60	6.50	4.50
1961D	209,146,550	—	—	—	—	—	1.45	1.60	6.50	—
1962	75,668,019	—	—	—	—	—	1.45	1.60	7.00	4.50
1962D	334,948,380	—	—	—	—	—	1.45	1.60	7.00	—
1963	126,725,645	—	—	—	—	—	1.45	1.60	6.50	4.00
1963D	421,476,530	—	—	—	—	—	1.45	1.60	6.50	—
1964	933,310,762	—	—	—	—	—	1.45	1.60	6.00	4.00
1964D	1,357,517,180	—	—	—	—	—	1.45	1.60	6.00	—

Roosevelt Dime.

KM# 195a Designer: John R. Sinnock. **Diameter:** 17.9 **Weight:** 2.2700 g. **Composition:** Copper-Nickel Clad Copper **Notes:** The 1979-S and 1981-S Type II proofs have clearer mint marks than the Type I proofs of those years. On the 1982 no-mint-mark variety, the mint mark was inadvertently left off.

Mint mark 1968- present   1982 No mint mark

Date	Mintage	MS-65	Prf-65	Date	Mintage	MS-65	Prf-65
1965	1,652,140,570	1.00	—	1967	2,244,007,320	1.50	—
1966	1,382,734,540	1.00	—	1968	424,470,000	1.00	—

Date	Mintage	MS-65	Prf-65	Date	Mintage	MS-65	Prf-65
1968D	480,748,280	1.00	—	1993P	766,180,000	1.00	—
1968S	(3,041,506)	—	1.00	1993D	750,110,166	1.50	—
1969	145,790,000	3.00	—	1993S	(2,633,439)	—	7.00
1969D	563,323,870	1.00	—	1994P	1,189,000,000	1.00	—
1969S	(2,934,631)	—	0.80	1994D	1,303,268,110	1.00	—
1970	345,570,000	1.00	—	1994S	(2,484,594)	—	5.00
1970S No S	—	—	1,300	1995P	1,125,500,000	1.50	—
1970D	754,942,100	1.00	—	1995D	1,274,890,000	2.00	—
1970S	(2,632,810)	—	1.00	1995S	(2,010,384)	—	20.00
1971	162,690,000	2.00	—	1996P	1,421,163,000	1.00	—
1971D	377,914,240	1.00	—	1996D	1,400,300,000	1.00	—
1971S	(3,220,733)	—	1.00	1996W	1,457,949	25.00	—
1972	431,540,000	1.00	—	1996S	(2,085,191)	—	2.50
1972D	330,290,000	1.00	—	1997P	991,640,000	2.00	—
1972S	(3,260,996)	—	1.00	1997D	979,810,000	1.00	—
1973	315,670,000	1.00	—	1997S	(1,975,000)	—	11.00
1973D	455,032,426	1.00	—	1998P	1,163,000,000	1.00	—
1973S	(2,760,339)	—	1.00	1998D	1,172,250,000	1.25	—
1974	470,248,000	1.00	—	1998S	(2,078,494)	—	4.00
1974D	571,083,000	1.00	—	1999P	2,164,000,000	1.00	—
1974S	(2,612,568)	—	1.00	1999D	1,397,750,000	1.00	—
1975	585,673,900	1.00	—	1999S	(2,557,897)	—	4.00
1975D	313,705,300	1.00	—	2000P	1,842,500,000	1.00	—
1975S	(2,845,450)	—	2.00	2000D	1,818,700,000	1.00	—
1976	568,760,000	1.50	—	2000S	(3,097,440)	—	1.00
1976D	695,222,774	1.00	—	2001P	1,369,590,000	1.00	—
1976S	(4,149,730)	—	1.00	2001D	1,412,800,000	1.00	—
1977	796,930,000	1.00	—	2001S	(2,249,496)	—	1.00
1977D	376,607,228	1.00	—	2002P	1,187,500,000	1.00	—
1977S	(3,251,152)	—	2.00	2002D	1,379,500,000	1.00	—
1978	663,980,000	1.00	—	2002S	(2,268,913)	—	2.00
1978D	282,847,540	1.00	—	2003P	1,085,500,000	1.00	—
1978S	(3,127,781)	—	1.00	2003D	986,500,000	1.00	—
1979	315,440,000	1.00	—	2003S	(2,076,165)	—	2.00
1979D	390,921,184	1.00	—	2004P	1,328,000,000	1.00	—
1979 type I	—	—	1.00	2004D	1,159,500,000	1.00	—
1979S type I	(3,677,175)	—	1.00	2004S	(1,804,396)	—	4.75
1979S type II	Inc. above	—	2.00	2005P	1,412,000,000	1.00	—
1980P	735,170,000	1.00	—	2005D	1,423,500,000	1.00	—
1980D	719,354,321	.70	—	2005S	—	—	2.25
1980S	(3,554,806)	—	1.00	2006P	1,381,000,000	1.00	—
1981P	676,650,000	1.00	—	2006D	1,447,000,000	1.00	—
1981D	712,284,143	1.00	—	2006S	—	—	2.25
1981S type I	—	—	1.00	2007P	—	1.00	—
1981S type II	—	—	2.00	2007D	—	1.00	—
1982P	519,475,000	8.50	—	2007S	—	—	2.25
1982 no mint mark	Inc. above	300	—	2008P	—	1.00	—
1982D	542,713,584	3.00	—	2008D	—	1.00	—
1982S	(3,857,479)	—	2.00	2008S	—	—	2.25
1983P	647,025,000	7.00	—	2009P	—	1.00	—
1983D	730,129,224	2.50	—	2009D	—	1.00	—
1983S	(3,279,126)	—	2.00	2009S	—	—	2.25
1984P	856,669,000	1.00	—				
1984D	704,803,976	2.00	—				
1984S	(3,065,110)	—	2.00				
1985P	705,200,962	1.00	—				
1985D	587,979,970	1.00	—				
1985S	(3,362,821)	—	1.00				
1986P	682,649,693	2.00	—				
1986D	473,326,970	2.00	—				
1986S	(3,010,497)	—	2.75				
1987P	762,709,481	1.00	—				
1987D	653,203,402	1.00	—				
1987S	(4,227,728)	—	1.00				
1988P	1,030,550,000	1.00	—				
1988D	962,385,488	1.00	—				
1988S	(3,262,948)	—	3.00				
1989P	1,298,400,000	1.00	—				
1989D	896,535,597	1.00	—				
1989S	(3,220,194)	—	4.00				
1990P	1,034,340,000	1.00	—				
1990D	839,995,824	1.00	—				
1990S	(3,299,559)	—	2.00				
1991P	927,220,000	1.00	—				
1991D	601,241,114	1.00	—				
1991S	(2,867,787)	—	3.00				
1992P	593,500,000	1.00	—				
1992D	616,273,932	1.00	—				
1992S	(2,858,981)	—	4.00				

Roosevelt Dime.

KM# 195b **Designer:** John R. Sinnock. **Diameter:** 17.9 **Weight:** 2.5000 g. **Composition:** 0.9000 Silver, 0.0723 oz. ASW.

Date	Mintage	Prf-65
1992S	(1,317,579)	5.00
1993S	(761,353)	9.00
1994S	(785,329)	9.00
1995S	(838,953)	25.00
1996S	(830,021)	9.00
1997S	(821,678)	25.00
1998S	(878,792)	9.00
1999S	(804,565)	6.50
2000S	(965,921)	4.00
2001S	(849,600)	5.00
2002S	(888,826)	5.00
2003S	(1,090,425)	4.00
2004S	—	4.50
2005S	—	3.50
2006S	—	3.50
2007S	—	3.50
2008S	—	3.50
2009S	—	3.50

20 CENTS

Seated Liberty within circle of stars,
date below. Eagle with arrows in
talons, value below.

KM# 109 Designer: William Barber. **Diameter:** 22
Weight: 5.0000 g. **Composition:** 0.9000 Silver,
0.1447 oz. ASW.

Date	Mintage	G-4	VG-8	F-12	VF-20	XF-40	AU-50	MS-60	MS-65	Prf-65
1875	39,700	165	210	270	325	415	550	835	5,500	9,500
1875S	1,155,000	100.00	110	120	175	210	320	500	4,900	—
Note: 1875-S exists as a branch mint proof										
1875S Clear S	Inc. above	110	120	135	200	235	350	600	5,500	—
1875S over horizontal S	Inc. above	100.00	110	120	175	210	320	500	4,900	—
Note: Also known as filled S										
1875S as $	Inc. above	—	120	130	150	225	260	375	1,300	—
1875CC	133,290	335	385	475	600	775	1,150	1,650	10,000	—
1876	15,900	185	225	285	350	410	535	800	5,600	9,400
1876CC	10,000	20,000	25,000	30,000	35,000	50,000	60,000	—	—	175,000
Note: 1876CC, Eliasberg Sale, April 1997, MS-65, $148,500. Heritage 1999 ANA, MS-63, $86,500.										
1877 proof only	510	—	—	2,700	2,900	3,300	3,500	—	—	10,000
1878 proof only	600	—	—	2,000	2,300	2,400	2,800	—	—	9,500

QUARTER

Draped Bust Quarter.

Small eagle.

KM# 25 Designer: Robert Scot. **Diameter:** 27.5
Weight: 6.7400 g. **Composition:** 0.8920 Silver,
0.1933 oz. ASW.

Date	Mintage	G-4	VG-8	F-12	VF-20	XF-40	AU-50	MS-60	MS-65
1796	6,146	11,000	16,500	30,000	39,500	42,500	68,000	82,500	235,000

Draped Bust Quarter.

Draped bust right, flanked by stars,
date at angle below. Heraldic eagle.

KM# 36 Designer: Robert Scot. **Diameter:** 27.5
Weight: 6.7400 g. **Composition:** 0.8920 Silver,
0.1933 oz. ASW.

Date	Mintage	G-4	VG-8	F-12	VF-20	XF-40	AU-50	MS-60	MS-65
1804	6,738	5,500	6,750	9,000	14,500	46,500	54,500	88,500	335,000
1805	121,394	230	285	520	960	2,500	4,450	6,600	62,000
1806/5	206,124	250	375	650	1,400	2,850	5,000	7,150	72,000
1806	Inc. above	220	275	500	900	2,350	4,250	6,300	56,000
1807	220,643	220	275	500	925	2,350	4,250	6,300	58,000

QUARTER

Liberty Cap Quarter.

Draped bust left, flanked by stars, date below. Eagle with arrows in talons, banner above, value below.

KM# 44   Designer: John Reich. **Diameter:** 27 **Weight:** 6.7400 g. **Composition:** 0.8920 Silver, 0.1933 oz. ASW. **Notes:** The 1827 restrikes were produced privately using dies sold as scrap by the U.S. Mint.

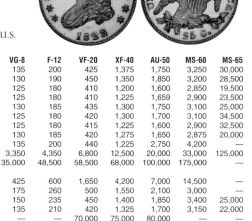

Date	Mintage	G-4	VG-8	F-12	VF-20	XF-40	AU-50	MS-60	MS-65
1815	89,235	100.00	135	200	425	1,375	1,750	3,250	30,000
1818/15	361,174	100.00	130	190	450	1,350	1,850	3,200	28,500
1818	Inc. above	95.00	125	180	410	1,200	1,600	2,850	19,500
1819 small 9	144,000	95.00	125	180	410	1,225	1,659	2,900	23,500
1819 large 9	Inc. above	95.00	130	185	435	1,300	1,750	3,100	25,000
1820 small O	127,444	95.00	125	180	420	1,300	1,700	3,100	34,500
1820 large O	Inc. above	95.00	125	180	415	1,225	1,600	2,900	32,500
1821	216,851	100.00	130	185	420	1,275	1,650	2,875	20,000
1822	64,080	110	135	200	440	1,225	2,750	4,200	—
1822 25/50C.	Inc. above	1,650	3,350	4,350	6,800	12,500	20,000	33,000	125,000
1823/22	17,800	30,000	35,000	48,500	58,500	68,000	100,000	175,000	—
Note: 1823/22, Superior, Aug. 1990, Proof, $62,500.									
1824/2	—	275	425	600	1,650	4,200	7,000	14,500	—
1825/22	168,000	125	175	260	500	1,550	2,100	3,000	—
1825/23	Inc. above	115	150	235	450	1,400	1,850	3,400	25,000
1825/24	Inc. above	100.00	135	210	420	1,325	1,700	3,150	22,000
1827 original curl base 2	4,000	—	—	—	70,000	75,000	80,000	—	—
Note: Eliasberg, April 1997, VF-20, $39,600.									
1827 restrike, square base 2	Inc. above	—	—	—	—	—	—	—	—
Note: 1827 restrike, Eliasberg, April 1997, Prf-65, $77,000.									
1828	102,000	90.00	120	180	400	1,100	1,650	3,000	26,000
1828 25/50C.	Inc. above	165	320	550	1,250	2,650	4,250	9,500	—

Liberty Cap Quarter.

Draped bust left, flanked by stars, date below. Eagle with arrows in talons, value below.

KM# 55   Designer: William Kneass. **Diameter:** 24.3 **Composition:** 0.8920 Silver ASW.

Date	Mintage	G-4	VG-8	F-12	VF-20	XF-40	AU-50	MS-60	MS-65
1831 small letter rev.	398,000	70.00	95.00	115	160	400	850	1,175	19,500
1831 large letter rev.	Inc. above	70.00	90.00	110	150	385	775	1,100	17,000
1832	320,000	70.00	90.00	110	150	385	775	1,075	22,750
1833	156,000	75.00	100.00	115	170	420	855	1,400	20,500
1834	286,000	70.00	90.00	110	150	385	775	1,100	17,000
1834 0 over O	Inc. above	—	—	—	—	—	—	—	—
1835	1,952,000	70.00	90.00	110	150	385	775	1,100	23,750
1836	472,000	70.00	90.00	110	150	385	775	1,100	18,850
1837	252,400	70.00	90.00	110	150	385	775	1,100	17,000
1838	832,000	70.00	90.00	110	150	385	775	1,100	19,500

Seated Liberty Quarter.

Seated Liberty, stars around top 1/2 of border, date below. Eagle with arrows in talons, value below.

KM# 64.1   Designer: Christian Gobrecht. **Diameter:** 24.3 **Weight:** 6.6800 g. **Composition:** 0.9000 Silver, 0.1933 oz. ASW.

Date	Mintage	G-4	VG-8	F-12	VF-20	XF-40	AU-50	MS-60	MS-65
1838	Inc. above	42.00	50.00	60.00	110	360	550	1,250	30,000
1839	491,146	36.00	44.00	52.00	85.00	350	550	1,250	34,000
1840O	425,200	46.00	54.00	75.00	135	375	575	1,350	38,500

Seated Liberty Quarter.
Drapery added to Liberty's left elbow, stars around top 1/2 of border. Eagle with arrows in talons, value below.

KM# 64.2 **Designer:** Christian Gobrecht.
Diameter: 24.3 **Weight:** 6.6800 g. **Composition:** 0.9000 Silver, 0.1933 oz. ASW.

Date	Mintage	G-4	VG-8	F-12	VF-20	XF-40	AU-50	MS-60	MS-65
1840	188,127	27.00	52.00	75.00	125	225	350	950	12,000
1840O	Inc. above	29.00	39.00	70.00	115	250	450	1,000	—
1841	120,000	65.00	90.00	125	170	275	385	750	11,000
1841O	452,000	21.50	27.50	50.00	85.00	165	350	700	10,000
1842 small date	88,000	—	—	—	—	—	—	—	—
Note: 1842 small date, Eliasberg, April 1997, Prf-63, $66,000.									
1842 large date	Inc. above	100.00	125	190	275	375	850	1,850	—
1842O small date	769,000	425	650	1,200	1,950	4,000	—	—	—
1842O large date	Inc. above	28.00	42.00	55.00	70.00	135	300	900	—
1843	645,600	22.00	26.00	34.00	45.00	75.00	175	400	6,750
1843O	968,000	25.00	31.50	55.00	125	250	750	2,000	11,000
1844	421,200	20.00	25.00	31.50	50.00	80.00	160	450	5,500
1844O	740,000	25.00	28.50	40.00	75.00	140	280	1,000	6,000
1845	922,000	20.00	25.00	31.50	45.00	70.00	150	465	5,000
1846	510,000	20.00	25.00	36.50	55.00	85.00	175	475	6,000
1847	734,000	20.00	25.00	31.50	50.00	70.00	150	450	5,000
1847O	368,000	30.00	45.00	70.00	135	300	750	1,900	—
1848	146,000	40.00	60.00	110	185	225	375	1,000	10,000
1849	340,000	20.00	30.00	45.00	65.00	125	275	750	9,000
1849O	—	550	750	1,150	1,850	3,250	5,750	—	—
1850	190,800	40.00	50.00	80.00	125	175	275	800	—
1850O	412,000	20.00	30.00	60.00	110	175	450	1,300	—
1851	160,000	60.00	75.00	125	225	285	400	850	8,500
1851O	88,000	185	275	425	700	1,250	2,250	4,000	—
1852	177,060	50.00	60.00	100.00	185	225	350	500	4,800
1852O	96,000	195	275	475	800	1,350	3,500	8,000	—
1853 recut date	44,200	450	650	900	1,100	1,350	1,800	2,600	9,000

Seated Liberty Quarter.
Seated Liberty, arrows at date. Rays around eagle.

KM# 78 **Designer:** Christian Gobrecht. **Diameter:** 24.3 **Weight:** 6.2200 g. **Composition:** 0.9000 Silver, 0.1800 oz. ASW.

Date	Mintage	G-4	VG-8	F-12	VF-20	XF-40	AU-50	MS-60	MS-65	Prf-65
1853	15,210,020	20.00	23.00	32.00	46.00	150	275	950	16,500	100,000
1853/4	Inc. above	40.00	65.00	100.00	200	275	750	1,750	—	—
1853O	1,332,000	18.00	35.00	50.00	100.00	275	1,100	2,750	—	—

Seated Liberty Quarter.
Seated Liberty, arrows at date. Eagle with arrows in talons, value below.

KM# 81 **Designer:** Christian Gobrecht. **Diameter:** 24.3 **Weight:** 6.6800 g. **Composition:** 0.9000 Silver, 0.1933 oz. ASW.

Date	Mintage	G-4	VG-8	F-12	VF-20	XF-40	AU-50	MS-60	MS-65	Prf-65
1854	12,380,000	15.00	20.00	27.50	35.00	75.00	225	440	7,500	17,500
1854O	1,484,000	17.00	24.00	35.00	60.00	125	300	1,750	—	—
1854O huge O	Inc. above	800	1,350	2,850	4,750	7,500	12,500	17,000	—	—
1855	2,857,000	15.00	20.00	27.50	35.00	75.00	225	440	8,500	18,500
1855O	176,000	50.00	75.00	110	240	475	950	2,750	—	—
1855S	396,400	40.00	60.00	80.00	225	500	1,250	2,000	—	—

Seated Liberty Quarter.

Seated Liberty, date below. Eagle with arrows in talons, value below.

KM# A64.2 **Designer:** Christian Gobrecht. **Diameter:** 24.3 **Weight:** 6.2200 g. **Composition:** 0.9000 Silver, 0.1800 oz. ASW.

Date	Mintage	G-4	VG-8	F-12	VF-20	XF-40	AU-50	MS-60	MS-65	Prf-65
1856	7,264,000	15.00	20.00	27.50	35.00	60.00	145	290	4,250	15,000
1856O	968,000	20.00	30.00	40.00	60.00	110	250	1,000	8,500	—
1856S	286,000	45.00	65.00	110	250	450	900	2,200	—	—
1856S/S	Inc. above	150	275	500	1,250	2,000	—	—	—	—
1857	9,644,000	15.00	20.00	27.50	35.00	60.00	145	290	4,000	9,500
1857O	1,180,000	15.00	20.00	29.00	40.00	80.00	275	975	—	—
1857S	82,000	125	175	275	450	700	950	2,750	—	—
1858	7,368,000	15.00	20.00	27.50	35.00	60.00	160	300	4,000	6,500
1858O	520,000	25.00	30.00	45.00	70.00	135	360	1,350	—	—
1858S	121,000	70.00	110	175	300	750	1,250	—	—	—
1859	1,344,000	17.00	24.00	30.00	40.00	75.00	175	375	6,000	7,000
1859O	260,000	25.00	30.00	50.00	80.00	150	400	1,000	15,000	—
1859S	80,000	125	150	250	500	1,500	2,500	—	—	—
1860	805,400	18.00	22.00	28.00	33.00	60.00	160	500	—	5,250
1860O	388,000	20.00	30.00	40.00	55.00	100.00	275	1,200	—	—
1860S	56,000	200	350	600	975	4,000	6,000	—	—	—
1861	4,854,600	16.00	19.00	27.00	32.00	55.00	150	290	4,200	5,500
1861S	96,000	90.00	145	235	400	1,250	2,750	—	—	—
1862	932,550	18.00	22.00	33.00	40.00	65.00	165	300	4,350	5,350
1862S	67,000	80.00	125	200	325	700	1,600	2,750	—	—
1863	192,060	30.00	45.00	60.00	120	185	300	650	4,350	5,500
1864	94,070	90.00	120	160	245	345	400	650	5,000	5,500
1864S	20,000	400	600	900	1,350	2,350	3,750	7,000	—	—
1865	59,300	85.00	115	150	235	325	375	875	9,500	5,500
1865S	41,000	125	175	250	425	750	1,250	2,350	11,500	—
1866 unique	—	—	—	—	—	—	—	—	—	—

Seated Liberty Quarter.

Seated Liberty, date below. IN GOD WE TRUST above eagle.

KM# 98 **Designer:** Christian Gobrecht. **Diameter:** 24.3 **Weight:** 6.2200 g. **Composition:** 0.9000 Silver, 0.1800 oz. ASW. **Notes:** The 1873 closed-3 and open-3 varieties are distinguished by the amount of space between the upper left and lower left serifs in the 3.

Date	Mintage	G-4	VG-8	F-12	VF-20	XF-40	AU-50	MS-60	MS-65	Prf-65
1866	17,525	475	600	750	1,000	1,200	1,500	2,250	7,500	3,000
1866S	28,000	325	375	675	1,050	1,450	2,000	3,000	—	—
1867	20,625	250	325	500	675	850	975	1,200	—	2,450
1867S	48,000	275	385	600	900	1,350	1,700	—	—	—
1868	30,000	200	250	325	400	500	650	900	7,000	3,450
1868S	96,000	95.00	110	195	300	625	1,350	2,000	—	—
1869	16,600	350	450	600	800	900	1,000	1,275	—	2,500
1869S	76,000	110	135	225	375	700	1,400	2,400	16,000	—
1870	87,400	55.00	80.00	145	245	295	425	850	6,000	2,750
1870CC	8,340	4,500	6,500	9,500	15,000	—	—	—	—	—
1871	119,160	40.00	65.00	75.00	150	195	350	650	6,000	2,500
1871CC	10,890	3,500	4,500	7,500	12,500	18,000	—	—	—	—
1871S	30,900	375	500	700	950	1,200	1,850	3,000	10,000	—
1872	182,950	30.00	40.00	80.00	110	155	300	600	6,500	2,500
1872CC	22,850	1,100	1,500	2,250	3,750	6,500	7,500	14,000	—	—
1872S	83,000	900	1,250	1,750	2,400	3,500	4,500	7,500	—	—
1873 closed 3	212,600	250	350	475	800	1,200	1,800	2,800	—	2,600
1873 open 3	Inc. above	30.00	42.50	80.00	120	175	250	450	5,000	—
1873CC 6 known	4,000	—	75,000	—	—	—	—	—	—	—

Note: 1873CC, Heritage, April 1999, MS-62, $106,375.

Seated Liberty Quarter.
Seated Liberty, arrows at date. IN GOD WE TRUST above eagle.
KM# 106 Designer: Christian Gobrecht.
Diameter: 24.3 **Weight:** 6.2500 g. **Composition:**
0.9000 Silver, 0.1808 oz. ASW.

Date	Mintage	G-4	VG-8	F-12	VF-20	XF-40	AU-50	MS-60	MS-65	Prf-65
1873	1,271,700	16.00	23.00	30.00	60.00	200	400	775	4,250	8,000
1873CC	12,462	3,500	4,500	8,000	11,000	17,000	—	—	—	—
1873S	156,000	25.00	40.00	85.00	140	275	550	1,200	8,000	—
1874	471,900	20.00	26.00	40.00	70.00	220	420	850	4,000	6,750
1874S	392,000	23.00	30.00	50.00	110	240	425	900	4,500	—

Seated Liberty Quarter.
Seated Liberty, date below. IN GOD WE TRUST above eagle.
KM# A98 Designer: Christian Gobrecht.
Diameter: 24.3 **Weight:** 6.2500 g. **Composition:**
0.9000 Silver, 0.1808 oz. ASW. **Notes:** The 1876-CC
fine-reeding variety has a more finely reeded edge.

Date	Mintage	G-4	VG-8	F-12	VF-20	XF-40	AU-50	MS-60	MS-65	Prf-65
1875	4,293,500	14.00	17.00	25.00	30.00	50.00	135	225	1,600	2,300
1875CC	140,000	75.00	110	225	350	550	850	1,600	15,000	—
1875S	680,000	25.00	36.00	67.00	110	175	275	575	3,200	—
1876	17,817,150	14.00	17.00	25.00	30.00	50.00	135	225	1,600	2,250
1876CC	4,944,000	30.00	40.00	50.00	65.00	90.00	150	325	3,600	—
1876CC fine reeding	Inc. above	30.00	40.00	50.00	65.00	90.00	150	325	3,600	—
1876S	8,596,000	16.00	19.00	25.00	30.00	50.00	135	225	2,000	—
1877	10,911,710	14.00	17.00	25.00	30.00	50.00	135	225	1,600	2,250
1877CC	4,192,000	30.00	40.00	50.00	65.00	90.00	150	325	2,000	—
1877S	8,996,000	14.00	17.00	25.00	30.00	50.00	135	225	1,600	—
1877S over horizontal S	Inc. above	45.00	60.00	95.00	175	250	375	650	—	—
1878	2,260,800	16.00	18.00	28.00	34.00	55.00	145	250	2,750	2,300
1878CC	996,000	35.00	45.00	55.00	80.00	110	150	450	3,500	—
1878S	140,000	165	200	300	400	650	875	1,450	—	—
1879	14,700	190	235	285	325	400	485	575	1,700	2,250
1880	14,955	190	235	285	325	400	485	575	1,600	2,250
1881	12,975	200	250	300	350	425	500	600	1,650	2,200
1882	16,300	200	250	300	350	425	500	600	1,850	2,200
1883	15,439	210	265	315	365	435	525	625	2,450	2,200
1884	8,875	375	450	550	650	750	750	850	1,900	2,200
1885	14,530	210	265	315	365	435	525	625	2,600	2,200
1886	5,886	500	600	700	800	900	1,000	1,250	2,600	2,400
1887	10,710	300	350	450	550	650	750	850	2,350	2,200
1888	10,833	275	325	425	500	600	700	800	2,000	2,350
1888S	1,216,000	15.00	20.00	27.50	30.00	60.00	160	245	2,450	—
1889	12,711	250	300	375	425	500	575	675	1,750	2,350
1890	80,590	65.00	85.00	100.00	125	200	300	425	—	2,350
1891	3,920,600	15.00	20.00	27.50	30.00	60.00	160	245	1,750	2,350
1891O	68,000	150	225	325	550	950	1,250	3,000	14,500	—
1891S	2,216,000	16.00	22.00	29.00	65.00	52.50	185	275	2,400	—

Barber Quarter.
Laureate head right, flanked by stars, date below. Heraldic eagle.
KM# 114 Designer: Charles E. Barber. **Diameter:**
24.3 **Weight:** 6.2500 g. **Composition:** 0.9000 Silver,
0.1808 oz. ASW.

Date	Mintage	G-4	VG-8	F-12	VF-20	XF-40	AU-50	MS-60	MS-65	Prf-65
1892	8,237,245	10.00	14.50	35.00	65.00	100.00	150	285	—	2,450
1892 Type 2 Rev	Inc. above	7.50	8.50	26.00	46.00	75.00	115	210	1,550	2,450
1892O	2,640,000	22.00	30.00	55.00	90.00	155	235	400	—	—
1892O Type 2 Rev	Inc. above	15.00	21.50	43.50	63.50	100.00	150	290	2,000	—
1892S	964,079	50.00	75.00	135	200	300	465	650	—	—
1892S Type 2 Rev	Inc. above	35.00	57.50	95.00	145	195	300	450	4,650	—

Date	Mintage	G-4	VG-8	F-12	VF-20	XF-40	AU-50	MS-60	MS-65	Prf-65
1893	5,484,838	6.50	9.00	27.50	41.50	70.00	115	210	1,650	2,450
1893O	3,396,000	13.50	22.00	44.00	75.00	165	285	390	—	—
1893O MM far right	Inc. above	9.00	15.00	31.00	57.50	115	170	265	2,100	—
1893S	1,454,535	26.00	47.50	82.00	158	255	390	635	—	—
1893S MM far right	Inc. above	21.00	38.00	67.50	125	195	310	450	7,950	—
1894	3,432,972	5.50	9.50	34.00	50.00	93.50	140	235	1,550	2,450
1894O	2,852,000	12.50	24.00	50.00	95.00	165	285	415	—	—
1894O MM far right	Inc. above	10.00	18.50	43.00	80.00	142	220	325	2,650	—
1894S	2,648,821	11.00	17.00	50.00	100.00	180	265	410	—	—
1894S MM far right	Inc. above	8.25	13.50	38.00	68.50	128	195	295	2,750	—
1895	4,440,880	6.50	10.50	31.50	41.50	78.00	130	225	1,850	2,450
1895O	2,816,000	17.50	27.50	60.00	92.00	175	290	525	—	—
1895O MM far right	Inc. above	12.50	19.50	46.00	75.00	145	225	390	2,850	—
1895S	1,764,681	28.00	40.00	85.00	165	235	375	560	—	—
1895S MM far right	Inc. above	22.00	30.00	68.50	120	175	290	425	4,450	—
1896	3,874,762	5.00	7.00	25.00	41.50	80.00	130	225	1,550	2,450
1896O	1,484,000	32.00	53.50	122	250	435	725	815	9,850	—
1896S	188,039	900	1,650	2,350	3,350	4,650	6,250	9,750	56,000	—
1897	8,140,731	5.00	6.25	21.50	33.50	72.00	115	210	1,550	2,450
1897O	1,414,800	19.50	40.00	130	255	400	625	900	3,950	—
1897S	542,229	75.00	115	235	290	440	665	900	7,000	—
1898	11,100,735	5.00	6.25	22.50	35.00	75.00	115	210	1,550	2,450
1898O	1,868,000	16.00	28.50	75.00	160	300	430	665	10,000	—
1898S	1,020,592	12.50	19.00	50.00	70.00	100.00	210	385	6,950	—
1899	12,624,846	5.00	6.25	22.50	35.00	75.00	115	210	1,550	2,450
1899O	2,644,000	14.00	21.00	38.50	72.00	145	290	415	3,750	—
1899S	708,000	18.00	28.50	70.00	92.50	145	275	410	3,650	—
1900	10,016,912	6.00	8.00	23.50	36.00	71.50	130	210	1,550	2,450
1900O	3,416,000	16.00	29.00	69.50	118	170	320	575	3,750	—
1900S	1,858,585	8.00	15.00	38.00	55.00	80.00	135	375	4,950	—
1901	8,892,813	11.00	13.00	25.00	41.50	80.00	135	215	1,850	2,450
1901O	1,612,000	42.50	60.00	145	275	455	665	885	5,850	—
1901S	72,664	6,250	14,000	17,500	25,500	30,000	35,000	40,000	82,500	—
1902	12,197,744	6.00	8.50	19.50	32.50	65.00	120	210	1,400	2,450
1902O	4,748,000	8.50	16.00	52.50	89.00	150	245	485	5,000	—
1902S	1,524,612	14.50	22.00	55.00	95.00	170	260	525	3,750	—
1903	9,670,064	6.75	8.50	19.50	32.50	62.00	112	210	2,600	2,450
1903O	3,500,000	8.00	13.50	41.50	65.00	125	260	435	6,250	—
1903S	1,036,000	15.50	26.00	46.00	88.00	145	285	435	2,900	—
1904	9,588,813	8.00	9.75	20.00	34.50	69.00	120	220	1,500	2,450
1904O	2,456,000	11.50	21.50	62.50	120	225	460	850	3,250	—
1905	4,968,250	13.50	15.00	27.50	39.50	72.00	120	210	1,650	2,450
1905O	1,230,000	18.50	33.50	82.50	170	265	365	500	6,600	—
1905S	1,884,000	12.75	15.00	43.50	66.00	110	220	335	3,650	—
1906	3,656,435	6.75	8.50	18.50	32.50	65.00	112	205	1,400	2,450
1906D	3,280,000	7.00	8.50	25.00	42.50	69.00	155	220	2,250	—
1906O	2,056,000	7.00	13.50	41.50	60.00	110	200	290	1,700	—
1907	7,192,575	5.50	8.00	16.50	32.50	62.00	112	205	1,400	2,450
1907D	2,484,000	6.00	9.00	29.00	52.50	78.00	175	240	2,750	—
1907O	4,560,000	5.50	13.50	19.00	38.50	66.00	135	205	2,600	—
1907S	1,360,000	10.00	18.50	47.50	75.00	135	275	465	4,250	—
1908	4,232,545	5.00	6.25	18.50	33.50	66.00	112	205	1,400	2,450
1908D	5,788,000	5.00	6.25	17.50	35.00	66.00	116	240	1,750	—
1908O	6,244,000	5.00	8.50	17.50	38.50	72.00	120	205	1,400	—
1908S	784,000	18.50	40.00	90.00	165	295	500	775	4,950	—
1909	9,268,650	5.00	6.25	17.50	33.50	66.00	108	205	1,400	2,450
1909D	5,114,000	6.25	8.00	22.00	41.50	88.00	160	205	2,350	—
1909O	712,000	19.50	45.00	95.00	200	375	600	800	8,500	—
1909S	1,348,000	8.00	13.50	37.50	57.50	96.00	200	300	2,500	—
1910	2,244,551	7.75	10.00	30.00	46.00	80.00	140	205	1,400	2,450
1910D	1,500,000	8.00	11.00	47.50	75.00	130	260	375	2,250	—
1911	3,720,543	6.25	8.50	19.50	33.50	72.50	125	215	1,400	2,450
1911D	933,600	9.00	19.50	95.00	215	330	500	700	6,250	—
1911S	988,000	7.00	13.00	51.50	90.00	180	300	400	1,600	—
1912	4,400,700	5.75	8.00	17.50	33.50	70.00	108	205	1,400	2,485
1912S	708,000	9.00	13.00	46.00	84.00	130	230	390	2,750	—
1913	484,613	16.00	26.00	75.00	190	390	535	960	5,000	2,485
1913D	1,450,800	12.50	14.50	38.50	58.50	94.00	185	275	1,400	—
1913S	40,000	1,850	2,450	5,000	7,750	10,500	12,850	15,000	37,500	—
1914	6,244,610	4.50	5.75	17.00	28.00	55.00	108	205	1,400	2,550
1914D	3,046,000	4.50	5.75	17.00	28.00	55.00	108	205	1,400	—
1914S	264,000	82.00	120	235	425	620	775	1,000	3,450	—
1915	3,480,450	4.50	5.75	17.00	28.00	55.00	108	205	1,400	2,485
1915D	3,694,000	4.50	5.75	17.00	28.00	55.00	108	205	1,400	—
1915S	704,000	9.00	13.00	35.00	57.50	110	220	285	1,500	—
1916	1,788,000	4.50	5.75	17.00	28.00	55.00	108	205	1,400	—
1916D	6,540,800	4.50	5.75	17.00	28.00	55.00	108	205	1,400	—
1916D/D	Inc. above	10.00	14.00	24.00	45.00	95.00	150	400	—	—

Standing Liberty Quarter.
Right breast exposed; Type 1.
KM# 141 Designer: Hermon A. MacNeil. **Diameter:** 24.3 **Weight:** 6.2500 g. **Composition:** 0.9000 Silver, 0.1808 oz. ASW.

Right breast exposed

Date	Mintage	G-4	VG-8	F-12	VF-20	XF-40	AU-50	MS-60	MS-65	-65FH
1916	52,000	3,500	6,350	9,500	13,000	14,500	16,500	18,500	30,000	37,500
1917	8,792,000	24.00	40.00	52.00	70.00	95.00	175	200	750	1,500
1917D	1,509,200	28.00	42.00	55.00	85.00	125	195	235	950	2,550
1917S	1,952,000	30.00	44.00	60.00	90.00	160	210	240	1,200	4,100

Standing Liberty Quarter.
Right breast covered; Type 2. Three stars below eagle.
KM# 145 Designer: Hermon A. MacNeil. **Diameter:** 24.3 **Weight:** 6.2500 g. **Composition:** 0.9000 Silver, 0.1808 oz. ASW.

Mint mark

Right breast covered

Date	Mintage	G-4	VG-8	F-12	VF-20	XF-40	AU-50	MS-60	MS-65	-65FH
1917	13,880,000	22.00	33.00	42.50	54.00	75.00	105	165	575	950
1917D	6,224,400	40.00	45.00	65.00	78.00	110	160	225	1,325	3,500
1917S	5,522,000	40.00	45.00	63.00	75.00	108	155	215	1,100	3,650
1918	14,240,000	17.00	21.00	29.00	35.00	46.00	80.00	135	560	1,750
1918D	7,380,000	26.00	36.00	66.00	78.00	122	195	250	1,485	4,850
1918S	11,072,000	17.00	21.00	32.00	35.00	48.00	95.00	185	1,250	13,500
1918/17S	Inc. above	1,550	2,250	3,850	5,200	7,500	13,500	17,850	110,000	320,000
1919	11,324,000	33.00	44.00	55.00	74.00	80.00	118	175	600	1,650
1919D	1,944,000	85.00	110	195	345	565	695	825	2,950	28,500
1919S	1,836,000	80.00	105	185	285	510	585	750	4,200	30,000
1920	27,860,000	15.00	18.00	25.00	37.00	51.00	90.00	165	600	2,100
1920D	3,586,400	48.00	65.00	88.00	120	160	215	325	2,250	7,200
1920S	6,380,000	19.00	25.00	30.00	37.00	57.00	110	235	2,650	24,000
1921	1,916,000	185	220	450	625	750	1,100	1,500	3,850	5,500
1923	9,716,000	15.00	18.00	35.00	37.00	55.00	95.00	155	620	4,000
1923S	1,360,000	300	425	675	985	1,250	1,650	2,300	4,750	6,500
1924	10,920,000	15.00	18.00	25.00	34.00	45.00	90.00	170	585	1,650
1924D	3,112,000	56.00	68.00	108	135	185	220	300	610	5,750
1924S	2,860,000	27.00	32.00	43.00	57.00	105	220	315	1,850	6,500
1925	12,280,000	4.00	4.75	7.00	18.50	44.00	90.00	150	575	950
1926	11,316,000	3.50	4.00	6.00	14.00	37.00	80.00	140	585	2,250
1926D	1,716,000	6.50	10.00	20.00	40.00	75.00	118	170	545	22,500
1926S	2,700,000	4.50	5.40	11.00	30.00	110	225	325	2,175	28,000
1927	11,912,000	3.50	4.00	6.00	12.00	32.00	70.00	105	550	1,300
1927D	976,400	14.00	19.00	32.00	70.00	140	210	250	600	2,650
1927S	396,000	35.00	48.00	110	285	1,000	2,650	4,750	12,000	165,000
1928	6,336,000	3.50	4.75	6.00	12.00	32.00	65.00	100.00	540	2,150
1928D	1,627,600	4.75	6.00	7.50	20.00	42.50	90.00	135	540	5,650
1928S Large S	2,644,000	6.00	7.50	10.00	25.00	65.00	115	200	—	—
1928S Small S	Inc. above	4.50	5.50	6.50	16.50	38.00	79.00	125	560	900
1929	11,140,000	3.50	4.75	6.00	12.00	32.00	65.00	100.00	540	900
1929D	1,358,000	4.25	5.50	6.75	16.00	38.50	79.00	135	540	5,850
1929S	1,764,000	4.00	5.50	6.50	15.00	34.00	75.00	120	540	875
1930	5,632,000	3.50	4.00	6.00	12.00	32.00	65.00	100.00	540	875
1930S	1,556,000	4.00	5.50	6.50	15.00	34.00	70.00	115	550	925

QUARTER

Washington Quarter.

KM# 164 **Designer:** John Flanagan. **Diameter:** 24.3 **Weight:** 6.2500 g. **Composition:** 0.9000 Silver, 0.1808 oz. ASW.

Mint mark 1932-64

Date	Mintage	G-4	VG-8	F-12	VF-20	XF-40	AU-50	MS-60	MS-65	Prf-65
1932	5,404,000	4.00	5.20	6.00	7.50	9.75	15.00	25.00	350	—
1932D	436,800	162	168	190	225	310	460	925	14,000	—
1932S	408,000	165	170	195	210	265	285	465	4,650	—
1934 Medium Motto	31,912,052	3.80	3.90	4.10	4.40	5.80	10.50	26.00	100.00	—
1934 Heavy Motto	Inc. above	5.50	7.00	9.00	12.50	18.00	30.00	50.00	265	—
1934 Light motto	Inc. above	4.40	5.25	6.00	10.00	15.00	26.00	45.00	400	—
1934 Doubled Die Obverse	Inc. above	75.00	100.00	165	200	320	450	800	8,000	—
1934D Medium Motto	3,527,200	5.00	6.00	8.50	16.50	29.00	90.00	235	1,150	—
1934D Heavy Motto	Inc. above	6.50	8.00	11.00	20.00	37.00	110	295	1,750	—
1935	32,484,000	3.90	4.00	4.10	4.20	4.30	10.00	21.00	100.00	—
1935D	5,780,000	4.10	3.40	7.50	14.00	30.00	125	250	675	—
1935S	5,660,000	4.10	4.20	5.00	7.50	15.00	36.50	95.00	290	—
1936	41,303,837	3.90	4.00	4.10	4.20	4.30	9.50	26.00	105	1,950
1936D	5,374,000	5.00	6.50	8.50	24.00	50.00	265	625	1,175	—
1936S	3,828,000	4.10	4.20	4.30	7.50	14.50	50.00	110	350	—
1937	19,701,542	3.90	4.00	4.10	4.20	4.30	16.50	22.00	87.00	665
1937 Double Die Obverse	Inc. above	—	100.00	235	340	450	850	1,850	11,500	—
1937D	7,189,600	4.10	4.20	5.00	7.25	17.00	32.00	64.00	135	—
1937S	1,652,000	4.30	5.00	7.00	20.00	34.00	95.00	160	360	—
1938	9,480,045	4.10	4.40	4.70	7.50	18.00	46.00	92.00	215	405
1938S	2,832,000	4.75	5.25	6.00	9.75	22.50	55.00	108	235	—
1939	33,548,795	3.90	4.00	4.10	4.20	4.30	7.00	16.00	48.00	345
1939D	7,092,000	4.00	4.10	4.30	5.25	12.00	20.00	42.00	110	—
1939S	2,628,000	4.30	4.40	5.25	10.50	24.00	60.00	110	310	—
1940	35,715,246	3.90	4.00	4.10	4.20	4.30	5.50	17.50	53.50	250
1940D	2,797,600	4.20	4.30	7.00	12.50	26.00	66.00	130	275	—
1940S	8,244,000	4.10	4.20	5.00	6.50	9.00	17.00	28.00	56.00	—
1941	79,047,287	—	—	—	—	3.00	5.00	9.50	37.00	205
1941D	16,714,800	—	—	—	3.70	7.50	15.00	33.00	68.00	—
1941S	16,080,000	—	—	—	3.90	6.50	12.50	30.00	67.00	—
1942	102,117,123	—	—	—	—	3.00	3.20	5.50	29.00	190
1942D Double Die Obv.	—	—	115	250	440	650	1,350	2,150	5,000	—
1942D Double Die Rev.	—	—	22.00	40.00	60.00	75.00	150	350	1,850	—
1942D	17,487,200	—	—	—	3.70	6.00	11.00	18.00	39.00	—
1942S	19,384,000	—	—	—	3.80	11.00	22.50	72.00	145	—
1943	99,700,000	—	—	—	—	3.20	4.50	5.25	40.00	—
1943D	16,095,600	—	—	—	3.90	8.00	16.50	29.00	51.00	—
1943S	21,700,000	—	—	3.60	5.00	7.50	15.00	27.00	52.50	—
1943S Double Die Obv.	Inc. above	40.00	75.00	125	175	225	275	500	3,500	—
1944	104,956,000	—	—	—	—	3.00	3.20	5.00	29.00	—
1944D	14,600,800	—	—	—	3.60	5.50	11.00	19.00	38.50	—
1944S	12,560,000	—	—	—	3.60	5.00	9.50	14.50	32.00	—
1945	74,372,000	—	—	—	—	3.00	3.20	5.00	37.50	—
1945D	12,341,600	—	—	—	3.70	6.50	11.00	18.00	42.50	—
1945S	17,004,001	—	—	—	3.60	4.10	6.00	8.50	32.50	—
1946	53,436,000	—	—	—	—	3.00	4.10	5.00	39.00	—
1946D	9,072,800	—	—	—	3.60	4.20	5.50	9.50	41.00	—
1946S	4,204,000	—	—	—	3.60	4.20	5.00	7.75	34.50	—
1947	22,556,000	—	—	—	—	4.20	5.00	11.50	40.00	—
1947D	15,338,400	—	—	—	3.60	4.10	4.30	11.00	40.00	—
1947S	5,532,000	—	—	—	3.60	4.10	4.30	9.25	28.50	—
1948	35,196,000	—	—	—	3.60	4.10	4.30	5.50	30.00	—
1948D	16,766,800	—	—	—	3.60	4.20	7.00	13.50	52.50	—
1948S	15,960,000	—	—	—	3.60	4.20	5.00	7.50	41.00	—
1949	9,312,000	—	—	—	3.70	6.50	15.00	36.00	53.00	—
1949D	10,068,400	—	—	—	3.50	5.00	10.00	17.00	48.00	—
1950	24,971,512	—	—	—	—	3.00	3.80	5.50	25.00	65.00
1950D	21,075,600	—	—	—	—	3.00	3.70	5.00	34.00	—
1950D/S	Inc. above	30.00	33.00	40.00	60.00	140	215	275	3,400	—
1950S	10,284,004	—	—	—	—	3.50	4.50	9.00	32.00	—
1950S/D	Inc. above	32.00	36.00	44.00	70.00	180	315	400	850	—
1950S/S	Inc. above	4.00	5.00	6.00	8.00	12.50	17.50	22.00	100.00	—
1951	43,505,602	—	—	—	—	3.00	3.20	6.00	32.00	65.00

Date	Mintage	G-4	VG-8	F-12	VF-20	XF-40	AU-50	MS-60	MS-65	Prf-65
1951D	35,354,800	—	—	—	—	3.00	3.80	7.00	38.00	—
1951S	9,048,000	—	—	3.00	4.50	6.00	9.00	24.00	52.00	—
1952	38,862,073	—	—	—	—	3.00	3.20	5.50	36.00	46.00
1952D	49,795,200	—	—	—	—	3.00	3.20	5.00	32.00	—
1952S	13,707,800	—	—	—	4.00	7.50	12.50	22.00	47.00	—
1953	18,664,920	—	—	—	—	3.00	3.20	5.50	42.00	46.00
1953D	56,112,400	—	—	—	—	3.00	3.20	4.45	29.00	—
1953S	14,016,000	—	—	—	—	3.00	3.80	5.00	38.00	—
1954	54,645,503	—	—	—	—	3.00	3.20	5.00	30.00	21.00
1954D	42,305,500	—	—	—	—	3.00	3.20	4.75	30.00	—
1954S	11,834,722	—	—	—	—	3.00	3.20	4.45	26.00	—
1955	18,558,381	—	—	—	—	3.00	3.20	4.00	25.00	24.00
1955D	3,182,400	—	—	—	—	4.00	4.10	5.00	42.00	—
1956	44,813,384	—	—	—	—	3.00	3.20	4.00	26.00	23.00
1956 Double Bar 5	Inc. above	—	4.00	4.50	5.00	6.50	9.00	20.00	125	
1956 Type B rev, proof rev die	Inc. above	—	—	8.00	12.00	20.00	30.00	40.00	100.00	—
1956D	32,334,500	—	—	—	—	3.00	3.20	3.95	23.00	—
1957	47,779,952	—	—	—	—	3.00	3.20	3.95	20.00	10.00
1957 Type B rev, proof rev die	Inc. above	—	—	—	6.50	10.00	16.00	30.00	110	—
1957D	77,924,160	—	—	—	—	3.00	3.20	3.95	20.00	—
1958	7,235,652	—	—	—	—	3.00	3.20	3.95	16.00	11.00
1958 Type B rev, proof rev die	Inc. above	—	—	—	6.50	10.00	16.00	24.00	90.00	—
1958D	78,124,900	—	—	—	—	3.00	3.20	3.95	16.00	—
1959	25,533,291	—	—	—	—	3.00	3.20	3.95	18.00	10.00
1959 Type B rev, proof rev die	Inc. above	—	—	—	5.00	10.00	14.00	20.00	70.00	—
1959D	62,054,232	—	—	—	—	3.00	3.20	3.95	22.00	—
1960	30,855,602	—	—	—	—	3.00	3.20	3.95	26.00	8.00
1960 Type B rev, proof rev die	Inc. above	—	—	—	6.50	10.00	16.00	24.00	90.00	—
1960D	63,000,324	—	—	—	—	3.00	3.20	3.95	15.00	—
1961	40,064,244	—	—	—	—	3.00	3.20	3.95	20.00	8.00
1961 Type B rev, proof rev die	Inc. above	—	—	—	5.00	10.00	14.00	20.00	70.00	—
1961D	83,656,928	—	—	—	—	3.00	3.20	3.95	36.00	—
1962	39,374,019	—	—	—	—	3.00	3.20	3.95	18.00	6.00
1962 Type B rev, proof rev die	Inc. above	—	—	—	10.00	15.00	25.00	60.00	175	—
1962D	127,554,756	—	—	—	—	3.00	3.20	3.95	45.00	—
1963	77,391,645	—	—	—	—	3.00	3.20	3.95	20.00	6.00
1963 Type B rev, proof rev die	Inc. above	—	—	—	5.00	6.00	8.00	15.00	50.00	—
1963D	135,288,184	—	—	—	—	3.00	3.20	3.95	22.00	—
1964	564,341,347	—	—	—	—	3.00	3.20	3.95	14.00	6.00
1964 Type B rev, proof rev die	Inc. above	—	—	—	5.00	10.00	14.00	20.00	70.00	—
1964 SMS	Inc. above	—	—	—	—	—	250	750	1,400	—
1964D	704,135,528	—	—	—	—	3.00	3.20	3.95	15.00	—
1964D Type C rev, clad rev die	Inc. above	—	—	—	40.00	55.00	75.00	125	450	—

Washington Quarter.

Designer: John Flanagan. **Diameter:** 24.3 **Weight:** 5.6700 g. **Composition:** Copper-Nickel Clad Copper

KM# 164a

Date	Mintage	MS-65	Prf-65	Date	Mintage	MS-65	Prf-65
1965	1,819,717,540	9.00	—	1971	109,284,000	9.00	—
1965 SMS	—	7.50	—	1971D	258,634,428	8.00	—
1966	821,101,500	7.50	—	1971S	(3,220,733)	—	4.00
1966 SMS	—	9.00	—	1972	215,048,000	7.50	—
1967 SMS	—	10.00	—	1972D	311,067,732	10.00	—
1967	1,524,031,848	8.00	—	1972S	(3,260,996)	—	3.50
1968	220,731,500	7.50	—	1973	346,924,000	10.00	—
1968D	101,534,000	9.00	—	1973D	232,977,400	12.50	—
1968S	(3,041,506)	—	6.50	1973S	(2,760,339)	—	3.00
1969	176,212,000	14.00	—	1974	801,456,000	12.00	—
1969D	114,372,000	12.00	—	1974D	353,160,300	18.00	—
1969S	(2,934,631)	—	7.00	1974S	(2,612,568)	—	6.50
1970	136,420,000	12.00	—	1975 none minted	—	—	—
1970D	417,341,364	9.50	—	1975D none minted	—	—	—
1970S	(2,632,810)	—	7.00	1975S none minted	—	—	—

QUARTER

Washington Quarter.
Bicentennial design, drummer boy.

KM# 204 **Rev. Designer:** Jack L. Ahr. **Diameter:** 24.3 **Weight:** 5.6700 g. **Composition:** Copper-Nickel Clad Copper

Mint mark
1968-present

Date	Mintage	MS-60	MS-65	Prf-65
1976	809,784,016	.60	10.00	—
1976D	860,118,839	.60	10.00	—
1976S	(4,149,730)	—	—	3.25

Washington Quarter.
Bicentennial design, drummer boy.

KM# 204a **Rev. Designer:** Jack L. Ahr. **Diameter:** 24.3 **Weight:** 5.7500 g. **Composition:** Silver Clad

Date	Mintage	MS-60	MS-65	Prf-65
1976S	4,908,319	2.00	4.00	—
1976S	(3,998,621)	—	—	5.00

Washington Quarter.
Regular design resumed.

KM# A164a **Diameter:** 24.3 **Weight:** 5.6700 g. **Composition:** Copper-Nickel Clad Copper **Notes:** KM#164 design and composition resumed. The 1979-S and 1981 Type II proofs have clearer mint marks than the Type I proofs for those years.

Date	Mintage	MS-65	Prf-65
1977	468,556,000	10.00	—
1977D	256,524,978	9.00	—
1977S	(3,251,152)	—	5.00
1978	521,452,000	10.00	—
1978D	287,373,152	11.00	—
1978S	(3,127,781)	—	5.00
1979	515,708,000	10.00	—
1979D	489,789,780	9.00	—
1979S T-I	—	—	4.00
1979S T-II	—	—	8.00
1980P	635,832,000	11.00	—
1980D	518,327,487	8.50	—
1980S	(3,554,806)	—	5.00
1981P	601,716,000	10.00	—

Date	Mintage	MS-65	Prf-65
1981D	575,722,833	9.00	—
1981S T-I	—	—	5.00
1981S T-II	—	—	7.50
1982P	500,931,000	32.50	—
1982D	480,042,788	22.00	—
1982S	(3,857,479)	—	7.00
1983P	673,535,000	45.00	—
1983D	617,806,446	40.00	—
1983S	(3,279,126)	—	5.00
1984P	676,545,000	16.00	—
1984D	546,483,064	12.50	—
1984S	(3,065,110)	—	4.50
1985P	775,818,962	32.00	—
1985D	519,962,888	10.00	—
1985S	(3,362,821)	5.00	6.00
1986P	551,199,333	12.00	—
1986D	504,298,660	15.00	—
1986S	(3,010,497)	—	5.00
1987P	582,499,481	10.50	—
1987D	655,594,696	10.00	—
1987S	(4,227,728)	—	5.00
1988P	562,052,000	16.00	—
1988D	596,810,688	14.00	—
1988S	(3,262,948)	—	6.50
1989P	512,868,000	18.00	—
1989D	896,535,597	5.50	—
1989S	(3,220,194)	—	5.00
1990P	613,792,000	17.00	—
1990D	927,638,181	7.00	—
1990S	(3,299,559)	—	6.00
1991P	570,968,000	15.00	—
1991D	630,966,693	14.00	—
1991S	(2,867,787)	—	5.00
1992P	384,764,000	20.00	—
1992D	389,777,107	27.50	—
1992S	(2,858,981)	—	4.50
1993P	639,276,000	11.00	—
1993D	645,476,128	14.00	—
1993S	(2,633,439)	—	5.00
1994P	825,600,000	18.00	—
1994D	880,034,110	8.00	—
1994S	(2,484,594)	—	13.50
1995P	1,004,336,000	22.00	—
1995D	1,103,216,000	20.00	—
1995S	(2,010,384)	—	12.50
1996P	925,040,000	15.00	—
1996D	906,868,000	14.00	—
1996S	—	—	4.50
1997P	595,740,000	12.50	—
1997D	599,680,000	16.00	—
1997S	(1,975,000)	—	10.00
1998P	896,268,000	13.50	—
1998D	821,000,000	13.50	—
1998S	—	—	10.00

Washington Quarter.

KM# A164b **Weight:** 6.2000 g. **Composition:** 0.9000 Silver, 0.1794 oz. ASW.

Date	Mintage	Prf-65
1992S	(1,317,579)	5.00
1993S	(761,353)	6.50
1994S	(785,329)	13.50
1995S	(838,953)	18.00
1996S	—	16.00
1997S	—	17.00
1998S	—	10.00

50 State Quarters

Connecticut

KM# 297 **Weight:** 5.6700 g. **Composition:** Copper-Nickel Clad Copper

Date	Mintage	MS-63	MS-65	Prf-65
1999P	688,744,000	1.00	10.00	—
1999D	657,480,000	1.00	9.00	—
1999S	(3,713,359)	—	—	12.00

KM# 297a **Weight:** 6.2500 g. **Composition:** 0.9000 Silver, 0.1808 oz. ASW.

Date	Mintage	MS-63	MS-65	Prf-65
1999S	(804,565)	—	—	65.00

Delaware

KM# 293 **Diameter:** 24.3 **Weight:** 5.6700 g. **Composition:** Copper-Nickel Clad Copper

Date	Mintage	MS-63	MS-65	Prf-65
1999P	373,400,000	1.40	8.00	—
1999D	401,424,000	1.25	20.00	—
1999S	(3,713,359)	—	—	12.00

KM# 293a **Weight:** 6.2500 g. **Composition:** 0.9000 Silver, 0.1808 oz. ASW.

Date	Mintage	MS-63	MS-65	Prf-65
1999S	(804,565)	—	—	65.00

Georgia

KM# 296 **Weight:** 5.6700 g. **Composition:** Copper-Nickel Clad Copper

Date	Mintage	MS-63	MS-65	Prf-65
1999P	451,188,000	1.20	14.00	—
1999D	488,744,000	1.20	14.00	—
1999S	(3,713,359)	—	—	12.00

KM# 296a **Weight:** 6.2500 g. **Composition:** 0.9000 Silver, 0.1808 oz. ASW.

Date	Mintage	MS-63	MS-65	Prf-65
1999S	(804,565)	—	—	65.00

New Jersey

KM# 295 **Weight:** 5.6700 g. **Composition:** Copper-Nickel Clad Copper

Date	Mintage	MS-63	MS-65	Prf-65
1999P	363,200,000	1.00	10.00	—
1999D	299,028,000	1.00	9.00	—
1999S	(3,713,359)	—	—	12.00

KM# 295a **Weight:** 6.2500 g. **Composition:** 0.9000 Silver, 0.1808 oz. ASW.

Date	Mintage	MS-63	MS-65	Prf-65
1999S	(804,565)	—	—	65.00

Pennsylvania

KM# 294 **Diameter:** 24.3 **Weight:** 5.6700 g. **Composition:** Copper-Nickel Clad Copper

Date	Mintage	MS-63	MS-65	Prf-65
1999P	349,000,000	1.00	15.00	—
1999D	358,332,000	1.00	20.00	—
1999S	(3,713,359)	—	—	12.00

KM# 294a **Weight:** 6.2500 g. **Composition:** 0.9000 Silver, 0.1808 oz. ASW.

Date	Mintage	MS-63	MS-65	Prf-65
1999S	(804,565)	—	—	65.00

Maryland

KM# 306 **Weight:** 5.6700 g. **Composition:** Copper-Nickel Clad Copper

Date	Mintage	MS-63	MS-65	Prf-65
2000P	678,200,000	1.00	11.00	—
2000D	556,526,000	1.00	11.00	—
2000S	(4,078,747)	—	—	3.50

KM# 306a **Weight:** 6.2500 g. **Composition:** 0.9000 Silver, 0.1808 oz. ASW.

Date	Mintage	MS-63	MS-65	Prf-65
2000S	(965,921)	—	—	5.50

QUARTER

Massachusetts

KM# 305   Weight: 5.6700 g. **Composition:**
Copper-Nickel Clad Copper

Date	Mintage	MS-63	MS-65	Prf-65
2000P	629,800,000	1.00	10.00	—
2000D	535,184,000	1.00	12.00	—
2000S	(4,078,747)	—	—	3.50

KM# 305a   Weight: 6.2500 g. **Composition:**
0.9000 Silver, 0.1808 oz. ASW.

Date	Mintage	MS-63	MS-65	Prf-65
2000S	(965,921)	—	—	5.50

Virginia

KM# 309   Weight: 5.6700 g. **Composition:**
Copper-Nickel Clad Copper

Date	Mintage	MS-63	MS-65	Prf-65
2000P	943,000,000	1.00	8.00	—
2000D	651,616,000	1.00	8.00	—
2000S	(4,078,747)	—	—	3.35

KM# 309a   Weight: 6.2500 g. **Composition:**
0.9000 Silver, 0.1808 oz. ASW.

Date	Mintage	MS-63	MS-65	Prf-65
2000S	(965,921)	—	—	5.50

New Hampshire

KM# 308   Weight: 5.6700 g. **Composition:**
Copper-Nickel Clad Copper

Date	Mintage	MS-63	MS-65	Prf-65
2000P	673,040,000	1.00	12.50	—
2000D	495,976,000	1.00	10.00	—
2000S	(4,078,747)	—	—	3.50

KM# 308a   Weight: 6.2500 g. **Composition:**
0.9000 Silver, 0.1808 oz. ASW.

Date	Mintage	MS-63	MS-65	Prf-65
2000S	(965,921)	—	—	5.50

Kentucky

KM# 322   Weight: 5.6700 g. **Composition:**
Copper-Nickel Clad Copper

Date	Mintage	MS-63	MS-65	Prf-65
2001P	353,000,000	1.20	7.00	—
2001D	370,564,000	1.00	8.00	—
2001S	(3,009,800)	—	—	11.00

KM# 322a   Weight: 6.2500 g. **Composition:**
0.9000 Silver, 0.1808 oz. ASW.

Date	Mintage	MS-63	MS-65	Prf-65
2001S	(849,500)	—	—	21.00

South Carolina

KM# 307   Weight: 5.6700 g. **Composition:**
Copper-Nickel Clad Copper

Date	Mintage	MS-63	MS-65	Prf-65
2000P	742,756,000	1.40	9.00	—
2000D	566,208,000	1.40	12.00	—
2000S	(4,078,747)	—	—	3.50

KM# 307a   Weight: 6.2500 g. **Composition:**
0.9000 Silver, 0.1808 oz. ASW.

Date	Mintage	MS-63	MS-65	Prf-65
2000S	(965,921)	—	—	5.50

New York

KM# 318   Weight: 5.6700 g. **Composition:**
Copper-Nickel Clad Copper

Date	Mintage	MS-63	MS-65	Prf-65
2001P	655,400,000	1.00	8.50	—
2001D	619,640,000	1.00	8.50	—
2001S	(3,009,800)	—	—	11.00

KM# 318a   Weight: 6.2500 g. **Composition:**
0.9000 Silver, 0.1808 oz. ASW.

Date	Mintage	MS-63	MS-65	Prf-65
2001S	(849,600)	—	—	24.00

QUARTER

North Carolina

KM# 319 Weight: 5.6700 g. **Composition:** Copper-Nickel Clad Copper

Date	Mintage	MS-63	MS-65	Prf-65
2001P	627,600,000	1.00	7.50	—
2001D	427,876,000	1.00	8.50	—
2001S	(3,009,800)	—	—	11.00

KM# 319a Weight: 6.2500 g. **Composition:** 0.9000 Silver, 0.1808 oz. ASW.

Date	Mintage	MS-63	MS-65	Prf-65
2001S	(849,600)	—	—	22.00

Rhode Island

KM# 320 Weight: 5.6700 g. **Composition:** Copper-Nickel Clad Copper

Date	Mintage	MS-63	MS-65	Prf-65
2001P	423,000,000	1.00	6.50	—
2001D	447,100,000	1.00	8.00	—
2001S	(3,009,800)	—	—	11.00

KM# 320a Weight: 6.2500 g. **Composition:** 0.9000 Silver, 0.1808 oz. ASW.

Date	Mintage	MS-63	MS-65	Prf-65
2001S	(849,600)	—	—	19.00

Vermont

KM# 321 Weight: 5.6700 g. **Composition:** Copper-Nickel Clad Copper

Date	Mintage	MS-63	MS-65	Prf-65
2001P	423,400,000	1.20	7.00	—
2001D	459,404,000	1.00	7.00	—
2001S	(3,009,800)	—	—	11.00

KM# 321a Weight: 6.2500 g. **Composition:** 0.9000 Silver, 0.1808 oz. ASW.

Date	Mintage	MS-63	MS-65	Prf-65
2001S	(849,600)	—	—	19.00

Indiana

KM# 334 Weight: 5.6700 g. **Composition:** Copper-Nickel Clad Copper

Date	Mintage	MS-63	MS-65	Prf-65
2002P	362,600,000	1.00	6.00	—
2002D	327,200,000	1.00	6.50	—
2002S	(3,084,185)	—	—	4.00

KM# 334a Weight: 6.2500 g. **Composition:** 0.9000 Silver, 0.1808 oz. ASW.

Date	Mintage	MS-63	MS-65	Prf-65
2002S	(892,229)	—	—	9.00

Louisiana

KM# 333 Weight: 5.6700 g. **Composition:** Copper-Nickel Clad Copper

Date	Mintage	MS-63	MS-65	Prf-65
2002P	362,000,000	1.00	6.50	—
2002D	402,204,000	1.00	7.00	—
2002S	(3,084,185)	—	—	4.00

KM# 333a Weight: 6.2500 g. **Composition:** 0.9000 Silver, 0.1808 oz. ASW.

Date	Mintage	MS-63	MS-65	Prf-65
2002S	(892,229)	—	—	9.00

Mississippi

KM# 335 Weight: 5.6700 g. **Composition:** Copper-Nickel Clad Copper

Date	Mintage	MS-63	MS-65	Prf-65
2002P	290,000,000	1.00	5.00	—
2002D	289,600,000	1.00	6.00	—
2002S	(3,084,185)	—	—	4.00

KM# 335a Weight: 6.2500 g. **Composition:** 0.9000 Silver, 0.1808 oz. ASW.

Date	Mintage	MS-63	MS-65	Prf-65
2002S	(892,229)	—	—	9.00

QUARTER

Ohio

KM# 332   Weight: 5.6700 g. **Composition:**
Copper-Nickel Clad Copper

Date	Mintage	MS-63	MS-65	Prf-65
2002P	217,200,000	1.00	6.50	—
2002D	414,832,000	1.00	7.00	—
2002S	(3,084,185)	—	—	4.00

KM# 332a   Weight: 6.2500 g. **Composition:**
0.9000 Silver, 0.1808 oz. ASW.

Date	Mintage	MS-63	MS-65	Prf-65
2002S	(892,229)	—	—	9.00

Arkansas

KM# 347   Weight: 5.6700 g. **Composition:**
Copper-Nickel Clad Copper

Date	Mintage	MS-63	MS-65	Prf-65
2003P	228,000,000	1.00	7.00	—
2003D	229,800,000	1.00	7.00	—
2003S	(3,270,603)	—	—	3.50

KM# 347a   Weight: 6.2500 g. **Composition:**
0.9000 Silver, 0.1808 oz. ASW.

Date	Mintage	MS-63	MS-65	Prf-65
2003S	—	—	—	5.25

Tennessee

KM# 331   Weight: 5.6700 g. **Composition:**
Copper-Nickel Clad Copper

Date	Mintage	MS-63	MS-65	Prf-65
2002P	361,600,000	1.40	6.50	—
2002D	286,468,000	1.40	7.00	—
2002S	(3,084,185)	—	—	4.00

KM# 331a   Weight: 6.2500 g. **Composition:**
0.9000 Silver, 0.1808 oz. ASW.

Date	Mintage	MS-63	MS-65	Prf-65
2002S	(892,229)	—	—	9.00

Illinois

KM# 343   Weight: 5.6700 g. **Composition:**
Copper-Nickel Clad Copper

Date	Mintage	MS-63	MS-65	Prf-65
2003P	225,800,000	1.10	7.00	—
2003D	237,400,000	1.10	6.00	—
2003S	(3,270,603)	—	—	3.50

KM# 343a   Weight: 6.2500 g. **Composition:**
0.9000 Silver, 0.1808 oz. ASW.

Date	Mintage	MS-63	MS-65	Prf-65
2003S	—	—	—	5.25

Alabama

KM# 344   Weight: 5.6700 g. **Composition:**
Copper-Nickel Clad Copper

Date	Mintage	MS-63	MS-65	Prf-65
2003P	225,000,000	1.00	7.00	—
2003D	232,400,000	1.00	7.00	—
2003S	(3,270,603)	—	—	3.50

KM# 344a   Weight: 6.2500 g. **Composition:**
0.9000 Silver, 0.1808 oz. ASW.

Date	Mintage	MS-63	MS-65	Prf-65
2003S	—	—	—	5.25

Maine

KM# 345   Weight: 5.6700 g. **Composition:**
Copper-Nickel Clad Copper

Date	Mintage	MS-63	MS-65	Prf-65
2003P	217,400,000	1.00	6.50	—
2003D	213,400,000	1.00	8.00	—
2003S	(3,270,603)	—	—	3.50

KM# 345a   Weight: 6.2500 g. **Composition:**
0.9000 Silver, 0.1808 oz. ASW.

Date	Mintage	MS-63	MS-65	Prf-65
2003S	—	—	—	5.25

Missouri

KM# 346   Composition: Copper-Nickel Clad
Copper

Date	Mintage	MS-63	MS-65	Prf-65
2003P	225,000,000	1.00	7.00	—
2003D	228,200,000	1.00	7.00	—
2003S	(3,270,603)	—	—	3.50

KM# 346a   Weight: 6.2500 g. **Composition:**
0.9000 Silver, 0.1808 oz. ASW.

Date	Mintage	MS-63	MS-65	Prf-65
2003S	—	—	—	5.25

Michigan

KM# 355   Weight: 5.6700 g. **Composition:**
Copper-Nickel Clad Copper

Date	Mintage	MS-63	MS-65	Prf-65
2004P	233,800,000	.75	6.50	—
2004D	225,800,000	.75	6.50	—
2004S	—	—	—	5.00

KM# 355a   Weight: 6.2500 g. **Composition:**
0.9000 Silver, 0.1808 oz. ASW.

Date	Mintage	MS-63	MS-65	Prf-65
2004S	—	—	—	6.00

Florida

KM# 356   Weight: 5.6700 g. **Composition:**
Copper-Nickel Clad Copper

Date	Mintage	MS-63	MS-65	Prf-65
2004P	240,200,000	.75	6.50	—
2004D	241,600,000	.75	7.00	—
2004S	—	—	—	5.00

KM# 356a   Weight: 6.2500 g. **Composition:**
0.9000 Silver, 0.1808 oz. ASW.

Date	Mintage	MS-63	MS-65	Prf-65
2004S	—	—	—	6.00

Texas

KM# 357   Weight: 5.6700 g. **Composition:**
Copper-Nickel Clad Copper

Date	Mintage	MS-63	MS-65	Prf-65
2004P	278,800,000	.75	7.00	—
2004D	263,000,000	.75	7.00	—
2004S	—	—	—	5.00

KM# 357a   Weight: 6.2500 g. **Composition:**
0.9000 Silver, 0.1808 oz. ASW.

Date	Mintage	MS-63	MS-65	Prf-65
2004S	—	—	—	6.00

Iowa

KM# 358   Weight: 5.6700 g. **Composition:**
Copper-Nickel Clad Copper

Date	Mintage	MS-63	MS-65	Prf-65
2004P	213,800,000	.75	6.50	—
2004D	251,800,000	.75	7.00	—
2004S	—	—	—	5.00

KM# 358a   Weight: 6.2500 g. **Composition:**
0.9000 Silver, 0.1808 oz. ASW.

Date	Mintage	MS-63	MS-65	Prf-65
2004S	—	—	—	6.00

Wisconsin

KM# 359   Weight: 5.6700 g. **Composition:**
Copper-Nickel Clad Copper

Date	Mintage	MS-63	MS-65	Prf-65
2004P	226,400,000	1.00	8.00	—
2004D	226,800,000	1.00	10.00	—
2004D Extra Leaf Low	Est. 9,000	300	600	—
2004D Extra Leaf High	Est. 3,000	400	900	—
2004S	—	—	—	5.00

KM# 359a   Weight: 6.2500 g. **Composition:**
0.9000 Silver, 0.1808 oz. ASW.

Date	Mintage	MS-63	MS-65	Prf-65
2004S	—	—	—	6.00

QUARTER

California

KM# 370   Weight: 5.6700 g. **Composition:**
Copper-Nickel Clad Copper

Date	Mintage	MS-63	MS-65	Prf-65
2005P	257,200,000	.75	5.00	—
2005P Satin Finish	Inc. above	3.50	6.00	—
2005D	263,200,000	.75	5.00	—
2005D Satin Finish	Inc. above	3.50	6.00	—
2005S	—	—	—	3.00

KM# 370a   Weight: 6.2500 g. **Composition:**
0.9000 Silver, 0.1808 oz. ASW.

Date	Mintage	MS-63	MS-65	Prf-65
2005S	—	—	—	5.50

Oregon

KM# 372   Weight: 5.6700 g. **Composition:**
Copper-Nickel Clad Copper

Date	Mintage	MS-63	MS-65	Prf-65
2005P	316,200,000	.75	5.00	—
2005P Satin Finish	Inc. above	3.50	6.00	—
2005D	404,000,000	.75	5.00	—
2005D Satin Finish	Inc. above	3.50	6.00	—
2005S	—	—	—	3.00

KM# 372a   Weight: 6.2500 g. **Composition:**
0.9000 Silver, 0.1808 oz. ASW.

Date	Mintage	MS-63	MS-65	Prf-65
2005S	—	—	—	5.50

Kansas

KM# 373   Weight: 5.6700 g. **Composition:**
Copper-Nickel Clad Copper

Date	Mintage	MS-63	MS-65	Prf-65
2005P	263,400,000	.75	5.00	—
2005P Satin Finish	Inc. above	3.50	6.00	—
2005D	300,000,000	.75	5.00	—
2005D Satin Finish	Inc. above	3.50	6.00	—
2005S	—	—	—	3.00

KM# 373a   Weight: 6.2500 g. **Composition:**
0.9000 Silver, 0.1808 oz. ASW.

Date	Mintage	MS-63	MS-65	Prf-65
2005S	—	—	—	5.50

West Virginia

KM# 374   Weight: 5.6700 g. **Composition:**
Copper-Nickel Clad Copper

Date	Mintage	MS-63	MS-65	Prf-65
2005P	365,400,000	.75	5.00	—
2005P Satin Finish	Inc. above	3.50	6.00	—
2005D	356,200,000	.75	5.00	—
2005D Satin Finish	Inc. above	3.50	6.00	—
2005S	—	—	—	3.00

KM# 374a   Weight: 6.2500 g. **Composition:**
0.9000 Silver, 0.1808 oz. ASW.

Date	Mintage	MS-63	MS-65	Prf-65
2005S	—	—	—	5.50

Minnesota

KM# 371   Weight: 5.6700 g. **Composition:**
Copper-Nickel Clad Copper

Date	Mintage	MS-63	MS-65	Prf-65
2005P	226,400,000	.75	5.00	—
2005P Satin Finish	Inc. above	3.50	6.00	—
2005D	226,800,000	.75	5.00	—
2005D Satin Finish	Inc. above	3.50	6.00	—
2005S	—	—	—	3.00

KM# 371a   Weight: 6.2500 g. **Composition:**
0.9000 Silver, 0.1808 oz. ASW.

Date	Mintage	MS-63	MS-65	Prf-65
2005S	—	—	—	5.50

Colorado

KM# 384   Diameter: 24.2 **Weight:** 5.7100 g.
Composition: Copper-Nickel Clad Copper

Date	Mintage	MS-63	MS-65	Prf-65
2006P	274,800,000	.75	5.00	—
2006P Satin Finish	Inc. above	3.00	5.00	—
2006D	294,200,000	.75	5.00	—
2006D Satin Finish	Inc. above	3.00	5.00	—
2006S	—	—	—	5.00

KM# 384a   Weight: 6.2500 g. **Composition:** 0.9000
Silver, 0.1808 oz. ASW.

Date	Mintage	MS-63	MS-65	Prf-65
2006S	—	—	—	5.75

Nebraska

KM# 383 **Weight:** 5.6700 g. **Composition:** Copper-Nickel Clad Copper

Date	Mintage	MS-63	MS-65	Prf-65
2006P	318,000,000	.75	6.00	—
2006P Satin Finish	Inc. above	3.00	5.00	—
2006D	273,000,000	.75	6.00	—
2006D Satin Finish	Inc. above	3.00	5.00	—
2006S	—	—	—	5.00

KM# 383a **Weight:** 6.2500 g. **Composition:** 0.9000 Silver, 0.1808 oz. ASW.

Date	Mintage	MS-63	MS-65	Prf-65
2006S	—	—	—	5.75

Nevada

KM# 382 **Weight:** 5.6700 g. **Composition:** Copper-Nickel Clad Copper

Date	Mintage	MS-63	MS-65	Prf-65
2006P	277,000,000	.75	6.00	—
2006P Satin Finish	Inc. above	3.00	5.00	—
2006D	312,800,000	.75	6.00	—
2006D Satin Finish	Inc. above	3.00	5.00	—
2006S	—	—	—	5.00

KM# 382a **Weight:** 6.2500 g. **Composition:** 0.9000 Silver, 0.1808 oz. ASW.

Date	Mintage	MS-63	MS-65	Prf-65
2006S	—	—	—	5.75

North Dakota

KM# 385 **Diameter:** 24.2 **Weight:** 5.7200 g. **Composition:** Copper-Nickel Clad Copper

Date	Mintage	MS-63	MS-65	Prf-65
2006P	305,800,000	.75	5.00	—
2006P Satin Finish	Inc. above	3.00	5.00	—
2006D	359,000,000	.75	5.00	—
2006D Satin Finish	Inc. above	3.00	5.00	—
2006S	—	—	—	5.00

KM# 385a **Weight:** 6.2500 g. **Composition:** 0.9000 Silver, 0.1808 oz. ASW.

Date	Mintage	MS-63	MS-65	Prf-65
2006S	—	—	—	5.75

South Dakota

KM# 386 **Diameter:** 24.3 **Weight:** 5.6500 g. **Composition:** Copper-Nickel Clad Copper

Date	Mintage	MS-63	MS-65	Prf-65
2006P	245,000,000	.75	5.00	—
2006P Satin Finish	Inc. above	3.00	5.00	—
2006D	265,800,000	.75	5.00	—
2006D Satin Finish	Inc. above	3.00	5.00	—
2006S	—	—	—	5.00

KM# 386a **Weight:** 6.2500 g. **Composition:** 0.9000 Silver, 0.1808 oz. ASW.

Date	Mintage	MS-63	MS-65	Prf-65
2006S	—	—	—	5.75

Idaho

KM# 398 **Weight:** 5.6700 g. **Composition:** Copper-Nickel Clad Copper

Date	Mintage	MS-63	MS-65	Prf-65
2007P	294,600,000	.75	8.00	—
2007D	286,800,000	.75	8.00	—
2007S	—	—	—	4.00

KM# 398a **Weight:** 6.2500 g. **Composition:** 0.9000 Silver, 0.1808 oz. ASW.

Date	Mintage	MS-63	MS-65	Prf-65
2007S	Inc. above	—	—	6.50

Montana

KM# 396 **Weight:** 5.6700 g. **Composition:** Copper-Nickel Clad Copper

Date	Mintage	MS-63	MS-65	Prf-65
2007P	257,000,000	.75	8.00	—
2007D	256,240,000	.75	5.00	—
2007S	—	—	—	4.00

KM# 396a **Weight:** 6.2500 g. **Composition:** 0.9000 Silver, 0.1808 oz. ASW.

Date	Mintage	MS-63	MS-65	Prf-65
2007S	Inc. above	—	—	6.50

QUARTER

Utah

KM# 400   Composition: Copper-Nickel Clad Copper

Date	Mintage	MS-63	MS-65	Prf-65
2007P	255,000,000	.75	8.00	—
2007D	253,200,000	.75	8.00	—
2007S	—	—	—	4.00

KM# 400a   Weight: 6.2500 g. **Composition:** 0.9000 Silver, 0.1808 oz. ASW.

Date	Mintage	MS-63	MS-65	Prf-65
2007S	Inc. above	—	—	6.50

Alaska

KM# 424   Weight: 5.6700 g. **Composition:** Copper-Nickel Clad Copper

Date	Mintage	MS-63	MS-65	Prf-65
2008P	251,800,000	.75	8.00	—
2008D	254,000,000	.75	8.00	—
2008S	—	—	—	4.00

KM# 424a   Weight: 6.2500 g. **Composition:** 0.9000 Silver, 0.1808 oz. ASW.

Date	Mintage	MS-63	MS-65	Prf-65
2008S	—	—	—	6.50

Washington

KM# 397   Weight: 5.6700 g. **Composition:** Copper-Nickel Clad Copper

Date	Mintage	MS-63	MS-65	Prf-65
2007P	265,200,000	.75	8.00	—
2007D	280,000,000	.75	8.00	—
2007S	—	—	—	4.00

KM# 397a   Weight: 6.2500 g. **Composition:** 0.9000 Silver, 0.1808 oz. ASW.

Date	Mintage	MS-63	MS-65	Prf-65
2007S	Inc. above	—	—	6.50

Arizona

KM# 423   Weight: 5.6700 g. **Composition:** Copper-Nickel Clad Copper

Date	Mintage	MS-63	MS-65	Prf-65
2008P	244,600,000	.75	8.00	—
2008D	265,000,000	.75	8.00	—
2008S	—	—	—	4.00

KM# 423a   Weight: 6.2500 g. **Composition:** 0.9000 Silver, 0.1808 oz. ASW.

Date	Mintage	MS-63	MS-65	Prf-65
2008S	—	—	—	6.50

Wyoming

KM# 399   Weight: 5.6700 g. **Composition:** Copper-Nickel Clad Copper

Date	Mintage	MS-63	MS-65	Prf-65
2007P	243,600,000	.75	8.00	—
2007D	320,800,000	.75	8.00	—
2007S	—	—	—	4.00

KM# 399a   Weight: 6.2500 g. **Composition:** 0.9000 Silver, 0.1808 oz. ASW.

Date	Mintage	MS-63	MS-65	Prf-65
2007S	—	—	—	6.50

Hawaii

KM# 425   Weight: 5.6700 g. **Composition:** Copper-Nickel Clad Copper

Date	Mintage	MS-63	MS-65	Prf-65
2008P	254,000,000	.75	8.00	—
2008D	263,600,000	.75	8.00	—
2008S	—	—	—	4.50

KM# 425a   Weight: 6.2500 g. **Composition:** 0.9000 Silver, 0.1808 oz. ASW.

Date	Mintage	MS-63	MS-65	Prf-65
2008S	—	—	—	6.50

QUARTER

New Mexico

KM# 422 Weight: 5.6700 g. **Composition:** Copper-Nickel Clad Copper

Date	Mintage	MS-63	MS-65	Prf-65
2008P	244,200,000	.75	8.00	—
2008D	244,400,000	.75	8.00	—
2008S	—	—	—	4.00

KM# 422a Weight: 6.2500 g. **Composition:** 0.9000 Silver, 0.1808 oz. ASW.

Date	Mintage	MS-63	MS-65	Prf-65
2008S	—	—	—	6.50

Oklahoma

KM# 421 Weight: 5.6700 g. **Composition:** Copper-Nickel Clad Copper

Date	Mintage	MS-63	MS-65	Prf-65
2008P	222,000,000	.75	8.00	—
2008D	194,600,000	.75	8.00	—
2008S	—	—	—	4.00

KM# 421a Weight: 6.2500 g. **Composition:** 0.9000 Silver, 0.1808 oz. ASW.

Date	Mintage	MS-63	MS-65	Prf-65
2008S	—	—	—	6.50

DC and Territories

American Samoa

KM# 448 Diameter: 24 **Weight:** 5.6700 g. **Composition:** Copper-Nickel Clad Copper

Date	Mintage	MS-63	MS-65	Prf-65
2009P	—	.75	8.00	—
2009D	—	.75	8.00	—
2009S	—	—	—	4.00

KM# 448a Diameter: 24 **Weight:** 6.2500 g. **Composition:** 0.9000 Silver, 0.1808 oz. ASW.

Date	Mintage	MS-63	MS-65	Prf-65
2009S	—	—	—	6.50

Northern Mariana Islands

KM# 466 Weight: 5.6700 g. **Composition:** Copper-Nickel Clad Copper

Date	Mintage	MS-63	MS-65	Prf-65
2009P	—	.75	8.00	—
2009D	—	.75	8.00	—
2009S	—	—	—	4.00

KM# 466a Weight: 6.2500 g. **Composition:** 0.9000 Silver, 0.1808 oz. ASW.

Date	Mintage	MS-63	MS-65	Prf-65
2009S	—	—	—	6.50

District of Columbia

KM# 445 Diameter: 24 **Weight:** 5.6700 g. **Composition:** Copper-Nickel Clad Copper

Date	Mintage	MS-63	MS-65	Prf-65
2009P	83,600,000	.75	8.00	—
2009D	88,800,000	.75	8.00	—
2009S	—	—	—	4.00

KM# 445a Diameter: 24 **Weight:** 6.2500 g. **Composition:** 0.9000 Silver, 0.1808 oz. ASW.

Date	Mintage	MS-63	MS-65	Prf-65
2009S	—	—	—	6.50

Puerto Rico

KM# 446 Diameter: 24 **Weight:** 5.6700 g. **Composition:** Copper-Nickel Clad Copper

Date	Mintage	MS-63	MS-65	Prf-65
2009P	53,200,000	.75	8.00	—
2009D	86,000,000	.75	8.00	—
2009S	—	—	—	4.00

KM# 446a Diameter: 24 **Weight:** 6.2500 g. **Composition:** 0.9000 Silver, 0.1808 oz. ASW.

Date	Mintage	MS-63	MS-65	Prf-65
2009S	—	—	—	6.50

Guam

KM# 447 Diameter: 24 **Weight:** 5.6700 g. **Composition:** Copper-Nickel Clad Copper

Date	Mintage	MS-63	MS-65	Prf-65
2009P	—	.75	8.00	—
2009D	—	.75	8.00	—
2009S	—	—	—	4.00

KM# 447a Diameter: 24 **Weight:** 6.2500 g. **Composition:** 0.9000 Silver, 0.1808 oz. ASW.

Date	Mintage	MS-63	MS-65	Prf-65
2009S	—	—	—	6.50

US Virgin Islands

KM# 449 Diameter: 24 **Weight:** 0.6250 g. **Composition:** 0.9000 Copper-Nickel Clad Copper, 0.0181 oz.

Date	Mintage	MS-63	MS-65	Prf-65
2009P	—	.75	8.00	—
2009D	—	.75	8.00	—
2009S	—	—	—	4.00

KM# 449a Diameter: 24 **Weight:** 6.2500 g. **Composition:** 0.9000 Silver, 0.1808 oz. ASW.

Date	Mintage	MS-63	MS-65	Prf-65
2009S	—	—	—	6.50

QUARTER

HALF DOLLAR

Flowing Hair Half Dollar.

KM# 16 **Designer:** Robert Scot. **Diameter:** 32.5 **Weight:** 13.4800 g. **Composition:** 0.8920 Silver, 0.3866 oz. ASW. **Notes:** The 1795 "recut date" variety had the date cut into the dies twice, so both sets of numbers are visible on the coin. The 1795 "3 leaves" variety has three leaves under each of the eagle's wings on the reverse.

Date	Mintage	G-4	VG-8	F-12	VF-20	XF-40	MS-60
1794	23,464	2,850	5,750	8,850	19,500	37,500	225,000
1795	299,680	1,025	1,450	2,850	4,850	13,850	46,500
1795 recut date	Inc. above	1,040	1,470	2,895	5,200	14,250	46,500
1795 3 leaves	Inc. above	2,600	3,150	5,350	8,350	17,500	59,500

Draped Bust Half Dollar.
Small eagle.

KM# 26 **Designer:** Robert Scot. **Diameter:** 32.5 **Weight:** 13.4800 g. **Composition:** 0.8920 Silver, 0.3866 oz. ASW.

Date	Mintage	G-4	VG-8	F-12	VF-20	XF-40	MS-60
1796 15 stars	3,918	36,500	46,000	62,000	73,500	118,000	300,000
1796 16 stars	Inc. above	39,500	50,000	67,000	79,500	128,000	320,000
1797	Inc. above	36,700	46,300	62,500	74,300	121,000	310,000

Draped Bust Half Dollar.
Draped bust right, flanked by stars, date at angle below. Heraldic eagle.

KM# 35 **Designer:** Robert Scot. **Diameter:** 32.5 **Weight:** 13.4800 g. **Composition:** 0.8920 Silver, 0.3866 oz. ASW.

Date	Mintage	G-4	VG-8	F-12	VF-20	XF-40	MS-60
1801	30,289	850	1,250	2,550	4,250	10,500	50,000
1802	29,890	900	1,350	2,750	4,500	11,000	52,000

Date	Mintage	G-4	VG-8	F-12	VF-20	XF-40	MS-60
1803 small 3	188,234	255	325	425	825	2,325	17,250
1803 large 3	Inc. above	195	235	295	715	1,925	14,750
1805	211,722	195	235	295	685	1,865	10,750
1805/4	Inc. above	270	385	570	1,515	3,325	30,000
1806 knobbed 6, large stars	839,576	195	235	295	665	1,825	—
1806 knobbed 6, small stars	Inc. above	195	235	295	680	2,025	13,500
1806 knobbed 6, stem not through claw	Inc. above	20,000	35,000	42,000	57,500	95,000	—
1806 pointed-top 6, stem not through claw	Inc. above	195	235	295	665	1,825	15,250
1806 pointed-top 6, stem through claw	Inc. above	195	235	295	665	1,825	9,750
1806/5	Inc. above	215	270	355	775	2,050	10,075
1806 /inverted 6	Inc. above	255	355	845	1,615	4,375	28,500
1807	301,076	195	235	295	665	1,825	9,750

Capped Bust.

Draped bust left, flanked by stars, date at angle below. "50 C." below eagle.

KM# 37 **Designer:** John Reich. **Diameter:** 32.5 **Weight:** 13.4800 g. **Composition:** 0.8920 Silver, 0.3866 oz. ASW.

Date	Mintage	G-4	VG-8	F-12	VF-20	XF-40	AU-50	MS-60	MS-65
1807 small stars	750,500	125	175	350	750	1,900	6,500	9,850	54,000
1807 large stars	Inc. above	115	165	300	660	1,750	5,650	8,900	—
1807 50/20 C.	Inc. above	85.00	125	195	450	1,500	3,150	6,500	30,000
1807 bearded goddess	—	450	775	1,500	3,350	6,850	22,500	—	—
1808	1,368,600	67.00	84.00	93.00	145	350	550	1,800	20,000
1808/7	Inc. above	90.00	110	135	240	440	1,850	5,400	32,500
1809 Normal edge	1,405,810	65.00	82.00	90.00	140	375	750	1,500	14,000
1809 XXXX edge	Inc. above	80.00	105	135	185	550	950	4,450	—
1809 IIIIIII edge	Inc. above	85.00	110	140	210	450	850	4,000	—
1810	1,276,276	64.00	81.00	87.00	135	265	650	1,950	19,500
1811 small 8	1,203,644	70.00	80.00	84.00	125	350	800	2,350	28,500
1811 large 8	Inc. above	80.00	107	115	175	425	1,000	2,400	28,500
1811 dated 18.11	Inc. above	78.00	100.00	110	165	650	1,250	3,500	28,500
1812	1,628,059	64.00	81.00	84.00	110	254	405	1,350	14,800
1812/1 small 8	Inc. above	80.00	97.00	115	200	500	1,350	2,500	—
1812/1 large 8	Inc. above	1,650	2,450	4,500	6,750	12,000	21,000	—	—
1812 Single leaf below wing	Inc. above	750	950	1,250	2,400	4,000	6,800	12,500	—
1813	1,241,903	64.00	81.00	84.00	110	184	445	1,400	14,000
1813 50/UNI reverse	1,241,903	74.00	101	120	175	650	1,350	3,650	27,500
1814	1,039,075	64.00	81.00	84.00	120	285	650	1,650	12,800
1814/3	Inc. above	100.00	165	245	300	850	1,650	3,250	—
1814 E/A in States	Inc. above	85.00	110	150	225	385	950	3,950	—
1814 Single leaf below wing	Inc. above	75.00	97.00	120	190	575	1,350	2,250	—
1815/2	47,150	1,100	1,550	2,250	3,650	5,500	7,950	14,500	85,000
1817	1,215,567	67.00	84.00	87.00	115	185	415	1,300	13,000
1817/3	Inc. above	115	175	280	525	1,150	2,350	4,850	—
1817/4	—	60,000	80,000	150,000	200,000	240,000	—	—	—
1817 dated 181.7	Inc. above	100.00	87.00	90.00	100.00	575	1,350	3,950	27,500
1817 Single leaf below wing	Inc. above	75.00	98.00	120	205	550	2,100	2,750	—
1818	1,960,322	64.00	81.00	84.00	115	225	405	1,350	12,600
1818/7 Large 8	Inc. above	100.00	115	145	190	325	950	1,850	17,500
1818/7 Small 8	Inc. above	98.00	110	130	150	250	850	1,650	16,500
1819	2,208,000	64.00	81.00	84.00	115	175	395	1,350	15,000
1819/8 small 9	Inc. above	75.00	92.00	105	180	290	650	1,900	13,000
1819/8 large 9	Inc. above	85.00	105	150	275	385	850	2,000	27,000
1820 Curl Base 2, small date	751,122	70.00	85.00	92.00	120	285	950	2,250	13,000
1820 Square Base 2 with knob, large date	Inc. above	72.00	90.00	100.00	135	400	800	2,400	14,500
1820 Square Base 2 without know, large date	Inc. above	72.00	90.00	100.00	150	475	1,100	2,500	26,500
1820 E's without Serifs	Inc. above	260	450	900	2,150	3,500	5,500	—	—
1820/19 Square Base 2	Inc. above	110	130	165	240	775	1,650	3,250	25,000
1820/19 Curled Base 2	Inc. above	95.00	115	140	200	650	1,450	2,900	24,500
1821	1,305,797	58.00	76.00	85.00	97.00	185	575	1,350	12,600

Date	Mintage	G-4	VG-8	F-12	VF-20	XF-40	AU-50	MS-60	MS-65
1822	1,559,573	58.00	76.00	85.00	97.00	180	450	1,250	12,300
1822/1	Inc. above	83.00	100.00	125	275	385	800	1,900	—
1823	1,694,200	58.00	76.00	85.00	97.00	175	425	1,150	12,500
1823 broken 3	Inc. above	68.00	88.00	100.00	135	500	1,500	3,200	—
1823 patched 3	Inc. above	73.00	94.00	115	155	550	950	2,000	16,500
1823 ugly 3	Inc. above	78.00	99.00	125	180	750	1,750	4,200	—
1824	3,504,954	58.00	76.00	85.00	97.00	175	360	1,075	11,500
1824/21	Inc. above	63.00	82.00	95.00	122	275	650	2,000	17,000
1824/4	Inc. above	61.00	80.00	87.00	110	225	500	1,350	—
1824 1824/various dates	Inc. above	60.00	79.00	87.00	100.00	300	875	2,000	16,500
1825	2,943,166	58.00	76.00	85.00	97.00	175	350	1,050	11,500
1826	4,004,180	58.00	76.00	85.00	97.00	175	350	1,050	11,500
1827 curled 2	5,493,400	61.00	81.00	95.00	130	185	450	1,400	14,000
1827 square 2	Inc. above	58.00	76.00	85.00	97.00	175	350	1,050	11,500
1827/6	Inc. above	85.00	95.00	120	155	265	650	1,450	13,000
1828 curled-base 2, no knob	3,075,200	58.00	76.00	85.00	97.00	175	350	1,150	12,500
1828 curled-base 2, knobbed 2	Inc. above	78.00	99.00	125	180	245	460	1,300	—
1828 small 8s, square-base 2, large letters	Inc. above	60.00	80.00	95.00	120	175	350	1,050	14,000
1828 small 8s, square-base 2, small letters	Inc. above	58.00	76.00	85.00	102	250	750	1,900	—
1828 large 8s, square-base 2	Inc. above	58.00	76.00	85.00	97.00	175	350	1,050	12,500
1829	3,712,156	55.00	72.00	75.00	85.00	159	315	1,000	11,500
1829 Large letters	Inc. above	59.00	79.00	85.00	100.00	180	420	1,250	14,000
1829/7	Inc. above	78.00	99.00	125	170	200	475	1,250	14,000
1830 Small O rev	4,764,800	55.00	72.00	75.00	85.00	159	315	1,000	11,500
1830 Large O	Inc. above	60.00	78.00	84.00	105	189	550	2,000	14,500
1830 Large letter rev	Inc. above	1,500	2,250	3,000	3,750	4,800	9,800	—	—
1831	5,873,660	55.00	72.00	75.00	85.00	159	315	1,000	11,500
1832 small letters	4,797,000	55.00	72.00	75.00	85.00	159	315	1,000	11,500
1832 large letters	Inc. above	58.00	75.00	81.00	95.00	175	375	1,350	14,000
1833	5,206,000	55.00	72.00	75.00	85.00	159	325	1,000	11,750
1834 small date, large stars, small letters	6,412,004	55.00	74.00	77.00	87.00	163	325	1,025	11,750
1834 small date, small stars, small letters	Inc. above	55.00	74.00	77.00	87.00	163	325	1,025	11,750
1834 large date, small letters	Inc. above	55.00	74.00	77.00	87.00	163	325	1,025	11,750
1834 large date, large letters	Inc. above	55.00	72.00	75.00	85.00	159	315	1,000	11,500
1835	5,352,006	55.00	72.00	75.00	85.00	159	315	1,000	11,500
1836	6,545,000	55.00	72.00	75.00	85.00	159	315	1,000	11,500
1836	Inc. above	80.00	95.00	120	265	450	1,000	2,500	—
1836 50/00	Inc. above	93.00	112	125	165	300	800	1,750	19,500

Bust Half Dollar.

Draped bust left, flanked by stars, date at angle below. "50 Cents" below eagle.

KM# 58 Designer: Christian Gobrecht. **Diameter:** 30 **Weight:** 13.3600 g. **Composition:** 0.9000 Silver, 0.3866 oz. ASW.

Date	Mintage	G-4	VG-8	F-12	VF-20	XF-40	AU-50	MS-60	MS-65
1836	1,200	850	1,075	1,600	2,000	3,350	4,400	8,850	66,500
1837	3,629,820	58.00	73.00	80.00	115	200	345	1,100	24,500

Bust Half Dollar.
Draped bust left, flanked by stars, date below. HALF DOL. below eagle.
KM# 65 **Designer:** Christian Gobrecht. **Diameter:** 30 **Weight:** 13.3600 g. **Composition:** 0.9000 Silver, 0.3866 oz. ASW.

Date	Mintage	G-4	VG-8	F-12	VF-20	XF-40	AU-50	MS-60	MS-65
1838	3,546,000	58.00	70.00	82.00	120	205	360	1,125	21,500
1838O proof only	Est. 20	—	—	—	—	250,000	300,000	—	—
1839	1,392,976	60.00	76.00	92.00	130	245	410	1,350	39,500
1839O	178,976	240	325	425	650	1,350	2,350	4,500	46,500

Seated Liberty Half Dollar.
Seated Liberty, date below. HALF DOL. below eagle.
KM# 68 **Designer:** Christian Gobrecht. **Diameter:** 30.6 **Weight:** 13.3600 g. **Composition:** 0.9000 Silver, 0.3866 oz. ASW.

Date	Mintage	G-4	VG-8	F-12	VF-20	XF-40	AU-50	MS-60	MS-65
1839 no drapery from elbow	Inc. above	45.00	80.00	150	340	800	1,850	6,000	178,000
1839 drapery	Inc. above	38.00	50.00	59.00	86.00	165	265	1,000	25,000
1840 small letters	1,435,008	36.00	46.00	60.00	84.00	150	325	600	7,500
1840 reverse 1838	Inc. above	150	200	275	350	650	1,350	3,400	30,000
1840O	855,100	36.00	48.00	57.00	90.00	140	275	450	—
1841	310,000	50.00	65.00	100.00	150	235	325	1,200	6,850
1841O	401,000	30.00	44.00	56.00	82.00	180	230	600	7,000
1842 small date	2,012,764	38.00	55.00	75.00	120	175	325	1,300	13,500
1842 medium date	Inc. above	30.00	41.00	51.00	64.00	115	220	750	8,800
1842O small date	957,000	650	850	1,400	2,450	4,650	7,750	16,500	—
1842O medium date	Inc. above	35.00	42.00	55.00	90.00	185	500	1,250	10,500
1843	3,844,000	28.00	39.00	51.00	65.00	110	225	500	4,500
1843O	2,268,000	30.00	41.00	51.00	65.00	120	240	550	—
1844	1,766,000	30.00	41.00	51.00	65.00	110	210	440	4,500
1844O	2,005,000	30.00	41.00	51.00	70.00	110	225	550	—
1844/1844O	Inc. above	500	775	1,000	1,300	2,500	5,750	10,000	—
1845	589,000	35.00	45.00	65.00	125	210	325	850	12,000
1845O	2,094,000	30.00	41.00	51.00	70.00	135	240	550	9,400
1845O no drapery	Inc. above	35.00	47.00	70.00	115	185	375	750	—
1846 medium date	2,210,000	30.00	41.00	51.00	70.00	110	200	500	9,000
1846 tall date	Inc. above	35.00	47.00	70.00	85.00	145	250	650	12,000
1846 /horizontal 6	Inc. above	175	250	325	450	625	1,000	2,500	—
1846O medium date	2,304,000	30.00	41.00	51.00	65.00	110	225	550	12,000
1846O tall date	Inc. above	165	285	365	620	1,050	2,000	6,650	—
1847/1846	1,156,000	2,000	2,750	3,750	5,250	7,700	12,500	21,000	—
1847	Inc. above	35.00	45.00	54.00	67.00	105	250	480	9,000
1847O	2,584,000	30.00	41.00	51.00	65.00	120	275	640	7,000
1848	580,000	45.00	65.00	95.00	185	265	485	1,000	9,000
1848O	3,180,000	30.00	41.00	51.00	70.00	110	285	750	9,000
1849	1,252,000	35.00	45.00	54.00	67.00	108	365	1,250	15,000
1849O	2,310,000	30.00	41.00	51.00	70.00	110	250	650	9,000
1850	227,000	275	325	400	550	675	1,000	1,500	—
1850O	2,456,000	35.00	28.00	45.00	80.00	135	275	650	9,000

Date	Mintage	G-4	VG-8	F-12	VF-20	XF-40	AU-50	MS-60	MS-65
1851	200,750	335	450	550	850	950	1,200	2,250	—
1851O	402,000	40.00	55.00	95.00	120	185	300	700	9,000
1852	77,130	425	500	700	925	1,100	1,350	1,700	—
1852O	144,000	75.00	125	200	350	600	1,250	3,850	26,000
1853O mintage unrecorded	—	—	250,000	—	—	450,000	—	—	—

Note: 1853O, Eliasberg Sale, 1997, VG-8, $154,000.

Seated Liberty Half Dollar.
Seated Liberty, arrows at date. Rays around eagle.

KM# 79 **Designer:** Christian Gobrecht. **Weight:** 12.4400 g. **Composition:** 0.9000 Silver, 0.3599 oz. ASW.

Date	Mintage	G-4	VG-8	F-12	VF-20	XF-40	AU-50	MS-60	MS-65	Prf-65
1853	3,532,708	31.00	36.50	50.00	88.00	250	590	1,500	21,500	175,000
1853O	1,328,000	38.00	48.00	57.00	125	310	750	2,350	27,500	—

Seated Liberty Half Dollar.
Seated Liberty, arrows at date. HALF DOL. below eagle.

KM# 82 **Designer:** Christian Gobrecht. **Weight:** 12.4400 g. **Composition:** 0.9000 Silver, 0.3599 oz. ASW.

Date	Mintage	G-4	VG-8	F-12	VF-20	XF-40	AU-50	MS-60	MS-65	Prf-65
1854	2,982,000	28.00	38.00	47.00	60.00	100.00	270	675	8,000	37,500
1854O	5,240,000	28.00	38.00	47.00	60.00	100.00	270	600	8,000	—
1855	759,500	30.00	40.00	49.00	63.00	120	325	700	9,000	39,500
1855/4	Inc. above	65.00	84.00	160	250	375	600	2,000	17,500	37,000
1855O	3,688,000	28.00	38.00	47.00	60.00	100.00	270	650	8,000	—
1855S	129,950	350	475	800	1,500	3,150	6,850	19,500	—	—

Seated Liberty Half Dollar.
Seated Liberty, date below. HALF DOL. below eagle.

KM# A68 **Designer:** Christian Gobrecht. **Weight:** 12.4400 g. **Composition:** 0.9000 Silver, 0.3599 oz. ASW.

Date	Mintage	G-4	VG-8	F-12	VF-20	XF-40	AU-50	MS-60	MS-65	Prf-65
1856	938,000	32.00	38.00	50.00	70.00	110	195	425	6,500	12,500
1856O	2,658,000	28.00	38.00	52.00	60.00	100.00	190	385	12,500	—

Date	Mintage	G-4	VG-8	F-12	VF-20	XF-40	AU-50	MS-60	MS-65	Prf-65
1856S	211,000	85.00	120	160	260	500	1,250	3,500	19,000	—
1857	1,988,000	28.00	38.00	50.00	60.00	100.00	190	385	5,150	12,500
1857O	818,000	33.00	40.00	52.00	85.00	135	275	885	12,500	—
1857S	158,000	100.00	120	145	285	575	975	3,500	19,000	—
1858	4,226,000	28.00	38.00	47.00	60.00	90.00	190	385	6,500	12,500
1858O	7,294,000	28.00	38.00	47.00	60.00	90.00	190	385	12,500	—
1858S	476,000	38.00	48.00	62.00	110	215	400	950	12,500	—
1859	748,000	30.00	41.00	51.00	70.00	120	200	650	6,600	5,500
1859O	2,834,000	28.00	38.00	47.00	60.00	100.00	190	450	6,500	—
1859S	566,000	38.00	44.00	59.00	100.00	215	375	750	12,500	—
1860	303,700	38.00	42.00	51.00	100.00	150	350	1,000	6,500	5,500
1860O	1,290,000	30.00	41.00	52.00	70.00	100.00	190	450	5,150	—
1860S	472,000	38.00	40.00	51.00	85.00	135	245	850	12,500	—
1861	2,888,400	30.00	40.00	49.00	65.00	100.00	190	440	5,150	5,500
1861O	2,532,633	30.00	41.00	53.00	86.00	125	235	450	5,150	—
1861S	939,500	35.00	44.00	53.00	70.00	120	195	975	9,500	—
1862	253,550	38.00	51.00	57.00	120	200	295	750	5,150	5,500
1862S	1,352,000	30.00	41.00	52.00	75.00	120	195	460	9,000	—
1863	503,660	35.00	48.00	57.00	85.00	135	250	750	5,150	5,500
1863S	916,000	33.00	45.00	52.00	70.00	120	195	460	9,000	—
1864	379,570	30.00	48.00	57.00	120	195	250	750	5,150	5,500
1864S	658,000	33.00	45.00	51.00	70.00	125	215	675	9,000	—
1865	511,900	28.00	47.00	55.00	90.00	150	275	750	5,150	5,500
1865S	675,000	35.00	45.00	52.00	70.00	120	235	500	9,000	—
1866 proof, unique	—	—	—	—	—	—	—	—	—	—
1866S	60,000	460	575	850	1,250	2,550	3,350	5,400	68,000	—

Seated Liberty Half Dollar.
Seated Liberty, date below. IN GOD WE TRUST above eagle.
KM# 99 **Designer:** Christian Gobrecht. **Weight:** 12.4400 g. **Composition:** 0.9000 Silver, 0.3599 oz. ASW.

Date	Mintage	G-4	VG-8	F-12	VF-20	XF-40	AU-50	MS-60	MS-65	Prf-65
1866	745,625	35.00	45.00	53.00	80.00	120	225	350	4,800	3,750
1866S	994,000	33.00	43.00	51.00	70.00	110	275	650	5,000	—
1867	449,925	38.00	48.00	59.00	110	165	250	350	4,800	3,750
1867S	1,196,000	32.00	42.00	51.00	70.00	110	250	350	7,000	—
1868	418,200	48.00	55.00	95.00	185	225	300	525	7,100	3,750
1868S	1,160,000	32.00	42.00	51.00	70.00	110	250	350	7,000	—
1869	795,900	35.00	45.00	49.00	70.00	110	190	385	4,600	3,750
1869S	656,000	35.00	47.00	51.00	70.00	120	265	600	7,000	—
1870	634,900	35.00	45.00	50.00	80.00	125	250	475	7,000	3,750
1870CC	54,617	900	1,500	1,900	3,900	12,500	30,000	100,000	—	—
1870S	1,004,000	31.00	43.00	53.00	85.00	150	275	575	7,000	—
1871	1,204,560	32.00	42.00	52.00	75.00	120	165	350	7,000	3,750
1871CC	153,950	225	325	600	1,200	1,950	10,000	15,000	—	—
1871S	2,178,000	30.00	41.00	49.00	70.00	110	215	400	7,000	—
1872	881,550	32.00	40.00	49.00	75.00	120	195	430	2,850	3,750
1872CC	272,000	85.00	125	275	400	1,500	4,000	8,000	50,000	—
1872S	580,000	31.00	47.00	67.00	120	225	375	975	7,000	—
1873 closed 3	801,800	35.00	46.00	64.00	98.00	135	250	545	4,500	3,750
1873 open 3	Inc. above	2,650	3,400	4,350	5,500	7,900	13,500	30,000	—	—
1873CC	122,500	225	320	425	950	1,900	6,500	12,000	80,000	—
1873S no arrows	5,000	—	—	—	—	—	—	—	—	—

Note: 1873S no arrows, no specimens known to survive.

Seated Liberty Half Dollar.
Seated Liberty, arrows at date. IN GOD WE TRUST above eagle.
KM# 107 **Designer:** Christian Gobrecht. **Weight:** 12.5000 g. **Composition:** 0.9000 Silver, 0.3617 oz. ASW.

Date	Mintage	G-4	VG-8	F-12	VF-20	XF-40	AU-50	MS-60	MS-65	Prf-65
1873	1,815,700	32.00	49.00	60.00	90.00	230	400	850	17,500	9,000
1873CC	214,560	150	275	375	850	2,000	2,400	5,700	42,000	—
1873S	233,000	55.00	78.00	130	245	425	675	2,200	40,000	—
1874	2,360,300	32.00	42.00	56.00	85.00	210	400	850	12,750	9,000
1874CC	59,000	400	575	1,000	1,750	3,600	5,600	10,500	—	—
1874S	394,000	43.00	65.00	85.00	185	365	685	1,850	20,000	—

Seated Liberty Half Dollar.
Seated Liberty, date below. IN GOD WE TRUST above eagle.
KM# A99 **Designer:** Christian Gobrecht. **Weight:** 12.5000 g. **Composition:** 0.9000 Silver, 0.3617 oz. ASW.

Date	Mintage	G-4	VG-8	F-12	VF-20	XF-40	AU-50	MS-60	MS-65	Prf-65
1875	6,027,500	28.00	38.00	47.00	56.00	88.00	180	420	3,500	3,375
1875CC	1,008,000	50.00	56.00	75.00	125	200	325	650	8,350	—
1875S	3,200,000	28.00	38.00	47.00	63.00	100.00	165	360	2,700	—
1876	8,419,150	28.00	38.00	47.00	56.00	88.00	165	360	5,300	3,775
1876CC	1,956,000	50.00	56.00	75.00	115	180	275	560	4,200	—
1876S	4,528,000	28.00	38.00	47.00	56.00	88.00	165	360	2,700	—
1877	8,304,510	28.00	38.00	47.00	56.00	88.00	165	360	2,700	3,825
1877CC	1,420,000	50.00	56.00	75.00	115	180	275	630	3,250	—
1877S	5,356,000	28.00	38.00	47.00	56.00	88.00	165	360	2,700	—
1878	1,378,400	35.00	46.00	67.00	80.00	120	165	425	3,650	3,900
1878CC	62,000	450	600	1,000	1,500	3,150	4,850	7,000	43,500	—
1878S	12,000	23,500	37,500	45,000	47,500	52,000	60,000	70,000	175,000	—
1879	5,900	275	310	360	400	465	575	700	3,650	3,150
1880	9,755	260	280	315	355	410	535	700	3,750	3,150
1881	10,975	270	300	335	385	455	565	700	4,000	3,150
1882	5,500	340	365	385	450	525	600	750	3,850	3,150
1883	9,039	325	340	365	435	500	575	775	3,950	3,150
1884	5,275	385	375	415	500	560	635	800	3,850	3,150
1885	6,130	390	425	475	550	625	700	825	3,850	3,150
1886	5,886	400	500	600	700	775	875	1,000	3,900	3,150
1887	5,710	500	525	650	775	875	950	1,100	3,900	3,150
1888	12,833	280	300	365	400	485	550	800	3,900	3,150
1889	12,711	275	315	350	400	485	550	800	3,900	3,150
1890	12,590	285	310	365	415	500	550	800	3,850	3,150
1891	200,600	55.00	60.00	94.00	122	155	260	480	3,850	3,150

Barber Half Dollar.
Laureate head right, flanked by stars, date below. Heraldic eagle.

KM# 116 **Designer:** Charles E. Barber. **Diameter:** 30.6 **Weight:** 12.5000 g. **Composition:** 0.9000 Silver, 0.3617 oz. ASW.

Mint mark

HALF DOLLAR

Date	Mintage	G-4	VG-8	F-12	VF-20	XF-40	AU-50	MS-60	MS-65	Prf-65
1892	935,245	28.50	40.00	65.00	120	195	345	475	3,620	4,650
1892O	390,000	310	420	515	575	630	690	850	4,350	—
1892O micro O	Inc. above	2,000	3,750	4,500	7,000	10,000	17,500	24,000	64,000	—
1892S	1,029,028	250	330	425	530	600	700	940	4,850	—
1893	1,826,792	20.00	36.00	75.00	135	205	335	520	3,800	4,650
1893O	1,389,000	36.00	64.50	130	220	360	435	625	9,650	—
1893S	740,000	165	225	300	500	595	725	1,275	25,000	—
1894	1,148,972	32.50	50.00	115	200	280	355	500	3,850	4,650
1894O	2,138,000	22.00	34.00	90.00	170	290	365	525	6,250	—
1894S	4,048,690	18.00	28.00	67.00	125	230	345	490	9,850	—
1895	1,835,218	18.00	25.00	72.00	150	225	345	595	3,900	4,650
1895O	1,766,000	23.00	43.00	110	195	285	385	620	6,950	—
1895S	1,108,086	30.00	54.00	130	235	310	410	580	8,250	—
1896	950,762	21.50	28.00	88.00	160	265	355	565	5,450	4,650
1896O	924,000	42.00	56.00	185	290	475	775	1,750	14,750	—
1896S	1,140,948	115	145	210	350	495	750	1,450	10,500	—
1897	2,480,731	14.10	16.00	47.50	100.00	180	345	485	3,620	4,650
1897O	632,000	170	230	485	835	1,100	1,350	1,800	9,500	—
1897S	933,900	155	225	385	535	840	1,050	1,500	7,350	—
1898	2,956,735	14.10	16.00	38.50	94.00	180	335	485	3,650	4,650
1898O	874,000	37.50	75.00	225	355	525	625	1,250	9,450	—
1898S	2,358,550	27.50	52.50	87.50	175	340	440	950	10,250	—
1899	5,538,846	14.60	16.00	39.50	98.00	180	365	475	3,620	4,650
1899O	1,724,000	26.00	37.50	80.00	170	300	400	675	8,150	—
1899S	1,686,411	23.00	42.50	88.00	135	205	355	660	6,900	—
1900	4,762,912	14.60	16.00	36.50	90.00	180	335	475	3,750	4,650
1900O	2,744,000	17.50	22.50	62.00	165	285	335	860	15,500	—
1900S	2,560,322	15.00	18.50	46.50	98.00	200	335	640	10,000	—
1901	4,268,813	14.60	16.50	38.50	94.00	180	335	510	4,250	4,650
1901O	1,124,000	16.50	26.50	80.00	205	350	475	1,350	14,850	—
1901S	847,044	34.00	55.00	160	355	610	1,050	1,850	19,500	—
1902	4,922,777	13.10	14.50	32.50	86.00	180	335	475	4,600	4,650
1902O	2,526,000	13.50	17.00	52.50	105	225	355	725	11,500	—
1902S	1,460,670	16.00	19.00	62.50	150	260	420	750	7,750	—
1903	2,278,755	14.60	16.00	47.50	100.00	200	335	500	9,250	4,650
1903O	2,100,000	14.10	17.00	53.00	115	210	335	665	9,500	—
1903S	1,920,772	15.00	18.00	55.00	125	220	380	610	5,750	—
1904	2,992,670	13.10	14.50	33.00	85.00	180	345	475	6,450	4,650
1904O	1,117,600	20.00	30.00	80.00	220	385	590	1,100	12,500	—
1904S	553,038	38.50	75.00	260	555	1,075	1,775	9,000	41,500	—
1905	662,727	22.50	32.50	95.00	180	270	370	565	7,500	4,650
1905O	505,000	30.00	44.50	125	235	340	440	760	4,850	—
1905S	2,494,000	15.50	18.00	50.00	125	230	350	615	9,750	—
1906	2,638,675	13.10	14.50	32.00	83.00	180	335	465	3,800	4,650
1906D	4,028,000	13.10	14.50	33.00	89.00	180	335	465	4,500	—
1906O	2,446,000	13.10	14.50	44.00	98.00	190	350	600	6,350	—
1906S	1,740,154	14.60	16.50	57.50	110	215	380	590	5,950	—
1907	2,598,575	13.10	14.50	30.00	83.00	180	335	465	3,600	4,650
1907D	3,856,000	13.10	14.50	30.00	75.00	180	335	465	3,600	—
1907O	3,946,000	13.10	14.50	32.00	89.00	180	33.00	575	3,700	—
1907S	1,250,000	17.40	20.00	80.00	165	315	650	1,275	12,500	—
1908	1,354,545	13.10	14.50	30.00	80.00	180	335	465	4,350	4,650
1908D	3,280,000	13.10	14.50	30.00	80.00	180	335	485	4,250	—
1908O	5,360,000	13.10	14.50	30.00	89.00	180	345	540	3,600	—
1908S	1,644,828	18.50	25.00	72.00	160	285	435	850	6,350	—
1909	2,368,650	14.10	16.00	32.00	83.00	180	335	465	3,600	4,650
1909O	925,400	17.40	23.50	56.00	140	300	510	775	4,850	—
1909S	1,764,000	13.40	14.50	37.00	100.00	180	335	600	4,450	—
1910	418,551	20.00	28.50	90.00	170	330	445	610	3,900	4,650

Date	Mintage	G-4	VG-8	F-12	VF-20	XF-40	AU-50	MS-60	MS-65	Prf-65
1910S	1,948,000	16.60	16.50	36.00	100.00	180	355	625	6,650	—
1911	1,406,543	13.10	14.50	30.00	83.00	180	335	465	3,600	4,650
1911D	695,080	14.10	16.00	40.00	91.00	180	345	565	3,700	—
1911S	1,272,000	14.60	16.50	42.00	98.00	180	345	580	5,950	—
1912	1,550,700	13.10	14.50	30.00	83.00	180	335	465	4,100	4,650
1912D	2,300,800	13.10	14.50	30.00	81.00	180	335	465	3,600	—
1912S	1,370,000	16.40	19.50	41.50	100.00	180	335	535	5,850	—
1913	188,627	77.00	88.00	235	420	600	875	1,150	5,250	4,800
1913D	534,000	17.00	19.50	44.00	100.00	200	335	485	5,450	—
1913S	604,000	20.00	25.00	53.50	110	225	385	725	4,650	—
1914	124,610	155	175	325	550	775	1,025	1,400	11,500	5,000
1914S	992,000	16.40	19.00	41.00	98.00	190	355	575	4,950	—
1915	138,450	112	168	285	380	575	920	1,350	6,650	5,000
1915D	1,170,400	13.10	14.50	30.00	75.00	180	335	465	3,600	—
1915S	1,604,000	16.90	19.50	41.50	94.00	195	350	480	3,600	—

Walking Liberty Half Dollar.
Liberty walking left wearing U.S. flag gown, sunrise at left. Eagle advancing left.

KM# 142 Designer: Adolph A. Weinman. **Diameter:** 30.6 **Weight:** 12.5000 g. **Composition:** 0.9000 Silver, 0.3617 oz. ASW. **Notes:** The mint mark appears on the obverse below the word "Trust" on 1916 and some 1917 issues. Starting with some 1917 issues and continuing through the remainder of the series, the mint mark was changed to the reverse, at about the 8 o'clock position near the rim.

Obverse mint mark
1916-1917

Reverse mint mark
1917-1947

Date	Mintage	G-4	VG-8	F-12	VF-20	XF-40	AU-50	MS-60	MS-65	Prf-65
1916	608,000	47.00	55.00	95.00	170	240	275	345	1,950	—
1916D	1,014,400	48.50	55.00	80.00	135	220	255	360	2,500	—
1916S	508,000	108	129	280	440	600	725	1,050	6,250	—
1917D obv. mint mark	765,400	23.50	33.00	80.00	155	235	335	625	7,900	—
1917S obv. mint mark	952,000	27.00	44.00	135	365	700	1,200	2,300	22,500	—
1917	12,292,000	9.00	9.10	10.50	19.50	42.00	72.00	130	1,050	—
1917D rev. mint mark	1,940,000	10.00	16.00	45.00	135	275	555	940	18,500	—
1917S rev. mint mark	5,554,000	9.70	10.00	16.50	32.00	65.00	155	330	13,850	—
1918	6,634,000	9.70	10.00	15.50	64.00	150	265	565	3,800	—
1918D	3,853,040	10.10	12.50	35.00	90.00	225	500	1,300	24,500	—
1918S	10,282,000	9.70	10.00	16.00	34.00	60.00	190	485	17,750	—
1919	962,000	26.00	32.50	78.50	265	535	885	1,325	7,750	—
1919D	1,165,000	25.00	38.50	95.00	320	765	1,750	5,950	130,000	—
1919S	1,552,000	17.50	28.50	72.00	310	825	1,750	3,300	20,000	—
1920	6,372,000	9.70	10.00	15.50	42.00	75.00	155	330	5,250	—
1920D	1,551,000	10.40	17.50	65.00	240	460	920	1,485	17,500	—
1920S	4,624,000	9.70	10.00	19.00	78.00	235	510	850	14,500	—
1921	246,000	165	210	350	750	1,575	2,650	4,500	19,500	—
1921D	208,000	310	370	550	950	2,200	3,150	5,650	29,500	—
1921S	548,000	45.00	65.00	210	750	4,850	7,950	12,850	130,000	—
1923S	2,178,000	10.10	11.50	27.50	110	295	650	1,375	16,500	—
1927S	2,392,000	9.70	11.00	16.50	46.00	165	425	990	9,750	—
1928S	1,940,000	10.00	13.50	28.00	110	325	600	1,650	—	—
1928S	Inc. above	9.70	11.00	18.50	66.00	195	450	985	10,750	—
1929D	1,001,200	10.10	11.00	17.50	32.00	98.00	195	390	3,350	—
1929S	1,902,000	9.70	11.00	14.50	28.50	115	220	400	3,750	—
1933S	1,786,000	10.10	11.50	13.50	20.00	58.00	240	590	4,500	—
1934	6,964,000	7.40	7.80	7.90	8.50	11.00	25.00	85.00	565	—
1934D	2,361,400	737	8.20	11.60	17.50	36.00	88.00	150	1,625	—
1934S	3,652,000	7.40	8.00	8.50	10.70	30.00	100.00	385	4,800	—
1935	9,162,000	7.40	7.80	7.90	8.50	11.90	21.50	45.00	365	—
1935D	3,003,800	7.40	8.00	8.50	14.00	33.00	66.00	140	2,450	—
1935S	3,854,000	7.40	8.00	8.30	13.50	32.00	95.00	285	2,850	—
1936	12,617,901	7.40	7.80	7.90	8.50	11.90	21.00	37.50	265	6,600
1936D	4,252,400	7.40	8.00	8.30	12.50	20.00	52.00	78.00	665	—
1936S	3,884,000	7.40	8.00	8.30	12.50	21.50	58.00	132	1,000	—
1937	9,527,728	7.40	7.80	7.90	8.50	11.90	22.00	38.00	285	1,700
1937D	1,676,000	7.40	9.80	9.90	15.00	33.50	105	220	965	—
1937S	2,090,000	7.40	8.00	8.50	8.50	25.50	62.00	168	785	—
1938	4,118,152	7.40	8.00	8.30	8.50	13.40	38.00	66.00	460	1,275

Date	Mintage	G-4	VG-8	F-12	VF-20	XF-40	AU-50	MS-60	MS-65	Prf-65
1938D	491,600	70.00	75.00	100.00	125	185	250	475	1,750	—
1939	6,820,808	7.40	7.50	6.50	8.50	11.90	22.00	41.00	210	1,150
1939D	4,267,800	7.40	7.20	7.90	9.50	12.70	26.00	45.00	225	—
1939S	2,552,000	7.40	8.00	8.30	9.00	25.00	76.00	145	375	—
1940	9,167,279	7.40	7.50	7.00	7.50	11.40	13.00	31.00	185	1,000
1940S	4,550,000	7.40	7.80	7.90	8.50	12.00	21.00	50.00	315	—
1941	24,207,412	7.40	7.50	7.00	8.04	10.20	13.00	30.00	160	850
1941D	11,248,400	7.40	7.80	7.90	8.50	10.00	18.00	37.50	180	—
1941S	8,098,000	7.40	7.80	7.90	8.50	12.00	27.50	70.00	1,025	—
1942	47,839,120	7.40	7.50	7.00	8.04	10.20	13.00	30.00	160	850
1942D	10,973,800	7.40	7.80	7.90	8.50	10.00	19.00	37.00	325	—
1942S	12,708,000	7.40	7.80	7.90	8.50	10.00	17.50	37.00	610	—
1943	53,190,000	7.40	7.50	7.00	8.04	10.20	13.00	30.00	150	—
1943D	11,346,000	7.40	7.80	7.90	8.50	10.00	25.00	42.00	295	—
1943D Double Die Obverse	—	7.60	7.50	9.00	12.00	15.00	30.00	55.00	450	—
1943S	13,450,000	7.40	7.80	7.90	8.50	10.00	18.50	42.00	460	—
1944	28,206,000	7.40	7.50	7.00	8.04	10.20	13.00	30.00	180	—
1944D	9,769,000	7.40	7.80	7.90	8.50	10.00	20.00	37.00	210	—
1944S	8,904,000	7.40	7.80	7.90	8.50	10.00	18.00	36.00	575	—
1945	31,502,000	7.40	7.50	7.00	8.04	10.20	13.00	30.00	165	—
1945D	9,966,800	7.40	7.80	7.90	8.50	10.00	19.00	36.00	145	—
1945S	10,156,000	7.40	7.80	7.90	8.50	10.00	17.50	36.00	180	—
1946	12,118,000	7.40	7.50	7.00	8.04	10.20	13.00	30.00	200	—
1946 Double Die Reverse	Inc. above	16.00	24.00	35.00	50.00	85.00	175	325	2,750	—
1946D	2,151,000	7.40	8.00	7.90	8.50	25.50	38.50	47.50	150	—
1946S	3,724,000	7.40	7.80	7.90	8.50	12.00	19.00	43.50	175	—
1947	4,094,000	7.40	7.25	7.50	8.50	11.00	22.00	50.00	275	—
1947D	3,900,600	7.40	8.00	7.90	8.50	14.00	31.50	52.50	165	—

Franklin Half Dollar.

Franklin bust right. Liberty Bell, small eagle at right.

KM# 199   **Designer:** John R. Sinnock. **Diameter:** 30.6 **Weight:** 12.5000 g. **Composition:** 0.9000 Silver, 0.3617 oz. ASW.

Mint mark

Date	Mintage	VG-8	F-12	VF-20	XF-40	AU-50	MS-60	MS-65	-65FBL	-65CAM
1948	3,006,814	6.20	6.30	6.90	8.50	11.50	16.00	75.00	190	—
1948D	4,028,600	6.20	6.30	6.90	8.00	11.00	15.00	125	260	—
1949	5,614,000	—	—	8.00	12.00	38.50	145	250	—	
1949D	4,120,600	—	—	6.70	9.00	25.00	43.50	900	1,750	—
1949S	3,744,000	—	—	6.90	11.00	30.00	62.50	160	700	—
1950	7,793,509	—	—	—	6.30	10.00	26.00	110	285	2,000
1950D	8,031,600	—	—	—	7.30	11.50	22.00	425	900	—
1951	16,859,602	—	—	—	6.00	9.00	11.00	75.00	340	1,450
1951D	9,475,200	—	—	—	10.30	17.50	26.00	170	540	—
1951S	13,696,000	—	—	6.30	7.00	15.00	23.50	125	750	—
1952	21,274,073	—	—	—	6.20	9.00	9.40	70.00	210	775
1952D	25,395,600	—	—	—	6.20	9.00	9.40	130	450	—
1952S	5,526,000	—	6.30	8.90	16.00	32.00	52.00	140	1,500	—
1953	2,796,920	—	6.30	6.40	10.00	16.00	25.00	140	1,000	475
1953D	20,900,400	—	—	—	6.50	8.20	12.00	150	400	—
1953S	4,148,000	—	—	6.30	7.00	15.00	25.00	65.00	16,000	—
1954	13,421,503	—	—	—	6.00	9.00	10.20	75.00	225	175
1954D	25,445,580	—	—	—	6.00	9.00	10.00	110	235	—
1954S	4,993,400	—	—	—	6.40	9.40	13.50	42.00	440	—
1955	2,876,381	15.50	16.00	17.50	18.00	18.50	20.00	70.00	140	120
1955 Bugs Bunny	Inc. above	20.00	22.00	23.00	25.00	26.00	28.00	120	750	—
1956 Type 1 rev.	4,701,384	6.00	6.00	6.10	6.40	8.20	13.50	55.00	125	300
1956 Type 2 rev.	Inc. above	—	—	—	—	—	—	—	—	40.00
1957 Type 1 rev.	6,361,952	—	—	—	6.00	7.20	8.10	63.00	95.00	55.00
1957 Type 2 rev.	Inc. above	—	—	—	—	—	—	—	—	—
1957D	19,966,850	—	—	—	6.00	7.20	7.90	60.00	100.00	—
1958 Type 1 rev.	4,917,652	—	—	—	6.00	7.20	7.90	55.00	110	60.00
1958 Type 2 rev.	Inc. above	—	—	—	12.00	20.00	26.00	—	—	—
1958D	23,962,412	—	—	—	6.00	7.20	7.90	55.00	80.00	—

Date	Mintage	VG-8	F-12	VF-20	XF-40	AU-50	MS-60	MS-65	-65FBL	-65CAM
1959 Type 1 rev.	7,349,291	—	—	—	6.00	7.20	7.90	110	250	75.00
1959 Type 2 rev.	Inc. above	—	—	—	12.00	16.00	30.00	115	—	—
1959D	13,053,750	—	—	—	6.00	7.20	7.90	125	215	—
1960 Type 1 rev.	7,715,602	—	—	—	6.00	7.20	7.90	110	340	45.00
1960 Type 2 rev.	Inc. above	—	—	—	—	—	—	—	—	—
1960D	18,215,812	—	—	—	6.00	7.20	7.90	400	1,350	—
1961 Type 1 rev.	11,318,244	—	—	—	6.00	7.20	7.90	125	1,300	40.00
1961 Type 2 rev.	Inc. above	—	—	—	—	—	—	—	—	—
1961 Double die rev.	Inc. above	—	—	—	—	—	—	—	—	3,500
1961D	20,276,442	—	—	—	6.00	7.20	7.90	155	875	—
1962 Type 1 rev.	12,932,019	—	—	—	6.00	7.20	7.90	145	1,850	35.00
1962 Type 2 rev.	Inc. above	—	—	—	—	—	—	—	—	—
1962D	35,473,281	—	—	—	6.00	7.20	7.90	175	800	—
1963 Type 1 rev.	25,239,645	—	—	—	6.00	7.20	7.90	55.00	1,200	35.00
1963 Type 2 rev.	Inc. above	—	—	—	—	—	—	—	—	—
1963D	67,069,292	—	—	—	6.00	7.20	7.90	75.00	165	—

Kennedy Half Dollar.

KM# 202 Obv. Designer: Gilroy Roberts.
Rev. Designer: Frank Gasparro. **Diameter:** 30.6
Weight: 12.5000 g. **Composition:** 0.9000 Silver,
0.3617 oz. ASW.

Mint mark 1964

Date	Mintage	MS-60	MS-65	Prf-65
1964	277,254,766	6.00	20.00	12.00
1964 Accented Hair	Inc. above	—	—	40.00
1964D	156,205,446	6.20	24.00	—

Kennedy Half Dollar.

KM# 202a Obv. Designer: Gilroy Roberts.
Rev. Designer: Frank Gasparro. **Diameter:** 30.6
Weight: 11.5000 g. **Composition:** 0.4000 Silver,
0.1479 oz. ASW.

Mint mark 1968 - present

Date	Mintage	MS-60	MS-65	Prf-65
1965	65,879,366	3.10	18.00	—
1965 SMS	2,360,000	—	15.00	—
1966	108,984,932	3.10	14.00	—
1966 SMS	2,261,583	—	17.00	—
1967	295,046,978	3.10	22.00	—

Date	Mintage	MS-60	MS-65	Prf-65
1967 SMS	1,863,344	—	18.00	—
1968D	246,951,930	3.10	18.00	—
1968S	3,041,506	—	—	7.00
1969D	129,881,800	3.10	20.00	—
1969S	2,934,631	—	—	7.50
1970D	2,150,000	13.00	38.00	—
1970S	2,632,810	—	—	20.00

Kennedy Half Dollar.

KM# 202b Obv. Designer: Gilroy Roberts. **Rev.
Designer:** Frank Gasparro. **Diameter:** 30.6 **Weight:**
11.3400 g. **Composition:** Copper-Nickel Clad Copper

Date	Mintage	MS-60	MS-65	Prf-65
1971	155,640,000	1.00	15.00	—
1971D	302,097,424	1.00	15.00	—
1971S	3,244,183	—	—	8.00
1972	153,180,000	1.00	20.00	—
1972D	141,890,000	1.00	14.00	—
1972S	3,267,667	—	—	7.00
1973	64,964,000	1.00	14.00	—
1973D	83,171,400	—	12.00	—
1973S	(2,769,624)	—	—	7.00
1974	201,596,000	1.00	18.00	—
1974D	79,066,300	1.00	20.00	—
1974S	(2,617,350)	—	—	5.00
1975 none minted	—	—	—	—
1975D none minted	—	—	—	—
1975S none minted	—	—	—	—

Kennedy Half Dollar.
Bicentennial design, Independence Hall.

KM# 205 Rev. Designer: Seth Huntington.
Diameter: 30.5 **Weight:** 11.2000 g. **Composition:**
Copper-Nickel

Date	Mintage	MS-60	MS-65	Prf-65
1976	234,308,000	1.00	22.00	—
1976D	287,565,248	1.00	9.00	—
1976S	(7,059,099)	—	—	4.00

Kennedy Half Dollar.

Bicentennial design, Independence Hall.

KM# 205a   Rev. Designer: Seth Huntington.
Weight: 11.5000 g. **Composition:** 0.4000 Silver,
0.1479 oz. ASW.

Date	Mintage	MS-60	MS-65	Prf-65
1976S	4,908,319	—	12.00	—
1976S	3,998,625	—	—	6.00

Kennedy Half Dollar.

Regular design resumed.

KM# A202b   Diameter: 30.4 **Weight:** 11.1000 g.
Composition: Copper-Nickel Clad Copper **Notes:**
KM#202b design and composition resumed. The
1979-S and 1981-S Type II proofs have clearer mint
marks than the Type I proofs of those years.

Date	Mintage	MS-65	Prf-65
1977	43,598,000	18.00	—
1977D	31,449,106	20.00	—
1977S	(3,251,152)	—	4.50
1978	14,350,000	12.00	—
1978D	13,765,799	10.00	—
1978S	(3,127,788)	—	6.00
1979	68,312,000	11.00	—
1979D	15,815,422	9.00	—
1979S Type I	3,677,175	—	6.00
1979S Type II	Inc. above	—	20.00
1980P	44,134,000	9.00	—
1980D	33,456,449	6.50	—
1980S	(3,547,030)	—	6.00
1981P	29,544,000	8.00	—
1981D	27,839,533	8.50	—
1981S Type I	(4,063,083)	—	5.00
1981S Type II	Inc. above	—	17.50
1982P	10,819,000	10.00	—
1982P no initials FG	Inc. above	40.00	—
1982D	13,140,102	9.00	—
1982S	(38,957,479)	—	6.50
1983P	34,139,000	20.00	—
1983D	32,472,244	10.00	—
1983S	(3,279,126)	—	6.50
1984P	26,029,000	10.00	—
1984D	26,262,158	15.00	—
1984S	(3,065,110)	—	7.00
1985P	18,706,962	10.00	—
1985D	19,814,034	12.00	—
1985S	(3,962,138)	—	6.00
1986P	13,107,633	25.00	—
1986D	15,336,145	17.00	—
1986S	(2,411,180)	—	8.00
1987P	2,890,758	14.00	—
1987D	2,890,758	10.00	—
1987S	(4,407,728)	—	6.50

Date	Mintage	MS-65	Prf-65
1988P	13,626,000	16.00	—
1988D	12,000,096	12.00	—
1988S	(3,262,948)	—	6.00
1989P	24,542,000	18.00	—
1989D	23,000,216	14.00	—
1989S	(3,220,194)	—	8.00
1990P	22,780,000	20.00	—
1990D	20,096,242	15.00	—
1990S	(3,299,559)	—	7.00
1991P	14,874,000	15.00	—
1991D	15,054,678	18.00	—
1991S	(2,867,787)	—	16.00
1992P	17,628,000	18.00	—
1992D	17,000,106	8.00	—
1992S	(2,858,981)	—	8.00
1993P	15,510,000	15.00	—
1993D	15,000,006	14.00	—
1993S	(2,633,439)	—	14.00
1994P	23,718,000	8.00	—
1994D	23,828,110	8.00	—
1994S	(2,484,594)	—	11.00
1995P	26,496,000	9.00	—
1995D	26,288,000	8.00	—
1995S	(2,010,384)	—	35.00
1996P	24,442,000	11.00	—
1996D	24,744,000	8.00	—
1996S	(2,085,191)	—	16.00
1997P	20,882,000	14.00	—
1997D	19,876,000	10.00	—
1997S	(1,975,000)	—	34.00
1998P	15,646,000	14.00	—
1998D	15,064,000	14.00	—
1998S	(2,078,494)	—	22.00
1999P	8,900,000	9.00	—
1999D	10,682,000	9.00	—
1999S	(2,557,897)	—	24.00
2000P	22,600,000	9.00	—
2000D	19,466,000	7.00	—
2000S	(3,082,944)	—	8.00
2001P	21,200,000	9.00	—
2001D	19,504,000	9.00	—
2001S	(2,235,000)	—	10.00
2002P	3,100,000	10.00	—
2002D	2,500,000	10.00	—
2002S	(2,268,913)	—	8.00
2003P	2,500,000	14.00	—
2003D	2,500,000	14.00	—
2003S	2,076,165	—	6.00
2004P	2,900,000	14.00	—
2004D	2,900,000	14.00	—
2004S	1,789,488	—	13.00
2005P	3,800,000	9.00	—
2005P Satin finish	1,160,000	8.00	—
2005D	3,500,000	9.00	—
2005D Satin finish	1,160,000	10.00	—
2005S	2,275,000	—	7.00
2006P	2,400,000	12.00	—
2006P Satin finish	847,361	12.00	—
2006D	2,000,000	20.00	—
2006D Satin finish	847,361	14.00	—
2006S	1,934,965	—	10.00
2007P	—	7.00	—
2007P Satin finish	—	14.00	—
2007D	—	7.00	—
2007D Satin finish	—	14.00	—
2007S	—	—	10.00
2008P	—	7.00	—
2008D	—	7.00	—
2008S	—	—	10.00
2009P	—	7.00	—
2009D	—	7.00	—
2009S	—	—	10.00

Kennedy Half Dollar.

KM# A202c **Designer:** Gilroy Roberts. **Diameter:** 30.6 **Weight:** 12.5000 g. **Composition:** 0.9000 Silver, 0.3617 oz. ASW.

Date	Mintage	Prf-65
1993S	(761,353)	32.00
1994S	(785,329)	36.00
1995S	(838,953)	92.00
1996S	(830,021)	40.00
1997S	(821,678)	75.00
1998S	(878,792)	25.00
1998S Matte Proof	(62,350)	325
1999S	(804,565)	38.00
2000S	(965,921)	9.00
2001S	(849,600)	20.00
2002S	(888,816)	14.00
2003S	(1,040,425)	14.50
2004S	1,175,935	14.00
2005S	1,069,679	9.00
2006S	988,140	11.00
2007S	—	12.00
2008S	—	12.00
2009S	—	12.00

Date	Mintage	Prf-65
1992S	(1,317,579)	12.00

DOLLAR

Flowing Hair Dollar.

KM# 17 **Designer:** Robert Scot. **Diameter:** 39-40 **Weight:** 26.9600 g. **Composition:** 0.8920 Silver, 0.7731 oz. ASW. **Notes:** The two 1795 varieties have either two or three leaves under each of the eagle's wings on the reverse.

Date	Mintage	F-12	VF-20	XF-40	AU-50	MS-60	MS-63
1794	1,758	120,000	170,000	245,000	365,000	575,000	950,000
1795 2 leaves	203,033	4,450	7,800	16,150	25,500	80,500	196,500
1795 3 leaves	Inc. above	4,200	7,250	14,500	22,500	69,500	182,500
1795 Silver plug	Inc. above	9,850	13,950	28,500	48,500	115,000	235,000

Draped Bust Dollar.
Small eagle.

KM# 18 **Designer:** Robert Scot. **Diameter:** 39-40 **Weight:** 26.9600 g. **Composition:** 0.8920 Silver, 0.7731 oz. ASW.

Date	Mintage	F-12	VF-20	XF-40	AU-50	MS-60	MS-63
1795 Off-center bust	Inc. above	3,850	5,850	12,500	17,000	52,000	126,000

Date	Mintage	F-12	VF-20	XF-40	AU-50	MS-60	MS-63
1795 Centered bust	—	3,900	5,950	12,700	17,250	52,500	126,000
1796 small date, small letters	72,920	4,100	6,300	13,750	18,500	70,000	—
1796 small date, large letters	Inc. above	3,875	6,400	13,700	19,400	—	—
1796 large date, small letters	Inc. above	4,250	6,750	14,350	19,200	57,000	136,000
1797 9 stars left, 7 stars right, small letters	7,776	5,200	9,000	18,850	36,500	—	—
1797 9 stars left, 7 stars right, large letters	Inc. above	4,250	6,850	13,950	20,300	55,500	—
1797 10 stars left, 6 stars right	Inc. above	4,050	6,350	13,600	18,500	53,500	125,000
1798 13 stars	327,536	4,150	6,300	13,750	21,000	85,000	—
1798 15 stars	Inc. above	4,700	7,450	16,150	25,500	95,000	—

Draped Bust Dollar.

Draped bust right, flanked by stars, date below. Heraldic eagle.

KM# 32 **Designer:** Robert Scot. **Diameter:** 39-40 **Weight:** 26.9600 g. **Composition:** 0.8920 Silver, 0.7731 oz. ASW.

Date	Mintage	F-12	VF-20	XF-40	AU-50	MS-60	MS-63
1798 knob 9, 4 stripes	423,515	1,785	2,735	5,550	9,850	21,750	95,000
1798 knob 9, 10 arrows	Inc. above	1,785	2,735	5,550	9,850	21,750	87,000
1798 knob 9, 5 stripes	Inc. above	—	—	—	—	—	124,500
1798 pointed 9, 4 berries	Inc. above	1,785	2,735	5,550	9,850	21,750	43,500
1798 5 berries, 12 arrows	Inc. above	1,785	2,735	5,550	9,850	21,750	43,500
1798 high 8	Inc. above	1,785	2,735	5,550	9,850	21,750	43,500
1798 13 arrows	Inc. above	1,785	2,735	5,550	9,850	21,750	45,000
1799/98 13-star reverse	Inc. above	2,000	2,950	4,300	8,600	23,500	45,000
1799/98 15-star reverse	Inc. above	1,875	2,850	4,000	8,300	24,500	47,500
1799 irregular date, 13-star reverse	Inc. above	1,825	3,000	3,900	8,200	23,500	45,000
1799 irregular date, 15-star reverse	Inc. above	1,825	3,200	5,550	9,850	21,500	42,500
1799 perfect date, 7- and 6-star obverse, no berries	Inc. above	1,750	2,700	3,850	8,150	18,500	42,500
1799 perfect date, 7- and 6-star obverse, small berries	Inc. above	1,750	2,700	3,850	8,150	18,500	42,500
1799 perfect date, 7- and 6-star obverse, medium large berries	Inc. above	1,750	2,700	3,850	8,150	18,500	42,500
1799 perfect date, 7- and 6-star obverse, extra large berries	Inc. above	1,750	2,700	3,850	8,150	18,500	51,500
1799 8 stars left, 5 stars right on obverse	Inc. above	1,825	2,800	3,900	8,200	24,000	45,000
1800 "R" in "Liberty" double cut	220,920	1,825	2,775	5,550	9,850	21,500	45,000
1800 first "T" in "States" double cut	Inc. above	1,800	2,750	5,550	9,850	21,500	45,000
1800 both letters double cut	Inc. above	1,800	2,750	5,550	9,850	21,500	45,000
1800 "T" in "United" double cut	Inc. above	1,800	2,750	5,550	9,850	21,500	45,000
1800 very wide date, low 8	Inc. above	1,800	2,750	5,550	9,850	21,500	—
1800 small berries	Inc. above	1,850	2,800	3,900	8,200	22,000	48,500
1800 dot date	Inc. above	2,000	3,000	4,300	8,600	21,500	45,000
1800 12 arrows	Inc. above	1,825	3,200	5,550	9,850	31,000	—
1800 10 arrows	Inc. above	1,825	3,200	5,550	9,850	—	—
1800 "Americai"	Inc. above	2,000	3,300	4,300	8,600	21,500	49,000
1801	54,454	2,050	3,200	4,000	8,300	25,000	—
1801 proof restrike	—	—	—	—	—	—	—
1802/1 close	Inc. above	2,000	3,300	4,300	8,600	20,500	—
1802/1 wide	Inc. above	2,000	3,300	4,300	8,600	20,500	—
1802 close, perfect date	Inc. above	1,850	2,800	3,900	8,200	20,500	—
1802 wide, perfect date	Inc. above	1,825	2,775	3,950	8,250	21,500	—
1802 proof restrike, mintage unrecorded	—	—	—	—	—	—	—
1803 large 3	85,634	1,875	3,000	4,000	8,300	20,500	47,500
1803 small 3	Inc. above	2,000	3,300	4,300	8,600	21,500	48,500
1803 proof restrike, mintage unrecorded	—	—	—	—	—	—	—
1804 15 known	—	—	—	—	—	3,000,000	—

Note: 1804, Childs Sale, Aug. 1999, Prf-68, $4,140,000.

DOLLAR

Gobrecht Dollar.
"C Gobrecht F." in base. Eagle flying left amid stars.

KM# 59.1 Obv. Designer: Christian Gobrecht.
Diameter: 38.1 **Weight:** 26.7300 g. **Composition:** 0.9000 Silver, 0.7734 oz. ASW.

Date	Mintage	VF-20	XF-40	AU-50	Prf-60
1836	1,000	11,500	14,850	—	25,500

"C. Gobrecht F." in base. Eagle flying in plain field.

KM# 59.2 Obv. Designer: Christian Gobrecht..
Diameter: 38.1 **Weight:** 26.7300 g. **Composition:** 0.9000 Silver, 0.7734 oz. ASW.

Date	Mintage	VF-20	XF-40	AU-50	Prf-60
1836 Restrike	—	—	—	—	24,000

"C. Gobrecht F." in base.

KM# 59a.1 Diameter: 38.1 **Weight:** 26.7300 g.
Composition: 0.9000 Silver, 0.7734 oz. ASW.

Date	Mintage	VF-20	XF-40	AU-50	Prf-60
1836	600	—	—	—	—

"C. Gobrecht F." in base. Eagle flying left amid stars.

KM# 59a.2 Diameter: 38.1 **Weight:** 26.7300 g.
Composition: 0.9000 Silver, 0.7734 oz. ASW.

Date	Mintage	VF-20	XF-40	AU-50	Prf-60
1836 Restrike	—	—	—	—	—

Designer's name omitted in base. Eagle in plain field.

KM# 59a.3 Diameter: 38.1 **Weight:** 26.7300 g.
Composition: 0.9000 Silver, 0.7734 oz. ASW.

Date	Mintage	VF-20	XF-40	AU-50	Prf-60
1839	300	—	—	—	38,000

Designer's name omitted in base. Eagle in plain field.

KM# 59a.4 Diameter: 38.1 **Weight:** 26.7300 g.
Composition: 0.9000 Silver, 0.7734 oz. ASW.

Date	Mintage	VF-20	XF-40	AU-50	Prf-60
1839 Restrike	—	—	—	—	36,500

Note: All other combinations are restrikes of the late 1850's.

Seated Liberty Dollar.
Seated Liberty, date below. No motto above eagle.

KM# 71 **Designer:** Christian Gobrecht. **Diameter:** 38.1 **Weight:** 26.7300 g. **Composition:** 0.9000 Silver, 0.7734 oz. ASW.

Date	Mintage	G-4	VG-8	F-12	VF-20	XF-40	AU-50	MS-60	MS-63	MS-65	Prf-65
1840	61,005	260	300	330	400	500	925	3,950	21,500	—	—
1841	173,000	250	290	315	375	465	800	2,900	5,600	95,000	—
1842	184,618	250	290	315	375	465	800	2,450	5,100	—	—
1843	165,100	250	290	315	375	465	800	2,700	10,000	—	—
1844	20,000	265	308	360	435	785	1,250	6,400	15,000	100,000	—
1845	24,500	285	330	360	435	540	1,750	10,500	26,500	—	—
1846	110,600	260	308	345	470	650	1,100	2,700	5,950	98,000	120,000
1846O	59,000	270	325	370	460	650	1,325	8,750	20,000	—	—
1847	140,750	250	290	315	375	465	800	2,900	7,500	95,000	—
1848	15,000	310	380	475	775	1,200	1,635	4,050	9,500	65,000	—
1849	62,600	260	300	330	400	500	850	3,150	7,750	95,000	155,000
1850	7,500	450	540	645	775	1,750	2,650	7,850	15,000	—	80,000
1850O	40,000	335	400	500	750	1,550	3,950	12,850	34,500	—	—
1851	1,300	4,000	4,850	5,750	7,750	18,000	27,000	43,500	68,500	150,000	225,000
1851 Restrike	—	—	—	—	—	—	—	—	—	—	90,000
1852	1,100	3,500	4,150	5,200	7,000	15,000	26,000	38,500	60,000	150,000	200,000
1852 Restrike	—	—	—	—	—	—	—	—	—	—	70,000
1853 Restrike	—	—	400	550	660	1,100	1,425	4,000	7,950	100,000	—
1853	46,110	335	400	550	650	875	1,275	3,300	7,350	—	90,000
1854	33,140	1,000	1,450	2,000	2,850	4,500	5,750	8,500	13,500	95,000	80,000
1855	26,000	900	1,150	1,450	2,150	3,750	4,950	8,850	22,500	—	55,000
1856	63,500	400	450	650	775	1,650	2,850	4,350	11,500	—	39,500
1857	94,000	450	525	675	800	1,500	1,850	3,500	9,000	92,000	39,500
1858 proof only	Est. 800	3,200	3,600	4,000	4,800	7,250	8,850	—	—	—	42,500
Note: Later restrike.											
1859	256,500	270	330	390	495	635	1,000	2,800	6,600	92,000	17,500
1859O	360,000	250	290	315	375	465	800	2,200	4,600	56,000	—
1859S	20,000	315	390	510	750	1,550	3,500	15,000	36,500	—	—
1860	218,930	260	300	330	400	500	900	2,500	5,600	85,000	15,700
1860O	515,000	250	290	315	375	465	800	2,200	4,600	56,000	—
1861	78,500	600	760	900	985	1,500	1,975	2,950	5,650	90,000	15,700
1862	12,090	440	600	850	945	1,350	1,650	3,250	5,750	90,000	15,700
1863	27,660	375	525	575	660	975	1,400	3,250	6,000	90,000	18,000
1864	31,170	350	410	500	565	900	1,375	3,350	6,250	90,000	15,700
1865	47,000	300	350	420	550	900	1,350	3,250	6,250	90,000	15,700
1866 2 known without motto	—	—	—	—	—	—	—	—	—	—	—

Seated Liberty Dollar.

Seated Liberty, date below. IN GOD WE TRUST above eagle.

KM# 100 Designer: Christian Gobrecht. **Diameter:** 38.1 **Weight:** 26.7300 g. **Composition:** 0.9000 Silver, 0.7734 oz. ASW.

Date	Mintage	G-4	VG-8	F-12	VF-20	XF-40	AU-50	MS-60	MS-63	MS-65	Prf-65
1866	49,625	310	345	390	470	555	900	2,350	5,100	69,500	14,500
1867	47,525	305	340	385	465	550	895	2,385	5,150	71,500	14,500
1868	162,700	280	315	370	450	535	920	3,500	7,100	71,500	14,500
1869	424,300	315	350	395	475	560	885	2,350	5,100	69,500	14,500
1870	416,000	260	295	330	410	495	820	2,250	4,950	66,500	14,500
1870CC	12,462	465	600	765	1,350	2,250	6,850	23,500	42,500	—	—
1870S 12-15 known	—	150,000	235,000	350,000	475,000	625,000	1,200,000	1,750,000	2,500,000	—	—
Note: 1870S, Eliasberg Sale, April 1997, EF-45 to AU-50, $264,000.											
1871	1,074,760	260	295	330	410	495	820	2,250	4,950	66,500	14,500
1871CC	1,376	2,000	2,750	4,400	6,950	14,000	24,500	68,500	175,000	—	—
1872	1,106,450	260	295	330	410	495	820	2,250	4,950	68,500	14,500
1872CC	3,150	900	1,350	2,650	4,200	7,250	12,500	28,500	120,000	385,000	—
1872S	9,000	310	365	550	700	2,000	4,500	11,000	26,000	—	—
1873	293,600	265	305	340	420	510	840	2,300	5,000	66,500	14,500
1873CC	2,300	6,000	7,250	11,500	18,500	32,500	48,500	85,000	225,000	625,000	—
1873S none known	700	—	—	—	—	—	—	—	—	—	—

Trade Dollar.

Seated Liberty, IN GOD WE TRUST in base above date. TRADE DOLLAR below eagle.

KM# 108 Designer: William Barber. **Diameter:** 38.1 **Weight:** 27.2200 g. **Comp:** 0.9000 Silver, 0.7876 oz. ASW.

Date	Mintage	G-4	VG-8	F-12	VF-20	XF-40	AU-50	MS-60	MS-65	Prf-65
1873	397,500	100.00	125	144	200	250	360	1,050	12,500	11,000
1873CC	124,500	230	275	330	450	700	1,475	8,850	122,000	—
1873S	703,000	115	135	155	210	265	385	1,450	15,500	—
1874	987,800	100.00	130	150	185	250	365	1,150	13,850	10,800
1874CC	1,373,200	235	265	310	375	600	775	3,250	26,500	—
1874S	2,549,000	90.00	135	140	150	175	270	975	11,000	—
1875	218,900	160	185	375	460	590	850	2,450	13,000	10,700
1875CC	1,573,700	200	255	285	335	510	675	2,150	40,000	—
1875S	4,487,000	80.00	125	130	140	165	260	960	11,000	—
1875S/CC	Inc. above	220	285	375	560	925	1,450	4,650	65,000	—
1876	456,150	90.00	135	140	150	175	270	950	7,500	10,500
1876CC	509,000	235	265	300	365	525	720	6,000	78,500	—
1876S	5,227,000	80.00	125	130	140	165	260	940	11,000	—
1877	3,039,710	90.00	135	140	150	175	270	950	16,000	10,500

Date	Mintage	G-4	VG-8	F-12	VF-20	XF-40	AU-50	MS-60	MS-65	Prf-65
1877CC	534,000	235	275	320	410	700	800	2,450	60,000	—
1877S	9,519,000	80.00	125	130	140	165	260	940	11,000	—
1878 proof only	900	—	—	—	1,200	1,300	1,500	—	—	13,500
1878CC	97,000	425	525	710	1,050	2,400	4,200	12,000	112,000	—
1878S	4,162,000	80.00	125	130	140	165	260	940	11,000	—
1879 proof only	1,541	—	—	—	1,175	1,275	1,400	—	—	10,500
1880 proof only	1,987	—	—	—	1,150	1,250	1,350	—	—	10,500
1881 proof only	960	—	—	—	1,200	1,300	1,400	—	—	10,500
1882 proof only	1,097	—	—	—	1,175	1,275	1,375	—	—	10,500
1883 proof only	979	—	—	—	1,200	1,300	1,400	—	—	10,500
1884 proof only	10	—	—	—	—	—	100,000	—	—	—

Note: 1884, Eliasberg Sale, April 1997, Prf-66, $396,000.

Date	Mintage	G-4	VG-8	F-12	VF-20	XF-40	AU-50	MS-60	MS-65	Prf-65
1885 proof only	5	—	—	—	—	—	—	—	—	—

Note: 1885, Eliasberg Sale, April 1997, Prf-65, $907,500.

Morgan Dollar.

Laureate head left, date below flanked by stars. Eagle within 1/2 wreath.

KM# 110   Designer: George T. Morgan. **Diameter:** 38.1 **Weight:** 26.7300 g. **Composition:** 0.9000 Silver, 0.7734 oz. ASW. **Notes:** "65DMPL" values are for coins grading MS-65 deep-mirror prooflike. The 1878 "8 tail feathers" and "7 tail feathers" varieties are distinguished by the number of feathers in the eagle's tail. On the "reverse of 1878" varieties, the top of the top feather in the arrows held by the eagle is straight across and the eagle's breast is concave. On the "reverse of 1879 varieties," the top feather in the arrows held by the eagle is slanted and the eagle's breast is convex. The 1890-CC "tail-bar variety has a bar extending from the arrow feathers to the wreath on the reverse, the result of a die gouge. The Pittman Act of 1918 authorized the melting of 270 Million pieces of various dates. They were not indivudually recorded.

8 Tail feathers

7 Tail feathers

7/8 Tail feathers

Date	Mintage	VG-8	F-12	VF-20	XF-40	AU-50	MS-60	MS-63	MS-64	MS-65	65DMPL	Prf-65
1878 8 tail feathers	750,000	29.00	32.00	37.50	46.00	74.00	128	175	385	1,500	23,500	8,350
1878 7 over 8 tail feathers	9,759,550	21.00	24.50	27.50	41.50	75.00	145	325	500	2,350	17,000	—
1878 7 tail feathers, reverse of 1878	Inc. above	20.50	22.00	23.00	25.00	40.00	74.00	98.00	228	1,215	11,650	11,500
1878 7 tail feathers, reverse of 1879	Inc. above	21.00	23.00	25.00	27.00	43.50	80.00	175	500	2,650	24,500	185,000
1878CC	2,212,000	98.50	100.00	110	125	150	220	390	510	1,940	10,800	—
1878S	9,744,000	20.00	21.00	22.50	27.00	37.50	60.00	63.50	100.00	265	11,650	—
1879	14,807,100	19.80	18.60	21.10	22.30	27.10	39.90	60.00	129	895	17,250	7,550
1879CC	756,000	165	185	285	735	1,900	4,150	6,500	9,450	29,850	49,000	—
1879CC capped CC	Inc. above	160	175	270	700	1,800	4,000	6,350	9,650	46,500	63,500	—
1879O	2,887,000	19.80	18.60	21.10	23.30	33.10	75.00	185	525	4,000	28,500	—
1879S reverse of 1878	9,110,000	22.50	23.50	25.00	30.00	47.50	125	375	1,275	7,300	24,000	—
1879S reverse of 1879	9,110,000	19.80	18.60	21.10	22.30	25.10	41.90	47.00	55.00	133	1,300	—
1880	12,601,335	19.80	18.60	21.10	22.60	27.60	39.90	51.00	140	855	6,350	7,350
1880CC reverse of 1878	591,000	175	210	245	300	355	575	660	1,300	2,750	21,500	—
1880CC 80/79 reverse of 1878	Inc. above	190	230	270	335	410	640	850	1,700	4,000	—	—

Date	Mintage	VG-8	F-12	VF-20	XF-40	AU-50	MS-60	MS-63	MS-64	MS-65	65DMPL	Prf-65
1880CC 8/7 reverse of 1878	Inc. above	170	200	235	290	360	600	700	1,300	2,950	—	—
1880CC reverse of 1879	Inc. above	170	200	240	285	345	550	575	725	1,550	9,850	—
1880CC 8/7 high 7 reverse of 1879	Inc. above	175	205	245	290	355	575	620	800	1,850	—	—
1880CC 8/7 low 7 reverse of 1879	Inc. above	175	205	245	290	355	575	620	800	1,850	—	—
1880O	5,305,000	20.10	18.60	21.10	23.30	27.60	60.00	355	2,050	28,500	70,000	—
1880S	8,900,000	19.80	18.60	21.10	22.30	25.10	41.90	44.00	55.00	133	775	—
1880S 8/7 crossbar	—	23.80	23.60	28.10	45.00	75.00	90.00	265	335	450	—	—
1881	9,163,975	19.80	18.60	21.10	22.30	25.10	39.90	63.00	150	825	21,750	7,650
1881CC	296,000	375	385	410	425	460	555	525	680	1,170	2,850	—
1881O	5,708,000	19.80	18.60	21.10	22.30	25.10	39.50	47.00	220	1,675	35,000	—
1881S	12,760,000	19.80	18.60	21.10	22.30	25.10	40.90	44.00	55.00	133	850	—
1882	11,101,100	19.80	18.60	21.10	22.30	25.10	43.90	47.00	67.00	570	6,800	7,350
1882CC	1,133,000	92.00	100.00	110	130	155	220	235	265	525	1,950	—
1882O	6,090,000	20.10	18.60	21.10	23.30	27.10	39.00	52.00	110	1,385	6,900	—
1882O/S	Inc. above	30.00	40.00	48.00	72.00	115	255	1,150	3,250	61,500	65,000	—
1882S	9,250,000	19.80	18.60	21.10	22.30	25.10	40.90	47.00	60.00	135	3,850	—
1883	12,291,039	19.80	18.60	21.10	22.30	25.10	39.90	44.00	58.00	255	1,650	7,500
1883CC	1,204,000	92.00	100.00	110	130	155	215	215	250	505	1,675	—
1883O	8,725,000	19.80	18.60	21.10	22.30	25.10	36.90	44.00	55.00	210	1,400	—
1883S	6,250,000	19.80	19.60	24.60	33.50	145	635	2,700	5,250	50,000	94,500	—
1884	14,070,875	19.80	18.60	21.10	22.30	25.10	39.90	47.00	65.50	330	4,350	7,350
1884CC	1,136,000	125	135	160	175	195	215	220	235	475	1,500	—
1884O	9,730,000	19.80	18.60	21.10	22.30	25.10	37.90	44.00	55.00	165	1,000	—
1884S	3,200,000	19.80	19.10	23.10	43.00	310	5,750	30,500	110,000	235,000	220,000	—
1885	17,787,767	19.80	18.60	21.10	22.30	25.10	36.90	47.00	55.00	169	845	7,350
1885CC	228,000	550	585	600	630	632	640	665	660	1,275	2,650	—
1885O	9,185,000	19.80	18.60	21.10	22.30	25.10	36.90	44.00	55.00	133	1,000	—
1885S	1,497,000	21.00	28.00	40.00	64.00	125	240	305	745	1,950	42,500	—
1886	19,963,886	19.80	18.60	21.10	22.30	25.10	36.90	44.00	55.00	133	1,275	7,350
1886O	10,710,000	19.80	18.60	21.60	30.30	78.00	685	3,550	11,500	190,000	300,000	—
1886S	750,000	47.50	62.50	85.00	90.00	180	320	465	800	3,250	30,000	—
1887	20,290,710	19.80	18.60	21.10	22.30	25.10	36.90	44.00	55.00	133	1,200	7,350
1887/6	Inc. above	23.00	26.00	34.00	55.00	165	425	585	1,000	2,450	44,750	—
1887O	11,550,000	19.80	18.60	23.10	25.30	25.00	52.00	110	370	2,500	12,000	—
1887/6O	—	24.00	30.00	39.00	65.00	190	450	2,150	7,950	32,000	—	—
1887S	1,771,000	20.30	19.10	24.60	29.30	44.00	110	242	715	3,100	29,500	—
1888	19,183,833	19.80	18.60	21.10	22.30	25.10	39.90	44.00	55.00	205	3,000	7,500
1888O	12,150,000	19.80	18.60	21.10	22.30	25.10	39.90	48.00	73.00	690	2,850	—
1888O Hot Lips	Inc. above	55.00	125	250	600	3,000	—	—	—	—	—	—
1888S	657,000	115	190	210	225	235	300	465	900	2,850	16,500	—
1889	21,726,811	19.80	18.60	21.10	22.30	25.10	38.90	44.00	58.00	375	4,050	7,350
1889CC	350,000	610	935	1,275	2,700	5,500	22,500	41,500	58,500	320,000	—	—
1889O	11,875,000	20.40	18.60	23.10	24.00	31.50	130	365	825	7,000	14,500	—
1889S	700,000	37.50	60.00	65.00	82.00	125	195	345	610	2,000	38,500	—
1890	16,802,590	19.80	18.60	21.10	22.30	25.10	39.90	44.00	155	2,850	19,750	7,350
1890CC	2,309,041	96.00	100.00	110	160	245	450	785	1,550	5,750	15,500	—
1890CC tail bar	Inc. above	155	175	225	400	700	1,450	3,600	5,500	—	—	—
1890O	10,701,000	20.30	19.10	23.10	23.00	35.00	63.00	98.00	275	1,925	10,000	—
1890S	8,230,373	20.10	18.60	21.60	24.30	28.00	56.00	95.00	282	1,065	10,500	—
1891	8,694,206	20.30	18.60	22.10	24.30	26.00	55.00	175	885	8,250	27,500	7,350
1891CC	1,618,000	96.00	98.50	110	150	220	350	700	1,185	4,750	34,500	—
1891CC Spitting Eagle	Inc. above	105	115	135	185	260	425	900	1,600	6,000	—	—
1891O	7,954,529	20.30	18.60	21.60	24.30	35.00	128	320	775	9,850	37,500	—
1891S	5,296,000	20.30	18.60	22.10	24.30	32.60	56.00	125	300	1,475	20,500	—
1892	1,037,245	23.30	22.60	27.10	35.00	75.00	155	435	1,050	4,850	20,500	7,500
1892CC	1,352,000	190	210	290	485	725	1,485	1,800	2,625	8,950	39,500	—
1892O	2,744,000	23.30	22.60	27.10	35.00	67.50	145	288	750	7,150	52,500	—
1892S	1,200,000	26.00	32.00	136	320	1,750	34,500	63,500	115,000	205,000	225,000	—
1893	378,792	245	250	260	300	400	700	970	1,875	7,000	66,000	7,500
1893CC	677,000	265	345	725	1,850	2,350	3,700	5,650	9,850	70,000	90,000	—
1893O	300,000	205	250	380	620	975	2,250	7,500	17,850	210,000	215,000	—
1893S	100,000	3,450	4,200	5,550	8,400	23,500	90,000	205,000	350,000	715,000	735,000	—
1894	110,972	1,425	1,485	1,550	1,700	1,825	3,650	5,975	10,600	49,000	78,000	7,500
1894O	1,723,000	55.00	57.00	59.00	92.00	310	580	3,850	11,750	63,500	61,500	—
1894S	1,260,000	62.00	65.00	110	150	510	695	1,050	1,950	5,650	26,000	—
1895 proof only	12,880	21,500	29,500	36,500	38,500	40,500	—	—	—	—	—	80,000
1895O	450,000	315	350	480	585	1,275	15,500	57,500	85,000	165,000	—	—
1895S	400,000	450	510	775	1,175	1,875	3,850	6,650	7,000	27,500	42,500	—
1896	9,967,762	19.80	18.60	21.10	22.30	25.10	39.90	45.00	58.00	195	1,450	7,350
1896O	4,900,000	20.30	18.60	22.10	29.80	185	1,450	8,350	46,000	180,000	180,000	—
1896S	5,000,000	23.30	35.00	60.00	235	895	1,775	3,450	4,850	19,500	110,000	—
1897	2,822,731	19.80	18.60	21.10	22.30	25.10	39.90	45.00	62.00	345	3,950	7,350
1897O	4,004,000	20.30	19.60	23.10	38.30	110	735	4,850	15,900	70,000	72,500	—

Date	Mintage	VG-8	F-12	VF-20	XF-40	AU-50	MS-60	MS-63	MS-64	MS-65	65DMPL	Prf-65
1897S	5,825,000	20.30	18.60	22.10	24.30	30.60	58.00	115	175	600	3,250	—
1898	5,884,735	19.80	18.60	21.10	22.80	25.10	39.90	45.00	58.00	240	1,440	7,350
1898O	4,440,000	19.80	18.60	21.10	22.80	25.10	40.40	45.00	56.00	169	975	—
1898S	4,102,000	21.80	25.00	35.00	55.00	105	260	475	635	2,550	18,000	—
1899	330,846	170	185	215	240	265	295	310	395	1,000	2,850	7,350
1899O	12,290,000	19.80	18.60	21.10	22.30	25.10	39.90	44.00	60.00	175	1,550	—
1899S	2,562,000	22.30	26.00	37.50	62.50	125	320	460	775	2,075	26,000	—
1900	8,880,938	19.80	18.60	21.10	22.30	25.10	39.90	44.00	65.00	195	42,500	7,350
1900O	12,590,000	19.80	18.60	21.10	22.30	25.10	39.90	44.00	65.00	186	6,250	—
1900O/CC	Inc. above	37.50	47.50	62.50	100.00	190	285	780	960	2,000	19,000	—
1900S	3,540,000	21.80	21.00	25.00	40.00	85.00	325	420	615	1,450	38,500	—
1901	6,962,813	27.50	36.00	57.50	110	350	2,350	17,250	55,000	375,000	—	7,850
1901 doubled die reverse	Inc. above	275	450	900	2,000	3,850	—	—	—	—	—	—
1901O	13,320,000	19.80	20.60	21.10	22.30	28.10	39.90	44.00	58.00	225	10,000	—
1901S	2,284,000	20.30	23.10	31.50	46.50	220	470	715	1,050	3,900	22,000	—
1902	7,994,777	20.30	20.60	22.10	24.30	25.00	44.00	100.00	145	495	19,500	7,350
1902O	8,636,000	19.80	20.60	21.10	22.30	25.10	38.90	44.00	56.00	177	16,000	—
1902S	1,530,000	77.00	93.00	160	220	315	425	625	975	2,950	15,000	—
1903	4,652,755	48.00	50.00	52.00	58.00	60.00	75.00	85.00	100.00	310	36,850	7,350
1903O	4,450,000	325	350	375	395	400	412	425	465	685	5,950	—
1903S	1,241,000	95.00	130	215	425	1,750	3,950	6,500	7,750	11,850	40,000	—
1903S Micro S	Inc. above	135	225	450	1,150	3,000	—	—	—	—	—	—
1904	2,788,650	21.00	23.00	25.00	27.00	32.00	78.00	245	610	3,500	86,500	7,350
1904O	3,720,000	21.00	23.00	25.00	27.00	29.00	37.00	44.00	55.00	163	1,165	—
1904S	2,304,000	35.00	47.50	87.00	230	570	1,200	3,850	5,500	10,500	19,000	—
1921	44,690,000	18.10	20.10	20.50	21.30	23.20	27.40	35.00	44.00	145	11,500	—
1921D	20,345,000	18.20	20.30	20.80	21.50	24.30	43.00	57.50	155	420	10,000	—
1921S	21,695,000	18.20	20.30	20.80	21.40	24.20	43.00	69.00	170	1,425	31,000	—

Peace Dollar.

Liberty Head left. Eagle facing right perched on rock.

KM# 150   Designer: Anthony DeFrancisci. **Diameter:** 38.1 **Weight:** 26.7300 g. **Composition:** 0.9000 Silver, 0.7734 oz. ASW.

Mint mark

Date	Mintage	G-4	VG-8	F-12	VF-20	XF-40	AU-50	MS-60	MS-63	MS-64	MS-65
1921	1,006,473	100.00	125	135	140	150	170	260	440	735	1,675
1922	51,737,000	16.90	17.00	17.10	17.20	17.30	18.10	26.80	32.00	44.00	150
1922D	15,063,000	16.90	17.30	17.10	17.20	17.30	19.00	26.50	53.00	105	660
1922S	17,475,000	16.90	17.30	17.10	17.20	17.30	19.00	26.50	69.00	285	2,475
1923	30,800,000	16.90	17.00	17.10	17.20	17.30	18.10	26.80	32.00	44.00	145
1923D	6,811,000	16.90	16.00	16.50	17.00	18.00	22.00	52.00	138	290	1,350
1923S	19,020,000	16.90	17.30	17.10	17.20	17.30	19.00	28.50	74.00	355	8,500
1924	11,811,000	16.90	17.00	16.50	17.20	17.30	18.10	26.80	32.00	44.00	168
1924S	1,728,000	25.00	30.00	31.00	33.00	44.00	66.50	180	525	1,375	10,750
1925	10,198,000	16.90	17.00	16.50	17.20	17.30	18.10	23.00	32.00	44.00	177
1925S	1,610,000	17.80	19.50	21.00	25.00	29.00	46.00	75.00	210	825	27,500
1926	1,939,000	17.80	17.90	18.20	18.50	18.80	22.50	43.00	82.00	118	510
1926D	2,348,700	17.80	17.90	18.00	18.30	22.00	32.50	66.00	190	330	900
1926S	6,980,000	17.50	17.60	17.70	17.80	17.90	21.10	44.00	110	245	1,225
1927	848,000	25.00	29.00	32.00	33.00	38.00	50.00	70.00	185	535	3,650
1927D	1,268,900	24.00	28.00	30.00	31.00	34.00	80.00	148	350	1,050	5,600
1927S	866,000	24.00	28.00	31.00	32.00	35.00	80.00	148	430	1,125	10,850
1928	360,649	345	385	390	395	400	415	495	875	1,150	4,850
1928S Large S	1,632,000	30.00	36.00	40.00	46.00	54.00	90.00	220	800	2,100	29,500
1928S Small S	Inc. above	28.00	33.00	34.00	38.00	43.50	66.00	155	500	1,100	24,850
1934	954,057	20.00	20.00	21.00	21.50	22.50	46.00	120	245	400	725
1934D Large D	1,569,500	17.00	20.00	23.00	23.50	42.00	65.00	165	600	925	3,000
1934D Small D	Inc. above	17.80	17.90	21.00	21.50	36.00	46.00	135	385	655	1,925
1934S	1,011,000	26.00	31.00	48.00	85.00	200	475	1,800	3,850	4,850	8,400
1935	1,576,000	17.00	18.00	21.00	21.50	24.50	30.00	55.00	105	220	765
1935S	1,964,000	17.00	18.00	21.00	21.50	23.00	92.00	235	380	550	1,125

Eisenhower Dollar.

KM# 203 **Designer:** Frank Gasparro. **Diameter:** 38 **Weight:** 22.8000 g. **Composition:** Copper-Nickel Clad Copper

Date	Mintage	Proof	MS-63	Prf-65
1971	47,799,000	—	10.00	—
1971D	68,587,424	—	8.00	—
1972 Low Relief	75,890,000	—	6.50	—
1972 High Relief	Inc. above	—	175	—
1972 Modified High Relief	Inc. above	—	40.00	—
1972D	92,548,511	—	5.50	—
1973	2,000,056	—	14.00	—
1973D	2,000,000	—	15.00	—
1973S	—	2,769,624	—	12.00
1974	27,366,000	—	5.50	—
1974D	35,466,000	—	7.00	—
1974S	—	2,617,350	—	11.00

Eisenhower Dollar.

KM# 203a **Designer:** Frank Gasparro. **Diameter:** 38.1 **Weight:** 24.5900 g. **Composition:** 0.4000 Silver, 0.3162 oz. ASW.

Date	Mintage	Proof	MS-63	Prf-65
1971S	6,868,530	—	7.50	—
1971S	—	4,265,234	—	11.00
1971S Peg Leg "R" Variety	Inc. above	—	—	17.00
1971S Partial Peg Leg "R" Variety	Inc. above	—	—	18.00
1972S	2,193,056	—	7.50	—
1972S	—	1,811,631	—	14.00
1973S	1,833,140	—	8.50	—
1973S	—	1,005,617	—	35.00
1974S	1,720,000	—	7.50	—
1974S	—	1,306,579	—	14.00

Eisenhower Dollar.

Bicentennial design, moon behind Liberty Bell.

KM# 206 **Rev. Designer:** Dennis R. Williams. **Diameter:** 38.1 **Weight:** 22.6800 g. **Composition:** Copper-Nickel Clad Copper **Notes:** In 1976 the lettering on the reverse was changed to thinner letters, resulting in the Type II variety for that year. The Type I variety was minted 1975 and dated 1976.

Type I
Squared "T"

Type II
Slant-top "T"

Date	Mintage	Proof	MS-63	Prf-65
1976 type I	117,337,000	—	9.00	—
1976 type II	Inc. above	—	5.00	—
1976D type I	103,228,274	—	6.00	—
1976D type II	Inc. above	—	5.00	—
1976S type I	—	2,909,369	—	13.00
1976S type II	—	4,149,730	—	9.00

Eisenhower Dollar.
Bicentennial design, moon behind Liberty Bell.

KM# 206a   Rev. Designer: Dennis R. Williams. **Weight:** 24.5900 g. **Composition:** 0.4000 Silver, 0.3162 oz. ASW.

Date	Mintage	Proof	MS-63	Prf-65
1976S	4,908,319	—	12.50	—
1976S	—	3,998,621	—	20.00

Eisenhower Dollar.
Regular design resumed.

KM# A203   Diameter: 38.1 **Composition:** Copper-Nickel Clad Copper

Date	Mintage	Proof	MS-63	Prf-65
1977	12,596,000	—	7.00	—
1977D	32,983,006	—	7.00	—
1977S	—	3,251,152	—	10.00
1978	25,702,000	—	5.00	—
1978D	33,012,890	—	5.00	—
1978S	—	3,127,788	—	12.00

Susan B. Anthony Dollar.
Susan B. Anthony bust right. Eagle landing on moon, symbolic of Apollo manned moon landing.

KM# 207   Designer: Frank Gasparro. **Diameter:** 26.5 **Weight:** 8.1000 g. **Composition:** Copper-Nickel Clad Copper **Notes:** The 1979-S and 1981-S Type II coins have a clearer mint mark than the Type I varieties for those years.

Date	Mintage	MS-63	Prf-65
1979P Near date	360,222,000	70.00	—
1979P	Inc. above	2.50	—
1979D	288,015,744	3.00	—
1979S Proof, Type I	(3,677,175)	—	8.00
1979S Proof, Type II	Inc. above	—	110
1979S	109,576,000	3.00	—
1980P	27,610,000	3.00	—
1980D	41,628,708	3.00	—
1980S	20,422,000	3.50	—
1980S Proof	3,547,030	—	8.00
1981P	3,000,000	7.50	—
1981D	3,250,000	7.50	—
1981S	3,492,000	7.50	—
1981S Proof, Type I	4,063,083	—	8.00
1981S Proof, Type II	Inc. above	—	230
1999P	29,592,000	4.00	—
1999P Proof	Est. 750,000	—	25.00
1999D	11,776,000	4.00	—

Sacagawea Dollar.
Sacagawea bust right, with baby on back. Eagle in flight left.

KM# 310   Diameter: 26.4 **Weight:** 8.0700 g. **Composition:** Copper-Zinc-Manganese-Nickel Clad Copper

Date	Mintage	MS-63	Prf-65
2000P	767,140,000	2.00	—
2000D	518,916,000	2.00	—
2000S	4,048,865	—	10.00
2001P	62,468,000	2.00	—
2001D	70,909,500	2.00	—
2001S	(3,084,600)	—	100.00
2002P	3,865,610	2.00	—
2002D	3,732,000	2.00	—
2002S	(3,157,739)	—	28.50
2003P	3,090,000	3.00	—
2003D	3,090,000	3.00	—
2003S	(3,116,590)	—	20.00
2004P	2,660,000	2.50	—
2004D	2,660,000	2.50	—
2004S	—	—	22.50
2005P	2,520,000	2.50	—
2005D	2,520,000	2.50	—
2005S	—	—	22.50
2006P	4,900,000	2.50	—
2006D	2,800,000	5.00	—
2006S	—	—	22.50
2007P	—	2.50	—
2007D	—	2.50	—
2007S	—	—	22.50
2008P	—	2.50	—
2008D	—	2.50	—
2008S	—	—	22.50

Presidents
George Washington

KM# 401   Diameter: 26.4 **Weight:** 8.0700 g. **Composition:** Copper-Zinc-Manganese-Nickel Clad Copper **Notes:** Date and mint mark incuse on edge.

Date	Mintage	MS-63	MS-65	Prf-65
2007P	176,680,000	2.00	5.00	—
(2007) Plain edge error	Inc. above	75.00	—	—
2007D	163,680,000	2.00	5.00	—
2007S	—	—	—	8.00

DOLLAR

James Madison

KM# 404 Diameter: 26.4 **Weight:** 8.0700 g.
Composition: Copper-Zinc-Manganese-Nickel Clad
Copper **Notes:** Date and mint mark incuse on edge.

Date	Mintage	MS-63	MS-65	Prf-65
2007P	—	2.00	5.00	—
2007D	—	2.00	5.00	—
2007S	—	—	—	8.00

Andrew Jackson

KM# 428 Diameter: 26.4 **Weight:** 8.0700 g.
Composition: Copper-Zinc-Manganese-Nickel Clad
Copper **Notes:** Date and mint mark incuse on edge.

Date	Mintage	MS-63	MS-65	Prf-65
2008P	61,180,000	2.00	5.00	—
2008D	61,070,000	2.00	5.00	—
2008S	—	—	—	8.00

John Adams

KM# 402 Diameter: 26.4 **Weight:** 8.0700 g.
Composition: Copper-Zinc-Manganese-Nickel Clad
Copper **Notes:** Date and mint mark incuse on edge.

Date	Mintage	MS-63	MS-65	Prf-65
2007P	112,420,000	2.00	5.00	—
2007P Double edge lettering	Inc. above	250	—	—
2007D	102,810,000	2.00	5.00	—
2007S	—	—	—	8.00

James Monroe

KM# 426 Diameter: 26.4 **Weight:** 8.0700 g.
Composition: Copper-Zinc-Manganese-Nickel Clad
Copper **Weight:** Date and mint mark incuse on edge.

Date	Mintage	MS-63	MS-65	Prf-65
2008P	64,260,000	2.00	5.00	—
2008D	60,230,000	2.00	5.00	—
2008S	—	—	—	8.00

Thomas Jefferson

KM# 403 Diameter: 26.4 **Weight:** 8.0700 g.
Composition: Copper-Zinc-Manganese-Nickel Clad
Copper **Notes:** Date and mint mark incuse on edge.

Date	Mintage	MS-63	MS-65	Prf-65
2007P	—	2.00	5.00	—
2007D	—	2.00	5.00	—
2007S	—	—	—	8.00

John Quincy Adams

KM# 427 Diameter: 26.4 **Weight:** 8.0700 g.
Composition: Copper-Zinc-Manganese-Nickel Clad
Copper **Notes:** Date and mint mark incuse on edge.

Date	Mintage	MS-63	MS-65	Prf-65
2008P	57,540,000	2.00	5.00	—
2008D	57,720,000	2.00	5.00	—
2008S	—	—	—	8.00

Martin van Buren

KM# 429   **Diameter:** 26.4 **Weight:** 8.0700 g.
Composition: Copper-Zinc-Manganese-Nickel Clad
Copper **Notes:** Date and mint mark incuse on edge.

Date	Mintage	MS-63	MS-65	Prf-65
2008P	51,520,000	2.00	5.00	—
2008D	50,960,000	2.00	5.00	—
2008S	—	—	—	8.00

GOLD

Liberty Head - Type 1.

Liberty head left within circle of stars.
Value, date within 3/4 wreath.

KM# 73   **Designer:** James B. Longacre. **Diameter:**
13 **Weight:** 1.6720 g. **Composition:** 0.9000 Gold,
0.0484 oz. AGW. **Notes:** On the "closed wreath"
varieties of 1849, the wreath on the reverse extends
closer to the numeral 1.

Date	Mintage	F-12	VF-20	XF-40	AU-50	MS-60
1849 open wreath	688,567	120	175	220	300	650
1849 small head, no L	—	—	—	—	—	—
1849 closed wreath	Inc. above	120	160	200	215	260
1849C closed wreath	11,634	800	950	1,450	2,400	8,850
1849C open wreath	Inc. above	135,000	240,000	320,000	475,000	600,000
1849D open wreath	21,588	1,050	1,300	1,875	2,600	6,000
1849O open wreath	215,000	140	185	265	335	800
1850	481,953	120	160	200	295	260
1850C	6,966	900	1,150	1,600	2,350	9,000
1850D	8,382	1,050	1,250	1,725	2,950	12,500
1850O	14,000	200	275	390	775	3,300
1851	3,317,671	120	160	200	215	260
1851C	41,267	840	1,150	1,500	1,700	3,150
1851D	9,882	1,000	1,250	1,675	2,500	5,650
1851O	290,000	160	195	240	265	775
1852	2,045,351	120	160	200	215	260
1852C	9,434	845	1,040	1,400	1,700	5,100
1852D	6,360	1,025	1,250	1,675	2,300	10,000
1852O	140,000	130	175	260	385	1,400
1853	4,076,051	120	160	200	215	260
1853C	11,515	900	1,100	1,400	2,000	5,600
1853D	6,583	1,040	1,250	1,700	2,650	9,700
1853O	290,000	135	160	235	270	665
1854	736,709	120	160	200	215	260
1854D	2,935	1,050	1,400	2,350	6,000	13,000
1854S	14,632	260	360	525	775	2,450

Indian Head - Type 2.

Indian head with headdress left.
Value, date within wreath.

KM# 83   **Designer:** James B. Longacre. **Diameter:**
15 **Weight:** 1.6720 g. **Composition:** 0.9000 Gold,
0.0484 oz. AGW.

Date	Mintage	F-12	VF-20	XF-40	AU-50	MS-60
1854	902,736	225	310	440	575	2,350
1855	758,269	225	310	440	575	2,350
1855C	9,803	975	1,450	3,750	11,500	33,000
1855D	1,811	3,250	4,750	9,800	22,000	48,000
1855O	55,000	345	440	600	1,500	7,800
1856S	24,600	525	820	1,325	2,500	8,650

Indian Head - Type 3.
Indian head with headdress left.
Value, date within wreath.

KM# 86 Designer: James B. Longacre. **Diameter:**
15 **Weight:** 1.6720 g. **Composition:** 0.9000 Gold,
0.0484 oz. AGW. **Notes:** The 1856 varieties are
distinguished by whether the 5 in the date is slanted
or upright. The 1873 varieties are distinguished by
the amount of space between the upper left and lower
left serifs in the 3.

Date	Mintage	F-12	VF-20	XF-40	AU-50	MS-60	Prf-65
1856 upright 5	1,762,936	140	170	225	250	460	—
1856 slanted 5	Inc. above	135	160	200	215	310	55,000
1856D	1,460	2,350	3,650	5,800	8,000	32,000	—
1857	774,789	125	155	200	215	310	32,000
1857C	13,280	900	1,150	1,750	3,750	13,250	—
1857D	3,533	1,000	1,300	2,300	4,400	11,000	—
1857S	10,000	260	520	650	1,300	6,200	—
1858	117,995	125	155	200	215	310	28,500
1858D	3,477	1,025	1,250	1,600	2,850	10,000	—
1858S	10,000	300	400	575	1,450	5,350	—
1859	168,244	125	155	200	215	310	17,000
1859C	5,235	885	1,050	1,700	4,250	9,850	—
1859D	4,952	1,050	1,500	2,100	3,250	10,500	—
1859S	15,000	210	265	525	1,250	5,500	—
1860	36,668	125	155	200	215	310	16,500
1860D	1,566	2,150	2,500	4,200	7,000	13,500	—
1860S	13,000	300	380	500	750	1,650	—
1861	527,499	125	155	200	215	310	14,850
1861D mintage unrecorded	—	4,950	7,000	11,000	21,000	41,500	—
1862	1,361,390	125	155	200	215	310	15,000
1863	6,250	370	500	925	2,100	3,900	18,000
1864	5,950	290	370	475	825	1,050	18,000
1865	3,725	290	370	590	750	1,600	18,000
1866	7,130	300	385	470	685	1,025	18,000
1867	5,250	325	420	525	675	1,160	17,500
1868	10,525	265	290	415	500	1,025	19,000
1869	5,925	315	460	530	725	1,150	17,000
1870	6,335	255	290	410	500	875	16,000
1870S	3,000	300	475	785	1,250	2,650	—
1871	3,930	260	290	390	480	750	18,000
1872	3,530	260	295	400	480	975	18,500
1873 closed 3	125,125	325	425	825	950	1,650	—
1873 open 3	Inc. above	125	155	200	215	310	—
1874	198,820	125	155	200	215	310	30,000
1875	420	1,650	2,350	4,650	5,200	10,000	32,500
1876	3,245	240	300	360	475	725	16,750
1877	3,920	150	210	340	460	725	18,000
1878	3,020	195	250	365	480	675	15,500
1879	3,030	170	225	285	3,300	525	14,000
1880	1,636	150	180	215	245	425	14,000
1881	7,707	150	180	215	245	410	11,500
1882	5,125	160	185	215	245	410	10,500
1883	11,007	150	175	215	245	410	11,000
1884	6,236	150	175	215	245	410	10,000
1885	12,261	150	175	215	245	410	10,000
1886	6,016	150	175	215	245	410	10,000
1887	8,543	150	175	215	245	410	10,000
1888	16,580	150	175	215	245	410	10,000
1889	30,729	150	175	215	245	340	10,000

$2.50 (QUARTER EAGLE)

GOLD

Liberty Cap.
Liberty cap on head, right, flanked by stars. Heraldic eagle.
KM# 27 Designer: Robert Scot. **Diameter:** 20 **Weight:** 4.3700 g. **Composition:** 0.9160 Gold, 0.1287 oz. AGW. **Notes:** The 1796 "no stars" variety does not have stars on the obverse. The 1804 varieties are distinguished by the number of stars on the obverse.

Date	Mintage	F-12	VF-20	XF-40	MS-60
1796 no stars	963	30,000	42,000	70,000	165,000
1796 stars	432	28,000	40,000	63,000	140,000
1797	427	17,000	23,000	27,500	120,000
1798	1,094	4,750	10,000	12,500	55,000
1802/1	3,035	4,400	8,000	9,500	32,000
1804 13-star reverse	3,327	23,500	36,500	72,000	200,000
1804 14-star reverse	Inc. above	4,800	7,400	9,000	27,500
1805	1,781	6,000	7,500	9,000	21,000
1806/4	1,616	5,750	8,000	9,500	23,000
1806/5	Inc. above	6,000	8,000	18,000	77,000
1807	6,812	5,500	7,000	9.00	21,000

Turban Head.
Turban on head left flanked by stars. Banner above eagle.
KM# 40 Designer: John Reich. **Diameter:** 20 **Weight:** 4.3700 g. **Composition:** 0.9160 Gold, 0.1287 oz. AGW.

Date	Mintage	F-12	VF-20	XF-40	MS-60
1808	2,710	22,500	31,000	45,000	125,000

Turban Head.
Turban on head left within circle of stars. Banner above eagle.
KM# 46 Designer: John Reich. **Diameter:** 18.5 **Weight:** 4.3700 g. **Composition:** 0.9160 Gold, 0.1287 oz. AGW.

Date	Mintage	F-12	VF-20	XF-40	MS-60
1821	6,448	5,500	6,250	7,500	23,000
1824/21	2,600	5,500	6,250	7,250	22,000
1825	4,434	5,500	6,500	7,800	21,000
1826/25	760	6,000	7,000	8,500	36,000
1827	2,800	5,500	7,500	9,000	22,500

Turban Head.
Turban on head left within circle of stars. Banner above eagle.
KM# 49 Designer: John Reich. **Diameter:** 18.2 **Weight:** 4.3700 g. **Composition:** 0.9160 Gold, 0.1287 oz. AGW.

Date	Mintage	F-12	VF-20	XF-40	MS-60
1829	3,403	4,900	5,850	6,700	12,500
1830	4,540	4,950	5,850	6,700	12,500
1831	4,520	4,950	5,850	6,700	12,500
1832	4,400	4,950	5,850	6,700	12,500
1833	4,160	4,950	5,850	6,800	12,750
1834	4,000	8,800	12,000	16,000	36,000

Classic Head.
Classic head left within circle of stars. No motto above eagle.
KM# 56 Designer: William Kneass. **Diameter:** 18.2 **Weight:** 4.1800 g. **Composition:** 0.8990 Gold, 0.1208 oz. AGW.

Date	Mintage	VF-20	XF-40	AU-50	MS-60	MS-65
1834	112,234	475	675	965	3,300	27,000

Date	Mintage	VF-20	XF-40	AU-50	MS-60	MS-65	Date	Mintage	VF-20	XF-40	AU-50	MS-60	MS-65
1835	131,402	475	675	950	3,200	32,000	1839	27,021	500	900	1,900	5,500	—
1836	547,986	475	675	940	3,100	29,000	1839C	18,140	1,500	2,650	4,500	26,500	—
1837	45,080	500	800	1,500	4,000	35,000	1839/8 Inc. above	—	—	—	—	—	—
1838	47,030	500	625	1,100	3,200	30,000	1839D	13,674	1,750	3,450	8,000	24,000	—
1838C	7,880	1,700	3,000	8,000	27,000	55,000	1839O	17,781	700	1,100	2,500	7,250	—

Coronet Head.

Coronet head left within circle of stars. No motto above eagle.

KM# 72　Designer: Christian Gobrecht.　Diameter: 18 Weight: 4.1800 g. Composition: 0.9000 Gold, 0.1209 oz. AGW.

1848 "Cal." reverse

Date	Mintage	F-12	VF-20	XF-40	AU-50	MS-60	Prf-65
1840	18,859	160	190	900	2,950	6,000	—
1840C	12,822	975	1,400	1,600	6,000	13,000	—
1840D	3,532	2,000	3,200	8,700	15,500	35,000	—
1840O	33,580	250	400	825	2,100	11,000	—
1841	—	—	48,000	85,000	96,000	—	—
1841C	10,281	750	1,500	2,000	3,500	18,500	—
1841D	4,164	950	2,100	4,750	11,000	25,000	—
1842	2,823	500	900	2,600	6,500	20,000	140,000
1842C	6,729	700	1,700	3,500	8,000	27,000	—
1842D	4,643	900	2,100	4,000	11,750	38,000	—
1842O	19,800	240	370	1,200	2,500	14,000	—
1843	100,546	160	180	450	915	3,000	140,000
1843C small date, Crosslet 4	26,064	1,500	2,400	5,500	9,000	29,000	—
1843C large date, Plain 4	Inc. above	800	1,600	2,200	3,500	8,800	—
1843D small date, Crosslet 4	36,209	920	1,800	2,350	3,250	10,500	—
1843O small date, Crosslet 4	288,002	165	190	250	350	1,700	—
1843O large date, Plain 4	76,000	210	260	465	1,600	8,000	—
1844	6,784	225	365	850	2,000	7,500	140,000
1844C	11,622	700	1,600	2,600	7,000	20,000	—
1844D	17,332	785	1,650	2,200	3,200	7,800	—
1845	91,051	190	250	350	600	1,275	140,000
1845D	19,460	950	1,900	2,600	3,900	15,000	—
1845O	4,000	550	1,050	2,300	9,000	20,000	—
1846	21,598	200	275	500	950	6,000	140,000
1846C	4,808	725	1,575	3,500	8,950	18,750	—
1846D	19,303	800	1,400	2,000	3,000	12,000	—
1846O	66,000	170	280	400	1,150	6,500	—
1847	29,814	140	220	360	825	3,800	—
1847C	23,226	900	1,800	2,300	3,500	7,250	—
1847D	15,784	800	1,650	2,250	3,250	10,500	—
1847O	124,000	160	240	400	1,000	4,000	—
1848	7,497	315	500	850	2,400	7,000	125,000
1848 "CAL."	1,389	8,000	15,000	26,000	36,000	50,000	—
1848C	16,788	800	1,600	2,100	3,800	13,750	—
1848D	13,771	1,000	2,000	2,500	4,500	12,000	—
1849	23,294	180	275	475	1,000	2,600	—
1849C	10,220	800	1,475	2,150	5,150	23,500	—
1849D	10,945	950	2,000	2,500	4,500	18,000	—
1850	252,923	160	180	275	350	1,100	—
1850C	9,148	800	1,500	2,100	3,400	17,500	—
1850D	12,148	950	1,800	2,500	4,000	15,000	—
1850O	84,000	170	225	450	1,200	4,900	—
1851	1,372,748	145	180	200	225	325	—
1851C	14,923	900	1,750	2,300	4,800	13,000	—
1851D	11,264	950	1,700	2,600	4,200	13,000	—
1851O	148,000	160	200	220	1,000	4,650	—
1852	1,159,681	150	175	200	250	325	—
1852C	9,772	675	1,500	2,100	4,250	18,000	—
1852D	4,078	840	1,600	2,800	7,250	17,000	—
1852O	140,000	160	190	300	950	5,000	—
1853	1,404,668	150	180	200	225	350	—
1853D	3,178	950	2,100	3,400	4,900	18,000	—
1854	596,258	150	180	215	240	350	—
1854C	7,295	800	1,500	2,400	5,000	14,750	—
1854D	1,760	1,750	2,900	6,950	12,000	27,500	—
1854O	153,000	150	185	240	425	1,600	—
1854S	246	32,500	70,000	115,000	215,000	300,000	—

$2.50 GOLD

Date	Mintage	F-12	VF-20	XF-40	AU-50	MS-60	Prf-65
1855	235,480	145	180	225	250	360	—
1855C	3,677	800	1,675	3,300	6,500	25,000	—
1855D	1,123	1,750	3,250	7,500	24,000	46,000	—
1856	384,240	145	175	210	250	390	75,000
1856C	7,913	650	1,150	2,200	4,400	15,500	—
1856D	874	3,500	6,700	12,500	30,000	72,500	—
1856O	21,100	180	240	750	1,500	8,000	—
1856S	71,120	160	250	375	950	4,500	—
1857	214,130	150	190	205	230	380	75,000
1857D	2,364	875	1,750	2,900	3,850	13,000	—
1857O	34,000	155	210	350	1,100	4,600	—
1857S	69,200	160	210	340	900	5,500	—
1858	47,377	150	200	250	360	1,350	59,000
1858C	9,056	825	1,500	2,100	3,350	9,250	—
1859	39,444	150	185	265	400	1,250	61,000
1859D	2,244	1,000	1,900	3,300	4,900	20,000	—
1859S	15,200	200	350	1,000	2,800	7,000	—
1860	22,675	150	200	265	470	1,300	58,000
1860C	7,469	815	1,550	2,200	3,950	21,000	—
1860S	35,600	170	250	675	1,200	4,000	—
1861	1,283,878	150	180	210	230	325	31,500
1861S	24,000	200	400	1,000	3,700	7,400	—
1862	98,543	160	200	300	520	1,375	32,500
1862/1	Inc. above	450	950	2,000	4,000	8,000	—
1862S	8,000	500	1,000	2,100	4,500	17,000	—
1863	30	—	—	—	—	—	95,000
1863S	10,800	250	500	1,500	3,200	13,500	—
1864	2,874	2,500	5,500	8,800	21,500	37,500	27,000
1865	1,545	2,400	6,000	8,000	19,000	38,000	30,000
1865S	23,376	160	225	650	1,650	5,000	—
1866	3,110	650	1,300	3,500	6,000	11,500	25,000
1866S	38,960	180	300	650	1,600	6,250	—
1867	3,250	190	385	900	1,250	4,800	27,000
1867S	28,000	170	250	625	1,750	4,000	—
1868	3,625	170	235	400	675	1,600	27,000
1868S	34,000	150	200	300	1,100	4,000	—
1869	4,345	170	250	450	715	3,000	24,500
1869S	29,500	160	240	440	775	5,000	—
1870	4,555	165	225	425	740	3,800	22,750
1870S	16,000	155	215	400	800	4,900	—
1871	5,350	160	230	325	600	2,200	24,000
1871S	22,000	150	185	280	530	2,200	—
1872	3,030	200	400	750	1,100	4,650	22,000
1872S	18,000	155	225	415	900	4,500	—
1873 closed 3	178,025	155	170	210	260	535	22,500
1873 open 3	Inc. above	155	165	195	250	300	—
1873S	27,000	160	225	425	900	2,800	—
1874	3,940	170	240	380	720	2,100	32,000
1875	420	1,750	3,500	5,000	11,000	21,500	32,500
1875S	11,600	150	200	300	850	4,500	—
1876	4,221	170	275	675	925	3,200	22,000
1876S	5,000	170	225	525	980	3,300	—
1877	1,652	275	400	800	1,100	3,250	22,000
1877S	35,400	150	160	200	230	635	—
1878	286,260	150	160	200	225	275	26,000
1878S	178,000	150	160	200	235	340	—
1879	88,990	150	160	195	235	300	26,000
1879S	43,500	155	200	300	550	2,150	—
1880	2,996	170	210	335	600	1,300	20,250
1881	691	900	2,200	3,400	5,000	10,000	19,000
1882	4,067	160	210	290	400	700	15,000
1883	2,002	175	220	440	1,000	2,600	15,500
1884	2,023	175	225	420	600	1,600	16,000
1885	887	400	715	1,800	2,500	4,400	15,000
1886	4,088	170	190	270	425	1,100	16,500
1887	6,282	175	200	245	325	700	16,500
1888	16,098	160	180	240	285	340	15,000
1889	17,648	155	180	230	250	325	17,000
1890	8,813	170	190	240	280	500	13,750
1891	11,040	165	175	215	230	400	14,000
1892	2,545	170	180	250	325	765	15,000
1893	30,106	165	175	200	240	300	14,000
1894	4,122	170	180	225	325	800	13,500
1895	6,199	150	175	225	275	395	12,500
1896	19,202	150	175	225	235	285	12,500
1897	29,904	150	175	210	235	285	12,500
1898	24,165	150	175	210	235	285	12,500
1899	27,350	150	175	210	235	300	12,500
1900	67,205	150	175	240	320	415	12,500

Date	Mintage	F-12	VF-20	XF-40	AU-50	MS-60	Prf-65
1901	91,322	150	175	200	235	275	12,500
1902	133,733	150	170	200	235	275	12,500
1903	201,257	150	170	200	235	275	13,000
1904	160,960	150	170	200	240	275	12,500
1905	217,944	150	170	200	240	275	12,500
1906	176,490	150	170	200	240	275	12,500
1907	336,448	150	170	200	240	275	12,500

Indian Head.

KM# 128 **Designer:** Bela Lyon Pratt. **Diameter:** 18
Weight: 4.1800 g. **Composition:** 0.9000 Gold,
0.1209 oz. AGW.

Date	Mintage	VF-20	XF-40	AU-50	MS-60	MS-63	MS-65	Prf-65
1908	565,057	165	220	230	275	1,800	8,500	16,000
1909	441,899	175	220	230	275	2,600	11,000	30,000
1910	492,682	175	220	230	275	2,600	12,500	18,000
1911	704,191	175	220	230	280	1,600	12,500	16,000
1911D	55,680	2,500	3,650	5,000	9,850	24,500	90,000	16,000
1912	616,197	175	220	230	275	2,800	16,000	16,000
1913	722,165	175	220	230	280	1,725	14,000	16,500
1914	240,117	175	235	260	480	8,500	34,000	16,500
1914D	448,000	175	220	230	300	2,650	40,000	23,000
1915	606,100	175	220	230	275	1,650	13,500	15,250
1925D	578,000	175	220	230	275	1,450	7,000	—
1926	446,000	175	220	230	275	1,450	7,000	—
1927	388,000	175	220	230	275	1,450	7,000	—
1928	416,000	175	220	230	275	1,450	7,000	—
1929	532,000	180	230	250	340	1,600	10,000	—

$3

GOLD
Indian head with headdress, left.
Value, date within wreath.

KM# 84 **Designer:** James B. Longacre. **Diameter:**
20.5 **Weight:** 5.0150 g. **Composition:** 0.9000 Gold,
0.1451 oz. AGW. **Notes:** The 1873 "closed-3" and
"open-3" varieties are distinguished by the amount of
space between the upper left and lower left serifs of
the 3 in the date.

Date	Mintage	VF-20	XF-40	AU-50	MS-60	MS-65	Prf-65
1854	138,618	850	1,100	2,000	3,400	18,000	125,000
1854D	1,120	8,300	15,000	29,000	65,000	—	—
1854O	24,000	1,000	2,000	4,000	20,000	—	—
1855	50,555	900	1,100	2,000	3,300	32,000	120,000
1855S	6,600	1,025	2,150	5,700	25,000	—	—
1856	26,010	880	1,100	2,150	3,500	27,000	—
1856S	34,500	900	1,500	2,350	10,000	—	—
1857	20,891	900	1,100	2,100	3,500	—	62,500
1857S	14,000	950	2,200	5,500	18,000	—	—
1858	2,133	950	1,800	3,000	9,000	—	62,500
1859	15,638	900	1,800	1,800	3,000	—	60,000
1860	7,155	900	1,600	2,000	3,600	21,000	46,000
1860S	7,000	950	2,000	7,000	17,000	—	—
1861	6,072	925	1,500	2,200	3,600	27,000	46,000
1862	5,785	925	1,850	2,200	3,600	28,000	46,500
1863	5,039	900	1,450	2,200	3,600	20,000	43,000
1864	2,680	950	1,500	2,300	3,600	29,000	42,000
1865	1,165	1,350	2,500	6,000	10,000	39,000	40,000
1866	4,030	970	1,100	2,000	3,600	27,500	42,000
1867	2,650	950	1,100	2,400	4,000	28,000	41,500
1868	4,875	740	1,100	2,100	3,000	22,000	42,000
1869	2,525	1,150	2,200	2,600	4,000	—	46,000
1870	3,535	1,000	1,500	2,400	5,000	—	47,000
1870S unique	—	—	—	—	—	—	—

Note: H. W. Bass Collection. AU50, cleaned. Est. value, $1,250,000.

Date	Mintage	VF-20	XF-40	AU-50	MS-60	MS-65	Prf-65
1871	1,330	1,000	1,500	2,000	4,000	27,500	47,000
1872	2,030	900	1,800	2,250	3,600	—	33,000
1873 open 3, proof only	25	3,300	5,000	8,700	—	—	—
1873 closed 3, mintage unknown	—	4,000	6,000	10,000	—	—	42,000

$2.50 GOLD

Date	Mintage	VF-20	XF-40	AU-50	MS-60	MS-65	Prf-65
1874	41,820	800	1,300	1,900	3,000	16,000	42,000
1875 proof only	20	20,000	28,000	47,500	—	—	175,000
1876	45	6,000	10,000	16,500	—	—	60,000
1877	1,488	1,200	2,900	5,200	12,000	60,000	43,500
1878	82,324	800	1,300	1,900	3,000	16,000	43,000
1879	3,030	850	1,300	2,000	2,650	19,000	32,000
1880	1,036	850	1,700	3,000	4,000	20,000	29,500
1881	554	1,400	2,750	5,500	8,000	24,000	25,000
1882	1,576	925	1,400	2,000	3,500	22,000	25,000
1883	989	1,000	1,600	3,500	3,600	24,000	25,000
1884	1,106	1,250	1,700	2,200	3,600	24,000	24,000
1885	910	1,300	1,800	2,850	3,900	24,000	25,000
1886	1,142	1,250	1,800	3,000	4,000	20,000	24,000
1887	6,160	900	1,300	2,000	3,000	18,000	21,000
1888	5,291	950	1,500	2,000	3,300	20,000	23,000
1889	2,429	925	1,300	1,700	3,100	18,000	22,000

$5 (HALF EAGLE)

GOLD

Liberty Cap.
Liberty Cap on head, right, flanked by stars. Small eagle.
KM# 19   Weight: 8.7500 g. Composition: 0.9160 Gold, 0.2577 oz. AGW.

Date	Mintage	F-12	VF-20	XF-40	MS-60
1795	8,707	19,500	25,000	31,000	79,500
1796/95	6,196	20,500	25,350	32,750	84,500
1797 15 stars	Inc. above	23,000	27,500	42,250	—
1797 16 stars	Inc. above	21,000	25,850	41,000	210,000
1798	—	112,000	185,000	350,000	—

Liberty Cap.
Liberty cap on head, right, flanked by stars. Large Heraldic eagle.
KM# 28   Designer: Robert Scot. Diameter: 25 Weight: 8.7500 g. Composition: 0.9160 Gold, 0.2577 oz. AGW.

Date	Mintage	F-12	VF-20	XF-40	MS-60
1795	Inc. above	10,000	16,500	22,500	85,000
1797/95	3,609	10,850	17,500	24,000	155,000
1797 15 star obv.; Unique	—	—	—	—	—
Note: Smithsonian collection					
1797 16 star obv.; Unique	—	—	—	—	—
Note: Smithsonian collection					
1798 small 8	24,867	4,850	6,650	10,100	—
1798 large 8, 13-star reverse	Inc. above	4,050	5,050	8,350	33,500
1798 large 8, 14-star reverse	Inc. above	5,050	6,650	10,950	—
1799 small reverse stars	7,451	3,850	4,900	11,100	21,500
1799 large reverse stars	Inc. above	3,950	4,750	14,200	31,700
1800	37,628	3,850	4,650	7,100	15,850
1802/1	53,176	3,850	4,650	7,100	15,850
1803/2	33,506	3,850	4,650	7,100	15,850
1804 small 8	30,475	3,850	4,650	7,100	15,850
1804 small 8 over large 8	Inc. above	3,950	4,850	7,600	17,850
1805	33,183	3,850	4,650	7,100	15,850
1806 pointed 6	64,093	3,850	4,650	7,100	17,750
1806 round 6	Inc. above	3,850	4,650	7,100	15,850
1807	32,488	3,850	4,650	7,100	15,850

$5 GOLD

Turban Head.
Capped draped bust, left, flanked by stars. Heraldic eagle.
KM# 38 Designer: John Reich. **Diameter:** 25
Weight: 8.7500 g. **Composition:** 0.9160 Gold,
0.2577 oz. AGW.

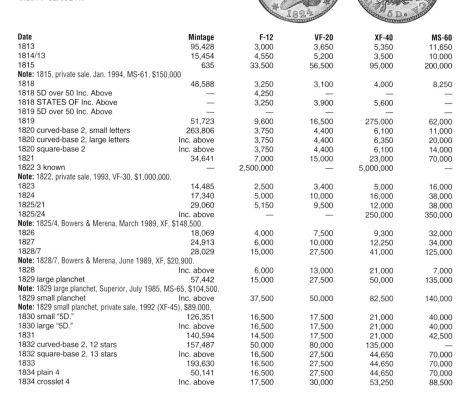

Date	Mintage	F-12	VF-20	XF-40	MS-60
1807	51,605	3,100	3,850	5,100	13,850
1808	55,578	3,600	4,500	5,950	18,850
1808/7	Inc. above	3,100	3,850	5,100	13,850
1809/8	33,875	3,100	3,850	5,100	13,850
1810 small date, small 5	100,287	17,500	32,500	48,500	125,000
1810 small date, large 5	Inc. above	3,100	3,850	5,100	16,250
1810 large date, small 5	Inc. above	17,500	37,500	60,000	135,000
1810 large date, large 5	Inc. above	3,100	3,850	5,100	13,850
1811 small 5	99,581	3,100	3,850	5,100	13,850
1811 tall 5	Inc. above	3,100	3,850	5,100	13,850
1812	58,087	3,100	3,850	5,100	13,850

Turban Head.
Capped head, left, within circle of stars. Heraldic eagle.
KM# 43 Designer: John Reich. **Diameter:** 25
Weight: 8.7500 g. **Composition:** 0.9160 Gold,
0.2577 oz. AGW.

Date	Mintage	F-12	VF-20	XF-40	MS-60
1813	95,428	3,000	3,650	5,350	11,650
1814/13	15,454	4,550	5,200	3,500	10,000
1815	635	33,500	56,500	95,000	200,000
Note: 1815, private sale, Jan. 1994, MS-61, $150,000					
1818	48,588	3,250	3,100	4,000	8,250
1818 5D over 50 Inc. Above	—	4,250	—	—	—
1818 STATES OF Inc. Above	—	3,250	3,900	5,600	—
1819 5D over 50 Inc. Above	—	—	—	—	—
1819	51,723	9,600	16,500	275,000	62,000
1820 curved-base 2, small letters	263,806	3,750	4,400	6,100	11,000
1820 curved-base 2, large letters	Inc. above	3,750	4,400	6,350	20,000
1820 square-base 2	Inc. above	3,750	4,400	6,100	14,000
1821	34,641	7,000	15,000	23,000	70,000
1822 3 known	—	2,500,000	—	5,000,000	—
Note: 1822, private sale, 1993, VF-30, $1,000,000.					
1823	14,485	2,500	3,400	5,000	16,000
1824	17,340	5,000	10,000	16,000	38,000
1825/21	29,060	5,150	9,500	12,000	38,000
1825/24	Inc. above	—	—	250,000	350,000
Note: 1825/4, Bowers & Merena, March 1989, XF, $148,500.					
1826	18,069	4,000	7,500	9,300	32,000
1827	24,913	6,000	10,000	12,250	34,000
1828/7	28,029	15,000	27,500	41,000	125,000
Note: 1828/7, Bowers & Merena, June 1989, XF, $20,900.					
1828	Inc. above	6,000	13,000	21,000	7,000
1829 large planchet	57,442	15,000	27,500	50,000	135,000
Note: 1829 large planchet, Superior, July 1985, MS-65, $104,500.					
1829 small planchet	Inc. above	37,500	50,000	82,500	140,000
Note: 1829 small planchet, private sale, 1992 (XF-45), $89,000.					
1830 small "5D."	126,351	16,500	17,500	21,000	40,000
1830 large "5D."	Inc. above	16,500	17,500	21,000	40,000
1831	140,594	14,500	17,500	21,000	42,500
1832 curved-base 2, 12 stars	157,487	50,000	80,000	135,000	—
1832 square-base 2, 13 stars	Inc. above	16,500	27,500	44,650	70,000
1833	193,630	16,500	27,500	44,650	70,000
1834 plain 4	50,141	16,500	27,500	44,650	70,000
1834 crosslet 4	Inc. above	17,500	30,000	53,250	88,500

Classic Head.

Classic head, left, within circle of stars. No motto above eagle.

KM# 57   Designer: William Kneass. **Diameter:** 22.5 **Weight:** 8.3600 g. **Composition:** 0.8990 Gold, 0.2416 oz. AGW.

Date	Mintage	VF-20	XF-40	AU-50	MS-60	MS-65
1834 plain 4	658,028	550	825	1,650	3,000	48,000
1834 crosslet 4	Inc. above	1,650	2,900	6,000	20,000	—
1835	371,534	550	825	1,700	3,150	—
1836	553,147	550	825	1,700	2,950	70,000
1837	207,121	550	825	1,900	3,500	75,000
1838	286,588	550	925	1,700	3,700	58,000
1838C	17,179	2,550	5,500	13,000	42,500	—
1838D	20,583	2,100	4,650	9,750	31,000	—

Coronet Head.

Coronet head, left, within circle of stars. No motto above eagle.

KM# 69   Designer: Christian Gobrecht. **Diameter:** 21.6 **Weight:** 8.3590 g. **Composition:** 0.9000 Gold, 0.2419 oz. AGW.

Date	Mintage	F-12	VF-20	XF-40	MS-60	Prf-65
1839	118,143	250	275	480	4,000	—
1839/8 curved date	Inc. above	275	325	700	2,250	—
1839C	17,205	1,250	2,300	2,900	24,000	—
1839D	18,939	1,125	2,200	3,200	22,000	—
1840	137,382	295	315	360	3,700	—
1840C	18,992	1,200	2,200	3,000	26,000	—
1840D	22,896	1,200	2,200	3,000	16,000	—
1840O	40,120	305	365	875	11,000	—
1841	15,833	305	400	875	5,500	—
1841C	21,467	1,200	1,850	2,400	20,000	—
1841D	30,495	1,400	1,800	2,350	15,000	—
1841O 2 known	50	—	—	—	—	—
1842 small letters	27,578	200	345	1,100	—	—
1842 large letters	Inc. above	350	750	2,000	11,000	—
1842C small date	28,184	4,500	10,000	23,000	110,000	—
1842C large date	Inc. above	900	1,800	2,200	18,000	—
1842D small date	59,608	1,000	2,000	2,300	15,000	—
1842D large date	Inc. above	1,400	2,350	6,500	48,000	—
1842O	16,400	550	1,000	3,400	22,000	—
1843	611,205	295	315	356	1,850	—
1843C	44,201	1,250	1,850	2,500	14,000	—
1843D	98,452	1,250	1,950	2,600	13,000	—
1843O small letters	19,075	300	660	1,700	26,000	—
1843O large letters	82,000	305	349	1,175	12,000	—
1844	340,330	295	315	356	2,000	—
1844C	23,631	1,300	1,900	3,000	24,000	—
1844D	88,982	1,500	1,950	2,400	12,000	—
1844O	364,600	329	349	375	4,700	—
1845	417,099	295	315	260	2,000	—
1845D	90,629	1,300	1,900	2,400	12,500	—
1845O	41,000	329	415	800	9,900	—
1846	395,942	295	315	330	2,400	—
1846C	12,995	1,350	1,900	3,000	24,000	—
1846D	80,294	1,250	1,800	2,400	13,000	—
1846O	58,000	329	375	1,000	11,500	—
1847	915,981	295	315	356	2,200	—
1847C	84,151	1,350	1,800	2,400	13,000	—
1847D	64,405	1,400	2,000	2,000	10,000	—
1847O	12,000	550	2,200	6,750	28,000	—
1848	260,775	295	315	275	1,500	—
1848C	64,472	1,400	1,900	2,250	19,250	—
1848D	47,465	1,450	2,000	2,350	14,500	—
1849	133,070	295	315	280	2,800	—
1849C	64,823	1,500	1,900	2,400	14,000	—
1849D	39,036	1,550	2,000	2,600	16,500	—
1850	64,491	295	300	625	4,250	—
1850C	63,591	1,350	1,850	2,300	14,000	—
1850D	43,984	1,450	1,950	2,500	33,000	—
1851	377,505	295	315	250	2,800	—

Date	Mintage	F-12	VF-20	XF-40	MS-60	Prf-65
1851C	49,176	1,300	1,900	2,350	17,500	—
1851D	62,710	1,400	1,950	2,400	15,000	—
1851O	41,000	280	590	1,500	13,000	—
1852	573,901	295	315	260	1,400	—
1852C	72,574	1,350	1,900	2,450	7,750	—
1852D	91,584	1,450	2,000	2,450	13,000	—
1853	305,770	295	315	250	1,400	—
1853C	65,571	1,500	1,950	2,350	8,500	—
1853D	89,678	1,550	2,000	2,500	11,000	—
1854	160,675	295	315	260	2,000	—
1854C	39,283	1,400	1,900	2,300	14,000	—
1854D	56,413	1,400	1,875	2,200	11,500	—
1854O	46,000	325	300	525	8,250	—
1854S	268	—	—	—	—	—
Note: 1854S, Bowers & Merena, Oct. 1982, AU-55, $170,000.						
1855	117,098	295	315	250	1,800	—
1855C	39,788	1,400	1,900	2,300	16,000	—
1855D	22,432	1,500	1,950	2,400	19,000	—
1855O	11,100	315	675	2,100	20,000	—
1855S	61,000	325	390	1,000	15,500	—
1856	197,990	295	315	356	2,850	—
1856C	28,457	1,450	1,875	2,400	20,000	—
1856D	19,786	1,475	1,950	2,600	15,000	—
1856O	10,000	370	650	1,600	14,000	—
1856S	105,100	305	300	700	6,750	—
1857	98,188	295	315	260	1,600	123,500
1857C	31,360	1,400	1,900	2,500	9,500	—
1857D	17,046	1,500	2,000	2,650	14,500	—
1857O	13,000	340	640	1,400	15,000	—
1857S	87,000	305	300	700	11,000	—
1858	15,136	305	240	550	3,850	190,000
1858C	38,856	1,400	1,900	2,350	11,000	—
1858D	15,362	1,500	2,000	2,450	12,500	—
1858S	18,600	400	825	2,350	31,000	—
1859	16,814	305	325	625	7,000	—
1859C	31,847	1,400	1,900	2,450	16,000	—
1859D	10,366	1,600	2,150	2,600	16,000	—
1859S	13,220	615	1,800	4,150	30,000	—
1860	19,825	200	280	575	3,650	100,000
1860C	14,813	1,500	2,100	3,000	15,000	—
1860D	14,635	1,500	1,900	2,600	15,000	—
1860S	21,200	500	1,100	2,100	27,000	—
1861	688,150	295	315	356	1,850	100,000
1861C	6,879	1,500	2,400	3,900	25,000	—
1861D	1,597	3,000	4,700	7,000	50,000	—
1861S	18,000	500	1,100	4,500	36,500	—
1862	4,465	400	800	1,850	20,000	96,000
1862S	9,500	1,500	3,000	6,000	62,000	—
1863	2,472	450	1,200	3,750	27,500	90,000
1863S	17,000	600	1,450	4,100	35,500	—
1864	4,220	350	650	1,850	15,000	72,000
1864S	3,888	2,300	4,750	16,000	55,000	—
1865	1,295	500	1,450	4,100	20,000	82,500
1865S	27,612	475	1,400	2,400	20,000	—
1866S	9,000	750	1,750	4,000	40,000	—

Coronet Head.

Coronet head, left, within circle of stars. IN GOD WE TRUST above eagle.

KM# 101   Designer: Christian Gobrecht.
Diameter: 21.6 **Weight:** 8.3590 g. **Composition:** 0.9000 Gold, 0.2419 oz. AGW.

Date	Mintage	VF-20	XF-40	AU-50	MS-60	MS-63	MS-65	Prf-65
1866	6,730	750	1,650	3,500	16,500	—	—	70,000
1866S	34,920	900	2,600	8,800	25,000	—	—	—
1867	6,920	500	1,500	3,300	11,500	—	—	70,000
1867S	29,000	1,400	2,900	8,000	34,500	—	—	—
1868	5,725	650	1,000	3,500	11,500	—	—	70,000
1868S	52,000	400	1,550	4,000	20,000	—	—	—
1869	1,785	925	2,400	3,500	17,500	34,000	—	65,000
1869S	31,000	500	1,750	4,000	26,000	—	—	—
1870	4,035	800	2,000	2,850	18,000	—	—	75,000
1870CC	7,675	5,250	15,000	30,000	110,000	137,500	200,000	—
1870S	17,000	950	2,600	8,250	29,000	—	—	—
1871	3,230	900	1,700	3,300	12,500	—	—	70,000

Date	Mintage	VF-20	XF-40	AU-50	MS-60	MS-63	MS-65	Prf-65
1871CC	20,770	1,250	3,000	12,000	60,000	—	—	—
1871S	25,000	500	950	2,950	13,000	—	—	—
1872	1,690	850	1,925	3,000	15,000	18,000	—	60,000
1872CC	16,980	1,250	5,000	20,000	60,000	—	—	—
1872S	36,400	460	800	3,400	13,500	—	—	—
1873 closed 3	49,305	347	361	440	1,200	6,500	24,000	70,000
1873 open 3	63,200	342	352	350	850	3,650	—	—
1873CC	7,416	2,600	12,500	27,500	60,000	—	—	—
1873S	31,000	525	1,400	3,250	21,000	—	—	—
1874	3,508	660	1,675	2,500	13,000	26,000	—	66,000
1874CC	21,198	850	1,700	9,500	36,000	—	—	—
1874S	16,000	640	2,100	4,800	22,500	—	—	—
1875	220	34,000	45,000	60,000	190,000	—	—	185,000
1875CC	11,828	1,400	4,500	11,500	52,000	—	—	—
1875S	9,000	715	2,250	5,000	16,500	32,500	—	—
1876	1,477	1,100	2,500	4,125	11,000	14,500	55,000	60,000
1876CC	6,887	1,450	5,000	14,000	46,500	82,500	165,000	—
1876S	4,000	2,000	3,600	9,500	30,000	—	—	—
1877	1,152	900	2,750	4,000	13,750	29,000	—	75,000
1877CC	8,680	1,000	3,300	11,000	52,500	—	—	—
1877S	26,700	400	650	1,400	9,200	—	—	—
1878	131,740	233	239	277	425	2,000	—	50,000
1878CC	9,054	3,100	7,200	20,000	60,000	—	—	—
1878S	144,700	231	234	3,000	675	4,250	—	—
1879	301,950	231	234	238	400	2,000	12,000	55,000
1879CC	17,281	575	1,500	3,150	22,000	—	—	—
1879S	426,200	233	239	277	950	3,300	—	—
1880	3,166,436	226	229	233	235	840	7,500	54,000
1880CC	51,017	425	815	1,375	9,900	—	—	—
1880S	1,348,900	226	229	233	235	800	5,750	—
1881	5,708,802	226	229	233	235	775	4,800	54,000
1881/80	Inc. above	330	600	750	1,500	4,500	—	—
1881CC	13,886	550	1,500	7,000	22,500	60,000	—	—
1881S	969,000	226	229	233	235	775	7,150	—
1882	2,514,568	226	229	233	235	800	6,150	54,000
1882CC	82,817	415	625	900	7,500	40,000	—	—
1882S	969,000	226	229	233	235	800	4,500	—
1883	233,461	243	246	250	260	1,200	—	40,000
1883CC	12,958	460	1,100	3,200	18,000	—	—	—
1883S	83,200	243	240	315	1,000	2,950	—	—
1884	191,078	243	246	250	650	2,250	—	35,000
1884CC	16,402	550	975	3,000	17,000	—	—	—
1884S	177,000	243	246	250	345	2,000	—	—
1885	601,506	226	229	233	260	825	4,800	35,000
1885S	1,211,500	226	229	233	235	790	4,000	—
1886	388,432	226	229	233	235	1,125	5,600	44,000
1886S	3,268,000	226	229	233	235	815	4,500	—
1887	87	—	14,500	20,000	—	—	—	120,000
1887S	1,912,000	226	229	233	235	800	4,800	—
1888	18,296	241	244	300	550	1,500	—	29,000
1888S	293,900	231	234	320	1,200	4,000	—	—
1889	7,565	350	440	515	1,150	2,400	—	30,000
1890	4,328	400	475	550	2,200	6,500	—	27,000
1890CC	53,800	330	460	615	1,600	8,000	55,000	—
1891	61,413	233	239	277	450	1,900	5,400	29,000
1891CC	208,000	325	415	525	750	3,150	31,500	—
1892	753,572	226	229	233	235	880	7,000	30,000
1892CC	82,968	340	400	575	1,500	6,000	33,500	—
1892O	10,000	515	1,000	1,375	3,300	—	—	—
1892S	298,400	226	229	238	525	3,300	—	—
1893	1,528,197	226	229	233	235	800	3,900	34,000
1893CC	60,000	360	465	770	1,400	6,350	—	—
1893O	110,000	241	340	480	950	6,500	—	—
1893S	224,000	226	229	238	245	825	9,000	—
1894	957,955	226	229	233	235	800	2,600	35,000
1894O	16,600	243	360	570	1,300	5,500	—	—
1894S	55,900	253	375	575	2,900	10,000	—	—
1895	1,345,936	226	229	233	235	800	4,500	29,000
1895S	112,000	231	275	400	3,150	6,500	26,000	—
1896	59,063	226	229	238	235	9,750	4,500	30,000
1896S	155,400	233	239	277	1,150	6,000	24,500	—
1897	867,883	226	229	233	235	825	4,500	35,000
1897S	354,000	226	229	238	865	5,150	—	—
1898	633,495	226	229	233	235	885	6,000	30,000
1898S	1,397,400	226	229	233	230	950	—	—
1899	1,710,729	226	229	233	235	730	3,600	30,000
1899S	1,545,000	226	229	233	235	1,000	9,600	—
1900	1,405,730	226	229	233	235	790	3,600	30,000
1900S	329,000	226	229	238	245	900	14,000	—

$5 GOLD

Date	Mintage	VF-20	XF-40	AU-50	MS-60	MS-63	MS-65	Prf-65
1901	616,040	226	229	233	235	750	3,650	27,000
1901S	3,648,000	226	229	233	235	730	3,600	—
1902	172,562	226	229	233	235	730	4,400	27,000
1902S	939,000	226	229	233	235	730	3,600	—
1903	227,024	226	229	233	235	730	4,000	27,000
1903S	1,855,000	226	229	233	235	730	3,600	—
1904	392,136	226	229	233	235	730	3,600	27,000
1904S	97,000	233	239	277	900	3,850	9,600	—
1905	302,308	226	229	233	235	740	4,000	27,000
1905S	880,700	226	229	233	235	1,500	9,600	—
1906	348,820	226	229	233	235	745	3,600	26,000
1906D	320,000	226	229	233	235	930	3,200	—
1906S	598,000	226	229	233	240	900	4,400	—
1907	626,192	226	229	233	235	730	3,400	23,000
1907D	888,000	226	229	233	235	730	3,400	—
1908	421,874	226	229	233	235	730	3,400	—

Indian Head.

KM# 129 **Designer:** Bela Lyon Pratt. **Diameter:** 21.6 **Weight:** 8.3590 g. **Composition:** 0.9000 Gold, 0.2419 oz. AGW.

Date	Mintage	VF-20	XF-40	AU-50	MS-60	MS-63	MS-65	Prf-65
1908	578,012	280	290	315	545	3,400	21,500	25,500
1908D	148,000	280	290	315	545	3,400	36,500	—
1908S	82,000	355	365	410	1,275	6,000	22,250	—
1909	627,138	280	290	315	525	3,400	21,500	36,000
1909D	3,423,560	280	290	315	525	2,850	21,500	—
1909O	34,200	2,150	3,350	7,250	27,500	64,500	475,000	—
1909S	297,200	310	330	375	1,350	11,000	45,000	—
1910	604,250	280	290	315	525	3,450	21,500	37,000
1910D	193,600	280	290	315	545	4,150	39,500	—
1910S	770,200	320	345	385	975	65,000	44,000	—
1911	915,139	280	290	315	525	2,850	21,500	28,500
1911D	72,500	575	700	1,100	4,650	38,500	255,000	—
1911S	1,416,000	290	325	370	600	5,850	41,500	—
1912	790,144	280	290	315	525	2,850	21,500	28,500
1912S	392,000	325	355	460	1,675	13,500	105,000	—
1913	916,099	280	290	315	525	3,400	22,250	28,000
1913S	408,000	320	350	500	1,450	11,500	125,000	—
1914	247,125	280	290	315	545	3,550	22,500	28,500
1914D	247,000	280	290	315	545	3,450	21,500	—
1914S	263,000	325	345	410	1,375	12,850	105,000	—
1915	588,075	280	290	315	525	34,750	21,500	39,000
1915S	164,000	335	365	495	1,950	17,000	110,000	—
1916S	240,000	305	325	395	710	5,750	28,500	—
1929	662,000	7,500	10,750	11,800	14,500	31,000	50,000	—

$10 (EAGLE)

GOLD

Liberty Cap.
Small eagle.

KM# 21 **Designer:** Robert Scot. **Diameter:** 33 **Weight:** 17.5000 g. **Composition:** 0.9160 Gold, 0.5154 oz. AGW.

Date	Mintage	F-12	VF-20	XF-40	MS-60
1795 13 leaves	5,583	28,500	33,850	48,500	122,500
1795 9 leaves	Inc. above	30,000	45,000	73,500	250,000
1796	4,146	27,500	36,000	50,000	135,000
1797 small eagle	3,615	31,500	40,000	55,000	200,000

Liberty Cap.

Liberty cap on head, right, flanked by stars. Heraldic eagle.

KM# 30   **Designer:** Robert Scot.   **Diameter:** 33 **Weight:** 17.5000 g. **Comp:** 0.9160 Gold, 0.5154 oz. AGW.

Date	Mintage	F-12	VF-20	XF-40	MS-60
1797 large eagle	10,940	9,800	12,850	21,400	58,500
1798/97CC 9 stars left, 4 right	900	13,500	19,000	34,500	127,500
1798/97 7 stars left, 6 right	842	28,500	38,500	87,500	235,000
1799 large star obv	37,449	9,350	10,750	18,200	37,500
1799 small star obv	Inc. above	9,350	10,750	18,200	37,500
1800	5,999	9,500	10,750	18,350	39,500
1801	44,344	9,250	10,900	17,400	37,500
1803 extra star	15,017	9,600	11,850	19,550	67,500
1803 large stars rev	Inc. above	9,250	11,400	17,800	37,500
1804 crosslet 4	3,757	16,500	22,750	31,500	92,500
1804 plain 4	—	—	—	—	400,000

Coronet Head.

Old-style head, left, within circle of stars. No motto above eagle.

KM# 66.1   **Designer:** Christian Gobrecht.
Diameter: 27 **Weight:** 16.7180 g. **Composition:** 0.9000 Gold, 0.4837 oz. AGW.

Date	Mintage	F-12	VF-20	XF-40	MS-60	Prf-65
1838	7,200	1,750	2,650	6,850	43,500	1,500,000
1839/8 Type of 1838	25,801	1,100	1,450	5,850	28,500	1,500,000
1839 large letters	Inc. above	800	1,150	2,150	32,000	—

Coronet Head.

New-style head, left, within circle of stars. No motto above eagle.

KM# 66.2   **Designer:** Christian Gobrecht.
Diameter: 27 **Weight:** 16.7180 g. **Composition:** 0.9000 Gold, 0.4837 oz. AGW.

Date	Mintage	F-12	VF-20	XF-40	MS-60	Prf-65
1839 small letters	12,447	975	1,550	6,850	75,000	—
1840	47,338	588	603	853	11,500	—
1841	63,131	568	593	753	9,000	—
1841O	2,500	1,750	3,450	6,950	—	—
1842 small date	81,507	568	593	678	15,000	—
1842 large date	Inc. above	568	593	668	9,500	—
1842O	27,400	568	603	983	22,500	—
1843	75,462	568	593	783	16,750	—
1843O	175,162	568	603	738	12,000	—
1844	6,361	800	1,350	3,200	16,750	—
1844O	118,700	568	603	923	15,000	—
1845	26,153	603	763	863	17,500	—
1845O	47,500	588	603	875	16,500	—
1845O repunched	Inc. above	663	963	3,850	—	—
1846	20,095	613	833	1,250	—	—
1846O	81,780	568	603	1,150	—	—

Date	Mintage	F-12	VF-20	XF-40	MS-60	Prf-65
1846/5	Inc. above	663	963	1,135	—	—
1847	862,258	568	593	613	3,250	—
1847O	571,500	568	593	613	6,500	—
1848	145,484	568	593	678	5,000	—
1848O	38,850	643	783	1,850	17,750	—
1849	653,618	568	593	613	3,400	—
1849O	23,900	643	783	2,450	27,500	—
1850 large date	291,451	568	593	613	4,500	—
1850 small date	Inc. above	643	783	1,150	8,500	—
1850O	57,500	588	618	1,275	19,500	—
1851	176,328	568	593	613	5,150	—
1851O	263,000	568	603	668	6,650	—
1852	263,106	568	593	613	5,250	—
1852O	18,000	643	763	1,650	27,500	—
1853	201,253	588	603	613	3,600	—
1853/2	Inc. above	588	618	948	14,950	—
1853O	51,000	568	618	678	14,500	—
1854	54,250	568	593	638	6,250	—
1854O small date	52,500	588	618	918	11,000	—
1854O large date	Inc. above	643	758	925	9,450	—
1854S	123,826	568	593	638	10,500	—
1855	121,701	568	593	613	4,750	—
1855O	18,000	588	618	2,100	28,000	—
1855S	9,000	900	1,950	3,250	—	—
1856	60,490	568	593	613	4,250	—
1856O	14,500	643	918	2,150	18,500	—
1856S	68,000	568	593	688	9,000	—
1857	16,606	588	618	1,050	13,500	—
1857O	5,500	743	1,800	3,650	—	—
1857S	26,000	588	603	1,050	11,500	—
1858	2,521	3,000	5,200	8,250	35,000	—
1858O	20,000	568	593	938	10,000	—
1858S	11,800	900	1,600	3,950	—	—
1859	16,093	588	618	798	10,500	—
1859O	2,300	2,000	4,250	10,500	—	—
1859S	7,000	1,450	2,600	5,250	—	—
1860	15,105	613	658	848	8,450	175,000
1860O	11,100	633	758	1,850	13,750	—
1860S	5,000	1,400	2,950	6,400	—	—
1861	113,233	568	593	613	6,250	170,000
1861S	15,500	690	1,600	3,750	—	—
1862	10,995	643	748	1,200	—	170,000
1862S	12,500	700	2,000	3,450	—	—
1863	1,248	2,400	4,000	10,000	52,500	165,000
1863S	10,000	700	1,600	3,750	29,500	—
1864	3,580	775	1,800	4,950	18,000	165,000
1864S	2,500	2,600	5,100	17,500	—	—
1865	4,005	900	1,950	4,850	34,500	165,000
1865S	16,700	1,700	4,850	12,500	—	—
1865S over inverted 186	Inc. above	1,300	3,450	8,750	50,000	—
1866S	8,500	1,000	2,650	5,950	—	—

Coronet Head.

New-style head, left, within circle of stars. IN GOD WE TRUST above eagle.

KM# 102 **Designer:** Christian Gobrecht.
Diameter: 27 **Weight:** 16.7180 g. **Composition:**
0.9000 Gold, 0.4837 oz. AGW.

Date	Mintage	VF-20	XF-40	AU-50	MS-60	MS-63	MS-65	Prf-65
1866	3,780	850	2,450	5,000	—	—	—	110,000
1866S	11,500	1,550	3,850	8,000	—	—	—	—
1867	3,140	1,500	2,600	5,000	33,000	—	—	—
1867S	9,000	2,350	6,650	9,850	—	—	—	—
1868	10,655	550	1,100	2,250	19,000	—	—	110,000
1868S	13,500	1,350	2,400	3,900	—	—	—	—
1869	1,855	1,550	3,000	5,650	36,000	—	—	—
1869S	6,430	1,500	2,700	6,250	25,000	—	—	—
1870	4,025	985	1,650	3,950	—	—	—	—
1870CC	5,908	13,000	30,000	52,500	—	—	—	—
1870S	8,000	1,150	2,850	7,400	33,500	—	—	—
1871	1,820	1,500	3,000	5,000	20,000	—	—	110,000
1871CC	8,085	2,600	6,400	22,500	65,000	—	—	—

Date	Mintage	VF-20	XF-40	AU-50	MS-60	MS-63	MS-65	Prf-65
1871S	16,500	1,300	2,200	6,000	30,000	—	—	—
1872	1,650	2,400	5,500	8,700	15,000	34,000	—	90,000
1872CC	4,600	2,850	9,850	24,500	—	—	—	—
1872S	17,300	675	1,175	1,900	—	—	—	—
1873 closed 3	825	4,500	9,750	17,500	55,000	—	—	—
1873CC	4,543	6,000	13,500	31,000	—	—	—	—
1873S	12,000	1,150	2,850	5,100	27,500	—	—	—
1874	53,160	559	589	599	2,100	7,250	42,500	110,000
1874CC	16,767	1,150	3,650	11,000	52,500	75,000	—	—
1874S	10,000	1,275	3,400	7,250	—	—	—	—
1875	120	40,000	67,500	80,000	—	—	—	—

Note: 1875, Akers, Aug. 1990, Proof, $115,000.

Date	Mintage	VF-20	XF-40	AU-50	MS-60	MS-63	MS-65	Prf-65
1875CC	7,715	4,250	9,850	25,000	71,500	—	—	—
1876	732	3,000	8,500	18,500	—	—	—	—
1876CC	4,696	3,600	7,750	21,500	—	—	—	—
1876S	5,000	1,300	2,950	7,500	—	—	—	—
1877	817	3,350	6,350	9,850	37,500	—	—	—
1877CC	3,332	2,400	6,750	15,000	—	—	—	—
1877S	17,000	550	1,250	2,450	33,500	—	—	—
1878	73,800	549	589	599	975	6,750	29,000	—
1878CC	3,244	3,850	10,000	19,000	—	—	—	—
1878S	26,100	589	775	2,150	16,500	29,500	—	—
1879	384,770	552	589	599	746	5,000	15,750	83,000
1879/78	Inc. above	559	601	884	1,250	2,850	—	—
1879CC	1,762	6,650	12,500	26,000	—	—	—	—
1879O	1,500	2,150	5,450	10,250	—	—	—	—
1879S	224,000	552	589	599	1,150	6,500	49,500	—
1880	1,644,876	534	551	561	601	3,650	—	—
1880CC	11,190	625	1,000	1,950	15,500	—	—	—
1880O	9,200	654	1,450	1,850	20,000	—	—	—
1880S	506,250	534	551	561	621	4,850	25,000	—
1881	3,877,260	534	551	561	601	1,015	16,500	63,000
1881CC	24,015	680	825	1,800	6,850	36,500	—	—
1881O	8,350	634	865	1,500	6,950	—	—	—
1881S	970,000	534	551	561	611	1,015	—	—
1882	2,324,480	534	551	561	601	1,015	19,500	63,000
1882CC	6,764	985	1,750	3,250	—	—	—	—
1882O	10,820	562	738	1,250	6,350	18,500	—	—
1882S	132,000	562	589	599	683	3,650	—	—
1883	208,740	534	551	561	611	3,100	—	63,000
1883CC	12,000	734	1,250	2,600	22,500	—	—	—
1883O	800	3,000	7,950	10,500	—	—	—	—
1883S	38,000	562	589	599	1,275	10,500	23,500	—
1884	76,905	562	589	599	781	5,100	15,000	53,000
1884CC	9,925	754	1,450	2,350	12,850	55,000	—	—
1884S	124,250	534	551	561	696	6,500	—	—
1885	253,527	534	551	561	601	4,850	—	53,000
1885S	228,000	534	551	561	601	4,400	—	—
1886	236,160	534	551	561	601	5,100	—	53,000
1886S	826,000	534	551	561	611	1,500	—	—
1887	53,680	562	589	599	800	4,750	—	53,000
1887S	817,000	534	551	561	611	3,500	—	—
1888	132,996	562	589	599	841	6,600	—	—
1888O	21,335	562	589	599	781	5,750	—	—
1888S	648,700	534	551	561	601	2,700	—	—
1889	4,485	592	778	1,100	2,700	—	—	53,000
1889S	425,400	534	551	561	611	1,500	18,500	—
1890	58,043	572	609	619	825	5,500	16,000	46,000
1890CC	17,500	674	771	935	3,850	18,500	—	—
1891	91,868	592	629	639	679	5,000	—	48,000
1891CC	103,732	674	731	840	1,300	7,150	—	—
1892	797,552	534	551	561	601	1,015	9,100	48,000
1892CC	40,000	674	731	825	3,800	22,500	—	—
1892O	28,688	592	589	599	659	11,000	—	—
1892S	115,500	562	613	623	663	4,500	—	—
1893	1,840,895	534	551	561	601	1,015	16,500	46,000
1893CC	14,000	674	771	1,800	8,500	—	—	—
1893O	17,000	562	589	641	881	5,300	—	—
1893S	141,350	562	589	599	639	5,250	19,500	—
1894	2,470,778	534	551	561	601	1,140	—	46,000
1894O	107,500	562	589	591	1,000	6,350	—	—
1894S	25,000	562	613	925	3,950	—	—	—
1895	567,826	534	551	561	601	1,015	17,500	43,500
1895O	98,000	562	589	611	751	8,000	—	—
1895S	49,000	562	601	675	2,400	9,500	—	—
1896	76,348	534	551	561	611	2,550	30,000	43,500
1896S	123,750	562	584	621	2,500	12,000	28,500	—
1897	1,000,159	534	551	561	601	1,140	10,000	—
1897O	42,500	562	589	599	800	5,850	27,500	—

Date	Mintage	VF-20	XF-40	AU-50	MS-60	MS-63	MS-65	Prf-65
1897S	234,750	562	584	594	870	5,750	22,500	—
1898	812,197	534	551	561	601	1,140	9,000	43,500
1898S	473,600	562	584	594	671	5,100	18,500	—
1899	1,262,305	534	551	561	601	1,015	5,950	43,500
1899O	37,047	562	589	601	781	8,450	—	—
1899S	841,000	534	551	561	611	3,650	12,850	—
1900	293,960	534	551	561	611	1,015	9,500	43,500
1900S	81,000	562	589	599	950	6,750	—	—
1901	1,718,825	534	551	561	601	1,015	5,950	43,500
1901O	72,041	562	589	599	721	3,750	12,500	—
1901S	2,812,750	534	551	561	601	1,015	6,250	—
1902	82,513	534	551	561	611	2,800	11,750	43,500
1902S	469,500	534	551	561	601	1,015	6,250	—
1903	125,926	534	551	561	611	2,450	13,500	43,500
1903O	112,771	562	589	599	711	3,250	18,000	—
1903S	538,000	534	551	561	611	1,040	5,950	—
1904	162,038	534	551	561	611	2,000	9,500	46,000
1904O	108,950	562	589	599	711	3,700	16,500	—
1905	201,078	534	551	561	601	1,450	8,500	43,500
1905S	369,250	562	584	626	1,100	5,600	22,500	—
1906	165,497	534	551	561	611	2,450	10,000	43,500
1906D	981,000	534	551	561	601	1,015	7,000	—
1906O	86,895	562	589	599	751	4,900	14,500	—
1906S	457,000	562	584	599	761	5,000	15,500	—
1907	1,203,973	534	551	561	601	1,015	5,950	43,500
1907D	1,030,000	534	551	561	611	2,250	—	—
1907S	210,500	562	584	621	801	5,450	17,000	—

Indian Head.
No motto next to eagle.

KM# 125 Designer: Augustus Saint-Gaudens.
Diameter: 27 **Weight:** 16.7180 g. **Composition:**
0.9000 Gold, 0.4837 oz. AGW. **Notes:** 1907 varieties
are distinguished by whether the edge is rolled or
wired, and whether the legend E PLURIBUS UNUM
has periods between each word.

Date	Mintage	VF-20	XF-40	AU-50	MS-60	MS-63	MS-65	Prf-65
1907 wire edge, periods before and after legend	500	11,000	16,850	19,500	26,500	43,500	83,500	—
1907 same, without stars on edge, unique	—	—	—	—	—	—	—	—
1907 rolled edge, periods	42	26,000	38,500	49,000	66,500	98,500	250,000	—
1907 without periods	239,406	651	715	750	815	3,400	10,000	—
1908 without motto	33,500	636	700	735	800	4,650	14,500	—
1908D without motto	210,000	636	700	735	840	6,350	37,500	—

Indian Head.
IN GOD WE TRUST left of eagle.

KM# 130 Designer: Augustus Saint-Gaudens.
Diameter: 27 **Weight:** 16.7180 g. **Composition:**
0.9000 Gold, 0.4837 oz. AGW.

Date	Mintage	VF-20	XF-40	AU-50	MS-60	MS-63	MS-65	Prf-65
1908	341,486	637	695	720	815	2,750	10,400	52,500
1908D	836,500	642	715	725	835	6,750	29,000	—
1908S	59,850	652	750	775	2,950	8,650	25,500	—
1909	184,863	637	695	720	795	3,550	16,500	54,500
1909D	121,540	642	700	725	860	6,100	34,500	—
1909S	292,350	642	700	725	860	6,350	17,500	—
1910	318,704	637	695	720	785	1,675	11,000	54,500
1910D	2,356,640	632	690	720	785	1,575	8,400	—
1910S	811,000	642	715	725	845	8,850	51,000	—
1911	505,595	632	690	715	800	1,650	9,250	52,500
1911D	30,100	702	975	1,450	5,850	25,000	122,500	—
1911S	51,000	672	720	765	1,050	9,000	17,000	—
1912	405,083	637	695	720	785	1,650	11,000	52,500
1912S	300,000	642	710	725	860	7,250	38,500	—
1913	442,071	637	695	720	785	1,700	11,500	52,500
1913S	66,000	687	720	825	4,000	28,500	100,000	—
1914	151,050	637	695	720	795	2,250	11,500	52,500

Date	Mintage	VF-20	XF-40	AU-50	MS-60	MS-63	MS-65	Prf-65
1914D	343,500	637	695	720	785	2,650	15,500	—
1914S	208,000	647	705	730	930	7,750	32,500	—
1915	351,075	637	695	720	785	250	12,750	55,000
1915S	59,000	687	460	775	3,150	15,250	58,500	—
1916S	138,500	672	730	755	850	6,350	20,000	—
1920S	126,500	9,800	16,500	20,000	36,500	86,000	245,000	—
1926	1,014,000	632	690	715	780	1,375	7,450	—
1930S	96,000	7,500	10,500	14,500	23,500	44,500	74,000	—
1932	4,463,000	632	690	715	780	1,375	7,500	—
1933	312,500	110,000	135,000	145,000	165,000	230,000	575,000	—

$20 (DOUBLE EAGLE)

GOLD

Liberty Head.

Coronet head, left, within circle of stars. TWENTY D. below eagle, no motto above eagle.

KM# 74.1 **Designer:** James B. Longacre. **Diameter:** 34 **Weight:** 33.4360 g. **Composition:** 0.9000 Gold, 0.9675 oz. AGW.

Date	Mintage	VF-20	XF-40	AU-50	MS-60	MS-63	MS-65	Prf-65
1849 unique, in Smithsonian collection	1	—	—	—	—	—	—	—
1850	1,170,261	1,355	1,425	3,000	8,500	43,500	175,000	—
1850O	141,000	1,250	3,500	9,800	45,000	—	—	—
1851	2,087,155	1,395	1,555	1,805	3,850	19,500	—	—
1851O	315,000	1,470	2,255	4,250	23,000	58,500	—	—
1852	2,053,026	1,395	1,555	1,705	3,950	17,500	—	—
1852O	190,000	1,250	2,650	3,800	22,500	—	—	—
1853	1,261,326	1,395	1,555	1,555	5,000	27,500	—	—
1853/2	Inc. above	1,475	2,250	6,850	33,500	—	—	—
1853O	71,000	1,485	3,650	4,850	32,500	65,000	—	—
1854	757,899	1,395	1,555	1,855	9,250	26,500	—	—
1854	Inc. above	1,635	2,350	6,000	—	—	—	—
1854O	3,250	95,000	225,000	365,000	—	—	—	—
1854S	141,468	1,475	1,325	3,000	6,000	15,500	52,500	—
1855	364,666	1,395	1,555	1,605	8,850	66,500	—	—
1855O	8,000	3,650	19,500	24,500	110,000	—	—	—
1855S	879,675	1,375	1,555	1,805	7,200	19,500	—	—
1856	329,878	1,395	1,555	1,605	8,400	24,500	—	—
1856O	2,250	97,500	165,000	300,000	525,000	750,000	—	—
1856S	1,189,750	1,375	1,555	1,605	5,900	15,000	30,000	—
1857	439,375	1,395	1,555	1,705	3,400	26,500	—	—
1857O	30,000	1,300	2,950	6,400	31,000	115,000	—	—
1857S	970,500	1,375	1,555	1,705	4,500	7,250	12,850	—
1858	211,714	450	1,100	1,605	5,500	34,500	—	—
1858O	35,250	1,950	3,850	7,500	42,000	—	—	—
1858S	846,710	1,375	1,575	1,895	8,500	—	—	—
1859	43,597	1,450	2,450	4,400	28,000	—	—	280,000
1859O	9,100	6,400	16,500	44,000	110,000	—	—	—
1859S	636,445	1,375	1,555	1,855	5,000	35,000	—	—
1860	577,670	1,375	1,555	1,705	4,650	18,000	63,500	—
1860O	6,600	3,650	14,500	24,000	100,000	—	—	—
1860S	544,950	1,395	1,845	1,895	7,350	18,500	48,000	—
1861	2,976,453	1,375	1,555	1,680	2,900	12,850	41,500	275,000
1861O	17,741	5,650	17,500	24,000	88,000	—	—	—
1861S	768,000	1,395	1,655	2,250	10,500	31,500	—	—

$20 GOLD

Liberty.
Coronet head, left, within circle of stars. Paquet design, TWENTY D. below eagle.

KM# 93   **Weight:** 33.4360 g. **Composition:** 0.9000 Gold, 0.9675 oz. AGW. **Notes:** In 1861 the reverse was redesigned by Anthony C. Paquet, but it was withdrawn soon after its release. The letters in the inscriptions on the Paquet-reverse variety are taller than on the regular reverse.

Date	Mintage	VF-20	XF-40	AU-50	MS-60	MS-63	MS-65	Prf-65
1861 2 Known	—	—	—	—	—	—	—	—
Note: 1861 Paquet reverse, Bowers & Merena, Nov. 1988, MS-67, $660,000.								
1861S	—	19,500	52,500	92,500	275,000	—	—	—
Note: Included in mintage of 1861S, KM#74.1								

Liberty.
Longacre design resumed.

KM# A74.1   **Weight:** 33.4360 g. **Composition:** 0.9000 Gold, 0.9675 oz. AGW.

Date	Mintage	VF-20	XF-40	AU-50	MS-60	MS-63	MS-65	Prf-65
1862	92,133	1,375	2,250	4,900	16,500	34,000	—	250,000
1862S	854,173	1,360	1,350	2,100	12,400	36,000	—	—
1863	142,790	1,375	1,900	3,950	19,500	39,500	—	250,000
1863S	966,570	1,360	1,510	1,850	7,350	32,500	—	—
1864	204,285	1,375	1,150	2,450	14,500	40,000	—	250,000
1864S	793,660	1,360	1,490	1,950	8,600	32,000	—	—
1865	351,200	1,375	1,510	1,645	6,200	26,000	—	250,000
1865S	1,042,500	1,360	1,510	1,560	4,200	9,000	19,500	—
1866S	Inc. below	3,400	13,500	44,500	—	—	—	—

Liberty.
Coronet head, left, within circle of stars. TWENTY D. below eagle. IN GOD WE TRUST above eagle.

KM# 74.2 **Designer:** James B. Longacre. **Diameter:** 34 **Weight:** 33.4360 g. **Composition:** 0.9000 Gold, 0.9675 oz. AGW.

Date	Mintage	VF-20	XF-40	AU-50	MS-60	MS-63	MS-65	Prf-65
1866	698,775	1,340	1,493	1,750	6,950	28,500	—	200,000
1866S	842,250	1,340	1,503	2,100	15,500	—	—	—
1867	251,065	1,340	1,513	1,200	3,250	30,000	—	200,000
1867S	920,750	1,340	1,503	1,900	15,000	—	—	—
1868	98,600	1,380	1,603	2,250	11,500	50,000	—	200,000
1868S	837,500	1,340	1,473	1,650	10,000	—	—	—
1869	175,155	1,350	1,463	1,600	6,800	22,750	—	210,000
1869S	686,750	1,340	1,493	1,493	7,000	45,000	—	—
1870	155,185	1,360	1,493	1,925	9,250	50,000	—	215,000
1870CC	3,789	125,000	195,000	360,000	—	—	—	—
1870S	982,000	1,340	1,448	1,495	5,450	34,000	—	—
1871	80,150	1,350	1,448	1,800	4,500	24,500	—	—
1871CC	17,387	9,500	19,500	40,000	97,500	300,000	650,000	—
1871S	928,000	1,340	1,463	1,535	4,750	22,000	—	—
1872	251,880	1,340	1,493	1,565	3,750	24,500	—	—
1872CC	26,900	2,450	5,450	8,950	38,500	—	—	—
1872S	780,000	1,340	1,493	1,540	3,250	23,500	—	—
1873 closed 3	Est. 208,925	1,340	1,553	1,600	3,350	—	—	200,000
1873 open 3	Est. 1,500,900	1,340	1,493	1,550	1,988	12,000	85,000	—
1873CC	22,410	2,900	4,750	11,750	37,500	115,000	—	—
1873S closed 3	1,040,600	1,340	1,463	1,543	2,150	20,000	—	—
1873S open 3	Inc. above	1,340	1,493	1,500	5,900	29,500	—	—
1874	366,800	1,340	1,493	1,540	1,978	19,500	—	—
1874CC	115,085	1,400	1,950	3,000	11,500	—	—	—
1874S	1,214,000	1,340	1,463	1,543	1,870	24,000	—	—
1875	295,740	1,340	1,493	1,540	1,900	13,500	—	—
1875CC	111,151	1,300	1,550	1,950	4,250	26,500	—	—
1875S	1,230,000	1,340	1,463	1,543	2,009	16,850	—	—
1876	583,905	1,340	1,483	1,543	1,275	13,500	78,500	—
1876CC	138,441	1,300	1,500	1,950	6,750	—	—	—
1876S	1,597,000	1,340	1,463	1,543	1,988	12,400	90,000	—

Liberty.
Coronet head, left, within circle of stars. TWENTY DOLLARS below eagle.

KM# 74.3 **Weight:** 33.4360 g. **Composition:** 0.9000 Gold, 0.9675 oz. AGW.

Date	Mintage	VF-20	XF-40	AU-50	MS-60	MS-63	MS-65	Prf-65
1877	397,670	1,230	1,370	1,413	1,545	11,500	—	—
1877CC	42,565	1,500	1,900	3,350	19,500	—	—	—
1877S	1,735,000	1,220	1,270	1,343	1,510	15,500	—	—

$20 GOLD

Date	Mintage	VF-20	XF-40	AU-50	MS-60	MS-63	MS-65	Prf-65
1878	543,645	1,240	1,370	1,423	1,630	12,500	—	—
1878CC	13,180	2,450	3,950	8,400	30,000	—	—	—
1878S	1,739,000	1,220	1,245	1,268	1,510	20,500	—	—
1879	207,630	1,300	1,370	1,373	1,510	16,500	—	—
1879CC	10,708	3,000	4,850	8,850	34,000	77,500	—	—
1879O	2,325	12,500	21,500	32,000	75,000	127,500	—	—
1879S	1,223,800	1,220	1,245	1,268	1,750	30,000	—	—
1880	51,456	1,330	1,400	1,448	3,150	25,000	—	110,000
1880S	836,000	1,220	1,245	1,278	1,950	17,500	—	—
1881	2,260	6,800	12,500	21,500	79,000	—	—	110,000
1881S	727,000	1,220	1,245	1,278	1,610	20,000	—	—
1882	630	11,500	29,500	50,000	110,000	185,000	—	130,000
1882CC	39,140	1,350	1,750	2,200	7,950	65,000	—	—
1882S	1,125,000	1,220	1,245	1,258	1,580	18,500	—	—
1883 proof only	92	—	—	14,000	—	—	—	195,000
1883CC	59,962	1,350	1,600	2,000	5,850	30,000	—	—
1883S	1,189,000	1,220	1,245	1,268	1,510	8,500	—	—
1884 proof only	71	—	—	15,000	—	—	—	225,000
1884CC	81,139	1,250	1,550	1,900	4,250	25,000	—	—
1884S	916,000	1,220	1,245	1,268	1,450	6,150	46,500	—
1885	828	8,800	13,850	18,500	48,500	100,000	—	115,000
1885CC	9,450	2,500	3,850	6,200	21,500	48,500	—	—
1885S	683,500	1,220	1,245	1,278	1,450	5,700	29,500	—
1886	1,106	12,500	29,500	42,500	73,500	140,000	—	105,000
1887	121	—	—	26,500	—	—	—	142,500
1887S	283,000	1,220	1,245	1,268	1,510	15,000	36,500	—
1888	226,266	1,220	1,245	1,288	1,560	7,900	36,500	93,500
1888S	859,600	1,220	1,245	1,268	1,450	4,650	—	—
1889	44,111	1,380	1,500	1,613	1,900	13,500	36,500	105,000
1889CC	30,945	1,500	1,750	2,350	6,650	25,500	—	—
1889S	774,700	1,220	1,245	1,268	1,460	5,400	—	—
1890	75,995	1,220	1,270	1,343	1,510	10,000	—	100,000
1890CC	91,209	1,250	1,450	1,850	4,750	32,500	—	—
1890S	802,750	1,220	1,245	1,268	1,450	6,350	30,000	—
1891	1,442	3,500	5,750	9,500	52,000	98,500	—	108,000
1891CC	5,000	4,800	9,000	9,850	26,500	71,500	—	—
1891S	1,288,125	1,220	1,245	1,268	1,450	3,000	—	—
1892	4,523	1,350	2,250	2,650	7,400	19,500	—	90,000
1892CC	27,265	1,350	1,750	2,350	6,950	36,500	—	—
1892S	930,150	1,220	1,245	1,323	1,440	2,950	24,500	—
1893	344,339	1,220	1,265	1,333	1,480	2,100	—	95,000
1893CC	18,402	1,550	1,900	2,500	5,950	29,500	—	—
1893S	996,175	1,180	1,200	1,218	1,285	2,850	28,500	—
1894	1,368,990	1,180	1,200	1,218	1,285	1,800	26,500	85,000
1894S	1,048,550	1,180	1,200	1,218	1,285	2,450	27,500	—
1895	1,114,656	1,180	1,200	1,218	1,285	1,650	17,500	82,500
1895S	1,143,500	1,180	1,200	1,218	1,285	2,200	15,500	—
1896	792,663	1,180	1,200	1,218	1,285	1,850	19,500	200,000
1896S	1,403,925	1,180	1,200	1,218	1,285	1,975	23,500	—
1897	1,383,261	1,180	1,200	1,218	1,285	2,285	18,500	200,000
1897S	1,470,250	1,180	1,200	1,218	1,285	1,450	21,500	—
1898	170,470	1,185	1,230	1,318	1,585	4,500	—	200,000
1898S	2,575,175	1,185	1,200	1,218	1,285	1,650	7,950	—
1899	1,669,384	1,180	1,200	1,218	1,285	1,625	12,500	200,000
1899S	2,010,300	1,180	1,200	1,218	1,285	1,750	21,500	—
1900	1,874,584	1,180	1,200	1,218	1,285	2,220	7,100	200,000
1900S	2,459,500	1,180	1,200	1,218	1,285	2,100	23,000	—
1901	111,526	1,180	1,200	1,218	1,285	2,220	5,850	200,000
1901S	1,596,000	1,180	1,200	1,218	1,285	3,850	21,500	—
1902	31,254	1,180	1,395	1,478	1,695	11,750	37,500	200,000
1902S	1,753,625	1,180	1,200	1,218	1,285	2,900	23,500	—
1903	287,428	1,180	1,200	1,218	1,285	2,220	5,500	200,000
1903S	954,000	1,180	1,200	1,218	1,285	2,250	13,500	—
1904	6,256,797	1,180	1,200	1,218	1,285	2,185	5,600	200,000
1904S	5,134,175	1,180	1,200	1,218	1,285	2,185	5,400	—
1905	59,011	1,185	1,220	1,253	1,585	14,500	—	200,000
1905S	1,813,000	1,180	1,200	1,218	1,285	3,250	20,500	—
1906	69,690	1,185	1,205	1,273	1,465	6,850	26,500	200,000
1906D	620,250	1,180	1,200	1,218	1,285	3,450	22,500	—
1906S	2,065,750	1,180	1,200	1,218	1,285	2,350	19,500	—
1907	1,451,864	1,180	1,200	1,218	1,285	2,185	8,200	200,000
1907D	842,250	1,180	1,200	1,218	1,285	2,650	7,350	—
1907S	2,165,800	1,180	1,200	1,218	1,285	2,650	27,000	—

Saint-Gaudens.
Roman numerals in date. No motto below eagle.

KM# 126 Designer: Augustus Saint-Gaudens. **Diameter:** 34 **Weight:** 33.4360 g. **Composition:** 0.9000 Gold, 0.9675 oz. AGW.

Date	Mintage	VF-20	XF-40	AU-50	MS-60	MS-63	MS-65	Prf-65
MCMVII (1907) high relief, unique, AU-55, $150,000	—	—	—	—	—	—	—	—
MCMVII (1907) high relief, wire rim	11,250	7,500	8,350	10,750	13,750	24,000	52,000	—
MCMVII (1907) high relief, flat rim	Inc. above	7,750	8,850	11,750	15,000	25,500	53,500	—

Saint-Gaudens.
Arabic numerals in date. No motto below eagle.

KM# 127 Designer: Augustus Saint-Gaudens. **Diameter:** 34 **Weight:** 33.4360 g. **Composition:** 0.9000 Gold, 0.9675 oz. AGW.

Date	Mintage	VF-20	XF-40	AU-50	MS-60	MS-63	MS-65	Prf-65
1907 large letters on edge, unique	—	—	—	—	—	—	—	—
1907 small letters on edge	361,667	1,210	1,230	1,260	1,360	1,735	3,350	—
1908	4,271,551	1,200	1,220	1,240	1,320	1,625	2,125	—
1908D	663,750	1,210	1,230	1,250	1,345	1,735	9,000	—

Saint-Gaudens.
Roman numerals in date. No motto below eagle.

KM# Pn1874 Designer: Augustus Saint-Gaudens. **Diameter:** 34 **Weight:** 33.4360 g. **Composition:** 0.9000 Gold, 0.9675 oz. AGW. **Notes:** The "Roman numerals" varieties for 1907 use Roman numerals for the date instead of Arabic numerals. The lettered-edge varieties have "E Pluribus Unum" on the edge, with stars between the words.

Date	Mintage	VF-20	XF-40	AU-50	MS-60	MS-63	MS-65	Prf-65
1907 extremely high relief, unique	—	—	—	—	—	—	—	—
1907 extremely high relief, lettered edge	—	—	—	—	—	—	—	—

Note: 1907 extremely high relief, lettered edge, Prf-68, private sale, 1990, $1,500,000.

$20 GOLD

Saint-Gaudens.
IN GOD WE TRUST below eagle.

KM# 131   Designer: Augustus Saint-Gaudens. **Diameter:** 34 **Weight:** 33.4360 g. **Composition:** 0.9000 Gold, 0.9675 oz. AGW.

Date	Mintage	VF-20	XF-40	AU-50	MS-60	MS-63	MS-65	Prf-65
1908	156,359	1,205	1,225	1,250	1,370	1,750	21,500	76,500
1908 Roman finish; Prf64 Rare	—	—	—	—	—	—	—	—
Note: Rare								
1908D	349,500	1,210	1,230	1,260	1,360	1,755	5,350	—
1908S	22,000	2,450	3,150	4,850	10,650	24,500	52,000	—
1909/8	161,282	1,210	1,230	1,300	1,850	6,950	32,500	—
1909	Inc. above	1,220	1,250	1,270	1,420	3,350	42,500	92,500
1909D	52,500	1,250	1,270	1,395	3,100	8,850	39,500	—
1909S	2,774,925	1,210	1,230	1,260	1,340	1,710	5,500	—
1910	482,167	1,205	1,225	1,250	1,370	1,725	7,350	84,500
1910D	429,000	1,205	1,225	1,250	1,345	1,695	2,600	—
1910S	2,128,250	1,210	1,230	1,265	1,350	1,760	8,000	—
1911	197,350	1,210	1,230	1,270	1,360	1,875	15,500	76,500
1911D	846,500	1,205	1,225	1,250	1,345	1,695	2,225	—
1911S	775,750	1,205	1,225	1,250	1,350	1,695	6,200	—
1912	149,824	1,210	1,230	1,265	1,385	2,050	19,500	76,500
1913	168,838	1,210	1,230	1,265	1,390	2,850	37,500	82,500
1913D	393,500	1,205	1,225	1,250	1,345	1,735	5,500	—
1913S	34,000	1,260	1,280	1,300	2,000	4,350	36,500	—
1914	95,320	1,220	1,240	1,300	1,275	3,900	25,000	81,500
1914D	453,000	1,205	1,225	1,250	1,345	1,705	3,250	—
1914S	1,498,000	1,205	1,225	1,250	1,345	1,695	2,000	—
1915	152,050	1,210	1,230	1,260	1,350	2,200	28,500	125,000
1915S	567,500	1,205	1,225	1,250	1,345	1,695	2,000	—
1916S	796,000	1,210	1,230	1,260	1,385	1,725	2,700	—
1920	228,250	1,200	1,220	1,240	1,345	1,755	75,000	—
1920S	558,000	14,500	18,500	28,500	53,000	105,000	355,000	—
1921	528,500	35,000	43,500	56,500	125,000	300,000	975,000	—
1922	1,375,500	1,200	1,220	1,240	1,320	1,645	2,450	—
1922S	2,658,000	1,320	1,150	1,300	2,450	4,850	42,500	—
1923	566,000	1,200	1,220	1,240	1,320	1,645	4,750	—
1923D	1,702,250	1,210	1,230	1,250	1,330	1,645	2,225	—
1924	4,323,500	1,200	1,220	1,240	1,320	1,625	2,125	—
1924D	3,049,500	1,423	1,550	1,800	3,100	9,150	75,000	—
1924S	2,927,500	1,320	1,550	1,850	3,000	9,850	135,000	—
1925	2,831,750	1,200	1,220	1,240	1,320	1,625	1,950	—
1925D	2,938,500	1,550	2,100	2,375	4,450	11,500	110,000	—
1925S	3,776,500	1,350	1,950	3,450	9,000	24,500	145,000	—
1926	816,750	1,200	1,220	1,240	1,320	1,625	2,125	—
1926D	481,000	10,000	15,500	20,500	28,500	45,000	175,000	—
1926S	2,041,500	1,403	1,550	1,725	3,150	5,650	31,500	—
1927	2,946,750	1,200	1,220	1,240	1,320	1,625	2,125	—
1927D	180,000	155,000	200,000	245,000	325,000	1,500,000	1,750,000	—
1927S	3,107,000	6,850	8,850	13,250	26,750	56,500	170,000	—
1928	8,816,000	1,200	1,220	1,240	1,320	1,625	2,125	—
1929	1,779,750	6,950	8,450	10,850	18,500	44,500	98,500	—
1930S	74,000	35,000	41,000	49,500	70,000	118,000	225,000	—
1931	2,938,250	10,500	13,500	20,500	31,500	69,500	120,000	—
1931D	106,500	8,850	11,500	21,500	42,500	88,500	145,000	—
1932	1,101,750	12,500	14,500	17,850	26,500	73,500	—	—
1933	445,500	—	—	—	—	—	9,000,000	—

Note: Sotheby/Stack's Sale, July 2002. Thirteen known, only one currently available.

COMMEMORATIVE COINAGE
1892-1954

All commemorative half dollars of 1892-1954 have the following specifications: diameter — 30.6 millimeters; weight — 12.5000 grams; composition — 0.9000 silver, 0.3617 ounces actual silver weight. Values for PDS sets contain one example each from the Philadelphia, Denver and San Francisco mints. Type coin prices are the most inexpensive single coin available from the date and mint mark combinations listed.

QUARTER

Columbian Exposition.
KM# 115 Obverse: Queen Isabella **Diameter:** 24.3 **Weight:** 6.2500 g. **Comp.:** 0.9000 Silver, 0.1808 oz. ASW.

Date	Mintage	AU-50	MS-60	MS-63	MS-64	MS-65
1893	24,214	590	665	875	1,400	4,200

Illinois Centennial-Lincoln.
KM# 143 Obv. Designer: George T. Morgan
Rev. Designer: John R. Sinnock

Date	Mintage	AU-50	MS-60	MS-63	MS-64	MS-65
1918	100,058	135	155	170	250	525

HALF DOLLAR

Columbian Exposition.
KM# 117 Obv. Designer: Charles E. Barber
Rev. Designer: George T. Morgan

Date	Mintage	AU-50	MS-60	MS-63	MS-64	MS-65
1892	950,000	18.50	28.00	85.00	180	650
1893	1,550,405	15.50	28.00	80.00	195	875

Maine Centennial.
KM# 146 Designer: Anthony de Francisci.

Date	Mintage	AU-50	MS-60	MS-63	MS-64	MS-65
1920	50,028	135	165	195	310	585

Panama-Pacific Exposition.
KM# 135 Designer: Charles E. Barber.

Date	Mintage	AU-50	MS-60	MS-63	MS-64	MS-65
1915S	27,134	465	550	825	1,550	2,650

Pilgrim Tercentenary.
KM# 147.1 Designer: Cyrus E. Dallin.

Date	Mintage	AU-50	MS-60	MS-63	MS-64	MS-65
1920	152,112	85.00	110	122	160	465

Missouri Centennial.

KM# 149.2 Designer: Robert Aitken. **Obverse:** 2 star 4 in field at left **Notes:** "Fake "2*4" counterstamps exist.

Date	Mintage	AU-50	MS-60	MS-63	MS-64	MS-65
1921	5,000	650	800	1,100	1,900	5,000

Alabama Centennial.

KM# 148.1 Designer: Laura G. Fraser.
Obverse: "2x2" at right above stars **Notes:** "Fake 2x2" counterstamps exist.

Date	Mintage	AU-50	MS-60	MS-63	MS-64	MS-65
1921	6,006	315	330	600	950	1,975

Pilgrim Tercentenary.

KM# 147.2 Designer: Cyrus E. Dallin. **Obverse:** 1921 date next to Pilgrim

Date	Mintage	AU-50	MS-60	MS-63	MS-64	MS-65
1921	20,053	175	200	225	285	600

Alabama Centennial.

KM# 148.2 Obv. Designer: Laura G. Fraser

Date	Mintage	AU-50	MS-60	MS-63	MS-64	MS-65
1921	59,038	190	215	525	685	1,800

Grant Memorial.

KM# 151.1 Designer: Laura G. Fraser.

Date	Mintage	AU-50	MS-60	MS-63	MS-64	MS-65
1922	67,405	115	125	160	290	800

Grant Memorial.

KM# 151.2 Designer: Laura G. Fraser. **Obverse:** Star above the word GRANT **Notes:** "Fake star" counterstamps exist.

Date	Mintage	AU-50	MS-60	MS-63	MS-64	MS-65
1922	4,256	950	1,300	2,100	2,850	7,250

Missouri Centennial.

KM# 149.1 Designer: Robert Aitken.

Date	Mintage	AU-50	MS-60	MS-63	MS-64	MS-65
1921	15,428	410	725	925	1,775	5,000

Monroe Doctrine Centennial.
KM# 153 Designer: Chester Beach.

Date	Mintage	AU-50	MS-60	MS-63	MS-64	MS-65
1923S	274,077	58.00	75.00	145	525	2,950

Lexington-Concord Sesquicentennial.
KM# 156 Designer: Chester Beach.

Date	Mintage	AU-50	MS-60	MS-63	MS-64	MS-65
1925	162,013	96.00	110	120	185	485

Huguenot-Walloon Tercentenary.
KM# 154 Designer: George T. Morgan. **Obverse:** Huguenot leader Gaspard de Coligny and William I of Orange

Date	Mintage	AU-50	MS-60	MS-63	MS-64	MS-65
1924	142,080	135	155	175	250	550

Stone Mountain Memorial.
KM# 157 Designer: Gutzon Borglum.

Date	Mintage	AU-50	MS-60	MS-63	MS-64	MS-65
1925	1,314,709	70.00	77.00	85.00	90.00	285

California Diamond Jubilee.
KM# 155 Designer: Jo Mora.

Date	Mintage	AU-50	MS-60	MS-63	MS-64	MS-65
1925S	86,594	215	240	280	520	1,125

Fort Vancouver Centennial.
KM# 158 Designer: Laura G. Fraser.

Date	Mintage	AU-50	MS-60	MS-63	MS-64	MS-65
1925	14,994	335	415	475	600	1,450

Oregon Trail Memorial.
KM# 159 Designer: James E. and Laura G. Fraser.

Date	Mintage	AU-50	MS-60	MS-63	MS-64	MS-65
1926	47,955	140	170	190	210	335
1926S	83,055	140	170	185	205	335
Type coin	—	150	180	190	210	320
1928	6,028	220	245	280	290	390
1933D	5,008	375	400	410	420	540
1934D	7,006	205	220	230	240	365
1936	10,006	150	190	200	210	325
1936S	5,006	170	190	210	220	360
1937D	12,008	180	205	210	215	325
1938	6,006	160	175	210	215	335
1938D	6,005	160	175	215	235	335
1938S	6,006	160	175	210	220	335
1939	3,004	525	620	630	655	720
1939D	3,004	525	620	640	675	735
1939S	3,005	525	620	630	655	725

U.S. Sesquicentennial.
KM# 160 Designer: John R. Sinnock.

Date	Mintage	AU-50	MS-60	MS-63	MS-64	MS-65
1926	141,120	88.00	115	150	600	4,400

Vermont Sesquicentennial.
KM# 162 Obv. Designer: Charles Keck

Date	Mintage	AU-50	MS-60	MS-63	MS-64	MS-65
1927	28,142	255	290	305	350	990

Hawaiian Sesquicentennial.
KM# 163 Designer: Juliette M. Fraser. **Notes:** Counterfeits exist.

Date	Mintage	AU-50	MS-60	MS-63	MS-64	MS-65
1928	10,008	1,750	2,650	3,500	4,500	6,850

Daniel Boone Bicentennial.
KM# 165.1 Designer: Augustus Lukeman.

Date	Mintage	AU-50	MS-60	MS-63	MS-64	MS-65
1934	10,007	125	135	140	150	275
1935	10,010	118	120	125	130	275
1935D	5,005	133	140	145	152	325
1935S	5,005	133	140	145	152	325

Daniel Boone Bicentennial.
KM# 165.2 Designer: Augustus Lukeman.
Reverse: "1934" added above the word PIONEER.

Date	Mintage	AU-50	MS-60	MS-63	MS-64	MS-65
1935	10,008	118	120	125	130	275
Type coin	—	130	135	145	150	240
1935D	2,003	375	415	430	485	860
1935S	2,004	375	415	430	450	890
1936	12,012	118	120	125	130	275
1936D	5,005	133	140	145	152	325
1936S	5,006	133	140	145	152	325
1937	9,810	125	130	135	980	285
1937D	2,506	285	385	390	385	560
1937S	2,506	285	385	390	415	590
1938	2,100	360	395	410	415	555
1938D	2,100	360	395	410	430	545
1938S	2,100	360	395	410	415	595

Maryland Tercentenary.
KM# 166 Designer: Hans Schuler.

Date	Mintage	AU-50	MS-60	MS-63	MS-64	MS-65
1934	25,015	160	180	195	215	350

Texas Centennial.
KM# 167 Designer: Pompeo Coppini.

Date	Mintage	AU-50	MS-60	MS-63	MS-64	MS-65
1934	61,463	140	145	155	160	290
Type coin	—	145	158	163	165	260
1935	9,994	140	145	155	160	290
1935D	10,007	140	145	155	160	290
1935S	10,008	140	145	155	160	290
1936	8,911	140	145	155	160	290
1936D	9,039	140	145	155	160	290
1936S	9,055	140	145	155	160	290
1937	6,571	142	148	160	165	295
1937D	6,605	142	148	160	165	295
1937S	6,637	142	148	160	165	295
1938	3,780	240	265	275	300	500
1938D	3,775	240	265	275	300	485
1938S	3,814	240	265	275	300	485

Arkansas Centennial.

KM# 168 Designer: Edward E. Burr.

Date	Mintage	AU-50	MS-60	MS-63	MS-64	MS-65
Type coin	—	110	115	125	130	210
1935	13,012	100.00	110	120	125	215
1935D	5,505	105	115	125	130	300
1935S	5,506	105	115	125	130	300
1936	9,660	100.00	110	120	125	230
1936D	9,660	100.00	110	120	125	230
1936S	9,662	100.00	110	120	125	230
1937	5,505	105	115	128	135	340
1937D	5,505	105	115	128	135	330
1937S	5,506	105	115	128	135	380
1938	3,156	165	190	210	210	620
1938D	3,155	165	190	195	210	610
1938S	3,156	165	190	195	210	675
1939	2,104	330	390	400	410	1,000
1939D	2,104	330	390	400	410	980
1939S	2,105	330	390	400	410	965

Connecticut Tercentenary.

KM# 169 Designer: Henry Kreiss.

Date	Mintage	AU-50	MS-60	MS-63	MS-64	MS-65
1935	25,018	255	290	310	380	540

Hudson, N.Y., Sesquicentennial.

KM# 170 Designer: Chester Beach.

Date	Mintage	AU-50	MS-60	MS-63	MS-64	MS-65
1935	10,008	750	925	1,250	1,675	2,250

Old Spanish Trail.

KM# 172 Designer: L.W. Hoffecker. **Notes:** Counterfeits exist.

Date	Mintage	AU-50	MS-60	MS-63	MS-64	MS-65
1935	10,008	1,250	1,375	1,700	1,900	2,250

San Diego-Pacific International Exposition.

KM# 171 Designer: Robert Aitken.

Date	Mintage	AU-50	MS-60	MS-63	MS-64	MS-65
1935S	70,132	105	130	145	150	170
1936D	30,092	105	135	150	160	170

Albany, N.Y., Charter Anniversary.

KM# 173 Designer: Gertrude K. Lathrop.

Date	Mintage	AU-50	MS-60	MS-63	MS-64	MS-65
1936	17,671	320	330	380	385	470

Arkansas Centennial.

KM# 187 Obv. Designer: Henry Kreiss **Rev. Designer:** Edward E. Burr **Obverse:** Sen. Joseph T. Robinson

Date	Mintage	AU-50	MS-60	MS-63	MS-64	MS-65
1936	25,265	145	150	165	180	420

Battle of Gettysburg 75th Anniversary.
KM# 181 Designer: Frank Vittor.

Date	Mintage	AU-50	MS-60	MS-63	MS-64	MS-65
1936	26,928	435	475	500	525	765

Columbia, S.C., Sesquicentennial.
KM# 178 Designer: A. Wolfe Davidson.

Date	Mintage	AU-50	MS-60	MS-63	MS-64	MS-65
1936	9,007	275	280	300	310	415
Type coin	—		280	290	330	335	385
1936D	8,009	275	280	300	310	415
1936S	8,007	275	280	300	310	415

Bridgeport, Conn., Centennial.
KM# 175 Designer: Henry Kreiss.

Date	Mintage	AU-50	MS-60	MS-63	MS-64	MS-65
1936	25,015	140	150	190	200	315

Delaware Tercentenary.
KM# 179 Designer: Carl L. Schmitz.

Date	Mintage	AU-50	MS-60	MS-63	MS-64	MS-65
1936	20,993	310	325	365	385	490

Cincinnati Music Center.
KM# 176 Designer: Constance Ortmayer.

Date	Mintage	AU-50	MS-60	MS-63	MS-64	MS-65
Type coin	—	335	345	375	560	700
1936	5,005	315	330	360	540	925
1936D	5,005	315	330	360	540	750
1936S	5,006	315	330	360	540	750

Elgin, Ill., Centennial.
KM# 180 Designer: Trygve Rovelstad.

Date	Mintage	AU-50	MS-60	MS-63	MS-64	MS-65
1936	20,015	245	265	280	295	355

Cleveland-Great Lakes Exposition.
KM# 177 Designer: Brenda Putnam.

Date	Mintage	AU-50	MS-60	MS-63	MS-64	MS-65
1936	50,030	135	140	150	160	245

Long Island Tercentenary.
KM# 182 Designer: Howard K. Weinman.

Date	Mintage	AU-50	MS-60	MS-63	MS-64	MS-65
1936	81,826	88.00	98.00	110	130	420

Lynchburg, Va., Sesquicentennial.
KM# 183 Designer: Charles Keck.

Date	Mintage	AU-50	MS-60	MS-63	MS-64	MS-65
1936	20,013	235	265	280	295	365

Norfolk, Va., Bicentennial. KM# 184
Designer: William M. and Marjorie E. Simpson.

Date	Mintage	AU-50	MS-60	MS-63	MS-64	MS-65
1936	16,936	535	565	590	610	650

Rhode Island Tercentenary. KM# 185
Designer: Arthur G. Carey and John H. Benson.

Date	Mintage	AU-50	MS-60	MS-63	MS-64	MS-65
1936	20,013	100.00	110	120	130	260
Type coin	—	105	110	125	128	290
1936D	15,010	100.00	110	120	130	275
1936S	15,011	100.00	110	120	130	290

San Francisco-Oakland Bay Bridge.
KM# 174 Designer: Jacques Schnier.

Date	Mintage	AU-50	MS-60	MS-63	MS-64	MS-65
1936	71,424	170	180	220	225	375

Wisconsin Territorial Centennial.
KM# 188 Designer: David Parsons.

Date	Mintage	AU-50	MS-60	MS-63	MS-64	MS-65
1936	25,015	230	255	275	315	400

York County, Maine, Tercentenary.
KM# 189 Designer: Walter H. Rich.

Date	Mintage	AU-50	MS-60	MS-63	MS-64	MS-65
1936	25,015	135	170	195	300	590

Battle of Antietam 75th Anniversary.
KM# 190 Designer: William M. Simpson.

Date	Mintage	AU-50	MS-60	MS-63	MS-64	MS-65
1937	18,028	725	760	790	850	985

Roanoke Island, N.C..
KM# 186 Designer: William M. Simpson.

Date	Mintage	AU-50	MS-60	MS-63	MS-64	MS-65
1937	29,030	255	285	310	330	340

New Rochelle, N.Y..
KM# 191
Designer: Gertrude K. Lathrop.

Date	Mintage	AU-50	MS-60	MS-63	MS-64	MS-65
1938	15,266	420	445	460	470	610

Booker T. Washington.
KM# 198 Designer: Isaac S. Hathaway. **Notes:**
Actual mintages are higher, but unsold issues were melted to produce Washington Carver issues.

Date	Mintage	AU-50	MS-60	MS-63	MS-64	MS-65
1946	1,000,546	14.00	18.00	19.50	21.00	50.00
Type coin	—	15.00	16.00	17.50	18.50	56.00
1946D	200,113	16.00	20.00	21.00	30.00	64.00
1946S	500,729	14.00	18.00	19.50	21.00	50.00
1947	100,017	25.00	35.00	55.00	65.00	95.00
1947D	100,017	25.00	35.00	55.00	70.00	115
1947S	100,017	25.00	35.00	55.00	65.00	90.00
1948	8,005	38.00	58.00	85.00	86.00	100.00
1948D	8,005	38.00	58.00	85.00	86.00	94.00
1948S	8,005	38.00	58.00	85.00	95.00	98.00
1949	6,004	67.00	83.00	92.00	98.00	120
1949D	6,004	67.00	83.00	92.00	98.00	120
1949S	6,004	67.00	83.00	95.00	104	110
1950	6,004	45.00	65.00	78.00	88.00	98.00
1950D	6,004	45.00	65.00	75.00	88.00	96.00
1950S	512,091	15.00	20.00	24.00	28.00	52.00

Date	Mintage	AU-50	MS-60	MS-63	MS-64	MS-65
1951	51,082	15.00	20.00	24.00	28.00	50.00
1951D	7,004	45.00	65.00	78.00	90.00	95.00
1951S	7,004	45.00	65.00	78.00	90.00	95.00

Iowa Statehood Centennial.
KM# 197 Designer: Adam Pietz.

Date	Mintage	AU-50	MS-60	MS-63	MS-64	MS-65
1946	100,057	115	120	125	130	260

Booker T. Washington and George Washington Carver.
KM# 200 Designer: Isaac S. Hathaway.

Date	Mintage	AU-50	MS-60	MS-63	MS-64	MS-65
1951	110,018	26.00	34.00	53.00	54.00	290
Type coin	—	14.00	16.00	18.50	20.00	52.50
1951D	10,004	35.00	43.00	60.00	58.00	140
1951S	10,004	35.00	43.00	60.00	58.00	140
1952	2,006,29 2	15.00	18.00	26.50	44.00	48.00
1952D	8,006	40.00	50.00	70.00	70.00	200
1952S	8,006	40.00	50.00	80.00	70.00	160
1953	8,003	35.00	47.00	75.00	85.00	260
1953D	8,003	35.00	47.00	75.00	85.00	175
1953S	108,020	26.00	33.00	50.00	55.00	120
1954	12,006	36.00	42.00	60.00	65.00	150
1954D	12,006	36.00	42.00	60.00	65.00	200
1954S	122,024	24.00	32.00	38.00	48.00	65.00

DOLLAR

La Fayette. **KM# 118 Designer:** Charles E. Barber. **Diameter:** 38.1 **Weight:** 26.7300 g. **Composition:** 0.9000 Silver, 0.7734 oz. ASW.

Date	Mintage	AU-50	MS-60	MS-63	MS-64	MS-65
1900	36,026	675	1,025	2,150	3,700	10,850

Louisiana Purchase Exposition - McKinley.
KM# 120 Obv. Designer: Charles E. Barber **Obverse:** William McKinley **Diameter:** 15 **Weight:** 1.6720 g. **Composition:** 0.9000 Gold, 0.0484 oz. AGW.

Date	Mintage	AU-50	MS-60	MS-63	MS-64	MS-65
1903	17,500	715	765	1,080	2,150	3,300

Louisiana Purchase Exposition - Jefferson.
KM# 119 Designer: Charles E. Barber. **Obverse:** Jefferson **Diameter:** 15 **Weight:** 1.6720 g. **Composition:** 0.9000 Gold, 0.0484 oz. AGW.

Date	Mintage	AU-50	MS-60	MS-63	MS-64	MS-65
1903	17,500	700	765	1,160	1,900	3,100

Lewis and Clark Exposition.
KM# 121 Obv. Designer: Charles E. Barber **Diameter:** 15 **Weight:** 1.6720 g. **Composition:** 0.9000 Gold, 0.0484 oz. AGW.

Date	Mintage	AU-50	MS-60	MS-63	MS-64	MS-65
1904	10,025	1,050	1,350	2,550	5,900	12,250
1905	10,041	1,300	1,625	3,300	7,000	18,500

Panama-Pacific Exposition.
KM# 136 Obv. Designer: Charles Keck **Diameter:** 15 **Weight:** 1.6720 g. **Composition:** 0.9000 Gold, 0.0484 oz. AGW.

Date	Mintage	AU-50	MS-60	MS-63	MS-64	MS-65
1915S	15,000	650	750	950	1,500	2,450

McKinley Memorial.
KM# 144 Obv. Designer: Charles E. Barber **Rev. Designer:** George T. Morgan **Diameter:** 15 **Weight:** 1.6720 g. **Composition:** 0.9000 Gold, 0.0484 oz. AGW.

Date	Mintage	AU-50	MS-60	MS-63	MS-64	MS-65
1916	9,977	625	685	800	1,550	2,350
1917	10,000	785	800	1,325	2,200	3,800

Grant Memorial.
KM# 152.1 Obv. Designer: Laura G. Fraser **Diameter:** 15 **Weight:** 1.6720 g. **Composition:** 0.9000 Gold, 0.0484 oz. AGW. **Notes:** Without an incuse "star" above the word GRANT on the obverse.

Date	Mintage	AU-50	MS-60	MS-63	MS-64	MS-65
1922	5,000	1,875	1,900	2,350	3,650	4,900

Grant Memorial.
KM# 152.2 Obv. Designer: Laura G. Fraser **Diameter:** 15 **Weight:** 1.6720 g. **Composition:** 0.9000 Gold, 0.0484 oz. AGW. **Notes:** Variety with an incuse "star" above the word GRANT on the obverse.

Date	Mintage	AU-50	MS-60	MS-63	MS-64	MS-65
1922	5,016	1,800	1,950	2,400	3,700	4,400

$2.50 (QUARTER EAGLE)

Panama-Pacific Exposition.
KM# 137 Obv. Designer: Charles E. Barber **Rev. Designer:** George T. Morgan **Diameter:** 18 **Weight:** 4.1800 g. **Composition:** 0.9000 Gold, 0.1209 oz. AGW.

Date	Mintage	AU-50	MS-60	MS-63	MS-64	MS-65
1915S	6,749	1,750	2,100	4,350	6,300	8,000

U.S. Sesquicentennial.
KM# 161 Obv. Designer: John R. Sinnock **Diameter:** 18 **Weight:** 4.1800 g. **Composition:** 0.9000 Gold, 0.1209 oz. AGW.

Date	Mintage	AU-50	MS-60	MS-63	MS-64	MS-65
1926	46,019	525	565	850	1,700	4,200

COMMEMORATIVE COINAGE 1892-1954

$50

Panama-Pacific Exposition Octagonal. KM# 139 Obv. Designer: Robert Aitken Diameter: 44
Weight: 83.5900 g. **Composition:** 0.9000 Gold, 2.4186 oz. AGW.

Date	Mintage	AU-50	MS-60	MS-63	MS-64	MS-65
1915S	645	52,500	55,000	80,000	99,500	148,000

Panama-Pacific Exposition Round. KM# 138 Obv. Designer: Robert Aitken Diameter: 44
Weight: 83.5900 g. **Composition:** 0.9000 Gold, 2.4186 oz. AGW.

Date	Mintage	AU-50	MS-60	MS-63	MS-64	MS-65
1915S	483	54,000	60,000	82,500	105,000	145,000

COMMEMORATIVE COINAGE 1982-PRESENT

All commemorative silver dollar coins of 1982-present have the following specifications: diameter — 38.1 millimeters; weight — 26.7300 grams; composition — 0.9000 silver, 0.7736 ounces actual silver weight. All commemorative $5 coins of 1982-present have the following specifications: diameter — 21.6 millimeters; weight — 8.3590 grams; composition: 0.9000 gold, 0.242 ounces actual gold weight.

Note: In 1982, after a hiatus of nearly 20 years, coinage of commemorative half dollars resumed. Those designated with a 'W' were struck at the West Point Mint. Some issues were struck in copper-nickel. Those struck in silver have the same size, weight and composition as the prior commemorative half-dollar series.

HALF DOLLAR

George Washington, 250th Birth Anniversary.
KM# 208 Obv. Designer: Elizabeth Jones **Diameter:** 30.6 **Weight:** 12.5000 g. **Composition:** 0.9000 Silver, 0.3617 oz. ASW.

Date	Mintage	Proof	MS-65	Prf-65
1982D	2,210,458	—	6.50	—
1982S	—	4,894,044	—	6.50

Statue of Liberty Centennial.
KM# 212 Obv. Designer: Edgar Z. Steever **Rev. Designer:** Sherl Joseph Winter **Weight:** 11.3400 g. **Composition:** Copper-Nickel Clad Copper

Date	Mintage	Proof	MS-65	Prf-65
1986D	928,008	—	5.25	—
1986S	—	6,925,627	—	5.25

Congress Bicentennial.
KM# 224 Obv. Designer: Patricia L. Verani

Rev. Designer: William Woodward and Edgar Z. Steever **Weight:** 11.3400 g. **Composition:** Copper-Nickel Clad Copper

Date	Mintage	Proof	MS-65	Prf-65
1989D	163,753	—	7.50	—
1989S	—	—	—	7.25

Mount Rushmore 50th Anniversary.
KM# 228 Obv. Designer: Marcel Jovine **Rev. Designer:** T. James Ferrell **Weight:** 11.3400 g. **Composition:** Copper-Nickel Clad Copper

Date	Mintage	Proof	MS-65	Prf-65
1991D	172,754	—	19.50	—
1991S	—	—	—	18.50

1992 Olympics.
KM# 233 Obv. Designer: William Cousins **Rev. Designer:** Steven M. Bieda **Weight:** 11.3400 g. **Composition:** Copper-Nickel Clad Copper

Date	Mintage	Proof	MS-65	Prf-65
1992P	161,607	—	8.50	—
1992S	—	519,645	—	9.00

Columbus Voyage - 500th Anniversary.

KM# 237 Designer: T. James Ferrell.
Weight: 11.3400 g. **Composition:** Copper-Nickel Clad Copper

Date	Mintage	Proof	MS-65	Prf-65
1992D	135,702	—	11.50	—
1992S	—	390,154	—	10.50

1994 World Cup Soccer.

KM# 246 Obv. Designer: Richard T. LaRoche
Rev. Designer: Dean McMullen **Weight:** 11.3400 g.
Composition: Copper-Nickel Clad Copper

Date	Mintage	Proof	MS-65	Prf-65
1994D	168,208	—	9.25	—
1994P	122,412	—	10.25	—
1994P	—	609,354	—	8.00

James Madison - Bill of Rights.

KM# 240 Obv. Designer: T. James Ferrell
Rev. Designer: Dean McMullen **Weight:** 12.5000 g. **Composition:** 0.9000 Silver, 0.3617 oz. ASW.

Date	Mintage	Proof	MS-65	Prf-65
1993W	173,224	—	18.50	—
1993S	—	559,758	—	15.00

1996 Atlanta Olympics - Baseball.

KM# 262 Obv. Designer: Edgar Z. Steever
Obverse: Baseball **Weight:** 11.3400 g.
Composition: Copper-Nickel Clad Copper

Date	Mintage	Proof	MS-65	Prf-65
1995S	164,605	—	20.50	—
1995S	—	118,087	—	18.00

World War II 50th Anniversary.

KM# 243 Obv. Designer: George Klauba **Rev. Designer:** William J. Leftwich **Weight:** 11.3400 g. **Composition:** Copper-Nickel Clad Copper

Date	Mintage	Proof	MS-65	Prf-65
(1993)P	192,968	—	27.50	—
(1993)P	—	290,343	—	24.50

1996 Atlanta Olympics - Basketball.

KM# 257 Obverse: Basketball **Weight:** 11.3400 g.
Composition: Copper-Nickel Clad Copper

Date	Mintage	Proof	MS-65	Prf-65
1995S	—	169,655	—	16.50
1995S	171,001	—	19.50	—

Civil War.

KM# 254 Obv. Designer: Don Troiani
Rev. Designer: T. James Ferrell **Weight:** 11.3400 g.
Composition: Copper-Nickel Clad Copper

Date	Mintage	Proof	MS-65	Prf-65
1995S	119,510	—	39.50	—
1995S	—	330,099	—	38.50

U. S. Capitol Visitor Center.

KM# 323 Obv. Designer: Dean McMullen
Rev. Designer: Alex Shagin and Marcel Jovine
Weight: 11.3400 g. **Composition:** Copper-Nickel
Clad Copper

Date	Mintage	Proof	MS-65	Prf-65
2001P	99,157	—	13.50	—
2001P	—	77,962	—	16.00

1996 Atlanta Olympics - Soccer.

KM# 271 Obverse: Soccer **Weight:** 11.3400 g.
Composition: Copper-Nickel Clad Copper

Date	Mintage	Proof	MS-65	Prf-65
1996S	52,836	—	138	—
1996S	—	122,412	—	100.00

First Flight Centennial.

KM# 348 Obv. Designer: John Mercanti
Rev. Designer: Donna Weaver **Weight:** 11.3400 g.
Composition: Copper-Nickel Clad Copper

Date	Mintage	Proof	MS-65	Prf-65
2003P	57,726	—	14.50	—
2003P	—	111,569	—	16.00

1996 Atlanta Olympics - Swimming.

KM# 267 Obverse: Swimming **Weight:** 11.3400 g.
Composition: Copper-Nickel Clad Copper

Date	Mintage	Proof	MS-65	Prf-65
1996S	49,533	—	150	—
1996S	—	114,315	—	34.50

American Bald Eagle.

KM# 438 Obverse: Two eaglets in nest with egg
Diameter: 30.6 **Weight:** 11.3400 g.
Composition: Copper-Nickel Clad Copper

Date	Mintage	Proof	MS-65	Prf-65
2008	750,000	—	—	—

DOLLAR

1984 Los Angeles Olympics - Discus.

KM# 209 Obv. Designer: Elizabeth Jones

Date	Mintage	Proof	MS-65	Prf-65
1983P	294,543	—	17.50	—
1983D	174,014	—	18.50	—
1983S	174,014	—	18.50	—
1983S	—	1,577,025	—	18.00

Statue of Liberty Centennial.

KM# 214 Obv. Designer: John Mercanti
Rev. Designer: John Mercanti and Matthew Peloso

Date	Mintage	Proof	MS-65	Prf-65
1986P	723,635	—	17.80	—
1986S	—	6,414,638	—	18.50

1984 Los Angeles Olympics - Stadium Statues.

KM# 210 Obv. Designer: Robert Graham

Date	Mintage	Proof	MS-65	Prf-65
1984P	217,954	—	17.50	—
1984D	116,675	—	18.50	—
1984S	116,675	—	18.50	—
1984S	—	1,801,210	—	18.50

Constitution Bicentennial.

KM# 220 Obv. Designer: Patricia L. Verani

Date	Mintage	Proof	MS-65	Prf-65
1987P	451,629	—	17.80	—
1987S	—	2,747,116	—	18.50

1988 Olympics.

KM# 222   Obv. Designer: Patricia L. Verani
Rev. Designer: Sherl Joseph Winter

Date	Mintage	Proof	MS-65	Prf-65
1988D	191,368	—	17.80	—
1988S	—	1,359,366	—	18.50

Eisenhower Centennial.

KM# 227   Obv. Designer: John Mercanti
Rev. Designer: Marcel Jovine and John Mercanti

Date	Mintage	Proof	MS-65	Prf-65
1990W	241,669	—	17.80	—
1990P	—	638,335	—	17.80

Congress Bicentennial.

KM# 225 Designer: William Woodward and Chester Y. Martin.

Date	Mintage	Proof	MS-65	Prf-65
1989D	135,203	—	21.50	—
1989S	—	762,198	—	20.50

Korean War - 38th Anniversary.

KM# 231 Obv. Designer: John Mercanti
Rev. Designer: T. James Ferrell

Date	Mintage	Proof	MS-65	Prf-65
1991D	213,049	—	19.50	—
1991P	—	618,488	—	20.00

Mount Rushmore 50th Anniversary.
KM# 229 Obv. Designer: Marika Somogyi
Rev. Designer: Frank Gasparro

Date	Mintage	Proof	MS-65	Prf-65
1991P	133,139	—	28.50	—
1991S	—	738,419	—	23.50

1992 Olympics - Baseball.
KM# 234 Obv. Designer: John R. Deecken and
Chester Y. Martin **Rev. Designer:** Marcel Jovine

Date	Mintage	Proof	MS-65	Prf-65
1992D	187,552	—	22.50	—
1992S	—	504,505	—	24.50

USO 50th Anniversary.
KM# 232 Obv. Designer: Robert Lamb
Rev. Designer: John Mercanti

Date	Mintage	Proof	MS-65	Prf-65
1991D	124,958	—	18.00	—
1991S	—	321,275	—	18.50

Columbus Discovery - 500th Anniversary.
KM# 238 Obv. Designer: John Mercanti
Rev. Designer: Thomas D. Rogers, Sr.

Date	Mintage	Proof	MS-65	Prf-65
1992D	106,949	—	26.00	—
1992P	—	385,241	—	29.00

White House Bicentennial.

KM# 236 Obv. Designer: Edgar Z. Steever
Rev. Designer: Chester Y. Martin

Date	Mintage	Proof	MS-65	Prf-65
1992D	123,803	—	26.00	—
1992W	—	375,851	—	28.00

Thomas Jefferson 250th Birth Anniversary.

KM# 249 Designer: T. James Ferrell.

Date	Mintage	Proof	MS-65	Prf-65
1993P	266,927	—	18.50	—
1993S	—	332,891	—	19.50

James Madison - Bill of Rights.

KM# 241 Obv. Designer: William Krawczewicz
and Thomas D. Rogers, Sr. **Rev. Designer:** Dean
McMullen and Thomas D. Rogers, Sr.

Date	Mintage	Proof	MS-65	Prf-65
1993D	98,383	—	18.50	—
1993S	—	534,001	—	20.50

World War II 50th Anniversary.

KM# 244 Designer: Thomas D. Rogers, Sr..

Date	Mintage	Proof	MS-65	Prf-65
1993D	94,708	—	39.50	—
1993W	—	322,422	—	37.50

1994 World Cup Sccer.

KM# 247 Obv. Designer: Dean McMullen and
T. James Ferrell

Date	Mintage	Proof	MS-65	Prf-65
1994D	81,698	—	22.50	—
1994S	—	576,978	—	23.50

U.S. Capitol Bicentennial.

KM# 253

Date	Mintage	Proof	MS-65	Prf-65
1994D	68,352	—	18.00	—
1994S	—	279,416	—	22.50

National Prisoner of War Museum.

KM# 251 Obv. Designer: Thomas Nielson and
Alfred Maletsky **Rev. Designer:** Edgar Z. Steever

Date	Mintage	Proof	MS-65	Prf-65
1994W	54,790	—	85.00	—
1994P	—	220,100	—	42.00

Vietnam Veterans Memorial.

KM# 250 Obv. Designer: John Mercanti
Rev. Designer: Thomas D. Rogers, Sr.

Date	Mintage	Proof	MS-65	Prf-65
1994W	57,317	—	79.00	—
1994P	—	226,262	—	30.00

Women in Military Service Memorial.

KM# 252 Obv. Designer: T. James Ferrell
Rev. Designer: Thomas D. Rogers, Sr.

Date	Mintage	Proof	MS-65	Prf-65
1994W	53,054	—	39.50	—
1994P	—	213,201	—	36.00

1996 Atlanta Olympics - Gymnastics.

KM# 260 Obverse: Gymnastics

Date	Mintage	Proof	MS-65	Prf-65
1995D	42,497	—	67.50	—
1995P	—	182,676	—	50.00

1996 Atlanta Olympics - Cycling.

KM# 263 Obv. Designer: John Mercanti
Obverse: Cycling

Date	Mintage	Proof	MS-65	Prf-65
1995D	19,662	—	142	—
1995P	—	118,795	—	46.00

1996 Atlanta Olympics - Track and field.

KM# 264 Obv. Designer: John Mercanti **Obverse:** Track and field

Date	Mintage	Proof	MS-65	Prf-65
1995D	24,796	—	92.00	—
1995P	—	136,935	—	49.00

1996 Atlanta Paralympics - Blind runner.

KM# 259 Obverse: Blind runner

Date	Mintage	Proof	MS-65	Prf-65
1995D	28,649	—	82.00	—
1995P	—	138,337	—	54.00

Special Olympics World Games.

KM# 266 Obv. Designer: Jamie Wyeth and T. James Ferrell **Rev. Designer:** Thomas D. Rogers, Sr.

Date	Mintage	Proof	MS-65	Prf-65
1995W	89,301	—	29.50	—
1995P	—	351,764	—	26.50

Civil War.

KM# 255 Obv. Designer: Don Troiani and Edgar Z. Steever **Rev. Designer:** John Mercanti

Date	Mintage	Proof	MS-65	Prf-65
1995P	45,866	—	69.00	—
1995S	—	437,114	—	69.00

1996 Atlanta Olympics - High Jump.

KM# A272 Rev. Designer: Thomas D. Rogers, Sr. **Obverse:** High jumper

Date	Mintage	Proof	MS-65	Prf-65
1996D	15,697	—	380	—
1996P	—	124,502	—	58.00

1996 Atlanta Olympics - Rowing.

KM# 272 **Rev. Designer:** Thomas D. Rogers, Sr.
Obverse: Rowing

Date	Mintage	Proof	MS-65	Prf-65
1996D	16,258	—	345	—
1996P	—	151,890	—	70.00

1996 Atlanta Paralympics - Wheelchair racer.

KM# 268 **Rev. Designer:** Thomas D. Rogers, Sr.
Obverse: Wheelchair racer

Date	Mintage	Proof	MS-65	Prf-65
1996D	14,497	—	365	—
1996P	—	84,280	—	82.00

1996 Atlanta Olympics - Tennis.

KM# 269 **Rev. Designer:** Thomas D. Rogers, Sr.
Obverse: Tennis

Date	Mintage	Proof	MS-65	Prf-65
1996D	15,983	—	315	—
1996P	—	92,016	—	85.00

National Community Service.

KM# 275 **Obv. Designer:** Thomas D. Rogers, Sr.
Rev. Designer: William C. Cousins

Date	Mintage	Proof	MS-65	Prf-65
1996S	23,500	—	220	—
1996S	—	101,543	—	76.00

Smithsonian Institution 150th Anniversary.

KM# 276 Obv. Designer: Thomas D. Rogers, Sr.
Rev. Designer: John Mercanti

Date	Mintage	Proof	MS-65	Prf-65
1996D	31,230	—	135	—
1996P	—	129,152	—	57.50

National Law Enforcement Officers Memorial.

KM# 281 Designer: Alfred Maletsky.

Date	Mintage	Proof	MS-65	Prf-65
1997P	—	110,428	—	105
1997P	28,575	—	160	—

Jackie Robinson.

KM# 279 Obv. Designer: Alfred Maletsky
Rev. Designer: T. James Ferrell

Date	Mintage	Proof	MS-65	Prf-65
1997S	30,007	—	98.00	—
1997S	—	110,495	—	118

U.S. Botanic Gardens 175th Anniversary.

KM# 278 Designer: Edgar Z. Steever.

Date	Mintage	Proof	MS-65	Prf-65
1997P	57,272	—	39.50	—
1997P	—	264,528	—	38.00

Black Revolutionary War Patriots.

KM# 288 Obv. Designer: John Mercanti **Rev. Designer:** Ed Dwight **Obverse:** Crispus Attucks

Date	Mintage	Proof	MS-65	Prf-65
1998S	37,210	—	160	—
1998S	—	75,070	—	96.00

Dolley Madison.

KM# 298 Designer: Tiffany & Co..

Date	Mintage	Proof	MS-65	Prf-65
1999P	22,948	—	42.00	—
1999P	—	158,247	—	34.50

Robert F. Kennedy.

KM# 287 Obv. Designer: Thomas D. Rogers, Sr. **Rev. Designer:** James M. Peed and Thomas D. Rogers, Sr.

Date	Mintage	Proof	MS-65	Prf-65
1998S	106,422	—	31.50	—
1998S	—	99,020	—	42.50

Yellowstone.

KM# 299 Obv. Designer: Edgar Z. Steever **Rev. Designer:** William C. Cousins

Date	Mintage	Proof	MS-65	Prf-65
1999P	23,614	—	49.50	—
1999P	—	128,646	—	45.00

Leif Ericson.

KM# 313 Obv. Designer: John Mercanti
Rev. Designer: T. James Ferrell

Date	Mintage	Proof	MS-65	Prf-65
2000P	28,150	—	87.00	—
2000 Iceland	—	15,947	—	25.00
2000P	—	58,612	—	70.00

American Indian - Bison.

KM# 325 Designer: James E. Fraser.

Date	Mintage	Proof	MS-65	Prf-65
2001D	197,131	—	175	—
2001P	—	272,869	—	180

Library of Congress Bicentennial.

KM# 311 Obv. Designer: Thomas D. Rogers, Sr.
Rev. Designer: John Mercanti

Date	Mintage	Proof	MS-65	Prf-65
2000P	52,771	—	38.00	—
2000P	—	196,900	—	33.00

Capitol Visitor Center.

KM# 324 Obv. Designer: Marika Somogyi
Rev. Designer: John Mercanti

Date	Mintage	Proof	MS-65	Prf-65
2001P	66,636	—	30.00	—
2001P	—	143,793	—	39.00

2002 Winter Olympics - Salt Lake City.

KM# 336 Obv. Designer: John Mercanti **Rev. Designer:** Donna Weaver

Date	Mintage	Proof	MS-65	Prf-65
2002P	35,388	—	30.00	—
2002P	—	142,873	—	38.00

First Flight Centennial.

KM# 349 Obv. Designer: T. James Ferrell **Rev. Designer:** Norman E. Nemeth **Obverse:** Orville and Wilbur Wright **Reverse:** Wright Brothers airplane

Date	Mintage	Proof	MS-65	Prf-65
2003P	53,761	—	33.50	—
2003P	—	193,086	—	28.50

U.S. Military Academy at West Point - Bicentennial.

KM# 338 Obv. Designer: T. James Ferrell **Rev. Designer:** John Mercanti

Date	Mintage	Proof	MS-65	Prf-65
2002W	103,201	—	18.50	—
2002W	—	288,293	—	18.50

Lewis and Clark Corps of Discovery Bicentennial.

KM# 363

Date	Mintage	Proof	MS-65	Prf-65
2004P	90,323	—	31.00	—
2004P	—	288,492	—	27.50

Thomas A. Edison - Electric Light 125th Anniversary.

KM# 362 Obv. Designer: Donna Weaver
Rev. Designer: John Mercanti

Date	Mintage	Proof	MS-65	Prf-65
2004P	68,031	—	34.00	—
2004P	—	213,409	—	34.50

U.S. Marine Corps, 230th Anniversary.

KM# 376

Date	Mintage	Proof	MS-65	Prf-65
2005P	130,000	—	37.00	—
2005P	—	370,000	—	39.00

John Marshall, 250th Birth Anniversary.

KM# 375 Obv. Designer: John Mercanti
Rev. Designer: Donna Weaver

Date	Mintage	Proof	MS-65	Prf-65
2005P	48,953	—	32.00	—
2005P	—	141,993	—	35.00

Benjamin Franklin, 300th Birth Anniversary.

KM# 387 Obv. Designer: Norman E. Nemeth
Obverse: Youthful Franklin flying kite
Reverse: Revolutionary era JOIN OR DIE snake cartoon illustration

Date	Mintage	Proof	MS-65	Prf-65
2006P	58,000	—	32.00	—
2006P	—	142,000	—	45.00

Benjamin Franklin, 300th Birth Anniversary.

KM# 388 Obverse: Bust 3/4 right, signature in oval below **Reverse:** Continental Dollar of 1776 in center

Date	Mintage	Proof	MS-65	Prf-65
2006P	58,000	—	33.00	—
2006P	—	142,000	—	44.00

Central High School Desegregation.

KM# 418 Obverse: Childrens feet walking left with adult feet in military boots **Reverse:** Little Rock's Central High School

Date	Mintage	Proof	MS-65	Prf-65
2007P	—	—	50.00	—
2007P	—	—	—	50.00

San Francisco Mint Museum.

KM# 394 Obverse: 3/4 view of building **Reverse:** Reverse of 1880s Morgan silver dollar

Date	Mintage	Proof	MS-65	Prf-65
2006S	—	—	41.00	—
2006S	—	—	—	42.00

Jamestown - 400th Anniversary.

KM# 405 Obverse: Two settlers and Native American **Reverse:** Three ships

Date	Mintage	Proof	MS-65	Prf-65
2007P	—	—	36.50	—
2007P	—	—	—	35.00

American Bald Eagle.

KM# 439 Obverse: Eagle with flight, mountain in background at right **Reverse:** Great Seal of the United States

Date	Mintage	Proof	MS-65	Prf-65
2008P	500,000	—	39.50	—
2008P	—	—	—	38.50

Louis Braille Birth Bicentennial.

KM# 455 Obv. Designer: Joel Iskowitz and Phebe Hemphill **Rev. Designer:** Susan Gamble and Joseph Menna **Obverse:** Louis Braille bust facing **Reverse:** School child reading book in Braille, BRL in Braille code above

Date	Mintage	Proof	MS-65	Prf-65
2009P	—	—	32.50	—
2009P	—	—	—	42.50

$5 (HALF EAGLE)

Lincoln Bicentennial.

KM# 454 Obv. Designer: Justin Kunz and Don Everhart **Rev. Designer:** Phebe Hemphill **Obverse:** 3/4 portrait facing right **Reverse:** Part of Gettysburg Address within wreath

Date	Mintage	Proof	MS-65	Prf-65
2009P	—	—	32.50	—
2009P Proof	—	—	—	42.50

Statue of Liberty Centennial.

KM# 215 Designer: Elizabeth Jones.

Date	Mintage	Proof	MS-65	Prf-65
1986W	95,248	—	266	—
1986W	—	404,013	—	266

Constitution Bicentennial.

KM# 221 Designer: Marcel Jovine.

Date	Mintage	Proof	MS-65	Prf-65
1987W	214,225	—	266	—
1987W	—	651,659	—	266

1988 Olympics.
KM# 223 Obv. Designer: Elizabeth Jones
Rev. Designer: Marcel Jovine

Date	Mintage	Proof	MS-65	Prf-65
1988W	62,913	—	266	—
1988W	—	281,456	—	266

Congress Bicentennial.
KM# 226 Obv. Designer: John Mercanti

Date	Mintage	Proof	MS-65	Prf-65
1989W	46,899	—	266	—
1989W	—	164,690	—	266

Mount Rushmore 50th Anniversary.
KM# 230 Obv. Designer: John Mercanti **Rev.
Designer:** Robert Lamb and William C. Cousins

Date	Mintage	Proof	MS-65	Prf-65
1991W	31,959	—	281	—
1991W	—	111,991	—	266

1992 Olympics.
KM# 235 Obv. Designer: James C. Sharpe and T.
James Ferrell **Rev. Designer:** James M. Peed

Date	Mintage	Proof	MS-65	Prf-65
1992W	27,732	—	321	—
1992W	—	77,313	—	266

Columbus Quincentenary.
KM# 239 Obv. Designer: T. James Ferrell

Rev. Designer: Thomas D. Rogers, Sr.

Date	Mintage	Proof	MS-65	Prf-65
1992W	—	79,730	—	266
1992W	24,329	—	331	—

James Madison - Bill of Rights.
KM# 242 Obv. Designer: Scott R. Blazek
Rev. Designer: Joseph D. Peña

Date	Mintage	Proof	MS-65	Prf-65
1993W	—	78,651	—	266
1993W	22,266	—	311	—

World War II 50th Anniversary.
KM# 245 Obv. Designer: Charles J. Madsen
Rev. Designer: Edward S. Fisher

Date	Mintage	Proof	MS-65	Prf-65
1993W	—	65,461	—	281
1993W	23,089	—	351	—

1994 World Cup Soccer.
KM# 248 Obv. Designer: William J. Krawczewicz
Rev. Designer: Dean McMullen

Date	Mintage	Proof	MS-65	Prf-65
1994W	22,464	—	321	—
1994W	—	89,619	—	266

1996 Olympics - Stadium.
KM# 265 Obverse: Stadium

Date	Mintage	Proof	MS-65	Prf-65
1995W	—	43,124	—	535
1995W	10,579	—	1,250	—

1996 Olympics - Torch runner.

KM# 261 Obverse: Torch runner

Date	Mintage	Proof	MS-65	Prf-65
1995W	—	57,442	—	375
1995W	14,675	—	850	—

Civil War.

KM# 256 Obv. Designer: Don Troiani
Rev. Designer: Alfred Maletsky

Date	Mintage	Proof	MS-65	Prf-65
1995W	12,735	—	785	—
1995W	—	55,246	—	331

1996 Olympics - Cauldron.

KM# 270 Obverse: Cauldron

Date	Mintage	Proof	MS-65	Prf-65
1996W	—	38,555	—	610
1996W	9,210	—	1,075	—

1996 Olympics - Flag bearer.

KM# 274 Obverse: Flag bearer

Date	Mintage	Proof	MS-65	Prf-65
1996W	—	32,886	—	635
1996W	9,174	—	1,060	—

Smithsonian Institution 150th Anniversary.

KM# 277 Obv. Designer: Alfred Maletsky

Rev. Designer: T. James Ferrell

Date	Mintage	Proof	MS-65	Prf-65
1996W	9,068	—	1,175	—
1996W	—	29,474	—	565

Franklin Delano Roosevelt.

KM# 282 Obv. Designer: T. James Ferrell **Rev. Designer:** James M. Peed and Thomas D. Rogers, Sr.

Date	Mintage	Proof	MS-65	Prf-65
1997W	11,894	—	800	—
1997W	—	29,474	—	425

Jackie Robinson.

KM# 280 Obv. Designer: William C. Cousins
Rev. Designer: James M. Peed

Date	Mintage	Proof	MS-65	Prf-65
1997W	5,202	—	4,950	—
1997W	—	24,546	—	665

George Washington Death Bicentennial.

KM# 300 Designer: Laura G. Fraser.

Date	Mintage	Proof	MS-65	Prf-65
1999W	22,511	—	385	—
1999W	—	41,693	—	310

Capitol Visitor Center.

KM# 326 Designer: Elizabeth Jones.

Date	Mintage	Proof	MS-65	Prf-65
2001W	6,761	—	1,350	—
2001W	—	27,652	—	360

2002 Winter Olympics.

KM# 337 Designer: Donna Weaver.

Date	Mintage	Proof	MS-65	Prf-65
2002W	10,585	—	475	—
2002W	—	32,877	—	360

San Francisco Mint Museum.

KM# 395 Obverse: Front entrance façade **Reverse:** Eagle as on 1860's $5. Gold

Date	Mintage	Proof	MS-65	Prf-65
2006	—	—	285	—

Jamestown - 400th Anniversary.

KM# 406 Obverse: Settler and Native American **Reverse:** Jamestown Memorial Church ruins

Date	Mintage	Proof	MS-65	Prf-65
2007W	—	—	266	—
2007W	—	—	—	266

American Bald Eagle.

KM# 440 Obverse: Two eagles on branch **Reverse:** Eagle with shield

Date	Mintage	Proof	MS-65	Prf-65
2008W	100,000	—	285	—
2008W	—	—	—	300

$10 (EAGLE)

1984 Olympics.

KM# 211 Obv. Designer: James M. Peed and John Mercanti **Rev. Designer:** John Mercanti **Diameter:** 27 **Weight:** 16.7180 g. **Composition:** 0.9000 Gold, 0.4837 oz. AGW.

Date	Mintage	Proof	MS-65	Prf-65
1984W	75,886	—	468	—
1984P	—	33,309	—	508
1984D	—	34,533	—	508
1984S	—	48,551	—	508
1984W	—	381,085	—	508

Library of Congress.

KM# 312 Obv. Designer: John Mercanti **Rev. Designer:** Thomas D. Rogers, Sr. **Weight:** 16.2590 g. **Composition:** Platinum-Gold-Alloy **Notes:** Composition is 48 percent platinum, 48 percent gold, and 4 percent alloy.

Date	Mintage	Proof	MS-65	Prf-65
2000W	6,683	—	2,750	—
2000W	—	27,167	—	1,175

First Flight Centennial.

KM# 350 Designer: Donna Weaver. **Weight:** 16.7180 g. **Composition:** 0.9000 Gold, 0.4837 oz. AGW.

Date	Mintage	Proof	MS-65	Prf-65
2003P	10,129	—	568	—
2003P	—	21,846	—	568

$20 (DOUBLE EAGLE)

KM# 464 Obverse: Liberty walking forward **Reverse:** Eagle in flight left, sunrise **Composition:** 0.9990 Gold, 0 oz. AGW. **Notes:** Ultra high relief

Date	Mintage	Proof	MS-65	Prf-65
2009	—	—	—	1,275

AMERICAN EAGLE BULLION COINS

GOLD $5

KM# 216 Obv. Designer: Augustus Saint-Gaudens. **Rev. Designer:** Miley Busiek. **Diameter:** 16.5 **Weight:** 3.3930 g. **Composition:** 0.9167 Gold, 0.1000 oz. AGW.

Date	Mintage	Unc	Prf.
MCMLXXXVI (1986)	912,609	142	—
MCMLXXXVII (1987)	580,266	134	—
MCMLXXXVIII (1988)	159,500	200	—
MCMLXXXVIII (1988)P	143,881	—	189
MCMLXXXIX (1989)	264,790	134	—
MCMLXXXIX (1989)P	82,924	—	194
MCMXC (1990)	210,210	134	—
MCMXC (1990)P	99,349	—	194
MCMXCI (1991)	165,200	142	—
MCMXCI (1991)P	70,344	—	189
1992	209,300	132	—
1992P	64,902	—	189
1993	210,709	134	—
1993P	58,649	—	189
1994	206,380	134	—
1994W	62,100	—	189
1995	223,025	132	—
1995W	62,650	—	189
1996	401,964	132	—
1996W	58,440	—	189
1997	528,515	132	—
1997W	35,000	—	189
1998	1,344,520	132	—
1998W	39,653	—	189
1999	2,750,338	132	—
1999W	48,426	—	165
1999 Die error	—	575	—
2000	569,153	184	—
2000W	50,000	—	189
2001	269,147	132	—
2001W	37,547	—	189
2002	230,027	132	—
2002W	40,864	—	189
2003	245,029	132	—
2003W	40,634	—	189
2004	250,016	132	—
2004W	35,481	—	189
2005	300,043	132	—
2005W	48,455	—	189
2006	—	132	—
2006W Burnished Unc.	—	140	—
2006W	—	—	189
2007	190,010	132	—
2007W Burnished Unc.	—	135	—
2007W	—	—	204
2008	—	142	—
2008	—	135	—
2008W	—	—	204
2009	—	142	—

GOLD $10

KM# 217 Obv. Designer: Augustus Saint-Gaudens. **Rev. Designer:** Miley Busiek. **Diameter:** 22 **Weight:** 8.4830 g. **Composition:** 0.9167 Gold, 0.2500 oz. AGW.

Date	Mintage	Unc	Prf.
MCMLXXXVI (1986)	726,031	295	—
MCMLXXXVII (1987)	269,255	335	—
MCMLXXXVIII (1988)	49,000	295	—
MCMLXXXVIII (1988)P	98,028	—	410
MCMLXXXIX (1989)	81,789	295	—
MCMLXXXIX (1989)P	53,593	—	410
MCMXC (1990)	41,000	295	—
MCMXC (1990)P	62,674	—	410
MCMXCI (1991)	36,100	375	—
MCMXCI (1991)P	50,839	—	410
1992	59,546	295	—
1992P	46,290	—	410
1993	71,864	295	—
1993P	46,271	—	410
1994	72,650	295	—
1994W	47,600	—	410
1995	83,752	295	—
1995W	47,545	—	410
1996	60,318	295	—
1996W	39,190	—	410
1997	108,805	295	—
1997W	29,800	—	410
1998	309,829	295	—
1998W	29,733	—	410
1999	564,232	295	—
1999W	34,416	—	410
1999 Die error	—	1,050	—
2000	128,964	295	—
2000W	36,000	—	410
2001	71,280	295	—
2001W	25,630	—	410
2002	62,027	295	—
2002W	29,242	—	410
2003	74,029	295	—
2003W	31,000	—	410
2004	72,014	295	—
2004W	29,127	—	410
2005	72,015	295	—
2005W	34,637	—	410
2006	60,004	295	—
2006W Burnished Unc.	—	335	—
2006W	—	—	410
2007	34,004	295	—
2007W Burnished Unc.	—	420	—
2007W	—	—	456
2008	—	295	—
2008W Burnished Unc.	—	315	—
2008W	—	—	456
2009	—	295	—

GOLD $25

GOLD $50

KM# 218 Obv. Designer: Augustus Saint-Gaudens. **Rev. Designer:** Miley Busiek. **Diameter:** 27 **Weight:** 16.9660 g. **Composition:** 0.9167 Gold, 0.5000 oz. AGW.

Date	Mintage	Unc	Prf.
MCMLXXXVI (1986)	599,566	576	—
MCMLXXXVII (1987)	131,255	635	—
MCMLXXXVII (1987)P	143,398	—	903
MCMLXXXVIII (1988)	45,000	745	—
MCMLXXXVIII (1988)P	76,528	—	903
MCMLXXXIX (1989)	44,829	800	—
MCMLXXXIX (1989)P	44,264	—	903
MCMXC (1990)	31,000	965	—
MCMXC (1990)P	51,636	—	903
MCMXCI (1991)	24,100	1,575	—
MCMXCI (1991)P	53,125	—	903
1992	54,404	655	—
1992P	40,982	—	903
1993	73,324	569	—
1993P	43,319	—	903
1994	62,400	569	—
1994W	44,100	—	903
1995	53,474	645	—
1995W	45,511	—	903
1996	39,287	569	—
1996W	35,937	—	903
1997	79,605	569	—
1997W	26,350	—	903
1998	169,029	569	—
1998W	25,896	—	903
1999	263,013	569	—
1999W	30,452	—	903
1999 Die error	—	—	—
2000	79,287	569	—
2000W	32,000	—	903
2001	48,047	569	—
2001W	23,261	—	903
2002	70,027	569	—
2002W	26,646	—	903
2003	79,029	569	—
2003W	29,000	—	903
2004	98,040	569	—
2004W	27,731	—	903
2005	80,023	569	—
2005W	33,598	—	903
2006	66,005	572	—
2006W Burnished Unc.	—	900	—
2006W	—	—	903
2007	47,002	572	—
2007W Burnished Unc.	—	845	—
2007W	—	—	903
2008	—	572	—
2008W Burnished Unc.	—	660	—
2008W	—	—	903
2009	—	572	—

KM# 219 Obv. Designer: Augustus Saint-Gaudens. **Rev. Designer:** Miley Busiek. **Diameter:** 32.7 **Weight:** 33.9310 g. **Composition:** 0.9167 Gold, 100000 oz. AGW.

Date	Mintage	Unc	Prf.
MCMLXXXVI (1986)	1,362,650	1,087	—
MCMLXXXVI (1986)W	446,290	—	1,745
MCMLXXXVII (1987)	1,045,500	1,087	—
MCMLXXXVII (1987)W	147,498	—	1,745
MCMLXXXVIII (1988)	465,000	1,087	—
MCMLXXXVIII (1988)W	87,133	—	1,745
MCMLXXXIX (1989)	—	1,087	—
MCMLXXXIX (1989)W	53,960	—	1,745
MCMXC (1990)	373,210	1,087	—
MCMXC (1990)W	62,401	—	1,745
MCMXCI (1991)	243,100	1,087	—
MCMXCI (1991)W	50,411	—	1,745
1992	275,000	1,087	—
1992W	44,835	—	1,745
1993	480,192	1,087	—
1993W	34,389	—	1,745
1994	221,633	1,087	—
1994W	36,300	—	1,745
1995	200,636	1,087	—
1995W	46,553	—	1,745
1996	189,148	1,087	—
1996W	37,302	—	1,745
1997	664,508	1,087	—
1997W	28,000	—	1,745
1998	1,468,530	1,087	—
1998W	26,060	—	1,745
1999	1,505,026	1,087	—
1999W	31,446	—	1,745
1999 Die error	—	1,800	—
2000	433,319	1,087	—
2000W	33,000	—	1,745
2001	143,605	1,087	—
2001W	24,580	—	1,745
2002	222,029	1,087	—
2002W	24,242	—	1,745
2003	416,032	1,087	—
2003W	29,000	—	1,745
2004	417,019	1,087	—
2004W	28,731	—	1,745
2005	356,555	1,087	—
2005W	34,695	—	1,745
2006	237,510	1,087	—
2006W Burnished Unc.	—	1,125	—
2006W	—	—	1,745
2006W Reverse Proof	10,000	—	2,600
2007	140,016	1,097	—
2007W Burnished Unc.	—	1,125	—
2007W	—	—	1,745
2008	—	1,087	—
2008 Burnished Unc.	—	1,165	—
2008W	—	—	1,745
2009	—	1,087	—

BULLION COINAGE

SILVER DOLLAR

KM# 273 Obv. Designer: Adolph A. Weinman.
Rev. Designer: John Mercanti. **Diameter:** 40.6
Weight: 31.1050 g. **Composition:** 0.9993 Silver,
0.9993 oz. ASW.

Date	Mintage	Unc	Prf.
1986	5,393,005	24.30	—
1986S	1,446,778	—	48.00
1987	11,442,335	23.60	—
1987S	904,732	—	48.00
1988	5,004,646	23.60	—
1988S	557,370	—	50.00
1989	5,203,327	20.80	—
1989S	617,694	—	50.00
1990	5,840,210	24.60	—
1990S	695,510	—	48.00
1991	7,191,066	23.60	—
1991S	511,924	—	48.00
1992	5,540,068	23.60	—
1992S	498,552	—	50.00
1993	6,763,762	23.60	—
1993P	403,625	—	136
1994	4,227,319	24.60	—
1994P	372,168	—	215
1995	4,672,051	26.10	—
1995P	395,400	—	127
1995W 10th Anniversary	30,125	—	3,150
1996	3,603,386	47.00	—
1996P	473,021	—	85.00
1997	4,295,004	23.60	—
1997P	429,682	—	132
1998	4,847,549	24.60	—
1998P	452,319	—	44.00
1999	7,408,640	24.60	—
1999P	549,769	—	47.00
2000	9,239,132	23.60	—
2000P	600,000	—	48.00
2001	9,001,711	20.80	—
2001W	746,154	—	48.00
2002	10,539,026	20.80	—
2002W	647,342	—	48.00
2003	8,495,008	20.80	—

Date	Mintage	Unc	Prf.
2003W	747,831	—	48.00
2004	8,882,754	20.80	—
2004W	783,219	—	48.00
2005	8,891,025	20.80	—
2005W	823,000	—	48.00
2006	10,676,522	23.10	—
2006W Burnished Unc.	470,000	75.00	—
2006W	—	—	48.00
2006P Reverse Proof	250,000	—	175
2006 20th Aniv. 3 pc. set	—	—	275
2007	9,028,036	21.10	—
2007W Burnished Unc.	—	20.00	—
2007W	—	—	48.00
2008	—	20.80	—
2008W Burnished Unc.	—	23.50	—
2008W Reverse of '07	—	465	—
2008	—	—	79.00
2009	—	20.80	—

PLATINUM $10

KM# 283 Obv. Designer: John Mercanti.
Rev. Designer: Thomas D. Rogers Sr. **Diameter:** 17
Weight: 3.1100 g. **Composition:** 0.9995 Platinum,
0.0999 oz.

Date	Mintage	Unc	Prf.
1997	70,250	253	—
1997W	36,996	—	221
1998	39,525	176	—
1998	—	—	—
1999	55,955	176	—
1999	—	—	—
2000	34,027	176	—
2000	—	—	—
2001	52,017	176	—
2001	—	—	—
2002	23,005	176	—
2002	—	—	—
2003	22,007	176	—
2003	—	—	—
2004	15,010	176	—
2004	—	—	—
2005	14,013	176	—
2005	—	—	—
2006	11,001	176	—
2006W Burnished Unc.	—	390	—
2006	—	—	—
2007	13,003	280	—
2007W Burnished Unc.	—	185	—
2007	—	—	—
2008	—	173	—
2008 Burnished Unc.	—	190	—
2008	—	—	—
2009	—	173	—
2009	—	—	—

KM# 289 Obv. Designer: John Mercanti.
Weight: 3.1100 g. **Composition:** 0.9995 Platinum,
0.0999 oz.

Date	Mintage	Unc	Prf.
1998W	19,832	—	221

KM# 301 Obv. Designer: John Mercanti.
Weight: 3.1100 g. **Composition:** 0.9995 Platinum, 0.0999 oz.

Date	Mintage	Unc	Prf.
1999W	19,123	—	221

KM# 314 Obv. Designer: John Mercanti.
Weight: 3.1100 g. **Composition:** 0.9995 Platinum, 0.0999 oz.

Date	Mintage	Unc	Prf.
2000W	15,651	—	221

KM# 327 Rev. Desc. Southwest desert cactus
Obv. Designer: John Mercanti. **Diameter:** 17
Weight: 3.1100 g. **Composition:** 0.9995 Platinum, 0.0999 oz.

Date	Mintage	Unc	Prf.
2001W	12,193	—	221

KM# 339 Obv. Designer: John Mercanti.
Diameter: 17 **Weight:** 3.1100 g. **Composition:** 0.9995 Platinum, 0.0999 oz.

Date	Mintage	Unc	Prf.
2002W	12,365	—	221

KM# 351 Rev. Desc. Eagle pearched on a Rocky
Mountain Pine branch against a flag backdrop **Obv.
Designer:** John Mercanti. **Rev. Designer:** Al
Maletsky. **Diameter:** 17 **Weight:** 3.1100 g.
Composition: 0.9995 Platinum, 0.0999 oz.

Date	Mintage	Unc	Prf.
2003W	8,161	—	255

KM# 364 Obv. Designer: John Mercanti.

Diameter: 17 **Weight:** 3.1100 g. **Composition:**
0.9995 Platinum, 0.0999 oz.

Date	Mintage	Unc	Prf.
2004W	6,846	—	595

KM# 377 Obv. Designer: John Mercanti. **Rev.
Designer:** Donna Weaver. **Diameter:** 17 **Weight:**
3.1100 g. **Composition:** 0.9995 Platinum, 0.0999 oz.

Date	Mintage	Unc	Prf.
2005W	8,000	—	218

KM# 389 Obv. Designer: John Mercanti.
Diameter: 17 **Weight:** 3.1100 g. **Composition:**
0.9995 Platinum, 0.0999 oz.

Date	Mintage	Unc	Prf.
2006W	—	—	190

KM# 414 Obv. Designer: John Mercanti.
Diameter: 17 **Weight:** 3.1100 g. **Composition:**
0.9995 Platinum, 0.0999 oz.

Date	Mintage	Unc	Prf.
2007W	—	—	221

KM# 434 Obv. Designer: John Mercanti.
Diameter: 17 **Weight:** 3.1100 g. **Composition:**
0.9995 Platinum, 0.0999 oz.

Date	Mintage	Unc	Prf.
2008W	—	—	405

KM# 460 Obv. Designer: John Mercanti.
Diameter: 17 **Weight:** 3.1100 g. **Composition:**
0.9995 Platinum, 0.0999 oz.

Date	Mintage	Unc	Prf.
2009W	—	—	245

PLATINUM $25

KM# 284 Rev. Desc. Eagle in flight over sunrise
Obv. Designer: John Mercanti. **Rev. Designer:**
Thomas D. Rogers Sr. **Diameter:** 22 **Weight:** 7.7857
g. **Composition:** 0.9995 Platinum, 0.2502 oz.

Date	Mintage	Unc	Prf.
1997	27,100	412	—
1997W	18,628	—	439
1998	38,887	412	—
1998	—	—	—
1999	39,734	412	—
1999	—	—	—
2000	20,054	412	—
2000	—	—	—
2001	21,815	412	—
2001	—	—	—
2002	27,405	412	—
2002	—	—	—

Date	Mintage	Unc	Prf.
2003	25,207	412	—
2003	—	—	—
2004	18,010	412	—
2004	—	—	—
2005	12,013	412	—
2005	—	—	—
2006	12,001	412	—
2006W Burnished Unc.	—	540	—
2006	—	—	—
2007	8,402	412	—
2007W Burnished Unc.	—	435	—
2007	—	—	—
2008	—	412	—
2008 Burnished Unc.	—	445	—
2008	—	—	—
2009	—	412	—
2009	—	—	—

KM# 290   Obv. Designer: John Mercanti.
Weight: 7.7857 g. **Composition:** 0.9995 Platinum, 0.2502 oz.

Date	Mintage	Unc	Prf.
1998W	14,860	—	439

KM# 302   Obv. Designer: John Mercanti.
Weight: 7.7857 g. **Composition:** 0.9995 Platinum, 0.2502 oz.

Date	Mintage	Unc	Prf.
1999W	13,514	—	439

KM# 315   Obv. Designer: John Mercanti.
Weight: 7.7857 g. **Composition:** 0.9995 Platinum, 0.2502 oz.

Date	Mintage	Unc	Prf.
2000W	11,995	—	439

KM# 328   Rev. Desc. Southwest desert cactus
Obv. Designer: John Mercanti. **Diameter:** 22
Weight: 7.7857 g. **Composition:** 0.9995 Platinum, 0.2502 oz.

Date	Mintage	Unc	Prf.
2001W	8,858	—	439

KM# 340   Obv. Designer: John Mercanti.
Diameter: 22 **Weight:** 7.7857 g. **Composition:** 0.9995 Platinum, 0.2502 oz.

Date	Mintage	Unc	Prf.
2002W	9,282	—	439

KM# 352   Rev. Desc. Eagle pearched on a Rocky
Mountain Pine branch against a flag backdrop. **Obv.
Designer:** John Mercanti. **Rev. Designer:** Al
Maletsky. **Diameter:** 22 **Weight:** 7.7857 g.
Composition: 0.9995 Platinum, 0.2502 oz.

Date	Mintage	Unc	Prf.
2003W	6,045	—	439

KM# 365   Obv. Designer: John Mercanti.
Diameter: 22 **Weight:** 7.7857 g. **Composition:** 0.9995 Platinum, 0.2502 oz.

Date	Mintage	Unc	Prf.
2004W	5,035	—	1,150

KM# 378   Obv. Designer: John Mercanti. **Rev.
Designer:** Donna Weaver. **Diameter:** 22 **Weight:**
7.7857 g. **Composition:** 0.9995 Platinum, 0.2502 oz.

Date	Mintage	Unc	Prf.
2005W	6,424	—	525

KM# 390   Obv. Designer: John Mercanti.
Diameter: 22 **Weight:** 7.7857 g. **Composition:** 0.9995 Platinum, 0.2502 oz.

Date	Mintage	Unc	Prf.
2006W	—	—	445

KM# 415   Obv. Designer: John Mercanti.
Diameter: 22 **Weight:** 7.7857 g. **Composition:** 0.9995 Platinum, 0.2502 oz.

Date	Mintage	Unc	Prf.
2007W	—	—	440

KM# 435   Obv. Designer: John Mercanti.
Diameter: 22 **Weight:** 7.7857 g. **Composition:**
0.9995 Platinum, 0.2502 oz.

Date	Mintage	Unc	Prf.
2008W	—	—	690

KM# 461   Obv. Designer: John Mercanti.
Diameter: 22 **Weight:** 7.7857 g. **Composition:**
0.9995 Platinum, 0.2502 oz.

Date	Mintage	Unc	Prf.
2009W	—	—	600

PLATINUM $50

KM# 285   Obv. Designer: John Mercanti. **Rev.
Designer:** Thomas D. Rogers Sr. **Diameter:** 27
Weight: 15.5520 g. **Composition:** 0.9995
Platinum, 0.4997 oz.

Date	Mintage	Unc	Prf.
1997	20,500	838	—
1997W	15,432	—	886
1998	32,415	838	—
1998	—	—	—
1999	32,309	838	—
1999	—	—	—
2000	18,892	838	—
2000	—	—	—
2001	12,815	838	—
2001	—	—	—
2002	24,005	838	—
2002	—	—	—
2003	17,409	838	—
2003	—	—	—
2004	—	838	—
2004	—	—	—
2005	9,013	838	—
2005	—	—	—
2006	9,602	838	—
2006W Burnished Unc.	—	885	—
2006	—	—	—
2007	—	838	—
2007W Burnished Unc.	—	800	—
2007	—	—	—
2008	—	838	—
2008 Burnished Unc.	—	815	—
2008	—	—	—
2009	—	838	—
2009	—	—	—

KM# 291   Obv. Designer: John Mercanti.
Weight: 15.5520 g. **Composition:** 0.9995
Platinum, 0.4997 oz.

Date	Mintage	Unc	Prf.
1998W	13,821	—	878

KM# 303   Obv. Designer: John Mercanti.
Weight: 15.5520 g. **Composition:** 0.9995
Platinum, 0.4997 oz.

Date	Mintage	Unc	Prf.
1999W	11,098	—	878

KM# 316   Obv. Designer: John Mercanti.
Weight: 15.5520 g. **Composition:** 0.9995
Platinum, 0.4997 oz.

Date	Mintage	Unc	Prf.
2000W	11,049	—	878

KM# 329   Obv. Designer: John Mercanti.
Diameter: 27 **Weight:** 15.5520 g. **Composition:**
0.9995 Platinum, 0.4997 oz.

Date	Mintage	Unc	Prf.
2001W	8,268	—	878

KM# 341   Obv. Designer: John Mercanti.
Diameter: 27 **Weight:** 15.5520 g. **Composition:**
0.9995 Platinum, 0.4997 oz.

Date	Mintage	Unc	Prf.
2002W	8,772	—	878

KM# 353   Rev. Desc. Eagle pearched on a Rocky
Mountain Pine branch against a flag backdrop. **Obv.
Designer:** John Mercanti. **Rev. Designer:** Al
Maletsky. **Diameter:** 27 **Weight:** 15.5520 g.
Composition: 0.9995 Platinum, 0.4997 oz.

Date	Mintage	Unc	Prf.
2003W	6,181	—	878

KM# 366 Obv. Designer: John Mercanti.
Diameter: 27 **Weight:** 15.5520 g. **Composition:**
0.9995 Platinum, 0.4997 oz.

Date	Mintage	Unc	Prf.
2004W	4,886	—	1,700

KM# 379 Obv. Designer: John Mercanti.
Rev. Designer: Donna Weaver. **Diameter:** 27
Weight: 15.5520 g. **Composition:** 0.9995
Platinum, 0.4997 oz.

Date	Mintage	Unc	Prf.
2005W	5,720	—	980

KM# 391 Obv. Designer: John Mercanti.
Diameter: 27 **Weight:** 15.5520 g. **Composition:**
0.9995 Platinum, 0.4997 oz.

Date	Mintage	Unc	Prf.
2006W	—	—	865

KM# 416 Obv. Designer: John Mercanti.
Diameter: 27 **Weight:** 15.5520 g. **Composition:**
0.9995 Platinum, 0.4997 oz.

Date	Mintage	Unc	Prf.
2007W	—	—	875

KM# 436 Obv. Designer: John Mercanti.
Diameter: 27 **Weight:** 15.5520 g. **Composition:**
0.9995 Platinum, 0.4997 oz.

Date	Mintage	Unc	Prf.
2008W	—	—	1,185

KM# 462 Obv. Designer: John Mercanti.
Diameter: 27 **Weight:** 15.5520 g. **Composition:**
0.9995 Platinum, 0.4997 oz.

Date	Mintage	Unc	Prf.
2009	—	—	—

PLATINUM $100

KM# 286 Rev. Desc. Eagle in flight over sun rise
Obv. Designer: John Mercanti. **Rev. Designer:**
Thomas D. Rogers Sr. **Diameter:** 33 **Weight:**
31.1050 g. **Comp:** 0.9995 Platinum, 0.9995 oz.

Date	Mintage	Unc	Prf.
1997	56,000	1,612	—
1997W	15,885	—	1,771
1998	133,002	1,612	—
1998	—	—	—
1999	56,707	1,612	—
1999	—	—	—
2000	18,892	1,612	—
2000	—	—	—
2001	14,070	1,612	—
2001	—	—	—
2002	11,502	1,612	—
2002	—	—	—
2003	8,007	1,612	—
2003	—	—	—
2004	7,009	1,612	—
2004	—	—	—
2005	6,310	1,612	—
2005	—	—	—
2006	6,000	1,612	—
2006W Burnished Unc.	—	1,585	—
2006	—	—	—
2007	—	1,612	—
2007W Burnished Unc.	—	1,585	—
2007	—	—	—
2008	—	1,612	—
2008 Burnished Unc.	—	1,600	—
2008	—	—	—
2009	—	1,612	—
2009	—	—	—

KM# 292 Rev. Desc. Eagle in flight over New
England costal lighthouse **Obv. Designer:** John
Mercanti. **Weight:** 31.1050 g. **Composition:**
0.9995 Platinum, 0.9995 oz.

Date	Mintage	Unc	Prf.
1998W	14,203	—	1,755

KM# 304 Rev. Desc. Eagle in flight over
Southeastern Wetlands **Obv. Designer:** John
Mercanti. **Weight:** 31.1050 g. **Composition:**
0.9995 Platinum, 0.9995 oz.

Date	Mintage	Unc	Prf.
1999W	—	—	1,755

KM# 317 Rev. Desc. Eagle in flight over Heartland **Obv. Designer:** John Mercanti. **Weight:** 31.1050 g. **Composition:** 0.9995 Platinum, 0.9995 oz.

Date	Mintage	Unc	Prf.
2000W	—	—	1,755

KM# 330 Rev. Desc. Eagle in flight over Southwestern cactus desert **Obv. Designer:** John Mercanti. **Diameter:** 33 **Weight:** 31.1050 g. **Composition:** 0.9995 Platinum, 0.9995 oz.

Date	Mintage	Unc	Prf.
2001W	8,990	—	1,755

KM# 342 Rev. Desc. Eagle fishing in America's Northwest **Obv. Designer:** John Mercanti. **Diameter:** 33 **Weight:** 31.1050 g. **Composition:** 0.9995 Platinum, 0.9995 oz.

Date	Mintage	Unc	Prf.
2002W	9,834	—	1,755

KM# 354 Rev. Desc. Eagle pearched on a Rocky Mountain Pine branch against a flag backdrop **Obv. Designer:** John Mercanti. **Rev. Designer:** Al Maletsky. **Diameter:** 33 **Weight:** 31.1050 g.

Composition: 0.9995 Platinum, 0.9995 oz.

Date	Mintage	Unc	Prf.
2003W	6,991	—	1,771

KM# 367 Rev. Desc. Inspired by the sculpture "America" by Daniel Chester French, 1907. The sculpture is outside the N.Y. Customs House, now part of the Smithsonian's Museum of the American Indian **Obv. Designer:** John Mercanti. **Rev. Designer:** Donna Weaver. **Diameter:** 33 **Weight:** 31.1050 g. **Composition:** 0.9995 Platinum, 0.9995 oz.

Date	Mintage	Unc	Prf.
2004W	5,833	—	2,150

KM# 380 Obv. Designer: John Mercanti. **Rev. Designer:** Donna Weaver. **Diameter:** 33 **Weight:** 31.1050 g. **Composition:** 0.9995 Platinum, 0.9995 oz.

Date	Mintage	Unc	Prf.
2005W	6,700	—	1,771

KM# 392 Obv. Designer: John Mercanti. **Diameter:** 33 **Weight:** 31.1050 g. **Composition:** 0.9995 Platinum, 0.9995 oz.

Date	Mintage	Unc	Prf.
2006W	—	—	1,755

KM# 417 Obv. Designer: John Mercanti. **Diameter:** 33 **Weight:** 31.1050 g. **Composition:** 0.9995 Platinum, 0.9995 oz.

Date	Mintage	Unc	Prf.
2007W	—	—	1,755

BULLION COINAGE

KM# 437　Obv. Designer: John Mercanti.
Diameter: 33　Weight: 31.1050 g.　Composition:
0.9995 Platinum, 0.9995 oz.

Date	Mintage	Unc	Prf.
2008W	—	—	2,250

KM# 463　Obv. Designer: John Mercanti.
Diameter: 33　Weight: 31.1020 g.　Composition:
0.9995 Platinum, 0.9994 oz.

Date	Mintage	Unc	Prf.
2009W	—	—	—

BISON BULLION COINAGE

GOLD $5

KM# 411　Obv. Desc. Indian Head right Rev.
Desc. Bison　Weight: 3.1100 g.　Composition:
0.9999 Gold, 0.1000 oz. AGW.

Date	Mintage	Unc	Prf.
2008W	—	450	—
2008W	—	—	470
2009W	—	450	—
2009W	—	—	470

GOLD $10

KM# 412　Obv. Desc. Indian Head right Rev.
Desc. Bison　Weight: 7.7857 g.　Composition:
0.9999 Gold, 0.2503 oz. AGW.

Date	Mintage	Unc	Prf.
2008W	—	600	—
2008W	—	—	765
2009W	—	600	—
2009W	—	—	765

GOLD $25

KM# 413　Obv. Desc. Indian Head right Rev.
Desc. Bison　Weight: 15.5520 g.　Composition:
0.9990 Gold, 0.4995 oz. AGW.

Date	Mintage	Unc	Prf.
2008W	—	990	—
2008W	—	—	1,085
2009W	—	990	—
2009W	—	—	1,085

GOLD $50

KM# 393　Obv. Desc. Indian head right Rev.
Desc. Bison standing left on mound Designer:
James E. Fraser. Diameter: 32　Weight: 31.1050 g.
Composition: 0.9999 Gold, 0.9999 oz. AGW.

Date	Mintage	Unc	Prf.
2006W	337,012	1,159	—
2006W	—	—	1,331
2007W	136,503	1,159	—
2007W	—	—	1,331
2008W	—	1,159	—
2008W	—	—	2,350
2008W Moy Family Chop	—	2,150	—
2009W	—	1,159	—
2009W	—	—	2,350

FIRST SPOUSE
GOLD BULLION COINAGE

GOLD $10

KM# 407　Obv. Desc. Bust 3/4 facing Rev. Desc.
Martha Washington seated sewing Weight: 15.5520
g. Composition: 0.9999 Gold, 0.4999 oz. AGW.

Date	Mintage	Unc	Prf.
2007W	20,000	553	—
2007W	20,000	—	575

KM# 408　Obv. Desc. Bust 3/4 facing Rev. Desc.
Abigail Adams seated at desk writing to John during
the Revolutionary War Weight: 15.5520 g.
Composition: 0.9999 Gold, 0.4999 oz. AGW.

Date	Mintage	Unc	Prf.
2007W	20,000	543	—
2007W	20,000	—	543

KM# 409   Obv. Desc. Bust design from coinage
Rev. Desc. Jefferson's tombstone **Weight:** 15.5520 g.
Composition: 0.9999 Gold, 0.4999 oz. AGW.

Date	Mintage	Unc	Prf.
2007W	20,000	553	—
2007W	20,000	—	575

KM# 410   Obv. Desc. Bust 3/4 facing **Rev. Desc.**
Dolley standing before painting of Washington, which
she saved from the White House **Weight:** 15.5520 g.
Composition: 0.9999 Gold, 0.4999 oz. AGW.

Date	Mintage	Unc	Prf.
2007W	40,000	553	—
2007W	Inc. above	—	575

KM# 430   Obv. Desc. Bust 3/4 facing right
Rev. Desc. Elizabeth standing before mirror
Weight: 15.5520 g. **Composition:** 0.9990 Gold,
0.4995 oz. AGW.

Date	Mintage	Unc	Prf.
2008W	40,000	553	—
2008W	Inc. above	—	575

KM# 431   Obv. Desc. Bust 3/4 facing right
Rev. Desc. Lousia and son Charles before entrance
Weight: 15.5520 g. **Composition:** 0.9990 Gold,
0.4995 oz. AGW.

Date	Mintage	Unc	Prf.
2008W	40,000	553	—
2008W	Inc. above	—	575

KM# 432   Obv. Desc. Capped and draped bust left
Rev. Desc. Andrew Jackson on horseback right
Weight: 15.5520 g. **Composition:** 0.9990 Gold,
0.4995 oz. AGW.

Date	Mintage	Unc	Prf.
2008W	40,000	553	—
2008W	Inc. above	—	575

KM# 433   Obv. Desc. Seated Liberty with shiled
Rev. Desc. Youthful van Buren seated under tree,
family tavern in distance **Weight:** 15.5520 g.
Composition: 0.9990 Gold, 0.4995 oz. AGW.

Date	Mintage	Unc	Prf.
2008W	40,000	553	—
2008W	Inc. above	—	575

KM# 456   Obv. Desc. Bust 3/4 left **Rev. Desc.** Anna
reading to her three children **Weight:** 15.5520 g.
Composition: 0.9990 Gold, 0.4995 oz. AGW.

Date	Mintage	Unc	Prf.
2009W	40,000	625	—
2009W	Inc. above	—	640

KM# 457   Obv. Desc. Bust facing **Rev. Desc.**
Letitia and two children playing outside of Cedar
Grove Plantation **Weight:** 15.5520 g.
Composition: 0.9990 Gold, 0.4995 oz. AGW.

Date	Mintage	Unc	Prf.
2009W	40,000	625	—
2009W	Inc. above	—	640

KM# 458   Obv. Desc. Bust facing **Rev. Desc.** Julia
and John Tyler dancing **Weight:** 15.5520 g.
Composition: 0.9990 Gold, 0.4995 oz. AGW.

Date	Mintage	Unc	Prf.
2009W	40,000	625	—
2009W	Inc. above	—	640

KM# 459   Obv. Desc. Bust 3/4 right **Rev. Desc.**
Sarah seated at desk as personal secretary to James
Polk **Weight:** 15.5520 g. **Composition:** 0.9990
Gold, 0.4995 oz. AGW.

Date	Mintage	Unc	Prf.
2009W	40,000	625	—
2009W	Inc. above	—	640

KM# 465   Obv. Desc. Bust 3/4 left **Rev. Desc.**
Margaret Taylor nurses wounded soldier during the
Seminole War **Weight:** 15.5520 g. **Composition:**
0.9990 Gold, 0.4995 oz. AGW.

Date	Mintage	Unc	Prf.
2009W	40,000	625	—
2009W	Inc. above	—	640

BULLION COINAGE

MINT SETS

Mint, or uncirculated, sets contain one uncirculated coin of each denomination from each mint produced for circulation that year. Values listed here are only for those sets sold by the U.S. Mint. Sets were not offered in years not listed. In years when the Mint did not offer the sets, some private companies compiled and marketed uncirculated sets. Mint sets from 1947 through 1958 contained two examples of each coin mounted in cardboard holders, which caused the coins to tarnish. Beginning in 1959, the sets have been packaged in sealed Pliofilm packets and include only one specimen of each coin struck for that year (both P & D mints). Listings for 1965, 1966 and 1967 are for "special mint sets," which were of higher quality than regular mint sets and were prooflike. They were packaged in plastic cases. The 1970 large-date and small-date varieties are distinguished by the size of the date on the coin. The 1976 three-piece set contains the quarter, half dollar and dollar with the Bicentennial design. The 1971 and 1972 sets do not include a dollar coin; the 1979 set does not include an S-mint-marked dollar. Mint sets issued prior to 1959 were double sets (containing two of each coin) packaged in cardboard with a paper overlay. Origional sets will always be toned and can bring large premiums if nicely preserved with good color.

Date	Sets Sold	Issue Price	Value
1947 Est. 5,000	—	4.87	1,350
1948 Est. 6,000	—	4.92	750
1949 Est. 5,200	—	5.45	935
1950 None issued	—	—	—
1951	8,654	6.75	900
1952	11,499	6.14	825
1953	15,538	6.14	565
1954	25,599	6.19	265
1955 flat pack	49,656	3.57	168
1956	45,475	3.34	165
1957	32,324	24.50	275
1958	50,314	4.43	150
1959	187,000	2.40	55.00
1960 large date	260,485	2.40	29.50
1961	223,704	2.40	45.00
1962	385,285	2.40	25.00
1963	606,612	2.40	25.00
1964	1,008,108	2.40	25.00
1965 Special Mint Set	2,360,000	4.00	4.80
1966 Special Mint Set	2,261,583	4.00	5.80
1967 Special Mint Set	1,863,344	4.00	9.50
1968	2,105,128	2.50	3.85
1969	1,817,392	2.50	4.10
1970 large date	2,038,134	2.50	15.00
1970 small date	Inc. above	2.50	70.00
1971	2,193,396	3.50	3.10
1972	2,750,000	3.50	3.25
1973	1,767,691	6.00	14.50
1974	1,975,981	6.75	7.25
1975	1,921,488	6.00	8.10
1976 3 coins	4,908,319	9.00	12.00

Date	Sets Sold	Issue Price	Value
1976	1,892,513	6.00	6.75
1977	2,006,869	7.00	7.50
1978	2,162,609	7.00	6.50
1979 Type I	2,526,000	8.00	4.75
1980	2,815,066	9.00	6.50
1981 Type I	2,908,145	11.00	12.85
1982 & 1983 None issued	—	—	—
1984	1,832,857	7.00	3.65
1985	1,710,571	7.00	4.40
1986	1,153,536	7.00	8.75
1987	2,890,758	7.00	5.00
1988	1,646,204	7.00	4.50
1989	1,987,915	7.00	4.00
1990	1,809,184	7.00	4.25
1991	1,352,101	7.00	5.50
1992	1,500,143	7.00	5.00
1993	1,297,094	8.00	5.50
1994	1,234,813	8.00	4.40
1995	1,038,787	8.00	7.25
1996	1,457,949	8.00	15.00
1997	950,473	8.00	12.50
1998	1,187,325	8.00	4.50
1999 9 piece	1,421,625	14.95	12.75
2000	1,490,160	14.95	10.00
2001	1,066,900	14.95	15.85
2002	1,139,388	14.95	21.00
2003	1,002,555	14.95	16.75
2004	844,484	16.95	31.50
2005	—	16.95	9.75
2006	—	16.95	14.00
2007	—	—	26.50
2008	—	—	46.50

SETS & ROLLS

MODERN COMMEMORATIVE COIN SETS

Olympic, 1983-1984

Date	Price
1983 & 1984 3 coin set: 1983 and one 1984 uncirculated dollar and 1984W uncirculated gold $10; KM209, 210, 211.	455
1983S & 1984S 3 coin set: proof 1983 and 1984 dollar and 1984W gold $10; KM209, 210, 211.	455
1983 & 1984 6 coin set: 1983S and 1984S uncirculated and proof dollars, 1984W uncirculated and proof gold $10; KM209, 210, 211.	910
1983S & 1984S 2 coin set: proof dollars.	22.50
1983 collectors 3 coin set: 1983 PDS uncirculated dollars; KM209.	37.50
1984 collectors 3 coin set: 1984 PDS uncirculated dollars; KM210.	38.50

Statue of Liberty

Date	Price
1986 2 coin set: uncirculated silver dollar and clad half dollar; KM212, 214.	17.00
1986 2 coin set: proof silver dollar and clad half dollar; KM212, 214.	17.00
1986 3 coin set: uncirculated silver dollar, clad half dollar and gold $5; KM212, 214, 215.	225
1986 3 coin set: proof silver dollar, clad half dollar and gold $5; KM212, 214, 215.	225
1986 6 coin set: 1 each of the proof and uncirculated issues; KM212, 214, 215.	450

Constitution

Date	Price
1987 2 coin set: uncirculated silver dollar and gold $5; KM220, 221.	220
1987 2 coin set: proof silver dollar and gold $5; KM220, 221.	220
1987 4 coin set: silver dollar and $5 gold proof and uncirculated issues; KM220, 221.	445

Olympic, 1988

Date	Price
1988 2 coin set: uncirculated silver dollar and gold $5; KM222, 223.	220
1988 2 coin set: proof silver dollar and gold $5; KM222, 223.	220
1988 4 coin set: silver dollar and $5 gold proof and uncirculated issues; KM222, 223.	440

Congress

Date	Price
1989 2 coin set: uncirculated silver dollar and clad half dollar; KM224, 225.	20.00
1989 2 coin set: proof silver dollar and clad half dollar; KM224, 225.	21.00
1989 3 coin set: uncirculated silver dollar, clad half and gold $5; KM224, 225, 226.	220
1989 3 coin set: proof silver dollar, clad half and gold $5; KM224, 225, 226.	220
1989 6 coin set: 1 each of the proof and uncirculated issues; KM224, 225, 226.	440

Mt. Rushmore

Date	Price
1991 2 coin set: uncirculated half dollar and silver dollar; KM228, 229.	45.00
1991 2 coin set: proof half dollar and silver dollar; KM228, 229.	45.00
1991 3 coin set: uncirculated half dollar, silver dollar and gold $5; KM228, 229, 230.	300
1991 3 coin set: proof half dollar, silver dollar and gold $5; KM228, 229, 230.	225
1991 6 coin set: 1 each of proof and uncirculated issues; KM228, 229, 230.	495

Olympic, 1992

Date	Price
1992 2 coin set: uncirculated half dollar and silver dollar; KM233, 234.	28.00
1992 2 coin set: proof half dollar and silver dollar; KM233, 234.	28.00
1992 3 coin set: uncirculated half dollar, silver dollar and gold $5; KM233, 234, 235.	275
1992 3 coin set: proof half dollar, silver dollar and gold $5; KM233, 234, 235.	240
1992 6 coin set: 1 each of proof and uncirculated issues; KM233, 234, 235.	520

Columbus Quincentenary

Date	Price
1992 2 coin set: uncirculated half dollar and silver dollar; KM237, 238.	35.00
1992 2 coin set: proof half dollar and silver dollar; KM237, 238.	39.00
1992 3 coin set: uncirculated half dollar, silver dollar and gold $5; KM237, 238, 239.	320
1992 3 coin set: proof half dollar, silver dollar and gold $5; KM237, 238, 239.	265
1992 6 coin set: 1 each of proof and uncirculated issues; KM237, 238, 239.	780

Jefferson

Date	Price
1993 Jefferson: dollar, 1994 matte proof nickel and $2 note; KM249, 192.	100.00

Madison / Bill of Rights

Date	Price
1993 2 coin set: uncirculated half dollar and silver dollar; KM240, 241.	28.00
1993 2 coin set: proof half dollar and silver dollar; KM240, 241.	29.00
1993 3 coin set: uncirculated half dollar, silver dollar and gold $5; KM240, 241, 242.	320
1993 3 coin set: proof half dollar, silver dollar and gold $5; KM240, 241, 242.	250
1993 6 coin set: 1 each of proof and uncirculated issues; KM240, 241, 242.	550

SETS & ROLLS

World War II

Date	Price
1993 2 coin set: uncirculated half dollar and silver dollar; KM243, 244.	49.00
1993 2 coin set: proof half dollar and silver dollar; KM243, 244.	55.00
1993 3 coin set: uncirculated half dollar, silver dollar and gold $5; KM243, 244, 245.	345
1993 3 coin set: proof half dollar, silver dollar and gold $5; KM243, 244, 245.	335
1993 6 coin set: 1 each of proof and uncirculated issues; KM243, 244, 245.	665

World Cup

Date	Price
1994 2 coin set: uncirculated half dollar and silver dollar; KM246, 247.	32.00
1994 2 coin set: proof half dollar and silver dollar; KM246, 247.	37.00
1994 3 coin set: uncirculated half dollar, silver dollar and gold $5; KM246, 247, 248.	290
1994 3 coin set: proof half dollar, silver dollar and gold $5; KM246, 247, 248.	250
1994 6 coin set: 1 each of proof and uncirculated issues; KM246, 247, 248.	525

U.S. Veterans

Date	Price
1994 3 coin set: uncirculated POW, Vietnam, Women dollars; KM250, 251, 252.	170
1994 3 coin set: proof POW, Vietnam, Women dollars; KM250, 251, 252.	120

Olympic, 1995-96

Date	Price
1995 4 coin set: uncirculated basketball half, $1 gymnast & blind runner, $5 torch runner; KM257, 259, 260, 261.	715
1995 4 coin set: proof basketball half, $1 gymnast & blind runner, $5 torch runner; KM257, 259, 260, 261.	415
1995P 2 coin set: proof $1 gymnast & blind runner; KM259, 260.	105
1995P 2 coin set: proof $1 track & field, cycling; KM263, 264.	95.00
1995-96 4 coin set: proof halves, basketball, baseball, swimming, soccer; KM257, 262, 267, 271.	140
1995 & 96 8 coins in cherry wood case: proof silver dollars: blind runner, gymnast, cycling, track & field, wheelchair, tennis, rowing, high jump; KM259, 260, 263, 264, 268, 269, 272, 272A.	2,150
1995 & 96 16 coins in cherry wood case: bu and proof silver dollars: blind runner, gymnast, cycling, track & field, wheelchair, tennis, rowing, high jump; KM259, 260, 263, 264, 268, 269, 272, 272A.	2,350
1995 & 96 16 coins in cherry wood case: proof half dollars: basketball, baseball, swimming, soccer, KM257, 262, 267, 271. Proof silver dollars: blind runner, gymnast, cycling, track & field, wheelchair, tennis, rowing, high jump, KM259, 260, 263, 264, 268, 269, 272, 272A. Proof $5 gold: torch runner, stadium, cauldron, flag bearer, KM 261, 265, 270, 274.	2,400
1995 & 96 32 coins in cherry wood case: bu & proof half dollars: basketball, baseball, swimming, soccer, KM257, 262, 267, 271. BU & proof silver dollars: blind runner, gymnast, cycling, track & field, wheelchair, tennis, rowing, high jump, KM259, 260, 263, 264, 268, 269, 272, 272A. BU & proof $5 gold: torch runner, stadium, cauldron, flag bearer, KM261, 265, 270, 274.	6,600
1996P 2 coin set: proof $1 wheelchair & tennis; KM268, 269.	160
1996P 2 coin set: proof $1 rowing & high jump; KM272, 272A.	130

Civil War

Date	Price
1995 2 coin set: uncirculated half and dollar; KM254, 255.	90.00
1995 2 coin set: proof half and dollar; KM254, 255.	100.00
1995 3 coin set: uncirculated half, dollar and gold $5; KM254, 255, 256.	800
1995 3 coin set: proof half, dollar and gold $5; KM254, 255, 256.	500
1995 6 coin set: 1 each of proof and uncirculated issues; KM254, 255, 256.	1,275

Smithsonian

Date	Price
1996 2 coin set: proof dollar and $5 gold; KM276, 277.	615
1996 4 coin set: proof and B.U. ; KM276, 277.	2,100

Jackie Robinson

Date	Price
1997 2 coin set: proof dollar & $5 gold; KM279, 280.	800
1997 4 coin set: proof & BU; KM279, 280.	5,750
1997 legacy set.	850

Botanic Garden

Date	Price
1997 2 coin set: dollar, Jefferson nickel and $1 note; KM278, 192.	230

Franklin Delano Roosevelt

Date	Price
1997W 2 coin set: uncirculated and proof; KM282.	1,350

Kennedy

Date	Price
1998 2 coin set: proof; KM287.	70.00
1998 2 coin collectors set: Robert Kennedy dollar and John Kennedy half dollar; KM287, 202b. Matte finished.	325

Black Patriots

Date	Price
1998S 2 coin set: uncirculated and proof; KM288.	200

George Washington

Date	Price
1999 2 coin set: proof and uncirculated gold $5; KM300.	800

Dolley Madison

Date	Price
1999 2 coin set: proof and uncirculated silver dollars; KM298.	77.00

Yellowstone National Park

Date	Price
1999 2 coin set: proof and uncirculated silver dollars; KM299.	88.00

Millennium Coin & Currency

Date	Price
2000 2 coin set: uncirculated Sacagewea $1, silver Eagle & $1 note.	72.00

Leif Ericson

Date	Price
2000 2 coin set: proof and uncirculated silver dollars; KM313.	84.00

Capitol Visitor Center

Date	Price
2001 3 coin set: proof half, silver dollar, gold $5; KM323, 324, 326.	445

American Buffalo

Date	Price
2001 2 coin set: 90% silver unc. & proof $1.; KM325.	460
2001 coin & currency set 90% unc. dollar & replicas of 1899 $5 silver cert.; KM325.	240

Winter Olympics - Salt Lake City

Date	Price
2002 2 coin set: proof 90% silver dollar KM336 & $5.00 Gold KM337.	420
2002 4 coin set: 90% silver unc. & proof $1, KM336 & unc. & proof gold 5, KM337.	940

First Flight Centennial

Date	Price
2003 3 coin set: proof gold ten dollar KM350, proof silver dollar KM349 & proof clad half dollar KM348.	575

Lewis and Clark Bicentennial

Date	Price
2004 Coin and pouch set.	100.00
2004 coin and currency set: Uncirculated silver dollar, two 2005 nickels, replica 1901 $10 Bison note, silver plated peace medal, three stamps & two booklets.	85.00
2004 Westward Journey Nickel series coin and medal set: Proof Sacagawea dollar, two 2005 proof nickels and silver plated peace medal.	35.00

Thomas Alva Edison

Date	Price
2004 Uncirculated silver dollar and light bulb.	60.00

U.S. Marine Corps.

Date	Price
2005 Uncirculated silver dollar and stamp set.	75.00
2005 American Legacy: Proof Marine Corps dollar, Proof John Marshall dollar and 10 piece proof set.	180

Chief Justice John Marshall

Date	Price
2005 Coin and Chronicles set: Uncirculated silver dollar, booklet and BEP intaglio portrait.	60.00
2005 American Legacy: Proof Marine Corps dollar, Proof John Marshall dollar and 10 piece proof set.	180

Benjamin Franklin Tercentennary

Date	Price
2006 Coin and Chronicles set: Uncirculated "Scientist" silver dollar, four stamps, Poor Richards Almanac and intaglio print.	65.00

PROOF SETS

Proof coins are produced through a special process involving specially selected, highly polished planchets and dies. They usually receive two strikings from the coin press at increased pressure. The result is a coin with mirrorlike surfaces and, in recent years, a cameo effect on its raised design surfaces. Proof sets have been sold off and on by the U.S. Mint since 1858. Listings here are for sets from what is commonly called the modern era, since 1936. Values for earlier proofs are included in regular date listings. Sets were not offered in years not listed. Since 1968, proof coins have been produced at the San Francisco Mint; before that they were produced at the Philadelphia Mint. In 1942 the five-cent coin was struck in two compositions. Some proof sets for that year contain only one type (five-coin set); others contain both types. Two types of packaging were used in 1955 -- a box and a flat, plastic holder. The 1960 large-date and small-date sets are distinguished by the size of the date on the cent. Some 1968 sets are missing the mint mark on the dime, the result of an error in the preparation of an obverse die. The 1970 large-date and small-date sets are distinguished by the size of the date on the cent. Some 1970 sets are missing the mint mark on the dime, the result of an error in the preparation of an obverse die. Some 1971 sets are missing the mint mark on the five-cent piece, the result of an error in the preparation of an obverse die. The 1976 three-piece set contains the quarter, half dollar and dollar with the Bicentennial designs. The 1979 and 1981 Type II sets have clearer mint marks than the Type I sets for those years. Some 1983 sets are missing the mint mark on the dime, the result of an error in the preparation of an obverse die. Prestige sets contain the five regular-issue coins plus a commemorative silver dollar from that year. Sets issued prior to 1956 came in transparent envelopes stapled together in a small square box. In mid 1955 sets were changed to a flat clear cellophane envelope. In 1968 sets were changed to a clear hard plastic case as they still are currently issued.

Date	Sets Sold	Issue Price	Value	Date	Sets Sold	Issue Price	Value
1795 (2006) XPn1-XPn3	—	—	—	1879 (2006) XPn18-20	—	—	—
1836 (2006) XPn4, 10-11	—	—	—	1879 (2006) XPn21-23	—	—	—
1863 (2006) XPn12-14	—	—	—	1936	3,837	1.89	7,500
1871 (2006) XPn15-17	—	—	—	1937	5,542	1.89	4,350

Date	Sets Sold	Issue Price	Value
1938	8,045	1.89	1,900
1939	8,795	—	1,800
1940	11,246	—	1,385
1941	15,287	—	1,450
1942 6 coins	21,120	1.89	1,475
1942 5 coins	Inc. above	1.89	1,375
1950	51,386	2.10	700
1951	57,500	2.10	625
1952	81,980	2.10	260
1953	128,800	2.10	235
1954	233,300	2.10	110
1955 box	378,200	2.10	110
1955 flat pack	Inc. above	2.10	155
1956	669,384	2.10	55.00
1957	1,247,952	2.10	24.50
1958	875,652	2.10	48.00
1959	1,149,291	2.10	23.00
1960 large date	1,691,602	2.10	20.50
1960 small date	Inc. above	2.10	33.50
1961	3,028,244	2.10	15.50
1962	3,218,019	2.10	15.50
1963	3,075,645	2.10	15.50
1964	3,950,762	2.10	15.75
1965 Special Mint Set	—	—	—
1966 Special Mint Set	—	—	—
1967 Special mint set	—	—	—
1968S	3,041,509	5.00	5.85
1968S no mint mark dime	Inc. above	5.00	17,500
1969S	2,934,631	5.00	6.75
1970S large date	2,632,810	5.00	7.25
1970S small date	Inc. above	5.00	100.00
1970S no mint mark dime	Inc. above	5.00	1,100
1971S	3,224,138	3.10	5.10
1971S no mint mark nickel Est. 1,655	1,655	5.00	1,850
1972S	3,267,667	5.50	5.50
1973S	2,769,624	7.00	6.50
1974S	2,617,350	7.00	7.25
1975S	2,909,369	7.00	7.75
1975S no mint mark dime	Inc. above	7.00	46,500
1976S 3 coins	3,998,621	13.00	12.00
1976S	4,149,730	7.00	6.35
1977S	3,251,152	9.00	6.25
1978S	3,127,788	9.00	7.50
1979S Type I	3,677,175	9.00	6.35
1979S Type II	Inc. above	9.00	80.00
1980S	3,547,030	10.00	5.35
1981S Type I	4,063,083	11.00	6.65
1981S Type II	Inc. above	11.00	335
1982S	3,857,479	11.00	3.25
1983S	3,138,765	11.00	5.00
1983S Prestige Set	140,361	59.00	60.00
1983S no mint mark dime	Inc. above	11.00	1,050
1984S	2,748,430	11.00	5.35
1984S Prestige Set	316,680	59.00	23.00
1985S	3,362,821	11.00	4.45
1986S	2,411,180	11.00	4.95
1986S Prestige Set	599,317	48.50	23.00
1987S	3,972,233	11.00	3.75
1987S Prestige Set	435,495	45.00	20.50
1988S	3,031,287	11.00	5.00
1988S Prestige Set	231,661	45.00	24.50
1989S	3,009,107	11.00	6.50
1989S Prestige Set	211,087	45.00	32.00
1990S	2,793,433	11.00	5.25
1990S no S 1¢	3,555	11.00	5,750
1990S Prestige Set	506,126	45.00	22.75
1990S Prestige Set, no S 1¢	Inc. above	45.00	5,800
1991S	2,610,833	11.00	9.65

Date	Sets Sold	Issue Price	Value
1991S Prestige Set	256,954	59.00	48.50
1992S	2,675,618	12.00	4.50
1992S Prestige Set	183,285	59.00	53.50
1992S Silver	1,009,585	21.00	13.50
1992S Silver premier	308,055	37.00	15.00
1993S	2,337,819	12.50	8.85
1993S Prestige Set	224,045	57.00	28.00
1993S Silver	570,213	21.00	23.50
1993S Silver premier	191,140	37.00	23.50
1994S	2,308,701	13.00	7.85
1994S Prestige Set	175,893	57.00	36.50
1994S Silver	636,009	21.00	26.50
1994S Silver premier	149,320	37.50	26.50
1995S	2,010,384	12.50	21.00
1995S Prestige Set	107,112	57.00	110
1995S Silver	549,878	21.00	66.50
1995S Silver premier	130,107	37.50	66.50
1996S	2,085,191	16.00	13.65
1996S Prestige Set	55,000	57.00	335
1996S Silver	623,655	21.00	31.50
1996S Silver premier	151,366	37.50	31.50
1997S	1,975,000	12.50	21.50
1997S Prestige Set	80,000	57.00	110
1997S Silver	605,473	21.00	48.50
1997S Silver premier	136,205	—	48.50
1998S	2,078,494	12.50	10.75
1998S Silver	638,134	21.00	18.50
1998S Silver premier	240,658	37.50	18.50
1999S 9 piece	2,557,899	19.95	36.50
1999S 5 quarter set	1,169,958	13.95	34.50
1999S Silver	804,565	31.95	250
2000S 10 piece	3,097,442	19.95	9.85
2000S 5 quarter set	995,803	13.95	6.00
2000S Silver	965,421	31.95	27.50
2001S 10 piece	2,249,498	19.95	77.50
2001S 5 quarter set	774,800	13.95	39.50
2001S Silver	849,600	31.95	105
2002S 10 piece	2,319,766	19.95	27.00
2002S 5 quarter set	764,419	13.95	16.50
2002S Silver	892,229	31.95	71.50
2003 X#207, 208, 209.2	—	44.00	28.75
2003S 10 piece	2,175,684	16.75	16.75
2003S 5 quarter set	1,225,507	13.95	10.00
2003S Silver	1,142,858	31.95	27.50
2004S 11 piece	1,804,396	22.95	28.00
2004S 5 quarter set	987,960	23.95	11.00
2004S Silver 11 piece	1,187,673	37.95	28.00
2004S Silver 5 quarter set	594,137	—	16.00
2005S American Legacy	—	—	88.00
2005S 11 piece	—	22.95	12.50
2005S 5 quarter set	—	15.95	8.85
2005S Silver 11 piece	—	37.95	28.50
2005S Silver 5 quarter set	—	23.95	16.00
2005S American Legacy	—	—	98.00
2006S 10 piece clad	—	22.95	28.50
2006S 5 quarter set	—	15.95	14.50
2006S Silver 10 piece	—	37.95	30.00
2006S Silver 5 quarter set	—	23.95	17.00
2007S 5 quarter set	—	13.95	15.25
2007S Silver 5 quarter set	—	22.95	19.00
2007S 14 piece clad	—	—	33.50
2007S Silver 14 piece	—	—	49.50
2007S Presidental $ set	—	—	20.75
2007S American Legacy	—	—	210
2008 14 pieces clad	—	—	69.00
2008S Silver 14 piece	—	—	66.50
2008S Presidental $ set	—	—	22.00
2008S 5 quarter set	—	22.95	33.00
2008S Silver 5 quarter set	—	—	26.50

UNCIRCULATED ROLLS

Listings are for rolls containing original uncirculated coins, unblemished well struck rolls can bring substantially more.Large date and small date varieties for 1960 and 1970 apply to the one cent coins.

Date	Cents	Nickels	Dimes	Quarters	Halves
1934	$585.00	$3,500.00	$2,350.00	$1,650.00	$2,350.00
1934D	$2,650.00	$4,350.00	$2,950.00	$9,000.00	Rare
1934S	—	—	—	—	Rare
1935	$885.00	$1,700.00	$1,450.00	$1,725.00	$1,250.00
1935D	$750.00	$3,150.00	$2,950.00	$8,850.00	$4,000.00
1935S	$2,500.00	$1,725.00	$1,950.00	$4,650.00	$6,500.00
1936	$285.00	$1,450.00	$885.00	$1,300.00	$1,750.00
1936D	$400.00	$1,450.00	$1,700.00	Rare	$2,750.00
1936S	$885.00	$1,800.00	$1,675.00	$6,250.00	$3,500.00
1937	$250.00	$1,100.00	$710.00	$1,250.00	$1,150.00
1937D	$250.00	$1,200.00	$1,550.00	$3,450.00	$5,000.00
1937S	$335.00	$1,285.00	$1,650.00	$4,850.00	$3,450.00
1938	$665.00	$535.00	$1,100.00	$3,100.00	$1,850.00
1938D Buffalo	—	$1,065.00	—	—	—
1938D	$710.00	$485.00	$1,000.00	—	Rare
1938S	$440.00	$355.00	$1,350.00	$3,250.00	—
1939	$180.00	$160.00	$630.00	$1,040.00	$1,250.00
1939D	$535.00	$3,850.00	$610.00	$1,875.00	$1,975.00
1939S	$265.00	$2,750.00	$1,900.00	$3,200.00	$2,350.00
1940	$225.00	$145.00	$535.00	$1,850.00	$975.00
1940D	$265.00	$120.00	$780.00	$5,350.00	—
1940S	$300.00	$265.00	$675.00	$1,275.00	$1,200.00
1941	$170.00	$215.00	$430.00	$475.00	$750.00
1941D	$335.00	$330.00	$710.00	$2,750.00	$1,200.00
1941S	$360.00	$295.00	$535.00	$2,450.00	$3,000.00
1942	$140.00	$315.00	$465.00	$450.00	$690.00
1942P	—	$600.00	—	—	—
1942D	$140.00	$2,550.00	$740.00	$1,060.00	$1,350.00
1942S	$585.00	$525.00	$1,050.00	$5,350.00	$1,475.00
1943	$60.00	$275.00	$470.00	$365.00	$725.00
1943D	$170.00	$210.00	$610.00	$2,000.00	$1,775.00
1943S	$310.00	$325.00	$650.00	$2,100.00	$1,365.00
1944	$30.00	$720.00	$460.00	$280.00	$715.00
1944D	$38.00	$680.00	$635.00	$725.00	$1,250.00
1944S	$120.00	$565.00	$660.00	$950.00	$1,300.00
1945	$125.00	$375.00	$410.00	$325.00	$730.00
1945D	$110.00	$315.00	$500.00	$1,000.00	$1,000.00
1945S	$80.00	$270.00	$525.00	575	$950.00
1946	$39.00	$80.00	$88.00	$365.00	$1,025.00
1946D	$36.50	$75.00	$92.00	$380.00	$900.00
1946S	$115.00	$50.00	$105.00	$275.00	$900.00
1947	$220.00	$58.00	$215.00	$735.00	$1,000.00
1947D	$46.50	$72.00	$275.00	$385.00	$1,000.00
1947S	$39.00	$72.00	$210.00	$415.00	—
1948	$72.50	$55.00	$188.00	$240.00	$450.00
1948D	$175.00	$155.00	$325.00	$645.00	$425.00
1948S	$165.00	$80.00	$255.00	$475.00	—
1949	$180.00	$330.00	$1,200.00	$2,350.00	$1,300.00
1949D	$125.00	$215.00	$550.00	$1,285.00	$1,475.00
1949S	$140.00	$138.00	$2,350.00	—	$2,250.00
1950	$115.00	$120.00	$525.00	$395.00	$750.00
1950D	$42.00	$410.00	$200.00	$440.00	$875.00
1950S	$78.00	—	$1,550.00	$850.00	—
1951	$165.00	$230.00	$120.00	$435.00	$390.00
1951D	$26.50	$285.00	$84.00	$325.00	$800.00
1951S	$60.00	$265.00	$690.00	$1,350.00	$750.00
1952	$165.00	$145.00	$110.00	$535.00	$385.00
1952D	$26.50	$260.00	$110.00	$300.00	$230.00
1952S	$300.00	$42.00	$290.00	$1,000.00	$1,585.00
1953	$42.00	$24.50	$120.00	$635.00	$490.00
1953D	$22.50	$17.00	$85.00	$165.00	$260.00
1953S	$35.00	$39.00	$85.00	$245.00	$850.00
1954	$39.00	$57.50	$82.00	$160.00	$185.00
1954D	$22.50	$24.00	$82.00	$160.00	$220.00
1954S	$22.50	$39.50	$82.00	$160.00	$410.00
1955	$24.50	$19.00	$83.00	$170.00	$300.00
1955D	$19.00	$7.00	$82.00	$185.00	—
1955S	$27.50	—	$80.00	—	—
1956	$10.50	$7.50	$80.00	$160.00	$222.00
1956D	$12.50	$9.25	$80.00	$158.00	—
1957	$10.00	$12.50	$80.00	$156.00	$172.00
1957D	$9.50	$4.75	$85.00	$158.00	$172.00
1958	$10.50	$6.50	$80.00	$156.00	$172.00
1958D	$9.75	$5.50	$80.00	$156.00	$166.00

SETS & ROLLS

Date	Cents	Nickels	Dimes	Quarters	Halves
1959	$2.50	$5.00	$80.00	$156.00	$168.00
1959D	$2.10	$5.25	$80.00	$156.00	$210.00
1960 LD	$1.60	$4.40	$80.00	$195.00	$168.00
1960 SD	$220.00	—	—	—	—
1960D LD	$1.60	$5.00	$80.00	$156.00	$175.00
1960D SD	$2.85	—	—	—	—
1961	$1.60	$4.25	$80.00	$156.00	$166.00
1961D	$1.90	$4.50	$80.00	$156.00	$166.00
1962	$1.65	$5.25	$80.00	$156.00	$170.00
1962D	$1.65	$5.50	$80.00	$156.00	$165.00
1963	$1.50	$4.25	$80.00	$156.00	$158.00
1963D	$1.65	$4.75	$80.00	$156.00	$158.00
1964	$1.50	$3.50	$80.00	$156.00	$156.00
1964D	$1.60	$3.50	$80.00	$156.00	$156.00
1965	$2.25	$8.75	$8.00	$25.00	$65.00
1966	$3.75	$6.00	$10.00	$53.00	$68.00
1967	$4.50	$9.75	$8.50	$25.00	$70.00
1968	$1.75	—	$8.50	$25.00	—
1968D	$1.70	$6.00	$9.50	$33.00	$68.00
1968S	$1.90	$6.25	—	—	—
1969	$7.75	—	$44.00	$100.00	—
1969D	$2.00	$6.25	$21.50	$82.00	$68.00
1969S	$3.75	$6.75	—	—	—
1970	$2.10	—	$8.00	$26.00	—
1970D	$2.10	$4.00	$7.75	$16.00	$235.00
1970S	$3.00	$4.50	—	—	—
1970S SD	$2,650.00	—	—	—	—
1971	$17.00	$26.50	$16.00	$50.00	$26.00
1971D	$3.00	$7.50	$9.50	$19.50	$15.50
1971S	$4.00	—	—	—	—
1972	$2.00	$6.50	$11.00	$23.00	$32.00
1972D	$6.00	$5.75	$10.00	$21.50	$23.00
1972S	$4.75	—	—	—	—
1973	$1.75	$6.25	$10.50	$22.00	$25.50
1973D	$1.75	$6.25	$9.00	$23.00	$18.00
1973S	$3.00	—	—	—	—
1974	$1.75	$4.50	$7.50	$18.50	$15.00
1974D	$1.75	$5.75	$7.75	$17.50	$21.00
1974S	$3.50	—	—	—	—
1975	$3.75	$12.50	$8.75	—	—
1975D	$1.75	$5.25	$15.50	—	—
1976	$1.75	$13.50	$21.00	$17.50	$18.00
1976D	$2.50	$11.00	$18.00	$17.50	$15.50
1977	$1.75	$6.25	$9.75	$16.50	$21.50
1977D	$2.85	$5.75	$8.50	$17.50	$24.00
1978	$3.00	$4.50	$7.25	$16.00	$32.00
1978D	$10.00	$5.00	$8.00	$16.50	$46.50
1979	$1.75	$4.75	$8.75	$17.00	$22.50
1979D	$3.00	$5.75	$8.00	$22.50	$22.50
1980	$1.75	$4.25	$8.00	$16.50	$20.50
1980D	$2.50	$4.50	$7.50	$16.50	$20.50
1981	$1.75	$4.25	$7.50	$16.50	$16.50
1981D	$1.85	$4.25	$8.00	$16.50	$19.00
1982 LD (pennies only)	$2.50	—	—	—	—
1982 SD (pennies only)	$25.00	$325.00	$270.00	$250.00	$98.00
1982D LD (pennies only)	$4.00	$54.00	$66.00	$165.00	$80.00
1982 LD, Copper plated Zinc	$8.00	—	—	—	—
1982 SD, Copper plated Zinc	$3.00	—	—	—	—
1982D LD, Copper plated Zinc	$35.00	—	—	—	—
1982D SD, Copper plated Zinc	$2.50	—	—	—	—
1983	$7.50	$90.00	$235.00	$945.00	$80.00
1983D	$17.50	$39.00	$39.00	$410.00	$120.00
1984	$5.50	$22.00	$8.50	$17.00	$26.00
1984D	$14.50	$6.50	$21.00	$29.00	$37.00
1985	$4.25	$10.00	$9.75	$31.00	$76.00
1985D	$9.75	$8.00	$9.25	$22.00	$44.00
1986	$20.00	$8.75	$25.00	$85.00	$75.00
1986D	$31.50	$24.50	$22.50	$210.00	$90.00
1987	$6.50	$6.00	$7.75	$15.50	$52.00
1987D	$13.50	$4.50	$8.75	$15.50	$52.00
1988	$6.25	$5.50	$9.75	$39.00	$75.00
1988D	$12.50	$9.00	$9.25	$22.50	$45.00
1989	$3.25	$5.50	$12.00	$19.50	$42.00
1989D	$3.50	$8.75	$12.50	$17.00	$25.00
1990	$4.00	$11.50	$14.50	$20.00	$39.00
1990D	$5.85	$13.75	$10.00	$25.00	$52.00
1991	$2.60	$12.00	$10.00	$29.00	$37.50
1991D	$11.50	$12.00	$11.00	$31.00	$33.00
1992	$3.00	$46.00	$8.00	$42.00	$21.00
1992D	$5.00	$9.00	$8.00	$27.50	$50.00

Date	Cents	Nickels	Dimes	Quarters	Halves
1993	$3.25	$13.50	$9.50	$39.00	$64.00
1993D	$7.50	$17.50	$13.00	$36.00	$17.00
1994	$2.00	$7.75	$12.00	$42.00	$15.00
1994D	$2.00	$8.00	$12.00	$47.50	$20.00
1995	$1.85	$10.50	$16.50	$45.00	$17.00
1995D	$2.00	$20.00	$19.50	$53.00	$40.00
1996	$2.25	$8.75	$11.00	$19.00	$17.00
1996D	$2.85	$8.25	$11.50	27.5	$19.00
1997	$2.75	$14.50	$29.00	$22.50	$20.00
1997D	$3.35	$60.00	$11.00	$39.00	$16.50
1998	$2.00	$13.75	$9.75	$17.00	$20.00
1998D	$1.85	$14.00	$12.00	$18.00	$16.50
1999P	$2.35	$5.50	$8.50	—	$20.00
1999D	$2.25	$6.25	$8.50	—	$19.00
2000P	$2.50	$6.25	$7.75	—	$15.00
2000D	$1.75	$4.75	$7.00	—	$17.00
2001P	$3.75	$4.75	$7.75	—	$16.50
2001D	$2.00	$6.50	$7.25	—	$16.00
2002P	$2.00	$4.00	$7.25	—	$20.00
2002D	$3.25	$4.10	$7.25	—	$20.00
2003P	$3.35	$7.50	$7.00	—	$22.50
2003D	$2.00	$3.50	$7.00	—	$19.50
2004P Peace Medal Nickel	$1.75	$6.75	$7.00	—	$30.00
2004D Peace Medal Nickel	$2.50	$7.00	$7.00	—	$30.00

50 STATE QUARTERS

Listings are for rolls containing uncirculated coins.

Date	Philadelphia	Denver	Date	Philadelphia	Denver
1999 Delaware	$19.75	$19.75	2004 Michigan	$15.00	$15.00
1999 Pennsylvania	$19.50	$19.75	2004 Florida	$15.25	$15.25
1999 New Jersey	$17.50	$17.00	2004 Texas	$14.50	$15.50
1999 Georgia	$57.50	$57.50	2004 Iowa	$15.25	$15.25
1999 Connecticut	$33.50	$33.50	2004 Wisconsin	$17.00	$17.75
2000 Massachusetts	$16.00	$16.00	2005 California	$22.00	$22.00
2000 Maryland	$16.00	$16.50	2005 Minnesota	$17.75	$18.00
2000 South Carolina	$17.50	$18.00	2005 Oregon	$14.50	$14.50
2000 New Hampshire	$14.75	$15.00	2005 Kansas	$15.00	$15.00
2000 Virginia	$15.00	$15.00	2005 West Virgina	$15.00	$14.00
2001 New York	$14.50	$14.50	2006 Nevada	$15.00	$15.00
2001 North Carolina	$16.50	$15.50	2006 Nebraska	$14.50	$14.50
2001 Rhode Island	$16.00	$16.00	2006 Colorado	$15.75	$14.75
2001 Vermont	$17.00	$15.00	2006 North Dakota	$14.00	$14.75
2001 Kentucky	$19.25	$19.50	2006 South Dakota	$15.00	$14.50
2002 Tennessee	$47.50	$47.50	2007 Montana	$17.75	$17.75
2002 Ohio	$22.50	$22.00	2007 Washington	$21.00	$21.00
2002 Louisiana	$15.00	$15.50	2007 Idaho	$16.00	$16.25
2002 Indiana	$16.50	$16.00	2007 Wyoming	$15.75	$16.00
2002 Mississippi	$16.50	$16.50	2007 Utah	$15.75	$15.00
2003 Illinois	$57.50	$57.50	2008 Oklahoma	$16.25	$16.50
2003 Alabama	$21.00	$21.00	2008 New Mexico	$17.00	$14.25
2003 Maine	$17.00	$16.25	2008 Arizona	$17.00	$15.25
2003 Missouri	$15.00	$15.50	2008 Alaska	$14.50	$15.25
2003 Arkansas	$15.75	$16.75	2008 Hawaii	$15.00	$15.00

TRUST TERRITORY QUARTERS

Listings are for rolls containing uncirculated coins.

Date	Philadelphia	Denver
2009 DC	$18.00	$15.50
2009 Puerto Rico	$15.00	$15.50
2009 Guam	$15.00	$16.50
2009 American Samoa	$15.00	$15.00
2009 Virgin Islands	$15.00	$15.00
2009 Marianna Islands	$15.00	$15.00

COLONIAL COINAGE

North America was initially explored by the Vikings, but it was not until the age of Discovery, that active and expansive colonization began. The French, Spanish, Dutch, English and Portuguese were all involved in colonizing North, Central and South America.

The Spanish were strongest in Central and South America, taking that whole continent except for Brazil, which went to Portugal. Their expansion also spread into what became modern day Florida, Texas, and California.

The French settled in the Mississippi River Delta, from New Orleans northward to St. Louis, then east to the Ohio River basin, and west to the Rockies; they also progressed to the north, in the St. Lawrence River area in Canada; Quebec and Montreal being their principal cities.

The Dutch had a presence from the 1620's through 1664, mainly in the New York region, but lost that territory to the English, and never again gained a stronghold on the mainland during this period.

The English settled on the East Coast of the United States, from Georgia north to what later became Maine, and east of the Allegheny and Appalachian Mountains. To the north in Canada, they worked their way into Nova Scotia, Newfoundland, and north of the French in Quebec, Ontario, and with the explorers of the Hudson Bay Company, westward on the plains to the Pacific North West.

On the basis of the voyage of John Cabot to the North American mainland in 1497, England initially claimed the entire continent. The first permanent English settlement was established at Jamestown, Va., in 1607. France and Spain had also claimed extensive territory in North America, but at the end of the French and Indian Wars in 1763, England acquired all of the territory east of the Mississippi River, including east and west Florida. From 1776 to 1781, the States were governed by the Continental Congress. From 1781 to 1789, they were organized under the Articles of Confederation, during which period the individual States, formed from the former 13 British-American colonies; New York, New Jersey, New Hampshire, Massachusetts, Rhode Island, Connecticut, Pennsylvania, Delaware, Maryland, Virginia, North Carolina, South Carolina and Georgia, had the right to issue money.

While British and Spanish silver coins circulated freely in the American Colonies, several of the Colonies and later States did issue copper or silver coins. In addition, both merchant and political tokens, mainly in copper, were issued in several locations. The most popularly circulated, and now collected, of these Colonial and State issues are listed here.

The population of the colonies during this political phase of America's history (1781-1789) was about 3 million, most of whom lived on self-sufficient family farms. Fishing, lumbering and the production of grains for export were major economic endeavors. Rapid strides were also being made in industry and manufacturing by 1775, when the North American colonies were accounting for one-seventh of the world's production of raw iron.

Independence from Great Britain was attained with the American Revolution in 1776. The Constitution organized and governs the present United States. It was ratified on Nov. 21, 1788.

MONETARY SYSTEM
12 Pence = 1 Shilling
5 Shillings = 1 Crown
21 Shillings = 1 Guinea

MARYLAND
LORD BALTIMORE
PENNY (DENARIUM)

KM#1 Composition: Copper. **Obverse Legend:**
CAECILIVS Dns TERRAE MARIAE.

Date	AG	Good	VG	Fine	VF	XF
(1659) 5 known	—	—	—	—	—	100,000

Note: Stack's Auction 5-04, proof realized $241,500

4 PENCE (GROAT)

KM#2 Composition: Silver. **Obverse:** Large bust.
Obverse Legend: CAECILIVS Dns TERRAE MARIAE.
Reverse: Large shield.

Date	AG	Good	VG	Fine	VF	XF
(1659)	1,250	1,850	3,500	6,250	13,500	20,000

KM#3 Composition: Silver. **Obverse:** Small bust.
Obverse Legend: CAECILIVS Dns TERRAE MARIAE.
Reverse: Small shield.

Date	AG	Good	VG	Fine	VF	XF
(1659) unique	—	—	—	—	—	—

Note: Norweb $26,400

6 PENCE

KM#4 Composition: Silver. **Obverse:** Small bust.
Obverse Legend: CAECILIVS Dns TERRAE MARIAE.
Note: Known in two other rare small-bust varieties and
two rare large-bust varieties.

Date	AG	Good	VG	Fine	VF	XF
(1659)	850	1,400	2,400	4,900	9,000	15,000

SHILLING

KM#6 Composition: Silver. **Obverse Legend:**
CAECILIVS Dns TERRAE MARIAE. **Note:** Varieties exist;
one is very rare.

Date	AG	Good	VG	Fine	VF	XF
(1659)	1,100	1,800	3,000	5,750	13,500	20,000

MASSACHUSETTS
NEW ENGLAND
3 PENCE

KM#1 Composition: Silver. **Obverse:** NE. **Reverse:** III.

Date	AG	Good	VG	Fine	VF	XF
(1652) Unique	—	—	—	—	—	—

Note: Massachusetts Historical Society specimen

6 PENCE

KM#2 Composition: Silver. **Obverse:** NE. **Reverse:** VI.

Date	AG	Good	VG	Fine	VF	XF
(1652) 8 known	—	25,000	50,000	90,000	175,000	—

Note: Garrett $75,000

SHILLING

KM#3 Composition: Silver. **Obverse:** NE.
Reverse: XII.

Date	AG	Good	VG	Fine	VF	XF
(1652)	—	35,000	65,000	100,000	200,000	—

OAK TREE
2 PENCE

KM#7 Composition: Silver. **Note:** Small 2 and large 2
vareites exist

Date	AG	Good	VG	Fine	VF	XF	Unc
1662	—	500	900	2,000	3,850	6,500	15,000

US COLONIAL AMERICA

3 PENCE

KM#8 **Composition:** Silver. **Note:** Two types of legends.

Date	AG	Good	VG	Fine	VF	XF	Unc
1652	350	600	1,000	2,500	5,500	9,000	—

6 PENCE

KM#9 **Composition:** Silver. **Note:** Three types of legends.

Date	AG	Good	VG	Fine	VF	XF	Unc
1652	400	900	1,100	2,700	6,400	9,500	25,000

SHILLING

KM#10 **Composition:** Silver. **Note:** Two types of legends.

Date	AG	Good	VG	Fine	VF	XF	Unc
1652	350	650	1,100	2,600	5,400	8,800	25,000

PINE TREE

3 PENCE

KM#11 **Composition:** Silver. **Obverse:** Tree without berries.

Date	AG	Good	VG	Fine	VF	XF	Unc
1652	250	500	700	1,650	3,000	5,600	17,500

KM#12 **Composition:** Silver. **Obverse:** Tree with berries.

Date	AG	Good	VG	Fine	VF	XF	Unc
1652	250	500	700	1,650	3,200	5,750	18,500

6 PENCE

KM#13 **Composition:** Silver. **Obverse:** Tree without berries; "spiney tree".

Date	AG	Good	VG	Fine	VF	XF	Unc
1652	400	700	1,400	2,000	3,750	6,500	20,000

KM#14 **Composition:** Silver. **Obverse:** Tree with berries.

Date	AG	Good	VG	Fine	VF	XF	Unc
1652	300	500	800	1,750	3,500	6,250	18,000

SHILLING

KM#15 **Composition:** Silver. **Note:** Large planchet. Many varieties exist; some are very rare.

Date	AG	Good	VG	Fine	VF	XF	Unc
1652	350	600	950	2,000	4,350	7,500	20,000

KM#16 **Composition:** Silver. **Note:** Small planchet; large dies. All examples are thought to be contemporary fabrications.

Date	AG	Good	VG	Fine	VF	XF	Unc
1652	—	—	—	—	—	—	—

KM#17 **Composition:** Silver. **Note:** Small planchet; small dies. Many varieties exist; some are very rare.

Date	AG	Good	VG	Fine	VF	XF	Unc
1652	285	525	800	1,700	3,750	6,950	22,500

WILLOW TREE

3 PENCE

KM#4 **Composition:** Silver.

Date	AG	Good	VG	Fine	VF	XF
1652 3 known	—	—	—	—	—	—

6 PENCE

KM#5 **Composition:** Silver.

Date	AG	Good	VG	Fine	VF	XF
1652						
14 known	9,000	17,500	30,000	57,500	125,000	200,000

SHILLING

KM#6 **Composition:** Silver.

Date	AG	Good	VG	Fine	VF	XF
1652	9,800	18,000	34,000	80,000	150,000	225,000

NEW JERSEY

ST. PATRICK OR MARK NEWBY

FARTHING

KM#1 **Composition:** Copper. Obverse **Legend:** FLOREAT REX. **Reverse Legend:** QUIESCAT PLEBS.

Date	AG	Good	VG	Fine	VF	XF	Unc
(1682)	70.00	125	285	700	2,250	4,500	—

Note: One very rare variety is known with reverse legend: QUIESAT PLEBS

KM#1a **Composition:** Silver. Obverse **Legend:** FLOREAT REX. **Reverse Legend:** QUIESCAT PLEBS.

Date	AG	Good	VG	Fine	VF	XF	Unc
(1682)	800	1,500	2,200	4,500	8,000	12,500	—

HALFPENNY

KM#2 **Composition:** Copper. Obverse **Legend:** FLOREAT REX. **Reverse Legend:** ECCE GREX.

Date	AG	Good	VG	Fine	VF	XF	Unc
(1682)	180	365	850	1,650	4,000	10,500	—

US COLONIAL AMERICA

EARLY AMERICAN TOKENS

AMERICAN PLANTATIONS

1/24 REAL

KM#Tn5.1   Composition: Tin. Obverse **Legend:** ET HIB REX.

Date	AG	Good	VG	Fine	VF	XF	Unc
(1688)	125	200	300	450	750	2,000	—

KM#Tn5.3   Composition: Tin. **Reverse:** Horizontal 4.

Date	AG	Good	VG	Fine	VF	XF	Unc
(1688)	275	400	900	1,500	2,700	5,000	—

KM#Tn5.4   Composition: Tin. Obverse **Legend:** ET HIB REX.

Date	AG	Good	VG	Fine	VF	XF	Unc
(1688)	—	250	450	750	1,400	2,650	9,000

KM#Tn6   Composition: Tin. **Reverse:** Arms of Scotland left, Ireland right.

Date	AG	Good	VG	Fine	VF	XF	Unc
(1688)	450	750	1,250	2,000	3,000	6,500	—

KM#Tn5.2   Composition: Tin. Obverse: Rider's head left of "B" in legend. **Note:** Restrikes made in 1828 from two Obverse dies.

Date	AG	Good	VG	Fine	VF	XF	Unc
(1828)	75.00	110	175	275	500	1,000	—

ELEPHANT

KM#Tn1.1   Weight: 15.5500 g. **Composition:** Copper. **Note:** Thick planchet.

Date	AG	Good	VG	Fine	VF	XF	Unc
(1664)	125	200	300	500	1,000	1,750	3,850

KM#Tn1.2   Composition: Copper. **Note:** Thin planchet.

Date	AG	Good	VG	Fine	VF	XF	Unc
(1664)	175	300	500	850	3,000	5,500	11,750

KM#Tn2   Composition: Copper. **Reverse:** Diagonals tie shield.

Date	AG	Good	VG	Fine	VF	XF	Unc
(1664)	250	450	650	2,250	6,500	10,000	17,500

KM#Tn3   Composition: Copper. **Reverse:** Sword right side of shield.

Date	AG	Good	VG	Fine	VF	XF
(1664) 3 known	—	—	—	—	12,500	—

Note: Norweb $1,320

KM#Tn4   Composition: Copper. **Reverse Legend:** LON DON.

Date	AG	Good	VG	Fine	VF	XF	Unc
(1684)	340	650	1,000	2,250	4,000	7,000	17,500

KM#Tn7   Composition: Copper. **Reverse Legend:** NEW ENGLAND.

Date	AG	Good	VG	Fine	VF	XF
(1694) 2 known	—	50,000	75,000	95,000	140,000	

Note: Norweb $25,300

KM#Tn8.1   Composition: Copper. **Reverse Legend:** CAROLINA (PROPRIETORS).

Date	AG	Good	VG	Fine	VF	XF
(1694) 5 known	—	—	4,750	6,500	14,000	22,500

Note: Norweb $35,200

KM#Tn8.2   Composition: Copper. **Reverse Legend:** CAROLINA (PROPRIETORS, O over E).

Date	AG	Good	VG	Fine	VF	XF
1694	1,300	2,500	4,000	6,000	12,000	17,500

Note: Norweb $17,600

GLOUCESTER

KM#Tn15 Composition: Copper. **Obverse Legend:** GLOVCESTER COVRTHOVSE VIRGINIA. **Reverse Legend:** RIGHAVLT DAWSON.ANNO.DOM.1714..

Date	AG	Good	VG	Fine	VF	XF
(1714) 2 known	—	—	—	—	—	—

Note: Garrett $36,000

HIBERNIA-VOCE POPULI

FARTHING

KM#Tn21.1 Composition: Copper. **Note:** Large letters

Date	AG	Good	VG	Fine	VF	XF	Unc
1760	125	200	325	600	1,600	3,000	8,500

KM#Tn21.2 Composition: Copper. **Note:** Small letters

Date	AG	Good	VG	Fine	VF	XF	Unc
1760	—	650	1,250	2,750	7,500	13,500	—

Note: Norweb $5,940.

HALFPENNY

KM#Tn22 Composition: Copper.

Date	AG	Good	VG	Fine	VF	XF	Unc
1700 Extremely rare	—	—	—	—	—	—	—

Note: Date is in error; ex-Roper $575. Norweb $577.50. Stack's Americana, VF, $2,900

1760	40.00	70.00	135	175	365	675	2,500
1760	50.00	80.00	135	195	425	775	3,500

Note: legend VOOE POPULI

1760 P below bust	65.00	100.00	185	350	700	1,750	8,000
1760 P in front of bust	55.00	90.00	170	325	600	1,400	6,500

HIGLEY OR GRANBY

KM#Tn16 Composition: Copper. **Obverse Legend:** CONNECTICVT. **Note:** THE VALVE OF THREE PENCE.

Date	AG	Good	VG	Fine	VF	XF
1737	—	10,000	18,000	40,000	80,000	—

Note: Garrett $16,000

KM#Tn17 Composition: Copper. **Obverse Legend:** THE VALVE OF THREE PENCE. **Reverse Legend:** I AM GOOD COPPER.

Date	AG	Good	VG	Fine	VF	XF
1737 2 known	—	11,000	20,000	40,000	85,000	—

Note: ex-Norweb $6,875

KM#Tn18.1 Composition: Copper. **Obverse Legend:** VALUE ME AS YOU PLEASE. **Reverse Legend:** I AM GOOD COPPER.

Date	AG	Good	VG	Fine	VF	XF
1737	6,500	10,000	18,000	40,000	80,000	—

KM#Tn18.2 Composition: Copper. **Obverse Legend:** VALVE.ME.AS.YOU.PLEASE.. **Reverse Legend:** I AM GOOD COPPER..

Date	AG	Good	VG	Fine	VF	XF
1737 2 known	—	—	—	—	—	275,000

KM#Tn19 Composition: Copper. **Reverse:** Broad axe.

Date	AG	Good	VG	Fine	VF	XF
(1737)	—	10,000	18,000	35,000	125,000	—

Note: Garrett $45,000

1739 5 known	—	—	—	—	—	—

Note: Eliasberg $12,650. Oechsner $9,900. Steinberg (holed) $4,400.

KM#Tn20 Composition: Copper. Obverse **Legend:**
THE WHEELE GOES ROUND. **Reverse:** J CUT MY WAY
THROUGH.

Date	AG	Good	VG	Fine	VF	XF
(1737) unique	—	—	—150,000	—	—	

Note: Roper $60,500

NEW YORKE

KM#Tn9 Composition: Brass. Obverse **Legend:**
NEW.YORK.IN.AMERICA.

Date	AG	Good	VG	Fine	VF	XF
1700	1,800	3,500	5,500	13,000	22,500	35,000

KM#Tn9a Composition: White Metal. Obverse
Legend: NEW.YORK.IN.AMERICA.

Date	AG	Good	VG	Fine	VF	XF
1700 4 known	—	—	6,000	15,000	28,000	50,000

PITT

KM#Tn23 Composition: Copper.

Date	AG	Good	VG	Fine	VF	XF
1766	—	—	—	7,500	22,000	35,000

HALFPENNY

KM#Tn24 Composition: Copper.

Date	AG	Good	VG	Fine	VF	XF	Unc
1766	140	250	400	700	1,500	2,750	7,500

KM#Tn24a Composition: Silver Plated Copper.

Date	AG	Good	VG	Fine	VF	XF	Unc
1766	—	—	—	—	2,250	5,000	12,000

ROYAL PATENT COINAGE

HIBERNIA

FARTHING

KM#20 Composition: Copper. **Note:** Pattern.

Date	AG	Good	VG	Fine	VF	XF	Unc
1722	135	235	375	500	1,000	2,600	7,750

KM#24 Composition: Copper. **Obverse:** 1722
Obverse. Obverse **Legend:** ...D:G:REX..

Date	AG	Good	VG	Fine	VF	XF	Unc
1723	20.00	40.00	60.00	90.00	150	350	—

KM#25 Composition: Copper. Obverse **Legend:** DEI
• GRATIA • REX •.

Date	AG	Good	VG	Fine	VF	XF	Unc
1723	25.00	45.00	60.00	180	300	550	950
1724	—	90.00	125	225	600	1,350	3,500

KM#25a Composition: Silver.

Date	AG	Good	VG	Fine	VF	XF	Unc
1723	—	—	1,600	2,250	4,000	5,500	10,000

HALFPENNY

KM#21 Composition: Copper. **Obverse:** Bust right.

Obverse **Legend:** GEORGIUS • DEI • GRATIA • REX •.
Reverse: Harp left, head left. **Reverse Legend:**
• HIBERNIA • 1722 •.

Date	AG	Good	VG	Fine	VF	XF	Unc
1722	50.00	90.00	110	160	325	700	1,750

KM#22 **Composition:** Copper. **Obverse:** Bust right.
Obverse **Legend:** GEORGIVS D: G: REX. **Reverse:** Harp
left, head right. **Reverse Legend:** • HIBERNIÆ •. **Note:**
"Rocks Reverse" pattern.

Date	AG	Good	VG	Fine	VF	XF	Unc
1722	—	—	—	2,750	3,850	8,500	—

KM#23.1 **Composition:** Copper. **Reverse:** Harp
right.

Date	AG	Good	VG	Fine	VF	XF	Unc
1722	35.00	60.00	80.00	120	285	600	1,400
1723	20.00	35.00	45.00	75.00	190	280	800
1723/22	35.00	60.00	80.00	150	375	750	1,750
1724	25.00	50.00	90.00	160	360	825	2,000

KM#23.2 **Composition:** Copper. **Obverse:** DEII error
in legend.

Date	AG	Good	VG	Fine	VF	XF	Unc
1722	75.00	125	160	325	750	1,400	2,750

KM#26 **Composition:** Copper. **Reverse:** Large head.
Note: Rare. Generally mint state only. Probably a pattern.

Date	AG	Good	VG	Fine	VF	XF	Unc
1723	—	—	—	—	—	—	—

KM#27 **Composition:** Copper. **Reverse:** Continuous
legend over head.

Date	AG	Good	VG	Fine	VF	XF	Unc
1724	45.00	80.00	150	300	900	1,500	3,500

ROSA AMERICANA

HALFPENNY

KM#1 **Composition:** Copper. **Obverse Legend:**
D • G • REX •.

Date	AG	Good	VG	Fine	VF	XF	Unc
1722	20.00	50.00	140	250	525	1,050	4,000

KM#2 **Composition:** Copper. **Obverse:** Uncrowned
rose. Obverse **Legend:** ... • DEI • GRATIA • REX •.
Note: Several varieties exist.

Date	AG	Good	VG	Fine	VF	XF	Unc
1722	50.00	90.00	135	250	450	950	3,500
1723	385	700	850	1,750	3,600	—	—

KM#3 **Composition:** Copper. **Reverse Legend:**
VTILE DVLCI.

Date	AG	Good	VG	Fine	VF	XF	Unc
1722	250	450	850	2,200	3,800	7,500	—

KM#9 **Composition:** Copper. **Reverse:** Crowned rose.

Date	AG	Good	VG	Fine	VF	XF	Unc
1723	45.00	85.00	110	165	425	1,000	4,500

PENNY

KM#4 **Composition:** Copper. **Reverse Legend:**
UTILE DULCI. **Note:** Several varieties exist.

Date	AG	Good	VG	Fine	VF	XF	Unc
1722	60.00	100.00	135	240	450	950	3,750

KM#5 **Composition:** Copper. **Note:** Several varieties
exist. Also known in two rare pattern types with long
hair ribbons, one with V's for U's on the Obverse.

Date	AG	Good	VG	Fine	VF	XF	Unc
1722	18.00	35.00	150	275	750	1,350	5,600

KM#10 Composition: Copper. **Note:** Several varieties exist.

Date	AG	Good	VG	Fine	VF	XF	Unc
1723	40.00	75.00	110	175	425	900	3,600

KM#12 Composition: Copper. **Note:** Pattern.

Date	AG	Good	VG	Fine	VF	XF
1724 2 known	—	—	—	—	—	—

KM#13 Composition: Copper. **Reverse Legend:** ROSA: SINE: SPINA •.

Date	AG	Good	VG	Fine	VF	XF
(1724) 5 known	—	—	—	—	—	—

Note: Norweb $2,035

KM#14 Composition: Copper. **Obverse:** George II. **Note:** Pattern.

Date	AG	Good	VG	Fine	VF	XF
1727 2 known	—	—	—	—	—	—

2 PENCE

KM#6 Composition: Copper. **Reverse:** Motto with scroll.

Date	AG	Good	VG	Fine	VF	XF	Unc
(1722)	80.00	150	200	425	700	1,200	6,250

KM#7 Composition: Copper. **Reverse:** Motto without scroll.

Date	AG	Good	VG	Fine	VF	XF
(1722) 3 known	—	—	—	—	—	—

KM#8.1 Composition: Copper. **Obverse Legend:** ...REX •. **Reverse:** Dated.

Date	AG	Good	VG	Fine	VF	XF	Unc
1722	70.00	125	175	275	750	1,500	5,500

KM#8.2 Comp.: Copper. **Obverse Legend:** ...REX.

Date	AG	Good	VG	Fine	VF	XF	Unc
1722	70.00	125	175	275	775	1,600	6,000

KM#11 Composition: Copper. **Obverse:** No stop after REX. **Reverse:** Stop after 1723. **Note:** Several varieties exist.

Date	AG	Good	VG	Fine	VF	XF	Unc
1723	65.00	120	160	285	550	1,200	3,500

KM#15 Composition: Copper. **Note:** Pattern. Two varieties exist; both extremely rare.

Date	AG	Good	VG	Fine	VF	XF	Unc
1724	—	—	—	—	—	—	—

Note: Stack's 5-05 choice AU realized $25,300. Ex-Garrett $5,775. Stack's Americana, XF, $10,925

KM#16 Composition: Copper. **Obverse:** Bust left. **Reverse:** Crowned rose. **Note:** Pattern.

Date	AG	Good	VG	Fine	VF	XF
1733 4 known	—	—	—	—	—	—

Note: Norweb $19,800

VIRGINIA HALFPENNY

KM#Tn25.1 Composition: Copper. **Reverse:** Small 7s in date.. **Note:** Struck on Irish halfpenny planchets.

Date	Good	VG	Fine	VF	XF	Unc	Proof
1773	—	—	—	—	—	— 22,000

KM#Tn25.2 Composition: Copper. Obverse **Legend:** GEORGIVS •.... **Reverse:** Varieties with 7 or 8 strings in harp.

Date	AG	Good	VG	Fine	VF	XF	Unc
1773	30.00	50.00	70.00	110	235	425	1,000

KM#Tn25.4 Composition: Copper. Obverse **Legend:** GEORGIVS.... **Reverse:** 8 harp strings, dot on cross.

Date	AG	Good	VG	Fine	VF	XF	Unc
1773	—	—	—	—	—	—	—

Note: ex-Steinberg $2,600

KM#Tn26 Composition: Silver. **Note:** So-called "shilling" silver proofs.

Date	AG	Good	VG	Fine	VF	XF
1774 6 known	—	—	—	—	—	—

Note: Garrett $23,000

KM#Tn25.3 Composition: Copper. Obverse **Legend:** GEORGIVS.... **Reverse:** Varieties with 6, 7 or 8 strings in harp.

Date	AG	Good	VG	Fine	VF	XF	Unc
1773	35.00	60.00	75.00	135	275	500	1,250

REVOLUTIONARY COINAGE

CONTINENTAL "DOLLAR".

KM#EA1 Composition: Pewter Obverse **Legend:** CURRENCY.

Date	AG	Good	VG	Fine	VF	XF	Unc
1776	—	7,500	9,350	12,000	21,000	32,500	70,000

KM#EA2 Composition: Pewter Obverse **Legend:** CURRENCY, EG FECIT.

Date	AG	Good	VG	Fine	VF	XF	Unc
1776	—	8,000	10,500	13,500	25,000	36,000	75,000

KM#EA2a Composition: Silver Obverse **Legend:** CURRENCY, EG FECIT.

Date	AG	Good	VG	Fine	VF	XF
1776 2 known	—	—	—300,000	450,000	—

KM#EA3 Composition: Pewter Obverse **Legend:** CURRENCEY

Date	AG	Good	VG	Fine	VF	XF
1776 extremely rare	—	—	—	—	— 100,000

KM#EA4 Composition: Pewter Obverse **Legend:** CURRENCY. **Reverse:** Floral cross.

Date	AG	Good	VG	Fine	VF	XF
1776 3 recorded	—	—	—	—	— 400,000

Note: Norweb $50,600. Johnson $25,300

KM#EA5 Composition: Pewter Obverse **Legend:** CURENCY.

Date	AG	Good	VG	Fine	VF	XF	Unc
1776	—	7,500	9,500	12,000	22,500	33,000	65,000

KM# 3.1 **Composition:** Copper **Obverse:** Mailed bust facing left.

Date	AG	Good	VG	Fine	VF	XF	Unc
1785	125	220	375	750	1,800	3,850	—
1786	30.00	50.00	90.00	175	475	1,200	—
1787	30.00	50.00	85.00	160	450	1,350	—
1788	30.00	50.00	80.00	160	435	1,100	—

KM# EA5a **Composition:** Brass **Obverse Legend:** CURENCY. **Note:** Two varieties exist.

Date	AG	Good	VG	Fine	VF	XF	Unc
1776	—	22,500	28,500	36,000	70,000	110,000	—

KM# EA5b **Composition:** Silver **Obverse Legend:** CURENCY.

Date	AG	Good	VG	Fine	VF	XF
1776 unique	—	—	—	300,000	450,000	—

Note: Romano $99,000

KM# 4 **Composition:** Copper **Obverse:** Small mailed bust facing left. **Reverse Legend:** ETLIB INDE.

Date	AG	Good	VG	Fine	VF	XF	Unc
1786	45.00	75.00	150	350	900	2,100	—

KM# 5 **Composition:** Copper **Obverse:** Small mailed bust facing right. **Reverse Legend:** INDE ET LIB.

Date	AG	Good	VG	Fine	VF	XF	Unc
1786	60.00	100.00	175	450	2,000	4,250	—

STATE COINAGE

CONNECTICUT

KM# 6 **Composition:** Copper **Obverse:** Large mailed bust facing right.

Date	AG	Good	VG	Fine	VF	XF	Unc
1786	55.00	90.00	160	400	1,750	3,750	—

KM# 1 **Composition:** Copper **Obverse:** Bust facing right.

Date	AG	Good	VG	Fine	VF	XF	Unc
1785	35.00	55.00	90.00	200	650	1,750	—

KM# 7 **Composition:** Copper **Obverse:** "Hercules head."

Date	AG	Good	VG	Fine	VF	XF	Unc
1786	60.00	110	220	600	2,500	5,800	—

KM# 2 **Comp.:** Copper **Obverse:** "African head."

Date	AG	Good	VG	Fine	VF	XF	Unc
1785	55.00	85.00	150	600	1,500	3,800	—

KM# 8.1   Composition: Copper **Obverse:** Draped bust.

Date	AG	Good	VG	Fine	VF	XF	Unc
1786	50.00	90.00	175	475	1,150	2,750	—

KM# 13   Composition: Copper **Obverse:** "Laughing head"

Date	AG	Good	VG	Fine	VF	XF	Unc
1787	35.00	60.00	120	240	650	1,800	—

KM# 9   Composition: Copper **Obverse:** Small head. **Reverse Legend:** ETLIB INDE.

Date	AG	Good	VG	Fine	VF	XF	Unc
1787	65.00	110	180	375	1,500	3,750	—

KM# 10   Composition: Copper **Obverse:** Small head. **Reverse Legend:** INDE ET LIB.

Date	AG	Good	VG	Fine	VF	XF	Unc
1787	75.00	135	200	450	2,000	4,000	—

KM# 11   Composition: Copper **Obverse:** Medium bust. **Note:** Two reverse legend types exist.

Date	AG	Good	VG	Fine	VF	XF	Unc
1787	60.00	90.00	150	350	1,500	3,000	—

KM# 14   Composition: Copper **Obverse:** "Horned head"

Date	AG	Good	VG	Fine	VF	XF	Unc
1787	30.00	50.00	80.00	165	450	1,200	—

KM# 15   Composition: Copper **Reverse Legend:** IND ET LIB

Date	AG	Good	VG	Fine	VF	XF
1787/8	50.00	85.00	170	450	1,500	4,000
1787/1887	85.00	150	225	600	1,750	4,500

KM# 16   Composition: Copper **Obverse Legend:** CONNECT. **Reverse Legend:** INDE ET LIB. **Note:** Two additional scarce reverse legend types exist.

Date	AG	Good	VG	Fine	VF	XF	Unc
1787	35.00	50.00	120	240	550	1,500	—

KM# 12   Composition: Copper **Obverse:** "Muttonhead" variety. **Note:** Extremely rare with legend INDE ET LIB.

Date	AG	Good	VG	Fine	VF	XF	Unc
1787	60.00	90.00	175	500	2,200	4,500	—

KM# 3.3   Composition: Copper **Obverse:** Perfect date. **Reverse Legend:** IN DE ET.

Date	AG	Good	VG	Fine	VF	XF	Unc
1787	50.00	80.00	125	350	750	1,500	—

KM# 8.2   Composition: Copper **Obverse:** Draped bust. **Note:** Many varieties.

Date	AG	Good	VG	Fine	VF	XF	Unc
1787	28.00	42.00	70.00	115	325	750	—

KM# 8.3   Composition: Copper **Obverse Legend:** AUCIORI.

Date	AG	Good	VG	Fine	VF	XF	Unc
1787	30.00	55.00	90.00	175	450	1,000	—

KM#8.4 **Composition:** Copper **Obverse Legend:** AUCTOPI.

Date	AG	Good	VG	Fine	VF	XF	Unc
1787	35.00	65.00	110	200	650	1,650	—

KM#8.5 **Composition:** Copper **Obverse Legend:** AUCTOBI.

Date	AG	Good	VG	Fine	VF	XF	Unc
1787	35.00	65.00	110	200	625	1,550	—

KM#8.6 **Composition:** Copper **Obverse Legend:** CONNFC.

Date	AG	Good	VG	Fine	VF	XF	Unc
1787	32.00	60.00	90.00	160	475	1,000	—

KM#8.7 **Composition:** Copper **Obverse Legend:** CONNLC.

Date	AG	Good	VG	Fine	VF	XF	Unc
1787	50.00	75.00	150	300	650	1,850	—

KM#8.8 **Composition:** Copper **Reverse Legend:** FNDE.

Date	AG	Good	VG	Fine	VF	XF	Unc
1787	35.00	55.00	80.00	160	475	1,400	—

KM#8.9 **Composition:** Copper **Reverse Legend:** ETLIR.

Date	AG	Good	VG	Fine	VF	XF	Unc
1787	32.00	50.00	75.00	150	440	1,175	—

KM#8.10 **Composition:** Copper **Reverse Legend:** ETIIB.

Date	AG	Good	VG	Fine	VF	XF	Unc
1787	35.00	50.00	75.00	150	450	1,200	—

KM#22.3 **Composition:** Copper **Obverse Legend:** CONNEC. **Reverse Legend:** INDE ET LIB.

Date	AG	Good	VG	Fine	VF	XF	Unc
1788	58.00	85.00	190	400	875	1,850	—

KM#22.4 **Composition:** Copper **Obverse Legend:** CONNEC. **Reverse Legend:** INDL ET LIB.

Date	AG	Good	VG	Fine	VF	XF	Unc
1788	58.00	85.00	190	400	875	1,850	—

MASSACHUSETTS

HALFPENNY

KM#20 **Composition:** Copper **Obverse:** Mailed bust facing right.

Date	AG	Good	VG	Fine	VF	XF	Unc
1788	28.00	40.00	85.00	180	550	1,450	—

KM#21 **Composition:** Copper **Obverse:** Small mailed bust facing right.

Date	AG	Good	VG	Fine	VF	XF	Unc
1788	850	1,500	2,950	4,150	9,500	18,500	—

KM#3.4 **Composition:** Copper **Obverse Legend:** CONNLC.

Date	AG	Good	VG	Fine	VF	XF	Unc
1788	44.00	60.00	120	240	650	1,850	—

KM#22.1 **Composition:** Copper **Obverse:** Draped bust facing left. **Reverse Legend:** INDE ET LIB.

Date	AG	Good	VG	Fine	VF	XF	Unc
1788	45.00	70.00	125	285	675	1,650	—

KM#22.2 **Composition:** Copper **Reverse Legend:** INDLET LIB.

Date	AG	Good	VG	Fine	VF	XF	Unc
1788	55.00	80.00	175	375	800	1,750	—

KM#17 **Composition:** Copper

Date	AG	Good	VG	Fine	VF	XF
1776 unique	—	—	—	200,000	—	—

Note: Garrett $40,000

PENNY

KM#18 **Composition:** Copper

Date	AG	Good	VG	Fine	VF	XF	Unc
1776 unique	—	—	—	—	—	—	—

HALF CENT

KM# 19 **Composition:** Copper **Note:** Varieties exist; some are rare.

Date	AG	Good	VG	Fine	VF	XF	Unc
1787	60.00	90.00	140	210	550	1,000	3,250
1788	70.00	110	175	260	585	1,100	3,500

CENT

KM# 20.1 **Composition:** Copper **Reverse:** Arrows in right talon

Date	Good	VG	Fine	VF	XF	Unc
1787 7 known	9,000	22,500	45,000	—	—	350,000

Note: Ex-Bushnell-Brand $8,800. Garrett $5,500

KM# 20.2 **Composition:** Copper **Reverse:** Arrows in left talon

Date	AG	Good	VG	Fine	VF	XF	Unc
1787	60.00	90.00	165	240	650	1,250	6,800

KM# 20.3 **Composition:** Copper **Reverse:** "Horned eagle" die break

Date	AG	Good	VG	Fine	VF	XF	Unc
1787	70.00	110	190	275	775	1,500	7,750

KM# 20.4 **Composition:** Copper **Reverse:** Without period after Massachusetts

Date	AG	Good	VG	Fine	VF	XF	Unc
1788	70.00	105	190	260	675	1,600	6,250

KM# 20.5 **Composition:** Copper **Reverse:** Period after Massachusetts, normal S's

Date	AG	Good	VG	Fine	VF	XF	Unc
1788	60.00	90.00	170	235	600	1,375	5,750

KM# 20.6 **Composition:** Copper **Reverse:** Period after Massachusetts, S's like 8's

Date	AG	Good	VG	Fine	VF	XF	Unc
1788	50.00	75.00	135	200	575	1,250	5,400

NEW HAMPSHIRE

KM# 1 **Composition:** Copper

Date	Good	VG	Fine	VF	XF
1776 extremely rare	—	75,000	—	—	—

Note: Garrett $13,000

NEW JERSEY

KM# 8 **Composition:** Copper **Obverse:** Date below draw bar.

Date	Good	VG	Fine	VF	XF
1786 extremely rare	—	—	48,000	110,000	—

Note: Garrett $52,000

KM# 9   Composition: Copper **Obverse:** Large horse head, date below plow, no coulter on plow.

Date	AG	Good	VG	Fine	VF	XF	Unc
1786	450	750	1,450	2,350	7,500	20,000	—

KM# 12.1   Composition: Copper **Reverse:** Plain shield. **Note:** Small planchet. Varieties exist.

Date	AG	Good	VG	Fine	VF	XF	Unc
1787	35.00	55.00	110	200	500	1,050	—

KM# 10   Composition: Copper **Reverse:** Narrow shield, straight beam.

Date	AG	Good	VG	Fine	VF	XF	Unc
1786	38.00	60.00	140	210	550	1,350	—

KM# 12.2   Composition: Copper **Reverse:** Shield heavily outlined. **Note:** Small planchet.

Date	AG	Good	VG	Fine	VF	XF	Unc
1787	38.00	60.00	120	215	550	1,150	—

KM# 11.1   Composition: Copper **Reverse:** Wide shield, curved beam. **Note:** Varieties exist.

Date	AG	Good	VG	Fine	VF	XF	Unc
1786	45.00	75.00	150	225	600	2,000	—

KM# 13   Composition: Copper **Obverse:** "Serpent head."

Date	AG	Good	VG	Fine	VF	XF	Unc
1787	55.00	85.00	200	375	1,500	3,750	—

KM# 14   Composition: Copper **Reverse:** Plain shield. **Note:** Large planchet. Varieties exist.

Date	AG	Good	VG	Fine	VF	XF	Unc
1787	45.00	60.00	135	240	750	1,650	—

KM# 11.2   Composition: Copper **Obverse:** Bridle variety (die break). **Note:** Reverse varieties exist.

Date	AG	Good	VG	Fine	VF	XF	Unc
1786	45.00	70.00	145	235	650	2,400	—

KM# 15   Composition: Copper **Reverse Legend:** PLURIBS.

Date	AG	Good	VG	Fine	VF	XF	Unc
1787	85.00	150	275	450	1,000	2,800	—

KM#16 **Composition:** Copper **Obverse:** Horse's head facing right. **Note:** Varieties exist.

Date	AG	Good	VG	Fine	VF	XF	Unc
1788	42.00	60.00	115	190	700	1,275	—

KM#3 **Composition:** Copper **Obverse:** Eagle on globe facing left. **Obverse Legend:** EXCELSIOR **Reverse Legend:** E. PLURIBUS UNUM

Date	AG	Good	VG	Fine	VF	XF	Unc
1787	1,250	2,000	3,500	6,500	16,500	32,000	—

KM#17 **Composition:** Copper **Reverse:** Fox before legend. **Note:** Varieties exist.

Date	AG	Good	VG	Fine	VF	XF	Unc
1788	75.00	135	285	550	1,750	4,400	—

KM#18 **Composition:** Copper **Obverse:** Horse's head facing left. **Note:** Varieties exist.

Date	AG	Good	VG	Fine	VF	XF	Unc
1788	235	400	850	1,500	4,800	13,000	—

KM#4 **Composition:** Copper **Obverse Legend:** EXCELSIOR **Reverse:** Large eagle, arrows in right talon. **Reverse Legend:** E. PLURIBUS UNUM

Date	AG	Good	VG	Fine	VF	XF	Unc
1787	—	4,500	9,000	16,500	35,000	55,000	—

Note: Norweb $18,700

NEW YORK

KM#5 **Composition:** Copper **Obverse:** George Clinton. **Reverse Legend:** EXCELSIOR

Date	AG	Good	VG	Fine	VF	XF
1787	4,500	7,500	14,500	26,000	48,500	125,000

KM#1 **Composition:** Copper **Obverse:** Bust right **Obverse Legend:** NON VI VIRTUTE VICI. **Reverse Legend:** NEO-EBORACENSIS

Date	AG	Good	VG	Fine	VF	XF	Unc
1786	3,250	5,000	7,500	15,000	35,000	—	—

KM#6 **Composition:** Copper **Obverse:** Indian. **Obverse Legend:** LIBERNATUS LIBERTATEM DEFENDO **Reverse:** New York arms. **Reverse Legend:** EXCELSIOR

Date	AG	Good	VG	Fine	VF	XF	Unc
1787	4,500	7,000	10,000	17,500	40,000	90,000	—

KM#2 **Composition:** Copper **Obverse:** Eagle on globe facing right. **Obverse Legend:** EXCELSIOR **Reverse Legend:** E. PLURIBUS UNUM

Date	AG	Good	VG	Fine	VF	XF	Unc
1787	1,400	2,250	3,850	7,000	17,500	32,500	—

KM#7 **Composition:** Copper **Obverse:** Indian.
Obverse Legend: LIBERNATUS LIBERTATEM
DEFENDO **Reverse:** Eagle on globe. **Reverse Legend:**
NEO EBORACUS EXCELSIOR

Date	AG	Good	VG	Fine	VF	XF
1787	6,000	11,000	15,000	27,500	55,000	120,000

KM#8 **Composition:** Copper **Obverse:** Indian.
Reverse: George III.

Date	AG	Good	VG	Fine	VF	XF
1787 3 Known	—	—60,000		—	—	—

MACHIN'S MILL

KM#9 **Composition:** Copper **Obverse:** Bust right
Obverse Legend: NOVA EBORAC. **Reverse:** Figure
seated right. **Reverse Legend:** VIRT.ET.LIB.

Date	AG	Good	VG	Fine	VF	XF	Unc
1787	75.00	115	220	360	1,150	2,700	—

KM#10 **Composition:** Copper **Obverse:** Bust right
Obverse Legend: NOVA EBORAC **Reverse:** Figure
seated left. **Reverse Legend:** VIRT.ET.LIB.

Date	AG	Good	VG	Fine	VF	XF	Unc
1787	60.00	100.00	200	325	825	1,750	—

KM#11 **Composition:** Copper **Obverse:** Small
head, star above. **Obverse Legend:** NOVA EBORAC.

Reverse: Figure seated left **Reverse Legend:**
VIRT.ET.LIB.

Date	AG	Good	VG	Fine	VF	XF	Unc
1787	2,450	3,500	5,200	7,500	20,000	55,000	—

KM#12 **Composition:** Copper **Obverse:** Large head,
two quatrefoils left. **Obverse Legend:** NOVA EBORAC.
Reverse: Figure seated left **Reverse Legend:**
VIRT.ET.LIB.

Date	AG	Good	VG	Fine	VF	XF	Unc
1787	350	600	1,250	2,250	7,500	15,000	—

KM#13 **Composition:** Copper **Note:** Crude,
lightweight imitations of the British Halfpenny were
struck at Machin's Mill in large quantities bearing the
Obverse legends: GEORGIVS II REX, GEORGIVS III
REX, and GEORGIUS III REX, with the BRITANNIA
reverse. There are many different mulings. Plain crosses
in the shield of Britannia are noticeable on high grade
pieces, unlike common British made imitations, which
usually have outlined crosses in the shield. Some
Machin's Mill varieties are very rare.

Date	AG	Good	VG	Fine	VF	XF
(1747-1788)	40.00	70.00	120	250	750	2,200

Note: Prices are for most common within date ranges. Examples are dated: 1747, 1771, 1772, 1774, 1775, 1776, 1777,
1778, 1784, 1785, 1786, 1787 and 1788. Other dates may exist

VERMONT

KM#1 **Composition:** Copper **Reverse Legend:**
IMMUNE COLUMBIA

Date	AG	Good	VG	Fine	VF	XF
(1785)	3,750	5,500	9,000	12,750	32,000	—

US COLONIAL AMERICA

KM#2 **Composition:** Copper **Obverse:** Sun rising over field with plow **Obverse Legend:** VERMONTIS. RES. PUBLICA. **Reverse:** Eye, with rays and stars **Reverse Legend:** QUARTA. DECIMA. STELLA.

Date	AG	Good	VG	Fine	VF	XF	Unc
1785	120	290	650	1,450	4,500	11,000	—

KM#6 **Composition:** Copper **Obverse:** Bust facing left. **Obverse Legend:** VERMON: AUCTORI: **Reverse:** Seated figure left **Reverse Legend:** INDE ETLIB

Date	AG	Good	VG	Fine	VF	XF
1786	115	175	350	800	2,800	4,750
1787						
extremely rare	—	—	4,500	11,000	27,500	44,000

KM#3 **Composition:** Copper **Obverse:** Sun rising over field with plow **Obverse Legend:** VERMONTS. RES. PUBLICA. **Reverse:** Eye, with rays and stars **Reverse Legend:** QUARTA. DECIMA. STELLA.

Date	AG	Good	VG	Fine	VF	XF	Unc
1785	150	275	600	1,250	3,100	7,500	—

KM#7 **Composition:** Copper Obverse: Bust facing right. **Obverse Legend:** VERMON. AUCTORI. **Reverse:** Seated figure left **Reverse Legend:** INDE ETLIB **Note:** Varieties exist.

Date	AG	Good	VG	Fine	VF	XF	Unc
1787	—	150	260	575	1,450	3,000	—

KM#4 **Composition:** Copper **Obverse:** Sun rising over field with plow **Obverse Legend:** VERMONTENSIUM.RES.PUBLICA **Reverse:** Eye, with pointed rays and stars **Reverse Legend:** QUARTA. DECIMA. STELLA.

Date	AG	Good	VG	Fine	VF	XF	Unc
1786	140	235	400	750	2,000	4,400	—

KM#8 **Composition:** Copper Obverse: Bust right **Obverse Legend:** VERMON AUCTORI **Reverse:** Seated figure left **Note:** Britannia mule.

Date	AG	Good	VG	Fine	VF	XF	Unc
1787	65.00	110	150	275	650	1,650	—

KM#9.2 **Composition:** Copper **Obverse:** Bust right. "C" backward in AUCTORI. **Reverse:** Seated figure left

Date	Good	VG	Fine	VF	XF
1788 extremely rare	4,200	7,000	17,500	38,000	—

Note: Stack's Americana, Fine, $9,775

KM#5 **Composition:** Copper **Obverse:** "Baby head." **Obverse Legend:** AUCTORI: VERMON: **Reverse:** Seated figure left **Reverse Legend:** ET:LIB: INDE

Date	AG	Good	VG	Fine	VF	XF	Unc
1786	200	350	650	1,750	4,800	12,500	—

KM# 10 **Composition:** Copper **Obverse:** Bust right **Reverse:** Seated figure left **Reverse Legend:** .ET LIB. .INDE.

Date	AG	Good	VG	Fine	VF	XF	Unc
1788	200	325	625	1,250	4,000	13,500	—

KM# 9.1 **Composition:** Copper Obverse: Bust right **Obverse Legend:** VERMON. AUCTORI. **Reverse:** Seated figure left **Reverse Legend:** INDE . ET LIB. **Note:** Varieties exist.

Date	AG	Good	VG	Fine	VF	XF	Unc
1788	200	325	625	1,350	4,000	11,500	—

KM# 11 **Composition:** Copper Obverse: Bust right **Reverse:** Seated figure left **Note:** George III Rex mule.

Date	AG	Good	VG	Fine	VF	XF	Unc
1788	300	550	900	2,250	4,500	12,000	—

EARLY AMERICAN TOKENS

ALBANY CHURCH "PENNY"

AUCTORI PLEBIS

KM#Tn54.1 **Composition:** Copper Obverse: Without "D" above church. **Note:** Uniface.

Date	AG	Good	VG	Fine	VF	XF
5 known	—	—	10,000	25,000	75,000	—

KM#Tn50 **Composition:** Copper **Obverse:** Bust left **Obverse Legend:** AUCTORI: PLEBIS: **Reverse:** Seated figure left **Reverse Legend:** INDEP: ET. LIBER

Date	AG	Good	VG	Fine	VF	XF	Unc
1787	—	100.00	165	340	800	2,100	15,000

BAR "CENT"

KM#Tn54.2 **Composition:** Copper Obverse: With "D" above church. **Note:** Uniface.

Date	AG	Good	VG	Fine	VF	XF	Unc
rare	—	—	9,000	22,500	67,500	—	—

KM#Tn49 **Composition:** Copper **Obverse:** USA monogram **Reverse:** Horizontal bars

Date	AG	Good	VG	Fine	VF	XF	Unc
(1785)	—	1,400	1,750	3,100	6,250	9,500	27,500

CASTORLAND
"HALF DOLLAR"

KM#Tn87.1 **Composition:** Silver **Obverse Legend:** FRANCO.AMERICANA COLONIA **Edge:** Reeded.

Date	AG	Good	VG	Fine	VF	XF	Unc
1796	—	—	—	—	—	5,000	13,500

KM#Tn87.1a **Composition:** Copper **Obverse Legend:** FRANCO.AMERICANA COLONIA **Edge:** Reeded.

Date	AG	Good	VG	Fine	VF	XF
1796 3 known	—	—	—	—	—	2,850

KM#Tn87.1b **Composition:** Brass **Obverse Legend:** FRANCO.AMERICANA COLONIA **Edge:** Reeded.

Date	AG	Good	VG	Fine	VF	XF	Unc
1796	—	—	—	—	—	200	650

KM#Tn87.2 **Composition:** Copper **Obverse Legend:** FRANCO.AMERICANA COLONIA **Edge:** Plain. **Note:** Thin planchet.

Date	AG	Good	VG	Fine	VF	XF
1796 unique	—	—	—	—	—	—

KM#Tn87.3 **Composition:** Silver **Obverse Legend:** FRANCO.AMERICANA COLONIA **Edge:** Reeded. **Note:** Thin planchet. Restrike.

Date	Good	VG	Fine	VF	XF	Unc	Proof
1796	—	—	—	—	—	500	—

KM#Tn87.4 **Composition:** Silver **Obverse Legend:** FRANCO.AMERICANA COLONIA **Edge:** Lettered. **Edge Lettering:** ARGENT. **Note:** Thin planchet. Restrike.

Date	Good	VG	Fine	VF	XF	Unc	Proof
1796	—	—	—	—	—	200	—

KM#Tn87.3a **Composition:** Copper **Obverse Legend:** FRANCO.AMERICANA COLONIA **Edge:** Reeded. **Note:** Thin planchet. Restrike.

Date	Good	VG	Fine	VF	XF	Unc	Proof
1796	—	—	—	—	—	450	—

KM#Tn87.5 **Composition:** Copper **Obverse Legend:** FRANCO.AMERICANA COLONIA **Edge:** Lettered. **Edge Lettering:** CUIVRE. **Note:** Thin planchet. Restrike.

Date	Good	VG	Fine	VF	XF	Unc	Proof
1796	—	—	—	—	—	150	—

CHALMERS

3 PENCE

KM#Tn45 **Composition:** Silver

Date	AG	Good	VG	Fine	VF	XF	Unc
1783	650	1,100	1,750	3,250	6,500	13,500	—

6 PENCE

KM#Tn46.1 **Composition:** Silver **Reverse:** Small date

Date	AG	Good	VG	Fine	VF	XF	Unc
1783	900	1,600	2,500	6,000	12,500	22,500	—

KM#Tn46.2 **Composition:** Silver **Reverse:** Large date

Date	AG	Good	VG	Fine	VF	XF	Unc
1783	775	1,450	2,250	6,000	11,500	18,500	—

SHILLING

KM#Tn47.1 **Composition:** Silver **Reverse:** Birds with long worm

Date	AG	Good	VG	Fine	VF	XF	Unc
1783	450	750	1,250	2,400	5,500	10,000	—

KM#Tn47.2 **Composition:** Silver **Reverse:** Birds with short worm

Date	AG	Good	VG	Fine	VF	XF	Unc
1783	450	750	1,250	2,350	5,000	10,000	—

KM#Tn48 **Composition:** Silver **Reverse:** Rings and stars

Date	AG	Good	VG	Fine	VF	XF
1783 4 known	—	—	—	—200,000	—	

Note: Garrett $75,000

COPPER COMPANY OF UPPER CANADA

HALFPENNY

KM#Tn86 Composition: Copper **Obverse Legend:** BRITISH SETTLEMENT KENTUCKY

Date	Good	VG	Fine	VF	XF	Unc	Proof
1796	—	—	—	—	—	—	10,500

FRANKLIN PRESS

KM#Tn73 Composition: Copper **Obverse:** Printing press **Obverse Legend:** SIC ORITUR DOCTRINA SURGETQUE LIBERTAS **Edge:** Plain.

Date	AG	Good	VG	Fine	VF	XF	Unc
1794	30.00	75.00	110	150	250	425	1,350

KENTUCKY TOKEN

KM#Tn70.1 Composition: Copper **Obverse Legend:** UNANIMITY IS THE STRENGTH OF SOCIETY **Reverse Legend:** E. PLURIBUS UNUM **Edge:** Plain. **Note:** 1793 date is circa.

Date	AG	Good	VG	Fine	VF	XF	Unc
(1793)	12.00	25.00	40.00	150	200	375	1,210

KM#Tn70.2 Composition: Copper **Obverse Legend:** UNANIMITY IS THE STRENGTH OF SOCIETY **Reverse Legend:** E. PLURIBUS UNUM **Edge:** Engrailed.

Date	AG	Good	VG	Fine	VF	XF	Unc
(1793)	35.00	75.00	125	200	500	950	3,400

KM#Tn70.3 Composition: Copper **Obverse Legend:** UNANIMITY IS THE STRENGTH OF SOCIETY **Reverse Legend:** E. PLURIBUS UNUM **Edge:** Lettered. **Edge Lettering:** PAYABLE AT BEDWORTH.

Date	AG	Good	VG	Fine	VF	XF
(1793) unique	—	—	—	—	—	1,980

KM#Tn70.4 Composition: Copper **Obverse Legend:** UNANIMITY IS THE STRENGTH OF SOCIETY **Reverse Legend:** E. PLURIBUS UNUM **Edge:** Lettered. **Edge Lettering:** PAYABLE AT LANCASTER.

Date	AG	Good	VG	Fine	VF	XF	Unc
(1793)	14.00	28.00	45.00	65.00	225	400	1,250

KM#Tn70.5 Composition: Copper **Obverse Legend:** UNANIMITY IS THE STRENGTH OF SOCIETY **Reverse Legend:** E. PLURIBUS UNUM **Edge:** Lettered. **Edge Lettering:** PAYABLE AT I.FIELDING.

Date	AG	Good	VG	Fine	VF	XF
(1793) unique	—	—	—	—	—	—

KM#Tn70.6 Composition: Copper **Obverse Legend:** UNANIMITY IS THE STRENGTH OF SOCIETY **Reverse Legend:** E. PLURIBUS UNUM **Edge:** Lettered. **Edge Lettering:** PAYABLE AT W. PARKERS.

Date	AG	Good	VG	Fine	VF	XF
(1793) unique	—	—	—	—	20,000	—

KM#Tn70.7 Composition: Copper **Obverse Legend:** UNANIMITY IS THE STRENGTH OF SOCIETY **Reverse Legend:** E. PLURIBUS UNUM **Edge:** Ornamented branch with two leaves.

Date	AG	Good	VG	Fine	VF	XF
(1793) unique	—	—	—	—	—	—

MOTT TOKEN

KM#Tn52.1 Composition: Copper **Obverse:** Clock **Reverse:** Eagle with shield **Note:** Thin planchet.

Date	AG	Good	VG	Fine	VF	XF	Unc
1789	50.00	80.00	150	250	400	750	1,750

KM#Tn52.2 Composition: Copper **Obverse:** Clock **Reverse:** Eagle with shield **Note:** Thick planchet. Weight generally about 170 grams.

Date	AG	Good	VG	Fine	VF	XF	Unc
1789	60.00	95.00	175	325	550	1,250	—

KM#Tn52.3 Composition: Copper **Obverse:** Clock **Reverse:** Eagle with shield **Edge:** Fully engrailed. **Note:** Specimens struck with perfect dies are scarcer and generally command higher prices.

Date	AG	Good	VG	Fine	VF	XF	Unc
1789	90.00	160	325	450	700	1,750	4,800

MYDDELTON TOKEN

KM#Tn85 **Composition:** Copper **Obverse Legend:** BRITISH SETTLEMENT KENTUCKY **Reverse Legend:** PAYABLE BY P.P.P.MYDDELTON.

Date	Good	VG	Fine	VF	XF	Unc	Proof
1796	—	—	—	—	—	—	37,500

KM#Tn85a **Composition:** Silver

Date	Good	VG	Fine	VF	XF	Unc	Proof
1796	—	—	—	—	—	—	12,000

NEW YORK THEATRE

KM#Tn90 **Composition:** Copper **Obverse:** Theater building **Obverse Legend:** THE.THEATRE.AT.NEW.YORK. AMERICA **Reverse:** Ships at sea, viewed from dock **Reverse Legend:** MAY.COMMERCE.FLOURISH **Note:** 1796 date is circa.

Date	AG	Good	VG	Fine	VF	XF	Unc
1796	—	—	—	—	7,000	9,500	25,000

NORTH AMERICAN

HALFPENNY

KM#Tn30 **Composition:** Copper **Obverse:** Seated figure left, with harp **Obverse Legend:** NORTH AMERICAN TOKEN **Reverse:** Ship **Reverse Legend:** COMMERCE

Date	AG	Good	VG	Fine	VF	XF	Unc
1781	32.00	50.00	65.00	130	300	750	3,250

RHODE ISLAND SHIP

KM#Tn27a **Composition:** Brass **Obverse:** Without wreath below ship.

Date	AG	Good	VG	Fine	VF	XF	Unc
1779	—	—	325	550	1,000	2,000	7,500

KM#Tn27b **Composition:** Pewter **Obverse:** Without wreath below ship.

Date	AG	Good	VG	Fine	VF	XF	Unc
1779	—	—	—	—	5,000	8,500	18,500

KM#Tn28a **Composition:** Brass **Obverse:** Wreath below ship.

Date	AG	Good	VG	Fine	VF	XF	Unc
1779	—	—	—	675	1,100	2,100	7,750

KM#Tn28b **Composition:** Pewter **Obverse:** Wreath below ship.

Date	AG	Good	VG	Fine	VF	XF	Unc
1779	—	—	—	—	5,500	9,000	20,000

KM#Tn29 **Composition:** Brass **Obverse:** VLUGTENDE below ship

Date	AG	Good	VG	Fine	VF	XF
1779 unique	—	—	—	—	—	35,000

Note: Garrett $16,000

STANDISH BARRY

3 PENCE

KM#Tn55 **Composition:** Silver **Obverse:** Bust left **Obverse Legend:** BALTIMORE.TOWN.JULY.4.90. **Reverse:** Denomination **Reverse Legend:** STANDISH BARRY.

Date	AG	Good	VG	Fine	VF	XF	Unc
1790	—	—	15,000	22,500	50,000	—	—

TALBOT, ALLUM & LEE

CENT

KM#Tn71.1 **Composition:** Copper **Reverse:** NEW YORK above ship **Edge:** Lettered. **Edge Lettering:** PAYABLE AT THE STORE OF

Date	AG	Good	VG	Fine	VF	XF	Unc
1794	32.00	50.00	85.00	165	275	550	2,000

KM#Tn71.2 **Composition:** Copper **Reverse:** NEW YORK above ship **Edge:** Plain. **Note:** Size of ampersand varies on Obverse and reverse dies.

Date	AG	Good	VG	Fine	VF	XF
1794 4 known	—	—	—	—	10,000	24,000

KM#Tn72.1 **Composition:** Copper **Reverse:** Without NEW YORK above ship **Edge:** Lettered. **Edge Lettering:** PAYABLE AT THE STORE OF

Date	AG	Good	VG	Fine	VF	XF	Unc
1794	200	375	600	3,500	6,500	10,500	22,000

KM#Tn72.2 **Composition:** Copper **Edge:** Lettered. **Edge Lettering:** WE PROMISE TO PAY THE BEARER ONE CENT.

Date	AG	Good	VG	Fine	VF	XF	Unc
1795	30.00	50.00	75.00	135	240	375	1,200

KM#Tn72.3 **Composition:** Copper **Edge:** Lettered. **Edge Lettering:** CURRENT EVERYWHERE.

Date	AG	Good	VG	Fine	VF	XF
1795 unique	—	—	—	—	—	—

KM#Tn72.4 **Composition:** Copper **Edge:** Olive leaf.

Date	AG	Good	VG	Fine	VF	XF
1795 unique	—	—	—	—	—	15,000

Note: Norweb $4,400

KM#Tn72.5 **Composition:** Copper **Edge:** Plain.

Date	AG	Good	VG	Fine	VF	XF
1795 plain edge; 2 known	—	—	—	—	—	—
1795 Lettered edge; unique	—	—	—	—	—	15,000

Note: Edge: Cambridge Bedford Huntington.X.X.; Norweb, $3,960

WASHINGTON PIECES

KM#Tn35 **Composition:** Copper **Obverse Legend:** GEORGIVS TRIUMPHO.

Date	AG	Good	VG	Fine	VF	XF	Unc
1783	—	95.00	125	260	325	750	—

KM#Tn36 **Composition:** Copper **Obverse:** Large military bust. **Note:** Varieties exist.

Date	AG	Good	VG	Fine	VF	XF	Unc
1783	—	—	50.00	85.00	180	450	2,600

KM#Tn37.1   Composition: Copper **Obverse:** Small military bust. **Edge:** Plain.

Date	AG	Good	VG	Fine	VF	XF	Unc
1783	—	—	70.00	95.00	220	525	3,600

Note: One proof example is known. Value: $25,000

KM#Tn37.2   Composition: Copper **Obverse:** Small military bust. **Edge:** Engrailed.

Date	AG	Good	VG	Fine	VF	XF	Unc
1783	—	75.00	110	150	300	750	4,250

KM#Tn38.1   Composition: Copper **Obverse:** Draped bust, no button on drapery, small letter.

Date	AG	Good	VG	Fine	VF	XF	Unc
1783	—	40.00	60.00	90.00	180	400	2,200

KM#Tn38.2   Composition: Copper **Obverse:** Draped bust, button on drapery, large letter.

Date	AG	Good	VG	Fine	VF	XF	Unc
1783	—	85.00	110	150	325	600	4,000

KM#Tn38.4   Composition: Copper **Edge:** Engrailed. **Note:** Restrike.

Date	Good	VG	Fine	VF	XF	Unc	Proof
1783	—	—	—	—	—	—	800

KM#Tn38.4a   Composition: Copper **Note:** Bronzed. Restrike.

Date	Good	VG	Fine	VF	XF	Unc	Proof
1783	—	—	—	—	—	—	—

KM#Tn83.3   Composition: Copper **Obverse:** Large modern lettering. **Edge:** Plain. **Note:** Restrike.

Date	Good	VG	Fine	VF	XF	Unc	Proof
1783	—	—	—	—	—	—	900

KM#Tn83.4b   Composition: Silver **Note:** Restrike.

Date	Good	VG	Fine	VF	XF	Unc	Proof
1783	—	—	—	—	—	—	1,600

KM#Tn83.4c   Composition: Gold AGW. **Note:** Restrike.

Date	AG	Good	VG	Fine	VF	XF
1783 2 known	—	—	—	—	—	—

KM#Tn60.1   Composition: Copper **Obverse Legend:** WASHINGTON PRESIDENT. **Edge:** Plain.

Date	AG	Good	VG	Fine	VF	XF
1792	850	1,450	3,000	7,500	16,000	—

Note: Steinberg $12,650. Garrett $15,500

KM#Tn60.2   Composition: Copper **Obverse Legend:** WASHINGTON PRESIDENT. **Edge:** Lettered. **Edge Lettering:** UNITED STATES OF AMERICA.

Date	AG	Good	VG	Fine	VF	XF	Unc
1792	—	—	—	—	—	—	—

KM#Tn61.1   Composition: Copper **Obverse Legend:** BORN VIRGINIA. **Note:** Varieties exist.

Date	AG	Good	VG	Fine	VF	XF	Unc
(1792)	500	1,000	2,000	4,000	7,500	12,000	—

KM#Tn61.2 **Composition:** Silver **Edge:** Lettered.
Edge Lettering: UNITED STATES OF AMERICA.

Date	AG	Good	VG	Fine	VF	XF
(1792) 2 known	—	—	—	—	—	—

KM#Tn61.1a **Composition:** Silver **Edge:** Plain.

Date	AG	Good	VG	Fine	VF	XF
(1792) 4 known	—	—	—	—	—	200,000

Note: Roper $16,500

KM#Tn62 **Composition:** Silver **Reverse:** Heraldic eagle. 1792 half dollar. **Note:** Mule.

Date	AG	Good	VG	Fine	VF	XF
(1792) 3 known	—	—	—	—	50,000	75,000

KM#Tn77.1 **Composition:** Copper **Obverse Legend:** LIBERTY AND SECURITY. **Edge:** Lettered. **Note:** "Penny."

Date	AG	Good	VG	Fine	VF	XF	Unc
(1795)	70.00	110	165	300	525	1,100	3,500

KM#Tn77.2 **Composition:** Copper **Edge:** Plain. **Note:** "Penny."

Date	AG	Good	VG	Fine	VF	XF
(1795) extremely rare	—	—	—	—	—	—

KM#Tn77.3 **Composition:** Copper **Note:** "Penny." Engine-turned borders.

Date	Good	VG	Fine	VF	XF	Unc
(1795) 12 known	275	450	650	1,250	2,400	7,500

KM#Tn78 **Composition:** Copper **Note:** Similar to "Halfpenny" with date on reverse.

Date	AG	Good	VG	Fine	VF	XF
1795 very rare	—	—	—	—	—	—

Note: Roper $6,600

HALFPENNY

KM#Tn56 **Composition:** Copper **Obverse Legend:** LIVERPOOL HALFPENNY

Date	AG	Good	VG	Fine	VF	XF	Unc
1791	40.00	70.00	1,000	125	300	550	3,250

KM#Tn66.1 **Composition:** Copper **Reverse:** Ship **Edge:** Lettered.

Date	AG	Good	VG	Fine	VF	XF	Unc
1793	20.00	30.00	60.00	200	425	800	3,400

KM#Tn66.2 **Composition:** Copper **Reverse:** Ship **Edge:** Plain.

Date	AG	Good	VG	Fine	VF	XF
1793 5 known	—	—	—	—	15,000	—

KM#Tn75.1 **Composition:** Copper **Obverse:** Large coat buttons **Reverse:** Grate **Edge:** Reeded.

Date	AG	Good	VG	Fine	VF	XF	Unc
1795	—	—	70.00	110	200	400	900

KM#Tn75.2 **Composition:** Copper **Reverse:** Grate **Edge:** Lettered.

Date	AG	Good	VG	Fine	VF	XF	Unc
1795	90.00	140	210	275	400	800	2,800

KM#Tn75.3 **Composition:** Copper **Obverse:** Small coat buttons **Reverse:** Grate **Edge:** Reeded.

Date	AG	Good	VG	Fine	VF	XF	Unc
1795	50.00	75.00	120	190	275	585	2,650

KM#Tn76.1   Composition: Copper **Obverse Legend:** LIBERTY AND SECURITY. **Edge:** Plain.

Date	AG	Good	VG	Fine	VF	XF	Unc
1795	18.00	35.00	60.00	160	350	700	3,250

KM#Tn76.2   Composition: Copper **Edge:** Lettered. **Edge Lettering:** PAYABLE AT LONDON ...

Date	AG	Good	VG	Fine	VF	XF	Unc
1795	40.00	65.00	90.00	140	300	625	2,850

KM#Tn76.3   Composition: Copper **Edge:** Lettered. **Edge Lettering:** BIRMINGHAM ...

Date	AG	Good	VG	Fine	VF	XF	Unc
1795	55.00	85.00	115	165	340	775	3,600

KM#Tn76.4   Composition: Copper **Edge:** Lettered. **Edge Lettering:** AN ASYLUM ...

Date	AG	Good	VG	Fine	VF	XF	Unc
1795	18.00	35.00	60.00	275	600	1,600	6,500

KM#Tn76.5   Composition: Copper **Edge:** Lettered. **Edge Lettering:** PAYABLE AT LIVERPOOL ...

Date	AG	Good	VG	Fine	VF	XF
1795 unique	—	—	—	—	—	—

KM#Tn76.6   Composition: Copper **Edge:** Lettered. **Edge Lettering:** PAYABLE AT LONDON-LIVERPOOL.

Date	AG	Good	VG	Fine	VF	XF
1795 unique	—	—	—	—	—	—

KM#Tn81.1   Composition: Copper **Reverse Legend:** NORTH WALES **Edge:** Plain.

Date	AG	Good	VG	Fine	VF	XF
(ca.1795)	60.00	110	175	265	625	1,750

KM#Tn82   Composition: Copper **Reverse:** Four stars at bottom **Reverse Legend:** NORTH WALES

Date	AG	Good	VG	Fine	VF	XF
(1795)	1,250	2,000	4,500	7,500	21,000	—

KM#Tn81.2   Composition: Copper **Reverse Legend:** NORTH WALES **Edge:** Lettered.

Date	AG	Good	VG	Fine	VF	XF	Unc
	350	550	1,150	1,750	5,500	9,500	—

CENT

KM#Tn39   Composition: Copper **Obverse:** Draped Bust left **Obverse Legend:** WASHINGTON & INDEPENDENCE **Reverse:** Denomination in wreath **Reverse Legend:** UNITY STATES OF AMERICA

Date	AG	Good	VG	Fine	VF	XF	Unc
1783	30.00	50.00	70.00	100.00	250	500	2,250

KM#Tn40   Composition: Copper **Note:** Double head.

Date	AG	Good	VG	Fine	VF	XF	Unc
(1783)	25.00	45.00	60.00	90.00	225	450	2,750

KM#Tn41   Composition: Copper **Obverse:** "Ugly head." **Note:** 3 known in copper, 1 in white metal.

Date	AG	Good	VG	Fine	VF	XF	Unc
1784	—	90,000	—	—	—	—	—

Note: Roper $14,850

KM#Tn57   Composition: Copper **Obverse:** Military bust left **Obverse Legend:** WASHINGTON PRESIDENT. **Reverse:** Small eagle

Date	AG	Good	VG	Fine	VF	XF	Unc
1791	—	—	350	500	725	1,000	4,750

KM#Tn58   Composition: Copper **Obverse:** Military bust left **Obverse Legend:** WASHINGTON PRESIDENT **Reverse:** Large eagle

Date	AG	Good	VG	Fine	VF	XF	Unc
1791	—	200	325	475	650	900	2,850

KM#Tn65   Composition: Copper **Obverse:** "Roman" head **Obverse Legend:** WASHINGTON PRESIDENT.

Date	AG	Good	VG	Fine	VF	XF	Unc
1792	—	—	—	—	—	—	—

HALF DOLLAR

KM#Tn59.1   Composition: Copper **Edge:** Lettered. **Edge Lettering:** UNITED STATES OF AMERICA

Date	AG	Good	VG	Fine	VF	XF
1792 2 known	—	—	—	—	—	75,000

Note: Roper $2,860. Benson, EF, $48,300.

KM#Tn59.2   Composition: Copper **Edge:** Plain.

Date	Good	VG	Fine	VF	XF
1792 3 known	—	—	—	125,000	200,000

KM#Tn59.1a   Composition: Silver **Edge:** Lettered. **Edge Lettering:** UNITED STATES OF AMERICA

Date	AG	Good	VG	Fine	VF	XF
1792 rare	—	—	—	—	40,000	65,000

Note: Roper $35,200

KM#Tn59.2a   Composition: Silver **Edge:** Plain.

Date	AG	Good	VG	Fine	VF	XF	Unc
1792 rare	—	—	—	—	—	—	—

KM#Tn59.1b   Composition: Gold AGW. **Edge:** Lettered. **Edge Lettering:** UNITED STATES OF AMERICA

Date	AG	Good	VG	Fine	VF	XF	Unc
1792 unique	—	—	—	—	—	—	—

KM#Tn63.1   Composition: Silver **Reverse:** Small eagle **Edge:** Plain.

Date	AG	Good	VG	Fine	VF	XF
1792	—	—	—	—	200,000	300,000

KM#Tn63.2   Composition: Silver **Edge:** Ornamented, circles and squares.

Date	Good	VG	Fine	VF	XF	Unc
1792 5 known	—	—	—	100,000	175,000	400,000

KM#Tn63.1a   Composition: Copper **Edge:** Plain.

Date	AG	Good	VG	Fine	VF	XF	Unc
1792	—	4,000	6,500	12,500	32,000	65,000	—

Note: Garrett $32,000

KM#Tn63.3   Composition: Silver **Edge:** Two olive leaves.

Date	AG	Good	VG	Fine	VF	XF	Unc
1792 unique	—	—	—	—	—	—	—

KM#Tn64   Composition: Silver **Reverse:** Large heraldic eagle

Date	AG	Good	VG	Fine	VF	XF	Unc
1792 unique	—	—	—	—	100,000	—	—

Note: Garrett $16,500

EARLY AMERICAN PATTERNS

CONFEDERATIO

KM#EA22 **Composition:** Copper **Obverse:** Standing figure with bow & arrow **Obverse Legend:** INIMICA TYRANNIS • AMERICANA • **Reverse:** Small circle of stars **Reverse Legend:** • CONFEDERATIO •

Date	AG	Good	VG	Fine	VF	XF	Unc
1785	—	—	—	—	50,000	95,000	—

KM#EA23 **Composition:** Copper **Obverse:** Standing figure with bow & arrow **Obverse Legend:** INIMICA TYRANNIS • AMERICANA • **Reverse:** Large circle of stars **Reverse Legend:** • CONFEDERATIO • **Note:** The Confederatio dies were struck in combination with 13 other dies of the period. All surviving examples of these combinations are extremely rare.

Date	AG	Good	VG	Fine	VF	XF
extremely rare	—	—	—	—	50,000	100,000

IMMUNE COLUMBIA

KM#EA20 **Composition:** Copper **Obverse:** George III **Obverse Legend:** GEORGIVS III • REX • **Reverse Legend:** IMMUNE COLUMBIA •

Date	AG	Good	VG	Fine	VF	XF	Unc
1785	3,500	5,000	7,500	9,500	22,500	—	—

KM#EA21 **Composition:** Copper **Obverse:** Head right **Obverse Legend:** VERMON AUCTORI **Reverse Legend:** IMMUNE COLUMBIA •

Date	AG	Good	VG	Fine	VF	XF	Unc
1785	—	5,500	8,500	11,500	35,000	—	—

KM#EA17a **Composition:** Silver **Obverse Legend:** IMMUNE COLUMBIA • **Reverse:** Eye, with pointed rays & stars **Reverse Legend:** NOVA CONSTELLATIO

Date	AG	Good	VG	Fine	VF	XF	Unc
1785	—	—	—	—	45,000	90,000	—

KM#EA19a **Composition:** Gold AGW. **Obverse Legend:** IMMUNE COLUMBIA • **Reverse:** Blunt rays **Reverse Legend:** NOVA CONSTELATIO •

Date	AG	Good	VG	Fine	VF	XF	Unc
1785 unique	—	—	—	—	—	—	—

Note: In the Smithsonian Collection

KM#EA17 **Composition:** Copper **Obverse Legend:** IMMUNE COLUMBIA. **Reverse:** Eye, with pointed rays & stars **Reverse Legend:** NOVA • CONSTELLATIO

Date	AG	Good	VG	Fine	VF	XF	Unc
1785	—	—	—	—	22,500	40,000	—

KM#EA18 **Composition:** Copper **Obverse Legend:** IMMUNE COLUMBIA • **Reverse:** Eye, with pointed rays & stars. Extra star in reverse legend **Reverse Legend:** NOVA • CONSTELLATIO *

Date	AG	Good	VG	Fine	VF	XF	Unc
1785	—	—	—	—	22,500	40,000	—

Note: Caldwell $4,675

KM#EA19 **Composition:** Copper **Obverse Legend:** IMMUNE COLUMBIA • **Reverse:** Blunt rays **Reverse Legend:** NOVA CONSTELLATIO

Date	AG	Good	VG	Fine	VF	XF
1785 2 known	—	—	—	—	—	100,000

Note: Norweb $22,000

KM#EA28 **Composition:** Copper **Obverse Legend:** IMMUNIS COLUMBIA **Reverse:** Eagle **Reverse Legend:** * E * PLURIBUS * UNUM *

Date	AG	Good	VG	Fine	VF	XF
1786 3 known	—	—	—	—	50,000	90,000

NOVA CONSTELLATIO

KM#EA24 **Composition:** Copper **Obverse:**
Washington **Reverse:** Stars in rayed circle **Reverse
Legend:** • CONFEDERATIO •

Date	AG	Good	VG	Fine	VF	XF
1786 3 known	—	—	—	—	50,000	—

Note: Garrett $50,000. Steinberg $12,650.

KM#EA6.1 **Composition:** Copper **Obverse:** Pointed
rays **Obverse Legend:** NOVA • CONSTELLATIO •
Reverse: Small "U•S"

Date	AG	Good	VG	Fine	VF	XF	Unc
1783	50.00	70.00	100.00	225	440	950	3,750

KM#EA25 **Composition:** Copper **Obverse:** Eagle,
raw shield **Obverse Legend:** * E • PLURIBUS UNUM •
Reverse: Shield **Reverse Legend:** * E * PLURIBUS *
UNUM *

Date	AG	Good	VG	Fine	VF	XF
1786 unique	—	—	—	—	—	—

Note: Garrett $37,500

KM#EA6.2 **Composition:** Copper **Obverse:** Pointed
rays **Obverse Legend:** NOVA • CONSTELLATIO •
Reverse: Large "US"

Date	AG	Good	VG	Fine	VF	XF	Unc
1783	55.00	75.00	110	250	600	1,400	6,000

KM#EA26 **Composition:** Copper **Obverse:**
Washington **Obverse Legend:** GEN • WASHINGTON •
Reverse: Eagle

Date	AG	Good	VG	Fine	VF	XF
1786 2 known	—	—	—	—	—	—

KM#EA7 **Composition:** Copper **Obverse:** Blunt rays
Obverse Legend: NOVA • CONSTELATIO •

Date	AG	Good	VG	Fine	VF	XF	Unc
1783	50.00	75.00	110	250	575	1,300	5,000

KM#EA27 **Composition:** Copper **Obverse Legend:**
IMMUNIS COLUMBIA • **Reverse:** Shield **Reverse
Legend:** * E * PLURIBUS * UNUM *

Date	AG	Good	VG	Fine	VF	XF
1786 extremely rare	—	—	—	—	40,000	—

Note: Rescigno, AU, $33,000. Steinberg, VF, $11,000

KM#EA8 **Composition:** Copper **Obverse:** Blunt rays
Obverse Legend: NOVA • CONSTELATIO •

Date	AG	Good	VG	Fine	VF	XF	Unc
1785	50.00	75.00	110	260	625	1,500	6,500

KM# EA9   Composition: Copper **Obverse:** Pointed rays **Obverse Legend:** NOVA • CONSTELLATIO •

Date	AG	Good	VG	Fine	VF	XF	Unc
1785	—	—	100.00	225	450	1,000	3,600

KM# EA10   Composition: Copper **Note:** Contemporary circulating counterfeit. Similar to previously listed coin.

Date	AG	Good	VG	Fine	VF	XF
1786 extremely rare	—	—	—	—	—	—

5 UNITS

KM# EA12   Composition: Copper **Obverse:** Eye, with pointed rays & stars **Obverse Legend:** NOVA CONSTELLATIO **Reverse Legend:** • LIBERTAS • JUSTITIA •

Date	AG	Good	VG	Fine	VF	XF	Unc
1783 unique	—	—	—	—	—	—	—

100 (BIT)

KM# EA13.1   Composition: Silver **Obverse:** Eye, with pointed rays & stars **Obverse Legend:** NOVA CONSTELLATIO **Reverse Legend:** • LIBERTAS • JUSTITIA • **Edge:** Leaf.

Date	AG	Good	VG	Fine	VF	XF	Unc
1783 2 known	—	—	—	—	—	—	—

Note: Garrett $97,500. Stack's auction, May 1991, $72,500

KM# EA13.2   Composition: Silver **Obverse:** Eye, with pointed rays & stars **Obverse Legend:** NOVA CONSTELLATIO **Reverse Legend:** • LIBERTAS • JUSTITIA • **Edge:** Plain

Date	AG	Good	VG	Fine	VF	XF	Unc
1783 unique	—	—	—	—	—	—	—

500 (QUINT)

KM# EA14   Composition: Silver **Obverse:** Eye with pointed rays & stars **Obverse Legend:** NOVA CONSTELLATIO **Reverse Legend:** • LIBERTAS • JUSTITIA •

Date	AG	Good	VG	Fine	VF	XF
1783 unique	—	—	—	—	—	250,000

Note: Garrett $165,000

KM# EA15   Composition: Silver **Obverse:** Eye, with rays & stars, no legend **Reverse Legend:** • LIBERTAS • JUSTITIA •

Date	AG	Good	VG	Fine	VF	XF
1783 unique	—	—	—	—	75,000	—

Note: Garrett $55,000

1000 (MARK)

KM# EA16   Composition: Silver **Obverse:** Eye, with pointed rays & stars **Obverse Legend:** NOVA CONSTELLATIO **Reverse Legend:** • LIBERTAS • JUSTITIA •

Date	AG	Good	VG	Fine	VF	XF
1783 unique	—	—	—	—	—	350,000

Note: Garrett $190,000

EARLY FEDERAL COINAGE

BRASHER

KM#Tn51.1 **Composition:** Gold AGW. **Obverse:** Sunrise over mountains. **Reverse:** Displayed eagle with shield on breast, EB counterstamp on wing.

Date	AG	Good	VG	Fine	VF	XF	Unc
1787 6 known	—	—	—	—	—	—	—

Note: Heritage FUN Sale, January 2005, AU-55, $2.415 million.

KM#Tn51.2 **Composition:** Gold AGW. **Obverse:** Sun rise over mountains **Reverse:** Displayed eagle with sheild on breast. EB counterstamp on breast.

Date	AG	Good	VG	Fine	VF	XF	Unc
1787 unique	—	—	—	—	—	—	—

Note: Heritage FUN Sale, January 2005, XF-45, $2.99 million. Foreign gold coins with the EB counterstamp exist. These are valued at over $5,000, with many much higher.

FUGIO "CENT"

KM#EA30.1 **Composition:** Copper **Obverse:** Club rays, round ends.

Date	AG	Good	VG	Fine	VF	XF	Unc
1787	225	325	450	850	2,000	3,850	—

KM#EA30.2 **Composition:** Copper **Obverse:** Club rays, concave ends.

Date	AG	Good	VG	Fine	VF	XF	Unc
1787	1,500	2,500	3,500	8,000	20,000	—	—

KM#EA30.3 **Composition:** Copper **Obverse Legend:** FUCIO.

Date	AG	Good	VG	Fine	VF	XF	Unc
1787	—	2,000	3,000	7,000	25,000	35,000	—

KM#EA31.1 **Composition:** Copper **Obverse:** Pointed rays. **Reverse:** UNITED above, STATES below.

Date	AG	Good	VG	Fine	VF	XF	Unc
1787	600	950	1,400	3,000	7,750	10,000	—

KM#EA31.2 **Composition:** Copper **Reverse:** UNITED STATES at sides of ring.

Date	AG	Good	VG	Fine	VF	XF	Unc
1787	110	175	275	550	850	1,600	3,500

KM#EA31.3 **Composition:** Copper **Reverse:** STATES UNITED at sides of ring.

Date	AG	Good	VG	Fine	VF	XF	Unc
1787	110	190	275	550	800	1,500	3,500

KM#EA31.4 **Composition:** Copper **Reverse:** Eight-pointed stars on ring.

Date	AG	Good	VG	Fine	VF	XF	Unc
1787	150	285	450	650	1,200	2,500	9,000

KM#EA31.5 **Composition:** Copper **Reverse:** Raised rims on ring, large lettering in center.

Date	AG	Good	VG	Fine	VF	XF	Unc
1787	185	325	500	900	2,400	5,250	17,500

KM#EA32.1 **Composition:** Copper **Obverse:** No cinquefoils, cross after date. **Obverse Legend:** UNITED STATES.

Date	AG	Good	VG	Fine	VF	XF	Unc
1787	300	485	750	1,450	3,500	6,500	—

KM#EA32.2 **Composition:** Copper **Obverse:** No cinquefoils, cross after date. **Obverse Legend:** STATES UNITED.

Date	AG	Good	VG	Fine	VF	XF	Unc
1787	—	—	750	1,500	3,750	6,800	—

KM#EA32.3 **Composition:** Copper **Obverse:** No cinquefoils, cross after date. **Reverse:** Raised rims on ring.

Date	AG	Good	VG	Fine	VF	XF	Unc
1787	—	—	—	—	22,500	—	—

KM#EA34 **Composition:** Brass **Note:** New Haven restrike.

Date	AG	Good	VG	Fine	VF	XF	Unc
1787	—	—	—	—	—	450	1,000

KM#EA34a **Composition:** Copper **Note:** New Haven restrike.

Date	AG	Good	VG	Fine	VF	XF	Unc
1787	—	—	—	—	450	750	1,000

KM#EA34b **Composition:** Silver **Note:** New Haven restrike.

Date	AG	Good	VG	Fine	VF	XF	Unc
1787(ca.1858)	—	—	—	—	—	1,500	4,000

KM#EA34c **Composition:** Gold AGW. **Note:** New Haven restrike.

Date	AG	Good	VG	Fine	VF	XF
1787(ca.1858) 2 known	—	—	—	—	—	—

Note: Norweb (holed) $1,430

KM#EA33 **Composition:** Copper **Obverse:** No cinquefoils, cross after date. **Reverse:** With rays. **Reverse Legend:** AMERICAN CONGRESS.

Date	AG	Good	VG	Fine	VF	XF
1787 extremely rare	—	—	—	—	275,000	—

Note: Norweb $63,800

ISSUES OF 1792

CENT

KM#PnE1 **Composition:** Bi-Metallic. **Weight:** Silver center in Copper ring

Date	AG	Good	VG	Fine	VF	XF
1792 12 known	—	—	—	175,000	300,000	450,000

Note: Norweb, MS-60, $143,000

KM#PnF1 **Comp.:** Copper **Note:** No silver center.

Date	AG	Good	VG	Fine	VF	XF
1792 8 known	—	—	—	250,000	500,000	750,000

Note: Norweb, EF-40, $35,200; Benson, VG-10, $57,500

KM#PnG1 **Composition:** Copper **Edge:** Plain **Note:** Commonly called "Birch cent."

Date	AG	Good	VG	Fine	VF	XF
1792 unique	—	—	—	—	—	500,000

KM#PnH1 **Composition:** Copper **Obverse:** One star in edge legend **Note:** Commonly called "Birch cent."

Date	AG	Good	VG	Fine	VF	XF
1792 2 known	—	—	—	150,000	350,000	450,000

Note: Norweb, EF-40, $59,400

KM#PnI1 **Composition:** Copper **Obverse:** Two stars in edge legend **Note:** Commonly called "Birch cent."

Date	AG	Good	VG	Fine	VF	XF
1792 6 known	—	—	—	—	—	—

Note: Hawn, strong VF, $57,750

KM#PnJ1 **Composition:** White Metal **Reverse:** "G.W.Pt." below wreath tie **Note:** Commonly called "Birch cent."

Date	AG	Good	VG	Fine	VF	XF
1792 unique	—	—	—	—	—	550,000

Note: Garrett, $90,000

HALF DISME

KM#5 **Composition:** Silver

Date	AG	VG	Fine	VF	XF	Unc
1792	25,000	35,000	55,000	90,000	125,000	450,000

KM#PnA1 **Composition:** Copper

Date	AG	Good	VG	Fine	VF	XF
1792 unique	—	—	—	—	—	—

DISME

KM#PnB1 **Composition:** Silver

Date	Good	VG	Fine	VF	XF
1792 3 known	—	—	—	700,000	1,000,000

Note: Norweb, EF-40, $28,600

KM#PnC1 **Composition:** Copper **Edge:** Reeded

Date	VG	Fine	VF	XF	Unc
1792 14 known	—	—	150,000	250,000	500,000

Note: Hawn, VF, $30,800; Benson, EF-45, $109,250

KM#PnD1 **Composition:** Copper **Edge:** Plain

Date	AG	Good	VG	Fine	VF	XF
1792 2 known	—	—	—	—	450,000	750,000

Note: Garrett, $45,000

QUARTER

KM#PnK1 **Composition:** Copper **Edge:** Reeded **Note:** Commonly called "Wright quarter."

Date	AG	Good	VG	Fine	VF	XF
1792 2 known	—	—	—	—	—	—

KM#PnL1 **Composition:** White Metal **Edge:** Plain **Note:** Commonly called "Wright quarter."

Date	AG	Good	VG	Fine	VF	XF
1792 2 known	—	—	—	—	—	—

Note: Norweb, VF-30 to EF-40, $28,600

KM#PnM1 **Composition:** White Metal **Note:** Commonly called "Wright quarter."

Date	AG	Good	VG	Fine	VF	XF
1792 die trial	—	—	—	—	—	—

Note: Garrett, $12,000

US TERRITORIAL GOLD

Territorial gold pieces (also referred to as "Private" and "Pioneer" gold) are those struck outside the U.S. Mint and not recognized as official issues by the federal government. The pieces so identified are of various shapes, denominations, and degrees of intrinsic value, and were locally required because of the remoteness of the early gold fields from a federal mint and/or an insufficient quantity of official coinage in frontier areas.

The legality of these privately issued pieces derives from the fact that federal law prior to 1864 prohibited a state from coining money, but did not specifically deny that right to an individual, providing that the privately issued coins did not closely resemble those of the United States.

In addition to coin-like gold pieces, the private minters of the gold rush days also issued gold in ingot and bar form. Ingots were intended for circulation and were cast in regular values and generally in large denominations. Bars represent a miner's deposit after it had been assayed, refined, cast into convenient form (generally rectangular), and stamped with the appropriate weight, fineness, and value. Although occasionally cast in even values for the convenience of banks, bars were more often of odd denomination, and when circulated were rounded off to the nearest figure. Ingots and bars are omitted from this listing.

CALIFORNIA

Fractional and Small Size Gold Coinage

During the California gold rush a wide variety of U.S. and foreign coins were used for small change, but only limited quantities of these coins were available. Gold dust was in common use, although this offered the miner a relatively low value for his gold.

By 1852 California jewelers had begun to manufacture 25¢, 50¢ and $1 gold pieces in round and octagonal shapes. Makers included M. Deriberpe, Antoine Louis Nouizillet, Isadore Routhier, Robert B. Gray, Pierre Frontier, Eugene Deviercy, Herman J. Brand, and Herman and Jacob Levison. Reuben N. Hershfield and Noah Mitchell made their coins in Leavenworth, Kansas and most of their production was seized in August 1871. Herman Kroll made California gold coins in New York City in the 1890s. Only two or three of these companies were in production at any one time. Many varieties bear the makers initials. Frontier and his partners made most of the large Liberty Head, Eagle reverse, and Washington Head design types. Most of the small Liberty Head types were made first by Nouizillet and later by Gray and then the Levison brothers and lastly by the California Jewelry Co. Coins initialed "G.G." are apparently patterns made by Frontier and Deviercy for the New York based firm of Gaime, Guillemot & Co.

Most of the earlier coins were struck from gold alloys and had an intrinsic value of about 50-60 percent of face value. They were generally struck from partially hubbed dies and with reeded collars. A few issues were struck with a plain collar or a collar with reeding on only 7 of the 8 sides. Many issues are too poorly struck or too thin to have a clear and complete image of the collar. The later coins and some of the earlier coins were struck from laminated or plated gold planchets, or from gold plated silver planchets. Most of the last dates of issue are extremely thin and contain only token amounts of gold.

Circumstantial evidence exists that the coins issued through 1856 circulated as small change. The San Francisco mint was established in 1854, and by 1856 it had ramped up its production enough to satisfy the local need for small change. However, some evidence exists that these small gold coins may have continued to circulate on occasion through 1871. After 1871, the gold content of the coins dramatically decreases and it is very unlikely that any of these last issues circulated.

Although the Private Coinages Act of 1864 outlawed all private coinage, this law was not enforced in California and production of small denominated gold continued through 1882. In the spring of 1883, Col. Henry Finnegass of the U.S. Secret Service halted production of the denominated private gold pieces. Non-denominated tokens (lacking DOLLARS, CENTS or the equivalent) were also made during this latter period, sometimes by the same manufacturing jeweler using the same obverse die and the same planchets as the small denomination gold coins. Production of these tokens continues to this day, with most issues made after the 1906 earthquake and fire being backdated to 1847-1865 and struck from brass or gold plated brass planchets.

Approximately 25,000 pieces of California small denomination gold coins are estimated to exist, in a total of over 500 varieties. A few varieties are undated, mostly gold rush era pieces; and a few of the issues are backdated, mostly those from the 1880's. This listing groups varieties together in easily identified categories. The prices quoted are for the most common variety in each group. UNC prices reflect the median auction prices realized of MS60 to MS62 graded coins. BU prices reflect the median auction prices realized of MS63 to MS64 graded coins. Pre-1871 true MS-65 coins are rare and sell for substantial premiums over the prices on this list. Post-1871 coins are rarely found with wear and often have a cameo proof appearance. Auction prices realized are highly volatile and it is not uncommon to find recent records of sales at twice or half of the values shown here. Many of the rarity estimates published in the 1980s and earlier have proven to be too high, so caution is advised when paying a premium for a rare variety. In addition, many varieties that have a refined appearance command higher prices than equivalent grade but scarcer varieties that have a more crude appearance.

Several counterfeits of California Fractional Gold coins exist. Beware of 1854 and 1858 dated round 1/2 dollars, and 1871 dated round dollars that have designs that do not match any of the published varieties. Beware of reeded edge Kroll coins being sold as originals (see the listings below).

For further information consult "California Pioneer Fractional Gold" by W. Breen and R.J. Gillio and "The Brasher Bulletin" the official newsletter of The Society of Private and Pioneer Numismatists.

CALIFORNIA

1/4 DOLLAR (OCTAGONAL)

KM# 1.1   Obverse: Large Liberty head, left **Reverse:** Value and date within beaded circle

Date	Fine	VF	XF	Unc	BU
1853	—	—	—	250	350
1854	—	—	—	300	400
1855	—	—	—	300	400
1856	—	—	—	310	425

KM# 1.10   Obverse: "Oriental" Liberty head, left, above date **Reverse:** 1/4 CALDOLL withn wreath

Date	Fine	VF	XF	Unc	BU
1881	—	—	—	1,000	3,000

KM# 1.11   Obverse: Large Liberty head, left, above 1872 **Reverse:** Value and 1871 within wreath

Date	Fine	VF	XF	Unc	BU
1872-71	—	—	—	1,000	3,000

KM# 1.2   Obverse: Liberty head, left **Reverse:** Value and date within wreath

Date	Fine	VF	XF	Unc	BU
1859	—	—	—	200	450
1864	—	—	—	250	400
1866	—	—	—	250	400
1867	—	—	—	250	400
1868	—	—	—	200	350
1869	—	—	—	200	350
1870	—	—	—	200	350
1871	—	—	—	200	350

KM# 1.3   Obverse: Large Liberty head, left, above date **Reverse:** 1/4 DOLLAR and CAL within wreath

Date	Fine	VF	XF	Unc	BU
1872	—	—	—	250	400
1873	—	—	—	175	300

KM# 1.4   Obverse: Small Liberty head, left **Reverse:** Value and date within beaded circle

Date	Fine	VF	XF	Unc	BU
1853	—	—	200	325	475

KM# 1.5   Obverse: Small Liberty head, left, above date **Reverse:** Value within wreath

Date	Fine	VF	XF	Unc	BU
1854	—	—	—	300	400

KM# 1.6   Obverse: Small Liberty head, left **Reverse:** Value and date within wreath

Date	Fine	VF	XF	Unc	BU
1855	—	—	—	300	400
1856	—	—	—	275	350
1857 Plain edge	—	—	—	100	150
Note: Kroll type date					
1857 Reeded edge	—	—	—	75.00	110
Note: Kroll type date					
1860 Rare	—	—	—	—	—
1860	—	—	—	200	300
1870	—	—	—	250	350

KM# 1.7   Obverse: Liberty head, left **Reverse:** 1/4 in shield, DOLLAR and date below, all within wreath

Date	Fine	VF	XF	Unc	BU
1863	—	—	—	500	—
1864	—	—	—	240	350
1865	—	—	—	250	550
1866	—	—	—	250	400
1867	—	—	—	200	400
1868	—	—	—	200	—
1869	—	—	—	190	300
1870	—	—	—	200	350

KM# 1.8   Obverse: Small Liberty head, left, above date **Reverse:** 1/4 DOLLAR and CAL, all within wreath

Date	Fine	VF	XF	Unc	BU
1870	—	—	—	225	300
1871	—	—	—	200	250
1871	—	—	—	200	250
1873	—	—	—	400	—
1874	—	—	—	200	275
1875/3	—	—	—	1,000	—
1876	—	—	—	225	300

KM# 1.9   Obverse: "Goofy" Liberty head, left **Reverse:** Value and date within wreath

Date	Fine	VF	XF	Unc	BU
1870	—	—	—	200	300

KM# 2.1   Obverse: Large Indian head, left, above date **Reverse:** Value within wreath

Date	Fine	VF	XF	Unc	BU
1852	—	—	—	340	500
Note: Back dated issue					
1868	—	—	—	340	500
Note: Back dated issue					

Date	Fine	VF	XF	Unc	BU
1874	—	—	—	320	450

Note: Back dated issue

Date	Fine	VF	XF	Unc	BU
1876	—	—	—	320	450
1878/6	—	—	—	450	650
1880	—	—	—	300	400
1881	—	—	—	320	450

KM# 2.2   Obverse: Large Indian head, left, above date **Reverse:** Value and CAL within wreath

Date	Fine	VF	XF	Unc	BU
1872	—	—	65.00	260	350
1873/2	—	—	200	600	850
1873	—	—	90.00	300	400
1874	—	—	65.00	260	350
1875	—	—	90.00	300	400
1876	—	—	90.00	300	400

KM# 2.3   Obverse: Small Indian head, left, above date **Reverse:** 1/4 DOLLAR and CAL, all within wreath

Date	Fine	VF	XF	Unc	BU
1875	—	—	—	250	350
1876	—	—	—	250	500
1881	—	—	—	500	1,100

KM# 2.4   Obverse: "Aztec" Indian head, left, above date **Reverse:** Value and CAL within wreath

Date	Fine	VF	XF	Unc	BU
1880	—	—	—	210	300

KM# 2.6   Obverse: "Dumb" Indian head, left, above date **Reverse:** Value and CAL within wreath

Date	Fine	VF	XF	Unc	BU
1881	—	—	—	650	—

KM# 2.7   Obverse: "Young" Indian head, left, above date **Reverse:** Value within wreath

Date	Fine	VF	XF	Unc	BU
1881	—	—	—	750	—

KM# 2.8   Obverse: Indian head, left, above date **Reverse:** 1/4 DOLLAR and CAL, all within wreath

Date	Fine	VF	XF	Unc	BU
1882	—	—	—	500	750

KM# 3   Obverse: Washington head, left, above date **Reverse:** Value and CAL within wreath

Date	Fine	VF	XF	Unc	BU
1872	—	—	—	900	1,400

1/4 DOLLAR (ROUND)

KM# 4   Obverse: Defiant eagle above date **Reverse:** 25 CENTS within wreath

Date	Fine	VF	XF	Unc	BU
1854	—	—	11,000	33,000	44,000

KM# 5.1   Obverse: Large Liberty head, left **Reverse:** Value and date within wreath

Date	Fine	VF	XF	Unc	BU
1853	—	—	400	1,000	1,500
1853	—	—	600	1,500	2,250
1853	—	—	600	1,500	2,250
1854	—	—	150	400	600
1858 Rare	—	—	—	—	—
1859	—	—	70.00	225	275
1865	—	—	90.00	250	350
1866	—	—	—	200	300
1867	—	—	—	200	300
1868	—	—	—	200	300
1870	—	—	—	200	300
1871	—	—	—	200	300

KM# 5.2   Obverse: Large Liberty head, left, above date **Reverse:** Value and CAL within wreath

Date	Fine	VF	XF	Unc	BU
1871	—	—	—	200	275
1872	—	—	—	250	325
1873	—	—	—	180	260

KM# 5.3   Obverse: Small Liberty head, left **Reverse:** 25 CENTS within wreath

Date	Fine	VF	XF	Unc	BU
	—	—	1,000	2,450	3,500

KM# 5.4   Obverse: Small Liberty head, left **Reverse:** "1/4 DOLL." or "DOLLAR" and date in wreath

Date	Fine	VF	XF	Unc	BU
	—	—	90.00	200	350

Note: Rare counterfeit exists

Date	Fine	VF	XF	Unc	BU
1853	—	—	500	1,200	2,500
1855 10 stars	—	—	120	275	365
1855 11 stars	—	—	—	50.00	100

Note: Kroll type

Date	Fine	VF	XF	Unc	BU
1856	—	—	100	250	350
1860	—	—	65.00	175	275
1864	—	—	75.00	200	300
1865	—	—	90.00	225	350
1866	—	—	125	600	350
1867	—	—	65.00	175	350
1869	—	—	65.00	175	300
1870	—	—	125	250	450

KM# 5.5 Obverse: Small Liberty head, left **Reverse:** Value in shield and date within wreath

Date	Fine	VF	XF	Unc	BU
1863/1860 Rare	—	—	—	—	—
Note: Struck over 1/4 Dollar KM#5.4					
1863	—	—	80.00	200	—
1870 Rare	—	—	—	—	—

KM# 5.6 Obverse: Small Liberty head, left, above date **Reverse:** 1/4 DOLLAR CAL within wreath

Date	Fine	VF	XF	Unc	BU
	—	—	100	500	—
1870	—	—	80.00	200	250
1871	—	—	80.00	200	250
1871	—	—	—	210	350
1873	—	—	—	300	500
1874	—	—	—	300	500
1875	—	—	—	250	475
1876	—	—	—	225	400

KM# 5.7 Obverse: "Goofy" Liberty head, left **Reverse:** Value and date within wreath

Date	Fine	VF	XF	Unc	BU
1870	—	—	110	220	250

KM# 5.8 Obverse: Liberty head left, H and date below **Reverse:** 1/4 DOLLAR CAL within wreath

Date	Fine	VF	XF	Unc	BU
1871	—	—	180	260	350

KM# 6.1 Obverse: Large Indian head left, date below **Reverse:** Value within wreath

Date	Fine	VF	XF	Unc	BU
1852	—	—	—	300	400
Note: Back dated issue					
1868	—	—	—	350	475
Note: Back dated issue					
1874	—	—	—	290	375
Note: Back dated issue					
1876	—	—	—	300	425
1878/6	—	—	—	300	400
1880	—	—	—	200	325
1881	—	—	—	200	325

KM# 6.2 Obverse: Large Indian head left, date below **Reverse:** 1/4 DOLLAR CAL within wreath

Date	Fine	VF	XF	Unc	BU
1872/1	—	—	—	200	300
1873	—	—	—	280	375
1874	—	—	—	180	275
1875	—	—	—	200	300
1876	—	—	—	200	300

KM# 6.3 Obverse: Small Indian head left, date below **Reverse:** Value within wreath

Date	Fine	VF	XF	Unc	BU
1875	—	—	75.00	250	400
1876	—	—	65.00	200	350
1881 Rare	—	—	—	—	—

KM# 6.4 Obverse: "Young" Indian head left, date below **Reverse:** 1/4 DOLLAR CAL within wreath

Date	Fine	VF	XF	Unc	BU
1882	—	—	400	1,225	1,750

KM# 7 Obverse: Washington head left, date below **Reverse:** 1/4 DOLLAR CAL within wreath

Date	Fine	VF	XF	Unc	BU
1872	—	—	—	1,100	1,400

1/2 DOLLAR (OCTAGONAL)

KM# 8.1 Obverse: Liberty head left, date below **Reverse:** 1/2 DOLLAR in beaded circle, CALIFORNIA GOLD around

Date	Fine	VF	XF	Unc	BU
1853	—	—	165	350	450
1854	—	—	110	285	350
Note: Rare counterfeit exists					
1854	—	—	165	350	450
1856	—	—	165	365	450

KM# 8.10 Obverse: "Goofy" Liberty head, left **Reverse:** Value and date within wreath

Date	Fine	VF	XF	Unc	BU
1870	—	—	55.00	200	300

KM# 8.11 Obverse: "Oriental" Liberty head left, date below **Reverse:** 1/2 CALDOLL within wreath

Date	Fine	VF	XF	Unc	BU
1881	—	—	250	750	1,150

KM# 8.2 Obverse: Liberty head, left **Reverse:** Small eagle with rays ("peacock")

Date	Fine	VF	XF	Unc	BU
1853	—	—	800	2,000	3,000

KM# 8.3 **Obverse:** Large Liberty head, left **Reverse:** Large eagle with date

Date	Fine	VF	XF	Unc	BU
1853	—	—	5,000	10,000	—

KM# 8.4 **Obverse:** Liberty head, left **Reverse:** Value and date within wreath

Date	Fine	VF	XF	Unc	BU
1859	—	—	—	200	275
1866	—	—	—	300	400
1867	—	—	—	225	300
1868	—	—	—	225	300
1869	—	—	—	250	350
1870	—	—	—	250	350
1871	—	—	—	225	300

KM# 8.5 **Obverse:** Large Liberty head left, date below **Reverse:** HALF / DOLLAR / CAL within wreath

Date	Fine	VF	XF	Unc	BU
1872	—	—	—	250	350
1873	—	—	—	225	300

KM# 8.6 **Obverse:** Liberty head, left **Reverse:** HALF DOL. CALIFORNIA GOLD around wreath, date within

Date	Fine	VF	XF	Unc	BU
1854	—	—	100	350	500
1855	—	—	90.00	300	400
1856	—	—	90.00	265	325
1856	—	—	165	1,100	—
Note: Back date issue struck in 1864					
1868	—	—	60.00	185	275
Note: Kroll type					

KM# 8.7 **Obverse:** Small Liberty head left **Reverse:** HALF / DOLLAR /date all within wreath

Date	Fine	VF	XF	Unc	BU
1864	—	—	—	275	350
Note: A rare silver strike of 1864G is known					
1870	—	—	—	275	—

KM# 8.8 **Obverse:** Liberty head left **Reverse:** CAL. GOLD / HALF DOL and date within wreath

Date	Fine	VF	XF	Unc	BU
1869	—	—	—	200	350
1870	—	—	—	200	350

KM# 8.9 **Obverse:** Small Liberty head left, date below **Reverse:** HALF DOLLAR CAL within wreath

Date	Fine	VF	XF	Unc	BU
1870	—	—	55.00	200	300
1871	—	—	55.00	200	250
1871	—	—	55.00	165	250
1873	—	—	85.00	300	600
1874	—	—	85.00	300	600
1875	—	—	250	1,000	—
1876	—	—	55.00	200	250

KM# 9.1 **Obverse:** Large Indian head left, date below **Reverse:** Value within wreath

Date	Fine	VF	XF	Unc	BU
1852	—	—	—	700	1,100
Note: Back dated issue					
1868	—	—	—	850	1,200
Note: Back dated issue					
1874	—	—	—	700	1,100
Note: Back dated issue					
1876	—	—	—	300	400
1880	—	—	—	300	400
1881	—	—	—	300	400

KM# 9.2 **Obverse:** Large Indian head left, date below **Reverse:** 1/2 DOLLAR CAL within wreath

Date	Fine	VF	XF	Unc	BU
1852	—	—	—	450	700
Note: Back dated issue					
1868	—	—	—	260	550
Note: Back dated issue					
1872	—	—	—	200	300
1873/2	—	—	—	200	400
1873	—	—	—	200	300
1874/3	—	—	—	250	350
1874	—	—	—	200	425
1875	—	—	—	250	300
1876	—	—	—	250	400
1878/6	—	—	—	250	400
1880	—	—	—	500	1,000
1881	—	—	—	250	400

KM# 9.3 **Obverse:** Small Indian head left, date below **Reverse:** Value and CAL within wreath

Date	Fine	VF	XF	Unc	BU
1875	—	—	—	225	350
1876	—	—	—	225	350

KM# 9.4 **Obverse:** "Young" Indian head left, date below **Reverse:** 1/2 DOLLAR CAL within wreath

Date	Fine	VF	XF	Unc	BU
1881	—	—	—	550	850
1882 Rare	—	—	—	—	—

1/2 DOLLAR (ROUND)

KM# 10   Obverse: Arms of California and date
Reverse: Eagle and legends

Date	Fine	VF	XF	Unc	BU
1853	—	—	—	—	—

KM# 11.1   Obverse: Liberty head, left **Reverse:**
Large eagle and legends

Date	Fine	VF	XF	Unc	BU
1854	—	—	1,000	6,000	—

Note: Similar obverse paired with reverse of KM#12.2, or an
eagle with no denomination are modern counterfeits

KM# 11.11   Obverse: "Goofy" Liberty head, left
Reverse: Value and date within wreath

Date	Fine	VF	XF	Unc	BU
1870	—	—	125	400	700

KM# 11.12   Obverse: Liberty head left, H and date
below **Reverse:** Value and CAL within wreath

Date	Fine	VF	XF	Unc	BU
1871	—	—	110	400	475

KM# 11.2   Obverse: Liberty head left, date below
Reverse: HALF DOL. CALIFORNIA GOLD around
wreath

Date	Fine	VF	XF	Unc	BU
1854	—	—	175	300	450

KM# 11.3   Obverse: Liberty head left **Reverse:** Date
in wreath, value and CALIFORNIA GOLD around
wreath

Date	Fine	VF	XF	Unc	BU
1852	—	—	145	275	400
1852	—	—	145	275	400
1853	—	—	145	275	400
1853	—	—	165	300	425
1853	—	—	165	300	425
1854	—	—	300	750	1,000
1854 Large head, small stars	—	—	750	1,500	3,000

Date	Fine	VF	XF	Unc	BU
1854 Small head, small stars	—	—	—	100	200
Note: Kroll type.					
1854 Large stars	—	—	—	—	—
Note: Common counterfeit					
1855	—	—	175	325	550
1856	—	—	100	225	325
1860/56	—	—	125	250	400

KM# 11.4   Obverse: Liberty head, left **Reverse:**
Small eagle and legends

Date	Fine	VF	XF	Unc	BU
1853 Rare	—	—	—	—	—
1853	—	—	5,000	10,000	15,000

KM# 11.5   Obverse: Liberty head left **Reverse:**
Value in wreath; CALIFORNIA GOLD and date around
wreath

Date	Fine	VF	XF	Unc	BU
1853	—	—	150	750	1,500

KM# 11.6   Obverse: Liberty head left **Reverse:**
Value and date within wreath

Date	Fine	VF	XF	Unc	BU
Rare	—	—	—	—	—
1854 13 stars	—	—	850	3,000	—
1854 12 stars	—	—	—	—	—
Note: Rare counterfeit without "FD" beneath truncation					
1855	—	—	155	450	600
1859	—	—	350	750	1,000
1859	—	—	—	250	400
1865	—	—	—	225	350
1866	—	—	—	250	400
1867	—	—	—	225	350
1868	—	—	—	250	400
1869	—	—	—	250	400
1870	—	—	—	225	350
1871	—	—	—	200	300
1873	—	—	—	250	450
Note: A rare counterfeit exists for this date					

KM# 11.7   Obverse: Liberty head left, date below
Reverse: Value and CAL within wreath

Date	Fine	VF	XF	Unc	BU
1870	—	—	—	250	400
1871	—	—	—	250	400
Note: Common, yet deceptive, counterfeits exist					
1871	—	—	—	400	—
1872	—	—	—	250	400
1873	—	—	—	400	1,000
1874	—	—	—	250	750
1875	—	—	—	300	800
1876	—	—	—	250	—

US TERRITORIAL GOLD

KM# 11.8 **Obverse:** Liberty head left **Reverse:** Value and date within wreath, CALIFORNIA GOLD around

Date	Fine	VF	XF	Unc	BU
1863	—	—	265	675	950

Note: This issue is a rare Kroll type. All 1858 dates of this type are counterfeits

KM# 12.4 **Obverse:** "Young" Indian head left, date above **Reverse:** Value and CAL within wreath

Date	Fine	VF	XF	Unc	BU
1882	—	—	—	850	—

DOLLAR (OCTAGONAL)

KM# 11.9 **Obverse:** Liberty head left **Reverse:** HALF DOLLAR and date within wreath

Date	Fine	VF	XF	Unc	BU
1864	—	—	100	250	350

Note: A rare silver strike is known

1866	—	—	500	800	1,000
1867	—	—	100	250	350
1868	—	—	100	250	350
1869	—	—	125	300	—
1870	—	—	—	350	—

KM# 13.1 **Obverse:** Liberty head left **Reverse:** Large eagle and legends

Date	Fine	VF	XF	Unc	BU
	—	—	1,000	2,000	4,000
1853	—	—	5,000	7,500	—
1854	—	—	2,000	3,000	5,000

KM# 12.1 **Obverse:** Large Indian head left, date below **Reverse:** Value within wreath **Note:** 1852, 1868 and 1874 are backdated issues

Date	Fine	VF	XF	Unc	BU
1852	—	—	—	350	675
1868	—	—	—	300	600
1874	—	—	—	300	600

Note: Similar obverse paired with reverse of KM#11.2 or an eagle with no denomination are modern counterfeits

1876	—	—	—	200	250
1878/6	—	—	—	300	450
1880	—	—	—	250	400
1881	—	—	—	250	400

KM# 13.2 **Obverse:** Liberty head left **Reverse:** Value and date in beaded circle; CALIFORNIA GOLD and initials around

Date	Fine	VF	XF	Unc	BU
1853	—	—	275	750	1,100
1853	—	—	450	1,100	—
1853	—	—	300	900	—
1853	—	—	275	750	1,200
1854	—	—	450	1,100	—
1854	—	—	300	900	1,600
1855	—	—	350	900	—
1856	—	—	2,100	5,000	—
1863 Reeded edge, restrike	—	—	—	100	150
1863 Plain edge	—	—	—	125	200

Note: Plain edge 1863 dates are original Kroll types, while reeded edge examples are Kroll restrikes

KM# 12.2 **Obverse:** Large Indian head left, date below **Reverse:** Value and CAL within wreath

Date	Fine	VF	XF	Unc	BU
1872	—	—	—	200	300
1873/2	—	—	—	350	650
1873	—	—	—	200	300
1874/3	—	—	—	300	450
1874	—	—	—	200	300
1875/3	—	—	—	200	300
1875	—	—	—	300	500
1876/5	—	—	—	200	300
1876	—	—	—	340	600

KM# 13.3 **Obverse:** Liberty head left **Reverse:** Value and date inside wreath; legends outside

Date	Fine	VF	XF	Unc	BU
1854 Rare	—	—	—	—	—

Note: Bowers and Marena sale 5-99, XF $9,775

1854	—	—	275	750	1,100
1855	—	—	275	750	1,100
1858	—	—	150	350	600

Note: 1858 dates are Kroll types

1859	—	—	1,900	—	—
1860	—	—	—	750	1,000
1868	—	—	—	750	1,100
1869	—	—	—	660	900
1870	—	—	—	600	900
1871	—	—	—	400	850

KM# 12.3 **Obverse:** Small Indian head left, date below **Reverse:** Value and CAL within wreath

Date	Fine	VF	XF	Unc	BU
1875	—	—	100	250	450
1876	—	—	75.00	200	300

KM# 13.4 **Obverse:** "Goofy" Liberty head, left **Reverse:** Value and date within wreath

Date	Fine	VF	XF	Unc	BU
1870	—	—	—	1,000	1,500

Note: Deceptive counterfeits exist

KM# 13.5 Obverse: Liberty head left, date below **Reverse:** Value and date within wreath; CALIFORNIA GOLD around

Date	Fine	VF	XF	Unc	BU
1871	—	—	—	600	900
1874	—	—	—	—	—
1875	—	—	—	—	—
1876	—	—	—	—	—

KM# 14.1 Obverse: Large Indian head left, date below **Reverse:** 1 DOLLAR within wreath; CALIFORNIA GOLD around

Date	Fine	VF	XF	Unc	BU
1872	—	—	—	600	900
1873/2	—	—	—	700	1,100
1873	—	—	—	750	—
1874	—	—	—	850	1,300
1875	—	—	—	600	1,000
1876/5	—	—	—	1,000	1,300

KM# 14.2 Obverse: Small Indian head left, date below **Reverse:** 1 DOLLAR CAL within wreath

Date	Fine	VF	XF	Unc	BU
1875	—	—	700	1,200	—
1876	—	—	—	1,400	—

KM# 14.3 Obverse: Indian head left, date below **Reverse:** 1 DOLLAR within wreath; CALIFORNIA GOLD around

Date	Fine	VF	XF	Unc	BU
1876	—	—	—	750	—

DOLLAR (ROUND)

KM# 15.1 Obverse: Liberty head left **Reverse:** Large eagle and legends

Date	Fine	VF	XF	Unc	BU
1853 Rare	—	—	—	—	—

Note: Superior sale Sept. 1987 MS-63 $35,200

KM# 15.2 Obverse: Liberty head left **Reverse:** Value and date within wreath; CALIFORNIA GOLD around

Date	Fine	VF	XF	Unc	BU
1854	—	—	3,000	—	—
1854	—	—	5,000	—	—
1854 Rare	—	—	—	—	—

Note: Superior sale Sept. 1988 Fine $13,200

Date	Fine	VF	XF	Unc	BU
1857 4 known	—	—	—	—	—
1870	—	—	500	2,000	—
1871	—	—	850	2,500	—

Note: Counterfeit exists

KM# 15.3 Obverse: Liberty head left, date below **Reverse:** Value within wreath; CALIFORNIA GOLD around

Date	Fine	VF	XF	Unc	BU
1870	—	—	500	1,400	2,000
1871	—	—	500	1,400	2,000

KM# 15.4 Obverse: "Goofy" Liberty head left **Reverse:** Value and date within wreath; CALIFORNIA GOLD around

Date	Fine	VF	XF	Unc	BU
1870	—	—	400	1,500	—

KM# 16 Obverse: Large Indian head left, date below **Reverse:** Value within wreath; CALIFORNIA GOLD outside

Date	Fine	VF	XF	Unc	BU
1872	—	—	650	1,800	2,400

U.S. Territorial Gold Coinage
Private Assay Office Issues

CALIFORNIA

Norris, Grieg & Norris produced the first territorial gold coin struck in California, a $5 piece struck in 1849 at Benicia City, though it bears the imprint of San Francisco. The coining facility was owned by Thomas H. Norris, Charles Greig, and Hiram A. Norris, members of a New York engineering firm. A unique 1850 variety of this coin has the name STOCKTON beneath the date, instead of SAN FRANCISCO.

Early in 1849, John Little Moffat, a New York assayer, established an assay office at San Francisco in association with Joseph R. Curtis, Philo H. Perry, and Samuel Ward. The first issues of the **Moffat & Co.** assay office consisted of rectangular $16 ingots and assay bars of various and irregular denominations. In early August, the firm began striking $5 and $10 gold coins which resemble those of the U.S. Mint in design, but carry the legend S.M.V. (Standard Mint Value) CALIFORNIA GOLD on the reverse. Five-dollar pieces of the same design were also issued in 1850.

On Sept. 30, 1850, Congress directed the Secretary of the Treasury to establish an official Assay Office in California. Moffat & Co. obtained a contract to perform the duties of the U.S. Assay Office. **Augustus Humbert**, a New York watchcase maker, was appointed U.S. Assayer of Gold in California. Humbert stamped the first octagonal coin-ingots of the Provisional Government Mint on Jan. 31, 1851. The $50 pieces were accepted at par with standard U.S. gold coins, but were not officially recognized as coins. Officially, they were designated as "ingots." Colloquially, they were known as slugs, quintuple eagles, or 5-eagle pieces.

The $50 ingots failed to alleviate the need of California for gold coins. The banks regarded them as disadvantageous to their interests and utilized them only when compelled to do so by public need or convenience. Being of sound value, the ingots drove the overvalued $5, $10, and $20 territorial gold coins from circulation, bringing about a return to the use of gold dust for everyday transactions. Eventually, the slugs became so great a nuisance that they were discounted 3 percent when accepted. This unexpected turn of events forced Moffat & Co. to resume the issuing of $10 and $20 gold coins in 1852. The $10 piece was first issued with the Moffat & Co. imprint on Liberty's coronet, and later with the official imprint of Augustus Humbert on reverse. The $20 piece was issued with the Humbert imprint.

On Feb. 14, 1852, John L. Moffat withdrew from Moffat & Co. to enter the diving bell business, and Moffat & Co. was reorganized as the **United States Assay Office of Gold**, composed of Joseph R. Curtis, Philo H. Perry, and Samuel Ward. The U.S. Assay Office of Gold issued gold coins in denominations of $50 and $10 in 1852, and $20 and $10 in 1853. With the exception of the $50 slugs, they carry the imprint of the Assay Office on reverse. The .900 fine issues of this facility reflect an attempt to bring the issues of the U.S. Assay Office into conformity with the U.S. Mint standard.

The last territorial gold coins to bear the imprint of Moffat & Co. are $20 pieces issued in 1853, after the retirement of John L. Moffat. These coins do not carry a mark of fineness, and generally assay below the U.S. Mint standard.

Templeton Reid, previously mentioned in connection with the private gold issues of Georgia, moved his coining equipment to California when gold was discovered there, and in 1849 issued $10 and $25 gold pieces. No specimens are available to present-day collectors. The only known $10 piece is in the Smithsonian Collection. The only known specimen of the $25 piece was stolen from the U.S. Mint Cabinet Collection in 1858 and was never recovered.

Little is known of the origin and location of the **Cincinnati Mining & Trading Co.** It is believed that the firm was organized in the East and was forced to abandon most of its equipment while enroute to California. A few $5 and $10 gold coins were struck in 1849. Base metal counterfeits exist.

The **Massachusetts & California Co.** was organized in Northampton, Mass., in May 1849 by Josiah Hayden, S. S. Wells, Miles G. Moies, and others. Coining equipment was taken to San Francisco where $5 gold pieces were struck in 1849. The few pieces extant are heavily alloyed with copper.

Wright & Co., a brokerage firm located in Portsmouth Square, San Francisco, issued an undated $10 gold piece in the autumn of 1849 under the name of **Miners' Bank**. Unlike most territorial gold pieces, the Miners' Bank eagle was alloyed with copper. The coinage proved to be unpopular because of its copper-induced color and low intrinsic value. The firm was dissolved on Jan. 14, 1850.

In 1849, Dr. **J. S. Ormsby** and Major William M. Ormsby struck gold coins of $5 and $10 denominations at Sacramento under the name of Ormsby & Co. The coinage, which is identified by the initials J. S. O., is undated. Ormsby & Co. coinage was greatly over-valued, the eagle assaying at as little as $9.37.

The **Pacific Co.** of San Francisco issued $5 and $10 gold coins in 1849. The clouded story of this coinage is based on conjecture. It is believed that the well-struck pattern coins of this type were struck in the East by the Pacific Co. that organized in Boston and set sail for California on Feb. 20, 1849, and that the crudely hand-struck pieces were made by the jewelry firm of Broderick and Kohler after the dies passed into their possession. In any event, the intrinsic value of the initial coinage exceeded face value, but by the end of 1849, when they passed out of favor, the coins had been debased so flagrantly that the eagles assayed for as little as $7.86.

Dubosq & Co., a Philadelphia jewelry firm owned by Theodore Dubosq Sr. and Jr. and Henry Dubosq, took melting and coining equipment to San Francisco in 1849, and in 1850 issued $5 and $10 gold coins struck with dies allegedly made by U.S. Mint Engraver James B. Longacre. Dubosq & Co. coinage was immensely popular with the forty-niners because its intrinsic worth was in excess of face value.

US TERRITORIAL GOLD

The minting equipment of David C. Broderick and Frederick D. Kohler (see Pacific Co.) was acquired in May 1850 by San Francisco jewelers George C. Baldwin and Thomas S. Holman, who organized a private minting venture under the name of **Baldwin & Co**. The firm produced a $5 piece of Liberty Head design and a $10 piece with Horseman device in 1850. Liberty Head $10 and $20 pieces were coined in 1851. Baldwin & Co. produced the first $20 piece issued in California.

Schultz & Co. of San Francisco, a brass foundry located in the rear of the Baldwin & Co. establishment, and operated by Judge G. W. Schultz and William T. Garratt, issued $5 gold coins from early 1851 until April of that year. The inscription "SHULTS & CO." is a misspelling of SCHULTZ & CO.

Dunbar & Co. of San Francisco issued a $5 gold piece in 1851, after Edward E. Dunbar, owner of the California Bank in San Francisco, purchased the coining equipment of the defunct Baldwin & Co.

The San Francisco-based firm of **Wass, Molitor & Co.** was owned by 2 Hungarian exiles, Count S. C. Wass and A. P. Molitor, who initially founded the firm as a gold smelting and assaying plant. In response to a plea from the commercial community for small gold coins, Wass, Molitor & Co. issued $5 and $10 gold coins in 1852. The $5 piece was coined with small head and large head varieties, and the $10 piece with small head, large head, and small close-date varieties. The firm produced a second issue of gold coins in 1855, in denominations of $10, $20, and $50.

The U.S. Assay Office in California closed its doors on Dec. 14, 1853, to make way for the newly established San Francisco Branch Mint. The Mint, however, was unable to start immediate quantity production due to the lack of refining acids. During the interim, John G. Kellogg, a former employee of Moffat & Co., and John Glover Richter, a former assayer in the U.S. Assay Office, formed **Kellogg & Co.** for the purpose of supplying businessmen with urgently needed coinage. The firm produced $20 coins dated 1854 and 1855, after which Augustus Humbert replaced Richter and the enterprise reorganized as Kellogg & Humbert Melters, Assayers & Coiners. Kellogg & Humbert endured until 1860, but issued coins, $20 pieces, only in 1855.

BALDWIN & COMPANY

5 DOLLARS

KM# 17 Obverse: Liberty head left, date below **Reverse:** Eagle

Date	Fine	VF	XF	Unc	BU
1850	7,500	11,500	20,000	45,000	—

10 DOLLARS

KM# 18 Obverse: Figure on horseback right, swinging rope, date and value below **Reverse:** Eagle

Date	Fine	VF	XF	Unc	BU
1850	30,000	60,000	97,500	175,000	—

Note: Bass Sale May 2000, MS-64 $149,500

KM# 19 Obverse: Coronet head left within circle of stars, date below **Reverse:** Eagle

Date	Fine	VF	XF	Unc	BU
1851	9,500	20,000	35,000	100,000	—

20 DOLLARS

KM# 20 Obverse: Coronet head, left, within circle of stars, date below **Reverse:** Eagle

Date	Fine	VF	XF	Unc	BU
1851 Rare	—	—	—	—	—

Note: Stack's Superior Sale Dec. 1988, XF-40 $52,800; Beware of copies cast in base metals

BLAKE & COMPANY

20 DOLLARS

KM# 21   Obverse: Value within small center circle, legend around **Reverse:** Coining screw press at centre, date and value below

Date	Fine	VF	XF	Unc	BU
1855	—	—	—	—	—

Note: No original specimens are known. Most experts believe this to be a counterfeit circa 1950. Many modern copies exist

J. H. BOWIE

5 DOLLARS

KM# 22   Obverse: Value at center, Company name above **Reverse:** Pine tree

Date	Fine	VF	XF	Unc	BU
1849 Rare	—	—	—	—	—

Note: Americana Sale Jan. 2001, AU-58 $253,000

CINCINNATI MINING AND TRADING COMPANY

5 DOLLARS

KM# 23   Obverse: Draped bust with headress left **Reverse:** Eagle with shield left, date below

Date	Fine	VF	XF	Unc	BU
1849 Rare	—	—	—	—	—

10 DOLLARS

KM# 24   Obverse: Draped bust with headdress left **Reverse:** Eagle with shield left, date below

Date	Fine	VF	XF	Unc	BU
1849 Rare	—	—	—	—	—

Note: Brand Sale 1984, XF $104,500

DUBOSQ & COMPANY

5 DOLLARS

KM# 26

Date	Fine	VF	XF	Unc	BU
1850	100,000	170,000	—	—	—

10 DOLLARS

KM# 27   Obverse: Coronet head left, within circle of stars, date below **Reverse:** Eagle

Date	Fine	VF	XF	Unc	BU
1850	100,000	180,000	260,000	—	—

DUNBAR & COMPANY

5 DOLLARS

KM# 28 Obverse: Coronet head left, within circle of stars, date below **Reverse:** Eagle

Date	Fine	VF	XF	Unc	BU
1851	112,500	162,500	275,000	—	—

Note: Spink & Son Sale 1988, AU $62,000

AUGUSTUS HUMBERT / UNITED STATES ASSAYER

10 DOLLARS

KM# 29.1 Obverse: Eagle with ribbon, value below **Reverse:** Inscription and date **Note:** "AUGUSTUS HUMBERT" imprint.

Date	Fine	VF	XF	Unc	BU
1852/1	3,000	5,300	8,300	30,000	—
1852	2,250	3,750	7,100	23,000	—

KM# 29.2 Obverse: Eagle with ribbon, value below **Reverse:** Inscription and date **Note:** Error: IINITED in obverse legend

Date	Fine	VF	XF	Unc	BU
1852/1 Rare	—	—	—	—	—
1852 Rare	—	—	—	—	—

20 DOLLARS

KM# 30 Obverse: Eagle with ribbon and shield **Reverse:** Inscription and date

Date	Fine	VF	XF	Unc	BU
1852/1	6,500	9,500	22,500	—	—

Note: Mory Sale June 2000, AU-53 $13,800; Garrett Sale March 1980, Humbert's Proof $325,000; Private Sale May 1989, Humbert's Proof (PCGS Pr-65) $1,350,000; California Sale Oct. 2000, Humbert's Proof (PCGS Pr-65) $552,000

50 DOLLARS

KM# 31.1 Obverse: Eagle with ribbon and shield **Reverse:** Target, 50 stamped incuse in center

Date	Fine	VF	XF	Unc	BU
1851	20,000	32,500	60,000	—	—

KM# 31.3   Obverse: Eagle with ribbon and shield **Reverse:** Target design, without value **Note:** ASSAYER inverted on edge.

Date	Fine	VF	XF	Unc	BU
1851 Unique	—	—	—	—	—

KM# 31.4   Obverse: Eagle with ribbon and shield **Reverse:** Target design, rays from center, without value

Date	Fine	VF	XF	Unc	BU
1851 Unique	—	—	—	—	—

KM# 31.1a   Obverse: 887 THOUS **Reverse:** 50 in center

Date	Fine	VF	XF	Unc	BU
1851	18,000	28,000	45,000	112,500	—

KM# 32.1   Obverse: Eagle with ribbon and shield **Reverse:** Target with circular center

Date	Fine	VF	XF	Unc	BU
1851	10,000	18,000	30,000	70,000	—

KM# 31.2   Obverse: Eagle with ribbon and shield **Reverse:** Target design, without value

Date	Fine	VF	XF	Unc	BU
1851	15,000	25,000	35,000	85,000	—

KM# 31.2a   Obverse: Eagle with ribbon and shield **Reverse:** Target design without value

Date	Fine	VF	XF	Unc	BU
1851	—	32,500	50,000	—	—

KM# 32.1a   Obverse: Eagle with ribbon and shield **Reverse:** Target with circular center, 50 stamped incuse

Date	Fine	VF	XF	Unc	BU
1851	5,000	8,000	16,000	35,000	—

Note: Garrett Sale March 1980, Humberts Proof $500,000

KM# 32.2 Obverse: Eagle with ribbon and shield
Reverse: Target, small design

Date	Fine	VF	XF	Unc	BU
1851	10,000	17,500	35,000	—	—
1852	9,500	16,500	32,000	80,000	—

Note: Bloomfield Sale December 1996, BU $159,500

KELLOGG & COMPANY

20 DOLLARS

KM# 33.4 Obverse: Coronet head left, thick date
Reverse: Eagle with shield, large and long arrows

Date	Fine	VF	XF	Unc	BU
1854	2,500	3,500	5,500	18,500	—
1855	2,650	3,750	6,000	20,000	—

Note: Garrett Sale March 1980 Proof $230,000

KM# 33.1 Obverse: Coronet head left, thick date
Reverse: Eagle with shield, short arrows

Date	Fine	VF	XF	Unc	BU
1854	2,500	3,500	5,500	18,500	—

KM# 33.2 Obverse: Coronet head left, medium date **Reverse:** Eagle with shield

Date	Fine	VF	XF	Unc	BU
1854	2,500	3,500	5,500	18,500	—

KM# 33.5 Obverse: Coronet head left, thick date
Reverse: Eagle with shield, medium arrows

Date	Fine	VF	XF	Unc	BU
1855	2,650	3,750	6,000	20,000	—

KM# 33.6 Obverse: Coronet head left **Reverse:**
Eagle with shield, short arrows

Date	Fine	VF	XF	Unc	BU
1855	2,650	3,750	6,000	20,000	—

KM# 33.3 Obverse: Coronet head left, thin date
Reverse: Eagle with shield, short arrows

Date	Fine	VF	XF	Unc	BU
1854	2,500	3,500	5,500	18,500	—

50 DOLLARS

KM# 34   Obverse: Coronet head left, within circle of stars **Reverse:** Banner above eagle, FIFTY DOLLS. in legend

Date	Fine	VF	XF	Unc	BU
1855	—	—	—	—	—

Note: Heritage FUN Sale January 2007, Pr64 $747,500. Heritage ANA Sale August 1977, Proof $156,500

MASSACHUSETTES AND CALIFORNIA COMPANY

5 DOLLARS

KM# 35   Obverse: Rearing equestrian figure within shield with bear and dear supporters **Reverse:** Value within wreath, date below

Date	Fine	VF	XF	Unc	BU
1849	100,000	150,000	250,000	—	—

MINERS BANK

10 DOLLARS

Date	Fine	VF	XF	Unc	BU
(1849)	—	18,500	35,000	90,000	—

Note: Garrett Sale March 1980, MS-65 $135,000

| (1849) | — | — | — | — | — |

Note: Rare, as most specimens have heavy copper alloy

MOFFAT & COMPANY

5 DOLLARS

KM# 37.1   Obverse: Coronet head left, within circle of stars, date below **Reverse:** Eagle with shiled

Date	Fine	VF	XF	Unc	BU
1849	1,250	2,250	3,750	12,500	—

KM# 37.2   Obverse: Coronet head left, within circle of stars, date below **Reverse:** Eagle with shield, die break at DOL

Date	Fine	VF	XF	Unc	BU
1849	1,250	2,250	3,750	12,500	—

KM# 37.3   Obverse: Coronet head left, within circle of stars, date below **Reverse:** Eagle with shield, die break on shield

Date	Fine	VF	XF	Unc	BU
1849	1,250	2,250	3,750	12,500	—

KM# 37.4   Obverse: Coronet head left, within circle of stars, date below **Reverse:** Eagle with shield, small letters

Date	Fine	VF	XF	Unc	BU
1850	1,350	2,500	4,250	14,000	—

KM# 37.5   Obverse: Coronet head left, within circle of stars, date below **Reverse:** Eagle with shield, large letters

Date	Fine	VF	XF	Unc	BU
1850	1,350	2,500	4,250	14,000	—

Note: Garrett Sale March 1980, MS-60 $21,000

10 DOLLARS

KM# 38.1 Obverse: Coronet head left, within circle of stars, date below **Reverse:** Eagle with shield, TEN DOL., middle arrow points below period at end of GOLD

Date	Fine	VF	XF	Unc	BU
1849	3,250	6,000	12,000	32,500	—

KM# 38.2 Obverse: Coronet head left, within circle of stars, date below **Reverse:** Eagle with shield, middle arrow points above period at end of GOLD.

Date	Fine	VF	XF	Unc	BU
1849	3,250	6,000	12,000	32,500	—

KM# 38.3 Obverse: Coronet head, left, within circle of stars, date below **Reverse:** Value: "TEN D.", large letters

Date	Fine	VF	XF	Unc	BU
1849	3,500	6,500	13,500	37,500	—

KM# 38.4 Obverse: Coronet head left, within circle of stars, date below **Reverse:** Eagle with shield, small letters

Date	Fine	VF	XF	Unc	BU
1849	3,500	6,500	13,500	37,500	—

KM# 39.1 Obverse: Coronet head left, within circle of stars, wide date below **Reverse:** Eagle with ribbon and shield **Note:** "MOFFAT & CO." imprint

Date	Fine	VF	XF	Unc	BU
1852	3,500	6,500	12,500	65,000	—

KM# 39.2 Obverse: Coronet head left, within circle of stars, date below, close date **Reverse:** Eagle with ribbon and shield, 880 THOUS. above **Note:** Struck by Augustus Humbert.

Date	Fine	VF	XF	Unc	BU
1852	3,000	6,000	11,500	60,000	—

20 DOLLARS

KM# 40 Obverse: Coronet head left, within circle of stars, date below **Reverse:** Eagle and shield, circle of stars and rays above **Note:** Struck by Curtis, Perry, & Ward.

Date	Fine	VF	XF	Unc	BU
1853	4,250	6,750	9,500	27,500	—

NORRIS, GREIG, & NORRIS

HALF EAGLE

KM# 41.1 Obverse: Date in center of circle of stars and legend **Reverse:** Eagle with laurel and arrows, period after ALLOY

Date	Fine	VF	XF	Unc	BU
1849	4,250	6,750	13,500	32,500	—

KM# 41.2 **Obverse:** Date in center of circle of stars and legend **Reverse:** Eagle with laurel and arrows, period after ALLOY

Date	Fine	VF	XF	Unc	BU
1849	4,250	6,750	13,500	32,500	—

KM# 41.3 **Obverse:** Date in center of circle of stars and legend **Reverse:** Eagle with laurel and arrows, period after ALLOY

Date	Fine	VF	XF	Unc	BU
1849	3,750	6,000	12,500	32,000	—

KM# 41.4 **Obverse:** Date in center of circle of stars and legend **Reverse:** Eagle with laurel and arrows, without period after ALLOY

Date	Fine	VF	XF	Unc	BU
1849	3,750	6,000	12,500	32,000	—

KM# 42 **Obverse:** STOCKTON beneath date **Reverse:** Eagle with laurel and arrows

Date	Fine	VF	XF	Unc	BU
1850 Unique	—	—	—	—	—

J. S. ORMSBY

5 DOLLARS

KM# 43.1 **Obverse:** J.S.O. in center **Reverse:** Value within circle of stars

Date	Fine	VF	XF	Unc	BU
(1849) Unique	—	—	—	—	—

KM# 43.2 **Obverse:** J.S.O. in center **Reverse:** Value within circle of stars

Date	Fine	VF	XF	Unc	BU
(1849) Unique	—	—	—	—	—

Note: Superior Auction 1989, VF $137,500

10 DOLLARS

KM# 44 **Obverse:** J.S.O. in center **Reverse:** Value in center circle of stars

Date	Fine	VF	XF	Unc	BU
(1849) Rare	—	—	—	—	—

Note: Garrett Sale March 1980, F-12 $100,000; Ariagno Sale June 1999, AU-50 $145,000

PACIFIC COMPANY

1 DOLLAR

KM# A45 **Obverse:** Liberty cap on pole, stars and rays around, value below **Reverse:** Eagle

Date	Fine	VF	XF	Unc	BU
(1849) Unique	—	—	—	—	—

Note: Stack's Old West Sale August 2006, AU $126,500. Mory Sale June 2000, EF-40 $57,500

5 DOLLARS

KM# 45 **Obverse:** Liberty cap on pole, stars and rays around, value below **Reverse:** Eagle

Date	Fine	VF	XF	Unc	BU
1849 Rare	—	—	—	—	—

Note: Garrett Sale March 1980, VF-30 $180,000

10 DOLLARS

KM# 46.1 **Obverse:** Liberty cap on pole, stars and rays around, value below **Reverse:** Eagle, date below

Date	Fine	VF	XF	Unc	BU
1849 Rare	—	—	—	—	—

Note: Waldorf Sale 1964, $24,000

KM# 46.2 **Obverse:** Liberty cap on pole, stars and rays around **Reverse:** Eagle

Date	Fine	VF	XF	Unc	BU
1849 Rare	—	—	—	—	—

TEMPLETON REID

10 DOLLARS

KM# 47   Obverse: Date in center **Reverse:** Value in center

Date	Fine	VF	XF	Unc	BU
1849 Unique	—	—	—	—	—

20 DOLLARS

KM# 48

Date	Fine	VF	XF	Unc	BU
1849 Unknown	—	—	—	—	—

Note: The only known specimen was stolen from the U.S. Mint in 1858 and has never been recovered. For additional listings of Templeton Reid, see listings under Georgia

SCHULTZ & COMPANY

5 DOLLARS

KM# 49   Obverse: Coronet head left, within circle of stars, date below **Reverse:** Eagle, shield on breast, value below

Date	Fine	VF	XF	Unc	BU
1851	20,000	55,000	75,000	—	—

UNITED STATES ASSAY OFFICE OF GOLD

10 DOLLARS

KM# 51.1   Obverse: Eagle with ribbon and shield **Reverse:** O of OFFICE below I of UNITED

Date	Fine	VF	XF	Unc	BU
1852	—	—	—	—	—

Note: Garrett Sale March 1980, MS-60 $18,000

KM# 51.2   Obverse: Eagle with ribbon and shield **Reverse:** O below N, strong beads

Date	Fine	VF	XF	Unc	BU
1852	1,750	3,000	5,000	16,500	—

KM# 51.3   Obverse: Eagle with ribbon and shield **Reverse:** Weak beads

Date	Fine	VF	XF	Unc	BU
1852	1,750	3,000	5,000	16,500	—

KM# 52   Obverse: Eagle with ribbon and shield **Reverse:** Inscription, date

Date	Fine	VF	XF	Unc	BU
1853	7,500	12,500	24,500	—	—

KM# 52a   Obverse: Eagle with ribbon and shield **Reverse:** Inscription, date

Date	Fine	VF	XF	Unc	BU
1853	3,750	6,500	9,500	—	—

Note: Garrett Sale March 1980, MS-60 $35,000

20 DOLLARS

KM# 53   Obverse: Eagle with ribbon and shield **Reverse:** Inscription, date

Date	Fine	VF	XF	Unc	BU
1853	8,500	12,500	18,500	42,500	—

KM# 53a Obverse: Eagle with ribbon and shield
Reverse: Inscription, date

Date	Fine	VF	XF	Unc	BU
1853	2,250	3,250	5,000	12,500	—

Note: 1853 Liberty Head listed under Moffat & Company

50 DOLLARS

KM# 54a Obverse: Eagle and ribbon with shield
Reverse: Target

Date	Fine	VF	XF	Unc	BU
1852	12,500	20,000	32,500	72,500	—

WASS, MOLITOR & COMPANY

5 DOLLARS

KM# 55.1 Obverse: Small Liberty head, rounded
bust **Reverse:** Eagle, shield on breast

Date	Fine	VF	XF	Unc	BU
1852	4,000	8,000	13,500	49,500	—

KM# 55.2 Obverse: Coronet head, left, within circle
of stars **Reverse:** Eagle, shield on breast **Note:** Thick
planchet.

Date	Fine	VF	XF	Unc	BU
1852 Unique	—	—	—	—	—

KM# 54 Obverse: Eagle with ribbon and shield
Reverse: Target

Date	Fine	VF	XF	Unc	BU
1852	11,500	18,500	28,500	67,500	—

KM# 56 Obverse: Large Liberty head, pointed bust
Reverse: Eagle, shield on breast

Date	Fine	VF	XF	Unc	BU
1852	4,000	9,000	17,000	52,500	—

US TERRITORIAL GOLD

10 DOLLARS

20 DOLLARS

KM# 57 **Obverse:** Liberty head with long neck, large date **Reverse:** Eagle, shield on breast

Date	Fine	VF	XF	Unc	BU
1852	4,750	9,250	17,000	—	—

KM# 60 **Obverse:** Large Liberty head **Reverse:** Eagle, shield on breast, value in banner above

Date	Fine	VF	XF	Unc	BU
1855 Rare	—	—	—	—	—

KM# 58 **Obverse:** Liberty head, short neck, wide date **Reverse:** Eagle, shield on breast

Date	Fine	VF	XF	Unc	BU
1852	2,500	4,650	7,500	27,500	—

KM# 59.1 **Obverse:** Liberty head, short neck, small date **Reverse:** Eagle, shield on breast

Date	Fine	VF	XF	Unc	BU
1852 Rare	—	—	—	—	—

Note: Eliasberg Sale May 1996, EF-45 $36,300; S.S. Central America Sale December 2000, VF-30 realized $12,650

KM# 59.2 **Obverse:** Plugged date **Reverse:** Eagle, shield on breast

Date	Fine	VF	XF	Unc	BU
1855	9,000	12,000	19,000	45,000	—

KM# 61 **Obverse:** Small head **Reverse:** Eagle, shield on breast, value in banner above

Date	Fine	VF	XF	Unc	BU
1855	12,500	22,500	35,000	—	—

Note: Heritage CSNS Sale May 2007, AU55 $43,125

US TERRITORIAL GOLD

50 DOLLARS

KM# 62 Obverse: Coronet head, left, within circle of stars, date below **Reverse:** Value within wreath

Date	Fine	VF	XF	Unc	BU
1855	20,000	30,000	50,000	—	—

Note: Heritage Baltimore Sale July-August 2008, MS-61 $207,000, AU-50 $63,250. Heritage FUN Sale January 2008, MS-60 $161,000. Bloomfield Sale December 1996, BU $170,500

COLORADO

The discovery of gold in Colorado Territory was accompanied by the inevitable need for coined money. Austin M. Clark, Milton E. Clark, and Emanuel H. Gruber, bankers of Leavenworth, Kansas, moved to Denver where they established a bank and issued $2.50, $5, $10, and $20 gold coins in 1860 and 1861. To protect the holder from loss by abrasion, **Clark, Gruber & Co.** made their coins slightly heavier than full value required. The 1860 issues carry the inscription PIKE'S PEAK GOLD on reverse. CLARK, GRUBER & CO. appears on the reverse of the 1861 issues, and PIKE'S PEAK on the coronet of Liberty. The government purchased the plant of Clark, Gruber & Co. in 1863 and operated it as a federal Assay Office until 1906.

In the summer of 1861, **John Parsons**, an assayer whose place of business was located in South Park at the Tarryall Mines, Colorado, issued undated gold coins in the denominations of $2.50 and $5. They, too, carry the inscription PIKE'S PEAK GOLD on reverse.

J. J. Conway & Co., bankers of Georgia Gulch, Colorado operated the Conway Mint for a short period in 1861. Undated gold coins in the denominations of $2.50, $5, and $10 were issued. A variety of the $5 coin does not carry the numeral 5 on reverse. The issues of the Conway Mint were highly regarded for their scrupulously maintained value.

CLARK, GRUBER & COMPANY

2-1/2 DOLLARS

KM# 63 Obverse: Coronet head, left, within circle of stars, date below **Reverse:** Eagle, shield on breast

Date	Fine	VF	XF	Unc	BU
1860	950	1,650	3,000	12,500	40,000

Note: Garrett Sale March 1980, MS-65 $12,000

KM# 64.1 Obverse: Coronet head, left, within circle of stars, date below **Reverse:** Eagle, shield on breast

Date	Fine	VF	XF	Unc	BU
1861	1,200	2,000	3,750	12,500	—

KM# 64.2 Obverse: Coronet head, left, within circle of stars, date below **Reverse:** Eagle, shield on breast
Note: Extra high edge.

Date	Fine	VF	XF	Unc	BU
1861	1,250	2,450	4,750	13,500	—

5 DOLLARS

KM# 65 Obverse: Coronet head, left, within circle of stars, date below **Reverse:** Eagle, shield on breast

Date	Fine	VF	XF	Unc	BU
1860	1,200	2,000	3,500	9,750	—

Note: Garrett Sale March 1980, MS-63 $9,000

KM# 66 Obverse: Coronet head, left, within circle of stars, date below **Reverse:** Eagle, shield on breast

Date	Fine	VF	XF	Unc	BU
1861	2,500	3,500	5,500	25,000	—

10 DOLLARS

KM# 67 Obverse: Mountain above value **Reverse:** Eagle, shield on breast

Date	Fine	VF	XF	Unc	BU
1860	5,250	8,750	14,500	40,000	—

KM# 68 Obverse: Coronet head, left, within circle of stars, date below **Reverse:** Eagle, shield on breast

Date	Fine	VF	XF	Unc	BU
1861	2,500	3,500	6,500	22,000	—

20 DOLLARS

KM# 69 Obverse: Mountain above value **Reverse:** Eagle, shield on breast

Date	Fine	VF	XF	Unc	BU
1860	50,000	100,000	175,000	400,000	—

Note: Heritage FUN Sale January 2006, MS-64 $690,000. Eliasberg Sale May 1996, AU $90,200. Schoonmaker Sale June 1997, VCF $62,700.

KM# 70 Obverse: Coronet head, left, within circle of stars, date below **Reverse:** Circle of stars and rays above eagle

Date	Fine	VF	XF	Unc	BU
1861	13,500	27,500	45,000	—	—

J. J. CONWAY

2-1/2 DOLLARS

KM# 71 Obverse: legend **Reverse:** Value in center

Date	Fine	VF	XF	Unc	BU
(1861)	—	112,500	175,000	—	—

5 DOLLARS

KM# 72.1 Obverse: Legend, ring of stars within **Reverse:** Large 5 in center

Date	Fine	VF	XF	Unc	BU
(1861) Rare	—	—	—	—	—

Note: Brand Sale June 1984, XF-40 $44,000

KM# 72.2 Obverse: Legend **Reverse:** Legend without large 5 in center

Date	Fine	VF	XF	Unc	BU
(1861) Unique	—	—	—	—	—

10 DOLLARS

KM# 73 Obverse: & CO. within circle **Reverse:** Numeral value within circle of stars

Date	Fine	VF	XF	Unc	BU
(1861) Rare	—	—	—	—	—

JOHN PARSONS

2-1/2 DOLLARS

KM# 74 Obverse: Assay office window and minting machine **Reverse:** Eagle, shield on breast, value below

Date	Fine	VF	XF	Unc	BU
(1861) Rare	—	—	—	—	—

Note: Garrett Sale March 1980, VF-20 $85,000

5 DOLLARS

KM# 75 Obverse: Assay office window and minting machine **Reverse:** Eagle, shield on breast, value below

Date	Fine	VF	XF	Unc	BU
(1861) Rare	—	—	—	—	—

Note: Garrett Sale March 1980, VF-20 $100,000

GEORGIA

The first territorial gold pieces were struck in 1830 by **Templeton Reid**, a goldsmith and assayer who established a private mint at Gainesville, Georgia, at the time gold was being mined on a relatively large scale in Georgia and North Carolina. Reid's pieces were issued in denominations of $2.50, $5, and $10. Except for an undated variety of the $10 piece, all are dated 1830.

CHRISTOPHER BECHTLER

2-1/2 DOLLARS

KM# 76.1 Obverse: 2.50 in center **Reverse:** 64. G. / 22. in center

Date	Fine	VF	XF	Unc	BU
	4,200	6,750	12,500	27,500	—

KM# 76.2 Obverse: 2.50 in center **Reverse:** 64. G. / 22. in center, even 22

Date	Fine	VF	XF	Unc	BU
	4,500	7,500	13,750	30,000	—

5 DOLLARS

KM# 77 Obverse: Value in center **Reverse:** 128 G / * in center

Date	Fine	VF	XF	Unc	BU
	4,000	7,000	11,000	28,500	—

KM# 78.1 Obverse: Value in center **Reverse:** 128. G. / * in center

Date	Fine	VF	XF	Unc	BU
	4,000	7,500	12,000	32,000	—

KM# 78.2 **Obverse:** Value in center **Reverse:** 128 G: in center

Date	Fine	VF	XF	Unc	BU
Rare	—	—	—	—	—

Note: Stack's Americana Sale January 2008 AU-58 $115,000. Akers Pittman Sale October 1997, VF-XF $26,400

TEMPLETON REID
2-1/2 DOLLARS

KM# 79 **Obverse:** Date in center **Reverse:** Value in center

Date	Fine	VF	XF	Unc	BU
1830	45,000	75,000	125,000	—	—

Note: Stack's Berngard/S.S. New York Sale July 2008 VF35 $103,500. Stack's Norweb Sale November 2006 AU55 $299,000

5 DOLLARS

KM# 80 **Obverse:** Value in center **Reverse:** Value in center

Date	Fine	VF	XF	Unc	BU
1830 Rare	—	—	—	—	—

Note: Garrett Sale November 1979, XF-40 $200,000

10 DOLLARS

KM# 81 **Obverse:** Date at center **Reverse:** Written value at center

Date	Fine	VF	XF	Unc	BU
1830 Rare	—	—	—	—	—

KM# 82 **Obverse:** Without date at center **Reverse:** Written value at center

Date	Fine	VF	XF	Unc	BU
(1830) Rare	—	—	—	—	—

Note: Also see listings under California

NORTH CAROLINA
AUGUST BECHTLER
DOLLAR

KM# 83.1 **Obverse:** Large 1 in center **Reverse:** 27. G. in center

Date	Fine	VF	XF	Unc	BU
(1842-52)	850	1,350	2,250	4,500	—

KM# 83.2 **Obverse:** Value in center **Reverse:** 27 G. in center

Date	Fine	VF	XF	Unc	BU
(1842-52)	850	1,350	2,250	4,500	—

5 DOLLARS

KM# 84 **Obverse:** Value in two lines in center **Reverse:** 134 G. at center

Date	Fine	VF	XF	Unc	BU
(1842-52)	2,650	5,300	9,000	32,500	—

KM# 85 **Obverse:** Value in two lines in center **Reverse:** 128 G. in center

Date	Fine	VF	XF	Unc	BU
(1842-52)	6,000	11,000	16,000	39,000	—

KM# 86 **Obverse:** Value in two lines in center **Reverse:** 141. G: in center

Date	Fine	VF	XF	Unc	BU
(1842-52)	5,500	9,700	15,000	37,500	—

Date	Fine	VF	XF	Unc	BU
(1842-52) Proof restrike	—	—	—	—	—

Note: Struck from original dies by Henry Chapman in 1908. Stack's Nerngard/S.S. New York Sale July 2008 Pr63 sold for $34,500. Akers Pittman Sale October 1997 chPr $14,300

CHRISTOPHER BECHTLER

DOLLAR

KM# 87   Obverse: 28 G. in center **Reverse:** ONE in center, N reversed

Date	Fine	VF	XF	Unc	BU
(1831-42)	1,250	2,200	3,000	7,500	—

KM# 88.1   Obverse: 28. G. centered in center **Reverse:** ONE at center

Date	Fine	VF	XF	Unc	BU
(1831-42)	2,400	4,000	6,000	24,000	—

KM# 88.2   Obverse: 28 G high in center **Reverse:** ONE in center

Date	Fine	VF	XF	Unc	BU
(1831-42)	5,000	8,500	12,500	32,500	—

KM# 89   Obverse: 30 G. /* in center **Reverse:** ONE at center

Date	Fine	VF	XF	Unc	BU
(1831-42)	1,650	2,750	4,250	15,000	—

2-1/2 DOLLARS

KM# 90   Obverse: 250 in center **Reverse:** 67 G. 21 CARATS at center

Date	Fine	VF	XF	Unc	BU
(1831-42)	2,500	5,500	11,500	25,000	—

Note: Stack's Old Coloney Sale December 2005 MS62 $23,000

KM# 91   Obverse: 250 in center **Reverse:** 70 G. 20 CARATS at center

Date	Fine	VF	XF	Unc	BU
(1831-42)	2,750	5,500	12,000	29,500	—

Note: Stack's Norweb Sale November 2006 MS60 $26,450. Stack's Allison Park Sale August 2004 MS62 $28,750. Bowers and Merena Long Sale May 1995, MS-63 $31,900

KM# 92.1   Obverse: RUTHERFORD in a circle, border of large beads **Reverse:** 250 / 20 C. / 75 G. in center

Date	Fine	VF	XF	Unc	BU
(1831-42)	12,500	22,500	34,500	75,000	—

KM# 92.2   Obverse: RUTHERFORD in circle **Reverse:** 250. / wide 20 C. in center

Date	Fine	VF	XF	Unc	BU
(1831-42)	15,000	25,000	35,000	85,000	—

Note: Stack's Norweb Sale November 2006 MS62 $83,375

KM# 93.1   Obverse: RUTHERFORD in a circle **Reverse:** 250 / 20 G in center

Date	Fine	VF	XF	Unc	BU
(1831-42) Unique	—	—	—	—	—

KM# 93.2   Obverse: * / 75 G in center, border finely serrated **Reverse:** 250. / 20 G. in center

Date	Fine	VF	XF	Unc	BU
(1831-42) Rare	—	—	—	—	—

5 DOLLARS

KM# 94 Obverse: two-line value in center **Reverse:** 134 G. / * in center

Date	Fine	VF	XF	Unc	BU
(1831-42)	2,750	5,500	8,500	22,500	—

KM# 95 Obverse: Two-line value in center **Reverse:** 134. G at center, 21 above CARATS, no star

Date	Fine	VF	XF	Unc	BU
(1831-42) Unique	—	—	—	—	—

KM# 96.1 Obverse: Value in center **Reverse:** 140 G. in center

Date	Fine	VF	XF	Unc	BU
1834	2,250	4,500	7,500	22,500	—

KM# 96.2 Obverse: Value in center **Reverse:** 140. G. in center

Date	Fine	VF	XF	Unc	BU
1834	6,500	12,500	20,000	60,000	—

KM# 97.1 Obverse: Value at center **Reverse:** 140 / G / in center, 20 close to CARATS

Date	Fine	VF	XF	Unc	BU
1834	3,500	7,500	12,500	33,500	—

KM# 97.2 Obverse: Value in center **Reverse:** 140 / G in center, 20 far away from CARATS

Date	Fine	VF	XF	Unc	BU
1834	2,500	6,500	11,500	32,500	—

Note: Stack's Berngard/S.S. New York Sale July 2008 AU58 $29,900

KM# 98 Obverse: Value in center **Reverse:** 141. G: in center

Date	Fine	VF	XF	Unc	BU
(1831-42) Proof restrike	—	—	—	—	—

Note: Struck from original dies by Henry Chapman in 1908. Heritage ANA Sale Auguust 2007 Pr65 $37,375

KM# 99.1 Obverse: Legend in double circle **Reverse:** 5 / DOLLARS / 20 CARATS / 150 G in center

Date	Fine	VF	XF	Unc	BU
(1831-42)	12,000	20,000	35,000	85,000	—

Note: Stack's Berngard/S.S. New York Sale July 2008 AU50 $69,000. Stack's Americana Sale January 2008 AU55 $74,750. Heritage ANA Sale August 2007 MS62 $97,750

KM# 99.2 Obverse: Legend in two circles **Reverse:** 5 / DOLLARS / 20 CARATS. in center

Date	Fine	VF	XF	Unc	BU
(1831-42) Rare	—	—	—	—	—

OREGON

OREGON EXCHANGE COMPANY

5 DOLLARS

KM# 100 Obverse: Beaver above date and sprigs **Reverse:** Weight and value in center

Date	Fine	VF	XF	Unc	BU
1849	22,500	37,500	70,000	—	—

Note: Heritage Internet Sale February 2009 AU53 $69,000. Heritage FUN Sale January 2009 VF25 $37,375

10 DOLLARS

KM# 101   Obverse: Beaver above date and sprigs **Reverse:** Weight and value within wreath

Date	Fine	VF	XF	Unc	BU
1849	65,000	125,000	225,000	—	—

Note: Heritage Long Beach Sale September 2002 XF40 $126,500

UTAH

MORMON ISSUES

2-1/2 DOLLARS

KM# 102   Obverse: Hat design above eye **Reverse:** Clasped hands above date

Date	Fine	VF	XF	Unc	BU
1849	8,000	13,500	25,000	65,000	—

5 DOLLARS

KM# 103   Obverse: Hat design above eye **Reverse:** Clasped hands above date

Date	Fine	VF	XF	Unc	BU
1849	7,500	12,500	22,500	55,000	—

KM# 104   Obverse: Hat design above eye and stars **Reverse:** Clasped hands above date

Date	Fine	VF	XF	Unc	BU
1850	8,500	15,000	25,000	65,000	—

Note: Heritage Long Beach Sale February 2009 MS61 $54,625

KM# 105   Obverse: Seated lion facing left above date **Reverse:** Beehive design on eagle breast

Date	Fine	VF	XF	Unc	BU
1860	12,500	25,000	45,000	85,000	—

Note: Heritage Los Angeles Sale August 2009 AU55 $63,250. Stack's Bergstrom/Husky Sale June 2008 MS61 $74,750

10 DOLLARS

KM# 106   Obverse: Hat design above eye **Reverse:** Clasped hands above date

Date	Fine	VF	XF	Unc	BU
1849		150,000	250,000	350,000	—	—

Note: Heritage ANA Sale July 1988, AU $93,000

20 DOLLARS

KM# 107   Obverse: Hat design above eye **Reverse:** Clasped hands above date

Date	Fine	VF	XF	Unc	BU
1849	65,000	125,000	200,000	—	—

Note: Stack's Old West Sale August 2006 XF45 $207,000

HAWAII

Hawaii, the 50th state, consists of eight main islands and numerous smaller islets of coral and volcanic origin. Situated in the central Pacific Ocean, 2,400 miles from San Francisco, the Hawaiian archipelago has an area of 6,450 square miles. Capital: Honolulu. The principal sources of income are in order: tourism, defense, and agriculture.

The Hawaiian Islands, originally populated by Polynesians from the Society Islands, were rediscovered by British navigator Capt. James Cook in 1778. He named them the Sandwich Islands. King Kamehameha I (the Great) united the islands under one kingdom, which endured until 1893, when Queen Lilioukalani was deposed and a provisional government established. This was followed in 1894 by a republic, which governed Hawaii until 1898, when the islands were ceded to the United States. Hawaii was organized as a territory in 1900 and attained statehood on Aug. 21, 1959.

Official coinage issued under the Kingdom of Hawaii was limited. The 1847 cent or Hapa Haneri coins were ordered by the Minister of Finance through an agent by the name of James Jackson Jarves. Jarves contracted the striking of 100,000 large copper coins from an unknown firm located somewhere in New England. The lack of acceptance by merchants limited the success of the 1847 coppers, which lead to a long gap before the next Hawaiian coinage issue in 1883.

The 1883 Kingdom coinage was contracted through Claus Spreckels, with circulation coins being struck at the San Francisco Mint. Very limited numbers of proof strikes were completed at the Philadelphia Mint, where Charles E. Barber designed these coins. Weights and measures on the 1883 Hawaiian coinage are the same as standard U.S. coins of the time period.

RULERS
Kamehameha I, 1795-1819
Kamehameha II, 1819-1824
Kamehameha III, 1825-1854
Kamehameha IV, 1854-1863
Kamehameha V, 1863-1872
Lunalilo, 1873-1874
Kalakaua, 1874-1891
Liliuokalani, 1891-1893
Provisional Government, 1893-1894
Republic, 1894-1898
Annexed to U.S., 1898-1900
Territory, 1900-1959

MONETARY SYSTEM
100 Hapa Haneri - Akahi Dala
100 Cents - 1 Dollar (Dala)

Date	Mintage	VG	F	VF	XF	Unc
1847	Inc. above	550	800	1,500	2,000	—

Note: Plain 4, 15 berries (7 left, 8 right)

KM# 1a CENT
Copper **Ruler:** Kamehameha III **Obv:** Uniformed bust, facing **Obv. Legend:** KAMEHAMEHA III.KA.MOI. **Rev:** Value within wreath **Rev. Legend:** AUPUNI HAWAII

Date	Mintage	VG	F	VF	XF	Unc
1847 Plain 4, 13 berries (6 left, 7 right)	100,000	200	275	350	500	900

KM# 1b CENT
Copper **Ruler:** Kamehameha III **Obv:** Uniformed bust, facing **Obv. Legend:** KAMEHAMEHA III.KA.MOI. **Rev:** Value within wreath **Rev. Legend:** AUPUNI HAWAII

Date	Mintage	VG	F	VF	XF	Unc
1847	Inc. above	200	275	350	500	950

Note: Plain 4, 15 berries (8 left, 7 right)

KM# 1f CENT
Copper **Ruler:** Kamehameha III **Obv:** Uniformed bust, facing **Obv. Legend:** KAMEHAMEHA III.KA.MOI. **Rev:** Value within wreath **Rev. Legend:** AUPUNI HAWAII

KM# 1c CENT
Copper **Ruler:** Kamehameha III **Obv:** Uniformed bust, facing **Obv. Legend:** KAMEHAMEHA III.KA.MOI. **Rev:** Value within wreath **Rev. Legend:** AUPUNI HAWAII

Date	Mintage	VG	F	VF	XF	Unc
1847	Inc. above	200	275	375	600	1,200

Note: Plain 4, 17 berries (8 left, 9 right)

KM# 1d CENT
Copper **Ruler:** Kamehameha III **Obv:** Uniformed bust, facing **Obv. Legend:** KAMEHAMEHA III.KA.MOI. **Rev:** Value within wreath **Rev. Legend:** AUPUNI HAWAII

Date	Mintage	VG	F	VF	XF	Unc
1847	Inc. above	200	275	350	500	950

Note: Crosslet 4, 15 berries (7 left, 8 right)

KM# 1e CENT
Copper **Ruler:** Kamehameha III **Obv:** Uniformed bust, facing **Obv. Legend:** KAMEHAMEHA III.KA.MOI. **Rev:** Value within wreath **Rev. Legend:** AUPUNI HAWAII

Date	Mintage	VG	F	VF	XF	Unc
1847	Inc. above	250	400	550	850	3,500

Note: Crosslet 4, 18 berries (9 left, 9 right)

KM# 2 5 CENTS (Pattern)
Nickel **Ruler:** Kalakaua I **Obv:** Head left, date below **Obv. Legend:** KALAKAUA KING OF SANDWICH ISLANDS **Rev:** Value within crowned belt

Date	Mintage	VG	F	VF	XF	Unc
1881	200	4,500	5,500	7,500	12,000	17,000

Note: All original specimens of this pattern were struck on thin nickel planchets, presumably in Paris and have "MAILLECHORT" stamped on the edge. In the early 1900's, deceptive replicas of the issue were produced in Canada, on thick and thin nickel and aluminum, and thin copper planchets (thick about 2.7 to 3.1mm; thin about 1.4 to 1.7mm). The original patterns can be easily distinguished from the replicas, because on the former, a small cross surmounts the crown on the reverse; on the replicas the originals have a cross, the replicas do not.

KM# 3 10 CENTS (Umi Keneta)
2.5000 g., 0.9000 Silver 0.0723 oz. ASW **Ruler:** Kalakaua I **Obv:** Head right, date below **Obv. Legend:** KALAKAUA I KING OF HAWAII **Rev:** Crown and value within wreath

Date	Mintage	VG	F	VF	XF	Unc
1883	250,000	45.00	60.00	95.00	250	1,000
1883 Proof	26	Value: 7,500				

KM# 4a 1/8 DOLLAR (Hapawalu)
Copper **Ruler:** Kalakaua I **Obv:** Head right **Obv. Legend:** KALAKAUA I KING OF HAWAII **Note:** Pattern issue.

Date	Mintage	VG	F	VF	XF	Unc
1883 Proof	18	Value: 20,000				

KM# 4 1/8 DOLLAR (Hapawalu)
0.9000 Silver **Ruler:** Kalakaua I **Obv:** Head right **Obv. Legend:** KALAKAUA I KING OF HAWAII **Note:** Pattern issue.

Date	Mintage	VG	F	VF	XF	Unc
1883 Proof	20	Value: 50,000				

KM# 5 1/4 DOLLAR (Hapaha)
6.2200 g., 0.9000 Silver 0.1800 oz. ASW **Ruler:** Kalakaua I **Obv:** Head right, date below **Obv. Legend:** KALAKAUA I KING OF HAWAII **Rev:** Crowned arms divides value **Rev. Legend:** UA MAU KE...

Date	Mintage	VG	F	VF	XF	Unc
1883	500,000	40.00	55.00	70.00	100	200
1883/1383	Inc. above	45.00	65.00	95.00	150	300
1883 Proof	26	Value: 10,000				

KM# 5a 1/4 DOLLAR (Hapaha)
Copper **Ruler:** Kalakaua I **Obv:** Head right, date below **Obv. Legend:** KALAKAUA I KING OF HAWAII **Rev:** Crowned arms divides value **Rev. Legend:** UA MAU KE... **Note:** Pattern issue.

Date	Mintage	VG	F	VF	XF	Unc
1883 Proof	18	Value: 8,500				

KM# 6 1/2 DOLLAR (Hapalua)
12.5000 g., 0.9000 Silver 0.3617 oz. ASW **Ruler:** Kalakaua I **Obv:** Head right, date below **Obv. Legend:** KALAKAUA I KING OF HAWAII **Rev:** Crowned arms divides value **Rev. Legend:** UA MAU KE...

Date	Mintage	VG	F	VF	XF	Unc
1883	700,000	100	125	175	300	1,200
1883 Proof	26	Value: 12,000				

KM# 6a   1/2 DOLLAR (Hapalua)
Copper   **Ruler:** Kalakaua I **Obv:** Head right, date below **Obv. Legend:** KALAKAUA I KING OF HAWAII **Rev:** Crowned arms divides value **Rev. Legend:** UA MAU KE... **Note:** Pattern issue.

Date	Mintage	VG	F	VF	XF	Unc
1883 Proof	18	Value: 10,000				

KM# 7a   DOLLAR (Akahi Dala)
Copper   **Ruler:** Kalakaua I **Obv:** Head right, date below **Obv. Legend:** KALAKAUA I KING OF HAWAII **Rev:** Crowned arms with supporters within crowned mantle **Rev. Legend:** UA MAU KE... **Note:** Pattern issue.

Date	Mintage	VG	F	VF	XF	Unc
1883 Proof	18	Value: 15,000				

Note: Official records indicate the following quantities of the above issues were redeemed and melted: KM#1 - 88,405; KM#3 - 79; KM#5 - 257,400; KM#6 - 612,245; KM#7 - 453,652. That leaves approximate net mintages of: KM#1 - 11,600; KM#3 - 250,000; KM#5 (regular date) - 242,600, (unknown) 40,000; KM#6 - 87,700; KM#7 - 46,300.

KM# 7   DOLLAR (Akahi Dala)
26.7300 g., 0.9000 Silver 0.7734 oz. ASW   **Ruler:** Kalakaua I **Obv:** Head right, date below **Obv. Legend:** KALAKAUA I KING OF HAWAII **Rev:** Crowned arms with supporters within crowned mantle **Rev. Legend:** UA MAU KE...

Date	Mintage	VG	F	VF	XF	Unc
1883	500,000	275	350	500	800	4,000
1883 Proof	26	Value: 15,000				

PHILIPPINES

UNITED STATES ADMINISTRATION

1899-1946

The Philippines, an archipelago in the western Pacific 500 miles (805 km.) from the southeast coast of Asia, has an area of 115,830 square miles (300,000 sq. km.) and a current population of 64.9 million. Its capital city is Manila. From its acquisition in 1898 until 1992, the U.S. has had a military presence in the Philippines.

Migration to the Philippines began about 30,000 years ago when land bridges connected the islands with Borneo and Sumatra. Ferdinand Magellan claimed the islands for Spain in 1521. Miguel de Legazpi established the first permanent settlement at Cebu in April 1565. Manila was established in 1572. A British expedition captured Manila and occupied the Spanish colony in October 1762, but returned it to Spain by the treaty of Paris, 1763. Spain held the Philippines despite growing Filipino nationalism until 1898 when they were ceded to the United States at the end of the Spanish-American War.

A military government was established on the Islands until a civil administration was put in place in 1901. The Philippines became a self-governing commonwealth under the United States in 1935. In 1942, during the Second World War, the Philippines were occupied by the Japanese. U.S forces and Filipinos both fought during 1944-45 to regain control of the Islands. On July 4, 1946, the Philippines became an independent Republic.

The coins listed here were issued under United States Administration of the Philippines. Coins dated 1903 to 1919 were struck at both the Philadelphia and San Francisco Mints, while coins dated 1920 and after were produced at the Manila Mint in the Philippines. With Japanese forces advancing in 1942, much of the Philippine Treasury's silver coinage was returned to the United States for safekeeping. Coinage that remained at the Mint in Manila was crated and dumped in the bay before the Japanese arrived. During the struggle to regain control of the Philippines near the end of WWII, coins dated 1944 to 1945 were struck by the U.S. Mint at Denver, San Francisco and Philadelphia.

Symbolically the first series of U.S. Philippines coins with its American eagle perched on a stars and stripes shield places emphasis on U.S. dominance of the islands. The second series, struck under Commonwealth authority began the move towards independence by placing a new Commonwealth of the Philippines shield on the reverses of all denominations.

MINT MARKS
D - Denver, 1944-1945
S - San Francisco, 1903-1947
M – Manila, 1920-1941

MONETARY SYSTEM
4 Quartos = 1 Real
8 Reales = 1 Peso
1 Peso = 100 Centavos

DECIMAL COINAGE

KM# 162 1/2 CENTAVO
Bronze **Obv:** Man seated beside hammer and anvil
Rev: Eagle above stars and striped shield

Date	Mintage	F	VF	XF	Unc	BU
1903	12,084,000	0.50	1.00	2.00	10.00	20.00
1903 Proof	2,558	Value: 65.00				
1904	5,654,000	0.50	1.25	2.00	15.00	35.00
1904 Proof	1,355	Value: 85.00				
1905 Proof	471	Value: 350				
1906 Proof	500	Value: 200				
1908 Proof	500	Value: 200				

KM# 163 CENTAVO
4.7000 g., Bronze **Obv:** Man seated beside hammer and anvil **Rev:** Eagle above stars and striped shield

Date	Mintage	F	VF	XF	Unc	BU
1903	10,790,000	0.50	1.25	2.50	20.00	40.00
1903 Proof	2,558	Value: 75.00				

Date	Mintage	F	VF	XF	Unc	BU
1904	17,040,000	0.50	1.25	2.50	15.00	30.00
1904 Proof	1,355	Value: 85.00				
1905	10,000,000	0.50	1.50	2.00	25.00	45.00
1905 Proof	471	Value: 175				
1906 Proof	500	Value: 150				
1908 Proof	500	Value: 150				
1908S	2,187,000	2.50	4.00	11.00	60.00	90.00
1909S	1,738,000	7.00	12.00	25.00	100	150
1910S	2,700,000	2.00	5.00	10.00	55.00	80.00
1911S	4,803,000	1.00	3.00	6.50	30.00	60.00
1912S	3,000,000	3.00	7.00	12.50	80.00	125
1913S	5,000,000	2.00	4.00	7.00	40.00	75.00
1914S	5,000,000	1.00	2.50	5.00	40.00	75.00
1915S	2,500,000	20.00	30.00	95.00	600	1,300
1916S	4,330,000	6.00	12.50	25.00	120	150
1917/6S	7,070,000	35.00	65.00	150	375	550
1917S	Inc. above	3.00	4.50	7.50	30.00	90.00
1918S	11,660,000	2.00	4.00	10.00	70.00	150
1918S Large S	Inc. above	100	175	300	1,300	1,900
1919S	4,540,000	0.75	2.50	6.50	60.00	125
1920S	2,500,000	4.50	9.50	15.00	150	300
1920	3,552,000	1.00	5.00	10.00	125	250
1921	7,283,000	0.75	3.50	5.00	50.00	100
1922	3,519,000	0.50	2.50	9.00	75.00	125
1925M	9,332,000	0.50	3.00	7.50	25.00	65.00
1926M	9,000,000	0.50	2.25	5.00	20.00	60.00
1927M	9,270,000	0.35	2.00	6.00	30.00	60.00
1928M	9,150,000	0.35	2.00	4.00	35.00	75.00
1929M	5,657,000	1.00	3.00	6.00	35.00	85.00
1930M	5,577,000	0.50	2.00	4.50	30.00	65.00
1931M	5,659,000	0.50	2.50	4.50	25.00	55.00
1932M	4,000,000	0.75	2.50	6.00	40.00	65.00
1933M	8,393,000	0.25	2.00	4.00	20.00	50.00
1934M	3,179,000	0.75	2.50	10.00	60.00	90.00
1936M	17,455,000	0.25	2.00	5.00	40.00	75.00

KM# 164   5 CENTAVOS
Copper-Nickel, 21.3 mm.   **Obv:** Man seated beside hammer and anvil **Rev:** Eagle above stars and striped shield

Date	Mintage	F	VF	XF	Unc	BU
1903	8,910,000	0.50	1.25	2.25	25.00	35.00
1903 Proof	2,558	Value: 85.00				
1904	1,075,000	0.75	2.00	5.00	27.00	40.00
1904 Proof	1,355	Value: 95.00				
1905 Proof	471	Value: 175				
1906 Proof	500	Value: 150				
1908 Proof	500	Value: 150				
1916S	300,000	35.00	60.00	125	600	1,100
1917S	2,300,000	2.00	5.00	10.00	125	250
1918/7S	—	3.00	9.00	18.50	150	—
1918S	2,780,000	2.00	6.00	12.50	120	200
1919S	1,220,000	2.50	10.00	15.50	150	300
1920	1,421,000	3.00	7.50	12.50	150	250
1921	2,132,000	2.00	5.00	10.00	90.00	180
1925M	1,000,000	10.00	17.50	25.00	160	250
1926M	1,200,000	5.00	6.50	17.50	125	175
1927M	1,000,000	2.00	5.00	8.50	55.00	100
1928M	1,000,000	3.00	5.00	7.50	50.00	75.00

KM# 173   5 CENTAVOS
Copper-Nickel **Obv:** Man seated beside hammer and anvil **Rev:** Eagle above stars and striped shield **Note:** Mule.

Date	Mintage	F	VF	XF	Unc	BU
1918S	—	250	600	1,750	4,000	8,000

KM# 175   5 CENTAVOS
4.7500 g., Copper-Nickel, 19 mm.   **Obv:** Man seated beside hammer and anvil **Rev:** Eagle above stars and striped shield

Date	Mintage	F	VF	XF	Unc	BU
1930M	2,905,000	1.00	2.50	5.00	35.00	65.00
1931M	3,477,000	1.00	2.70	5.00	50.00	75.00
1932M	3,956,000	1.00	2.50	4.50	40.00	60.00
1934M	2,154,000	1.00	3.50	7.00	65.00	125
1935M	2,754,000	1.00	1.75	6.50	80.00	120

KM# 165   10 CENTAVOS
2.6924 g., 0.9000 Silver 0.0779 oz. ASW   **Obv:** Female standing beside hammer and anvil **Rev:** Eagle above stars and striped shield

Date	Mintage	F	VF	XF	Unc	BU
1903	5,103,000	1.25	3.00	5.00	35.00	60.00
1903 Proof	2,558	Value: 85.00				
1903S	1,200,000	11.00	17.50	30.00	350	800
1904	11,000	15.00	25.00	35.00	80.00	135
1904 Proof	1,355	Value: 80.00				
1904S	5,040,000	1.50	3.50	5.00	50.00	95.00
1905 Proof	471	Value: 150				
1906 Proof	500	Value: 125				

KM# 169   10 CENTAVOS
2.0000 g., 0.7500 Silver 0.0482 oz. ASW   **Obv:** Female standing beside hammer and anvil **Rev:** Eagle above stars and striped shield

Date	Mintage	F	VF	XF	Unc	BU
1907	1,501,000	1.50	4.00	6.00	40.00	95.00
1907S	4,930,000	1.25	2.00	3.00	40.00	75.00
1908 Proof	500	Value: 125				
1908S	3,364,000	1.25	2.00	4.00	35.00	75.00
1909S	312,000	15.00	27.50	75.00	400	900
1910S	—	—	—			

Note: Unknown in any collection. Counterfeits of the 1910S are commonly encountered

1911S	1,101,000	3.00	6.50	15.00	125	300
1912S	1,010,000	2.25	6.00	14.00	125	260
1913S	1,361,000	1.50	5.00	9.00	110	200
1914S	1,180,000	2.00	5.00	15.00	175	300
1915S	450,000	6.00	24.00	35.00	300	650
1917S	5,991,000	1.00	1.50	4.00	40.00	65.00
1918S	8,420,000	1.00	1.50	3.00	25.00	40.00
1919S	1,630,000	1.25	2.00	5.00	45.00	90.00
1920	520,000	4.50	6.50	12.50	85.00	200
1921	3,863,000	1.00	1.50	2.75	25.00	40.00
1929M	1,000,000	1.25	1.50	5.00	25.00	35.00
1935M	1,280,000	1.25	1.50	2.25	20.00	30.00

KM# 166   20 CENTAVOS
5.3849 g., 0.9000 Silver 0.1558 oz. ASW   **Obv:** Female standing beside hammer and anvil **Rev:** Eagle above stars and striped shield

Date	Mintage	F	VF	XF	Unc	BU
1903	5,353,000	1.75	2.50	6.00	40.00	90.00
1903 Proof	2,558	Value: 125				
1903S	150,000	10.00	20.00	60.00	750	1,100
1904	11,000	16.00	30.00	40.00	100	175
1904 Proof	1,355	Value: 125				
1904S	2,060,000	3.00	5.00	12.50	100	175
1905 Proof	471	Value: 200				
1905S	420,000	7.50	15.00	35.00	200	700
1906 Proof	500	Value: 150				

KM# 170 20 CENTAVOS
4.0000 g., 0.7500 Silver 0.0964 oz. ASW **Obv:**
Female standing beside hammer and anvil **Rev:** Eagle
above stars and striped shield

Date	Mintage	F	VF	XF	Unc	BU
1907	1,251,000	2.25	4.00	10.00	125	200
1907S	3,165,000	2.25	3.00	6.00	35.00	125
1908 Proof	500	Value: 200				
1908S	1,535,000	2.25	4.50	12.50	60.00	125
1909S	450,000	10.00	30.00	75.00	375	950
1910S	500,000	15.00	25.00	70.00	400	950
1911S	505,000	10.00	30.00	60.00	275	850
1912S	750,000	5.00	15.00	35.00	200	350
1913S/S	949,000	9.00	20.00	50.00	250	400
1913S	Inc. above	3.00	7.50	15.00	175	300
1914S	795,000	3.50	8.00	25.00	200	450
1915S	655,000	12.50	17.50	45.00	425	950
1916S	1,435,000	6.00	10.00	20.00	125	225
1917S	3,151,000	1.75	3.00	5.00	45.00	85.00
1918S	5,560,000	1.75	2.50	5.00	35.00	75.00
1919S	850,000	1.75	5.00	10.00	100	200
1920	1,046,000	2.50	5.00	15.00	125	175
1921	1,843,000	BV	2.00	7.00	75.00	100
1929M	1,970,000	BV	2.50	5.00	25.00	50.00

KM# 171 50 CENTAVOS
10.0000 g., 0.7500 Silver 0.2411 oz. ASW **Obv:**
Female standing beside hammer and anvil **Rev:** Eagle
above stars and striped shield

Date	Mintage	F	VF	XF	Unc	BU
1907	1,201,000	6.00	11.00	40.00	200	450
1907S	2,112,000	4.00	8.00	35.00	125	300
1908 Proof	500	Value: 250				
1908S	1,601,000	5.00	10.00	30.00	250	2,000
1909S	528,000	6.00	15.00	70.00	300	800
1917S	674,000	10.00	15.00	25.00	150	300
1918S	2,202,000	4.00	5.00	10.00	100	150
1919S	1,200,000	4.00	5.00	14.00	125	175
1920	420,000	4.00	5.50	11.00	35.00	95.00
1921	2,317,000	BV	4.00	6.00	30.00	60.00

KM# 174 20 CENTAVOS
4.0000 g., 0.7500 Silver 0.0964 oz. ASW **Obv:**
Female standing beside hammer and anvil **Rev:** Eagle
above stars and striped shield **Note:** Mule.

Date	Mintage	F	VF	XF	Unc	BU
1928M	100,000	5.00	15.00	50.00	800	1,300

KM# 168 PESO
26.9568 g., 0.9000 Silver 0.7800 oz. ASW **Obv:**
Female standing beside hammer and anvil **Rev:** Eagle
above stars and striped shield

Date	Mintage	F	VF	XF	Unc	BU
1903	2,791,000	16.00	20.00	27.00	125	450
1903 Proof	2,558	Value: 250				
1903S	11,361,000	15.00	18.00	25.00	110	175
1904	11,000	65.00	75.00	110	265	400
1904 Proof	1,355	Value: 325				
1904S	6,600,000	15.00	18.00	25.00	160	240
1905S	6,056,000	15.00	25.00	35.00	225	350
curved serif on 1						
1905S	—	30.00	45.00	75.00	500	2,000
straight serif on 1						
1905 Proof	471	Value: 1,000				
1906 Proof	500	Value: 900				
1906S	201,000	1,000	1,600	2,600	16,000	30,000

Note: Counterfeits of the 1906S exist

KM# 167 50 CENTAVOS
13.4784 g., 0.9000 Silver 0.3900 oz. ASW **Obv:**
Female standing beside hammer and anvil **Rev:** Eagle
above stars and striped shield

Date	Mintage	F	VF	XF	Unc	BU
1903	3,102,000	4.00	6.50	11.00	55.00	85.00
1903 Proof	2,558	Value: 150				
1903S 2 Known	—	—	—	22,000	—	—
1904	11,000	25.00	40.00	70.00	125	225
1904 Proof	1,355	Value: 175				
1904S	2,160,000	5.00	11.00	15.00	125	200
1905 Proof	471	Value: 300				
1905S	852,000	8.00	17.50	35.00	600	2,000
1906 Proof	500	Value: 275				

KM# 180 5 CENTAVOS
4.8000 g., Copper-Nickel **Obv:** Male seated beside hammer and anvil **Rev:** Eagle with wings open above shield

Date	Mintage	F	VF	XF	Unc	BU
1937M	2,494,000	1.00	2.50	5.50	45.00	75.00
1938M	4,000,000	0.50	1.25	2.50	20.00	35.00
1941M	2,750,000	1.00	2.50	6.00	40.00	90.00

KM# 180a 5 CENTAVOS
4.9200 g., Copper-Nickel-Zinc, 19 mm. **Obv:** Male seated beside hammer and anvil **Rev:** Eagle with wings open above shield

Date	Mintage	F	VF	XF	Unc	BU
1944	21,198,000	—	0.50	1.00	2.00	3.00
1944S	14,040,000	—	0.25	0.30	1.25	2.50
1945S	72,796,000	—	0.25	0.30	1.00	2.50

KM# 172 PESO
20.0000 g., 0.8000 Silver 0.5144 oz. ASW **Obv:** Female standing beside hammer and anvil **Rev:** Eagle above stars and striped shield

Date	Mintage	F	VF	XF	Unc	BU
1907 Proof, 2 known	—	—	—	—	—	—
1907S	10,276,000	6.50	8.00	10.00	75.00	125
1908 Proof	500	Value: 750				
1908S	20,955,000	6.00	8.00	10.00	75.00	125
1909S	7,578,000	7.50	10.00	15.00	90.00	140
1910S	3,154,000	10.00	12.50	25.00	250	525
1911S	463,000	20.00	30.00	65.00	750	2,700
1912S	680,000	20.00	35.00	80.00	1,500	6,500

KM# 181 10 CENTAVOS
2.0000 g., 0.7500 Silver 0.0482 oz. ASW, 16.7 mm. **Obv:** Female standing beside hammer and anvil **Rev:** Eagle with wings open above shield

Date	Mintage	F	VF	XF	Unc	BU
1937M	3,500,000	1.00	2.00	3.00	20.00	30.00
1938M	3,750,000	BV	1.00	2.00	12.50	18.00
1941M	2,500,000	BV	1.50	2.50	10.00	15.00
1944D	31,592,000	—	—	BV	2.00	3.50
1945D	137,208,000	—	—	BV	2.00	3.00

Note: 1937, 1938, and 1941 dated strikes have inverted W's for M's

UNITED STATES ADMINISTRATION

Commonwealth

DECIMAL COINAGE

KM# 179 CENTAVO
5.3000 g., Bronze, 25 mm. **Obv:** Male seated beside hammer and anvil **Rev:** Eagle above shield

Date	Mintage	F	VF	XF	Unc	BU
1937M	15,790,000	0.25	2.00	3.00	20.00	35.00
1938M	10,000,000	0.25	1.50	3.00	15.00	25.00
1939M	6,500,000	0.25	2.00	4.00	30.00	50.00
1940M	4,000,000	0.25	1.25	2.25	15.00	25.00
1941M	5,000,000	0.25	2.00	3.50	20.00	35.00
1944S	58,000,000	—	0.25	0.50	1.50	3.00

KM# 182 20 CENTAVOS
4.0000 g., 0.7500 Silver 0.0964 oz. ASW, 21 mm. **Obv:** Female standing beside hammer and anvil **Rev:** Eagle with wings open above shield

Date	Mintage	F	VF	XF	Unc	BU
1937M	2,665,000	BV	1.75	3.00	20.00	35.00
1938M	3,000,000	BV	1.50	2.50	12.00	20.00
1941M	1,500,000	BV	1.50	2.50	10.00	20.00
1944D	28,596,000	—	—	BV	2.00	3.00
1944D/S	—	12.00	16.50	17.50	40.00	50.00
1945D	82,804,000	—	—	BV	2.00	3.00

KM# 176   50 CENTAVOS
10.0000 g., 0.7500 Silver 0.2411 oz. ASW, 27.5 mm.
Subject: Establishment of the Commonwealth **Obv:**
Busts facing each other **Rev:** Eagle above shield
Designer: Ambrosia Morales

Date	Mintage	F	VF	XF	Unc	BU
1936	20,000	—	30.00	65.00	110	150

KM# 178   PESO
20.0000 g., 0.9000 Silver 0.5787 oz. ASW, 35 mm.
Subject: Establishment of the Commonwealth **Obv:**
Conjoined busts left **Rev:** Eagle with wings open
above shield **Designer:** Ambrosia Morales

Date	Mintage	F	VF	XF	Unc	BU
1936	10,000	—	50.00	75.00	150	250

KM# 183   50 CENTAVOS
10.0000 g., 0.7500 Silver 0.2411 oz. ASW, 27.5 mm.
Obv: Female standing beside hammer and anvil **Rev:**
Eagle with wings open above shield

Date	Mintage	F	VF	XF	Unc	BU
1944S	19,187,000	—	—	BV	5.00	7.50
1945S	18,120,000	—	—	BV	5.00	7.50
1945S	18,120,000	—	—	BV	5.00	7.50

KM# 177   PESO
20.0000 g., 0.9000 Silver 0.5787 oz. ASW, 35 mm.
Subject: Establishment of the Commonwealth **Obv:**
Conjoined busts left **Rev:** Eagle with wings open
above shield **Designer:** Ambrosia Morales

Date	Mintage	F	VF	XF	Unc	BU
1936	10,000	—	50.00	75.00	150	250

PUERTO RICO

The Commonwealth of Puerto Rico, the eastern-most island of the Greater Antilles in the West Indies, has an area of approximately 3,435 square miles (9,104 sq. km.), with sandy beaches on the costal areas and much mountainous territory inland. Puerto Rico's capital, San Juan, affords the island one of the best natural harbors in the Caribbean and has become an important stop on the Mona Passage shipping route to the Panama Canal.

Columbus discovered Puerto Rico (*Rich Port*) and took possession for Spain on Nov. 19, 1493 - the only time Columbus set foot on the soil of what is now a possession of the United States. The first settlement, Caparra, was established by Ponce de Leon in 1508. The early years of the colony were not promising. Considerable gold was found, but the supply was soon exhausted. Efforts to enslave the Indians caused violent reprisals. Hurricanes destroyed crops and homes. French, Dutch, and English freebooters burned the towns. Puerto Rico remained a Spanish possession until 1898, when it was ceded to the United States following the Spanish-American War.

When the Spanish first colonized Puerto Rico, native populations were operating on a barter system of exchange. Spanish coinage was introduced and eventually accepted for exchange. As mints developed in the Americas, their coins, first cobs and later milled coins, were also circulated in Puerto Rico. This mix of Spanish and Spanish Colonial coins served Puerto Rico for several centuries, though copper and bronze coins were easier to keep in circulation, while silver and gold tended to be taken away by traders. Paper money was also used in Puerto Rico from the mid 18th century on, though counterfeiting lead to the devaluation of many of these banknotes. Economic conditions were in great disarray by the early part of the 19th century. All sorts of currency and coinage were in circulation with counterfeits diluting the money supply. Cob coins, Spanish coins, cut and countermarked coins of the various West Indies, along with several issues of bank notes were all in circulation, leading to confusion and lack of fluid acceptance.

In 1895 the first coinage specifically struck for the Island of Puerto Rico was produced by Spain. Additional denominations were struck in 1896 completing Puerto Rico's only official coinage series. These coins brought some semblance of order to the daily economic transactions on the island and remained in use until Puerto Rico was taken over by the United States in 1898. Redemption of all peso denominated coins took place from July 1900 until March 1901 at the rate of 60 U.S. cents to the peso.

RULER	ASSAYERS' INITIALS	MONETARY SYSTEM
Spanish, until 1898	G - Antonio Garcia Gonzalez	100 Centavos = 1 Peso
	P - Felix Miguel Peiro Rodrigo	

DECIMAL COINAGE

KM# 20 5 CENTAVOS
1.2500 g., 0.9000 Silver 0.0362 oz. ASW **Ruler:**
Alfonso XIII **Obv:** Value, date **Rev:** Crowned arms, pillars

Date	Mintage	F	VF	XF	Unc	BU
1896 PGV	600,000	30.00	50.00	90.00	225	—

KM# 21 10 CENTAVOS
2.5000 g., 0.9000 Silver 0.0723 oz. ASW **Ruler:**
Alfonso XIII **Obv:** Young head left **Rev:** Crowned arms, pillars

Date	Mintage	F	VF	XF	Unc	BU
1896 PGV	700,000	35.00	70.00	150	375	—

KM# 22 20 CENTAVOS
5.0000 g., 0.9000 Silver 0.1447 oz. ASW **Ruler:**
Alfonso XIII **Obv:** Young head left **Rev:** Crowned arms, pillars

Date	Mintage	F	VF	XF	Unc	BU
1895 PGV	3,350,000	45.00	80.00	165	400	—

KM# 23 40 CENTAVOS
10.0000 g., 0.9000 Silver 0.2893 oz. ASW **Ruler:**
Alfonso XIII **Obv:** Young head left **Rev:** Crowned arms, pillars

Date	Mintage	F	VF	XF	Unc	BU
1896 PGV	725,000	250	350	850	2,850	—

KM# 24 PESO
25.0000 g., 0.9000 Silver 0.7234 oz. ASW **Ruler:**
Alfonso XIII **Obv:** Young head left **Rev:** Crowned arms, pillars

Date	Mintage	F	VF	XF	Unc	BU
1895 PGV	8,500,000	300	450	900	2,500	3,250

Glossary

Adjustment marks: Marks made by use of a file to correct the weight of overweight coinage planchets prior to striking. Adjusting the weight of planchets was a common practice at the first U.S. Mint in Philadelphia and was often carried out by women hired to weigh planchets and do any necessary filing of the metal.

Altered coin: A coin that has been changed after it left the mint. Such changes are often to the date or mintmark of a common coin in an attempt to increase its value by passing to an unsuspecting buyer as a rare date or mint.

Alloy: A metal or mixture of metals added to the primary metal in the coinage composition, often as a means of facilitating hardness during striking. For example, most U.S. silver coins contain an alloy of 10 percent copper.

Anneal: To heat in order to soften. In the minting process planchets are annealed prior to striking.

Authentication: The act of determining whether a coin, medal, token or other related item is a genuine product of the issuing authority.

Bag marks: Scrapes and impairments to a coin's surface obtained after minting by contact with other coins. The term originates from the storage of coins in bags, but such marks can occur as coins leave the presses and enter hoppers. A larger coin is more susceptible to marks, which affect its grade and, therefore, its value.

Base metal: A metal with low intrinsic value.

Beading: A form of design around the edge of a coin. Beading once served a functional purpose of deterring clipping or shaving parts of the metal by those looking to make a profit and then return the debased coin to circulation.

Blank: Often used in reference to the coinage planchet or disc of metal from which the actual coin is struck. Planchets or blanks are punched out of a sheet of metal by what is known as a blanking press.

Business strike: A coin produced for circulation.

Cast copy: A copy of a coin or medal made by a casting process in which molds are used to produce the finished product. Casting imparts a different surface texture to the finished product than striking and often leaves traces of a seam where the molds came together.

Center dot: A raised dot at the center of a coin caused by use of a compass to aid the engraver in the circular positioning of die devices, such as stars, letters, and dates. Center dots are prevalent on early U.S. coinage.

Chop mark: A mark used by Oriental merchants as a means of guaranteeing the silver content of coins paid out. The merchants' chop marks, or stamped insignia, often obliterated the original design of the host coin. U.S. Trade dollars, struck from 1873 through 1878 and intended for use in trade with China, are sometimes found bearing multiple marks.

Clash marks: Marks impressed in the coinage dies when they come together without a planchet between them. Such marks will affect coins struck subsequently by causing portions of the obverse design to appear in raised form on the reverse, and vice versa.

Clipping: The practice of shaving or cutting small pieces of metal from a coin in circulation. Clipping was prevalent in Colonial times as a means of surreptitiously extracting precious metal from a coin before placing it back into circulation. The introduction of beading and a raised border helped to alleviate the problem.

Coin alignment: U.S. coins are normally struck with an alignment by which, when a coin is held by the top and bottom edge and rotated from side-to-side, the reverse will appear upside down.

Collar: A ring-shaped die between which the obverse and reverse coinage dies are held during striking. The collar contains the outward flow during striking and can be used to produce edge reeding.

Commemorative: A coin issued to honor a special event or person. United States commemorative coins have historically been produced for sale to collectors and not placed in circulation, though the 50-states quarters are circulating commemoratives.

Copy: A replica of an original issue. Copies often vary in quality and metallic composition from the original. Since passage of the Hobby Protection Act (Public Law 93-167) of Nov. 29, 1973, it has been illegal to produce or import copies of coins or other numismatic items that are not clearly and permanently marked with the word "Copy."

Counterfeit: A coin or medal or other numismatic item made fraudulently, either for entry into circulation or sale to collectors.

Denticles: The toothlike pattern found around a coin's obverse or reverse border.

Die: A cylindrical piece of metal containing an incuse image that imparts a raised image when stamped into a planchet.

Die crack: A crack that develops in a coinage die after extensive usage, or if the die is defective or is used to strike harder metals. Die cracks, which often run through border lettering, appear as raised lines on the finished coin.

Device: The principal design element.

Double eagle: Name adopted by the Act of March 3, 1849, for the gold coin valued at 20 units or $20.

Eagle: Name adopted by the Coinage Act of 1792 for a gold coin valued at 10 units or $10. Also a name used to refer to gold, silver, and platinum coins of the American Eagle bullion coinage program begun in 1986.

Edge: The cylindrical surface of a coin between the two sides. The edge can be plain, reeded, ornamented, or lettered.

Electrotype: A copy of a coin, medal, or token made by electroplating.

Exergue: The lower segment of a coin, below the main design, generally separated by a line and often containing the date, designer initials, and mintmark.

Face value: The nominal legal-tender value assigned to a given coin by the governing authority.

Fasces: A Roman symbol of authority consisting of a bound bundle of rods and an axe.

Field: The flat area of a coin's obverse or reverse, devoid of devices or inscriptions.

Galvano: A reproduction of a proposed design from an artist's original model produced in plaster or other substance and then electroplated with metal. The galvano is then used in a reducing lathe to make a die or hub.

Glory: A heraldic term for stars, rays or other devices placed as if in the sky or luminous.

Grading: The largely subjective practice of providing a numerical or adjectival ranking of the condition of a coin, token, or medal. The grade is often a major determinant of value.

Gresham's law: The name for the observation made by Sir Thomas Gresham, 16th century English financier, that when two coins with the same face value but different intrinsic values are in circulation at the same time, the one with the lesser intrinsic value will remain in circulation while the other is hoarded.

Half eagle: Name adopted by the Coinage Act of 1792 for a gold coin valued at five units or $5.

Hub: A piece of die steel showing the coinage devices in relief. The hub is used to produce a die that, in contrast, has the relief details incuse. The die is then used to produce the final coin, which looks much the same as the hub. Hubs may be reused to make new dies.

Legend: A coin' principal lettering, generally shown along its outer perimeter.

Lettered edge: Incuse or raised lettering on a coin's edge.

Matte proof: A proof coin on which the surface is granular or dull. On U.S. coins this type of surface was used on proofs of the early 20th century. The process has since been abandoned.

Magician's coin: A term sometimes used to describe a coin with two heads or two tails. Such a coin is considered impossible in normal production due to physical differences in obverse and reverse die mountings, though as of 2001 two have been certified as genuine by professional coin authenticators. The vast majority are products made outside the Mint as novelty pieces.

Medal: Made to commemorate an event or person. Medals differ from coins in that a medal is not legal tender and, in general, is not produced with the intent of circulating as money.

Medal alignment: Medals are generally struck with the coinage dies facing the same direction during striking. When held by the top and bottom edge and rotated from side-to-side, a piece struck in this manner will show both the obverse and reverse right side up.

Mintage: The total number of coins struck during a given time frame, generally one year.

Mintmark: A letter or other marking on a coin's surface to identify the mint at which the coin was struck.

Mule: The combination of two coinage dies not intended for use together.

Numismatics: The science, study or collecting of coins, tokens, medals, paper money, and related items.

Obverse: The front or "heads" side of a coin, medal, or token.

Overdate: Variety produced when one or more digits of the date are re-engraved over an old date on a die at the Mint, generally to save on dies or correct an error. Portions of the old date can still be seen under the new one.

Overmintmark: Variety created at the Mint when a different mintmark is punched over an already existing mintmark, generally done to make a coinage die already punched for one mint usable at another. Portions of the old mintmark can still be seen under the new one.

Overstrike: A coin, token or medal struck over another coin, token, or medal.

Pattern: A trial strike of a proposed coin design, issued by the Mint or authorized agent of a governing authority. Patterns can be in a variety of metals, thicknesses, and sizes.

Phrygian cap: A close-fitting, egg-shell-shaped hat placed on the head of a freed slave when Rome was in its ascendancy. Hung from a pole, it was a popular symbol of freedom during the French Revolution and in 18th century United States.

Planchet: A disc of metal or other material on which the image of the dies are impressed, resulting in a finished coin. Also sometimes called a blank.

Proof: A coin struck twice or more from specially polished dies and polished planchets. Modern proofs are prepared with a mirror finish. Early 20th century proofs were prepared with a matte surface.

Prooflike: A prooflike coin exhibits some of the characteristics of a proof despite having been struck by regular production processes. Many Morgan dollars are found with prooflike surfaces. The field will have a mirror background similar to that of a proof, and design details are frosted like some proofs.

Quarter eagle: Name adopted by the Coinage Act of 1792 for a gold coin valued at 2.5 units or $2.50.

Reeding: Serrated (toothlike) ornamentation applied to the coin's edge during striking.

Relief: The portion of a design raised above the surface of a coin, medal, or token.

Restrike: A coin, medal or token produced from original dies at a later date, often with the purpose of sale to collectors.

Reverse: The backside or "tails" side of a coin, medal or token, opposite from the principal figure of the design or obverse.

Rim: The raised area bordering the edge and surrounding the field.

Series: The complete group of coins of the same denomination and design and representing all issuing mints.

Token: A privately issued piece, generally in metal, with a represented value in trade or offer of service. Tokens are also produced for advertising purposes.

Type coin: A coin from a given series representing the basic design. A type coin is collected as an example of a particular design rather than for its date and mintmark.

Variety: Any coin noticeably different in dies from another of the same design, date and mint. Overdate and overmintmarks are examples of varieties.

Wire edge: Created when coinage metal flows between the coinage die and collar, producing a thin flange of coin metal at the outside edge or edges of a coin.

1 Dollar 251

1/2 Dollar 238

1/24 Real 206

1/4 Dollar 236

10 Dollars 143, 183, 244

100 Dollars 190

100 (Bit). 231

1000 (Mark) 231

1984 Los Angeles Olympics . . . . . .
. . . . 166, 183

1988 Olympics 167, 181

1992 Olympics 163, 168, 181

1994 World Cup Soccer . . . .
. . . . 164, 170, 181

1996 Atlanta Olympics . . . .
. . . . 164, 171, 181

1996 Atlanta Paralympics . . . .
. . . . 172, 173

2 Cents .67

2 Pence. 203, 210

20 Cents. 89

20 Dollars 183, 244

25 Dollars 185

2002 Winter Olympics . . 177, 182

2-1/2 Dollars 133, 161, 255

3 Dollars 136

3 Pence 203, 221, 224

4 Pence (Groat) 203

5 Cents 72

5 Dollars. 137, 180, 192, 244

5 Units. 231

50 Dollars 190, 246

50 State Quarters 99

500 (Quint) 231

6 Pence 203, 221

A

Alabama Centennial. 154

Alabama Quarter 102

Alaska Quarter 106

Albany Church "Penny". 220

Albany, N.Y., Charter
Anniversary 157

American Bald Eagle. 165, 180, 183

American Eagle Bullion Coins. 184

American Indian. 176

American Plantations. 206

American Samoa Quarter. 107

Andrew Jackson Dollar 130

Arizona Quarter 106

INDEX

Arkansas Centennial 157

Arkansas Quarter. 102

Auctori Plebis 220

August Bechtler 258

Augustus Humbert / United States
Assayer 246

B

Baldwin & Company. 244

Bar "Cent" 220

Barber Dime 84

Barber Half Dollar. 115

Barber Quarter. 93

Battle of Antietam 75th
Anniversary. 159

Battle of Gettysburg 75th
Anniversary. 158

Benjamin Franklin, 300th Birth
Anniversary. 178,

Bison Bullion Coinage 192

Black Revolutionary War
Patriots 175

Blake & Company 245

Booker T. Washington 160

Booker T. Washington and George
Washington Carver 160

Braided Hair Cent 61

Braided Hair Half Cent 57

Brasher Gold. 232

Bridgeport, Conn.,
Centennial. 158

Buffalo Nickel. 74

Bust Half Dollar 110

C

California Diamond Jubilee . . 155

California Gold 235, 243

California Quarter 104

Capitol Visitor Center . . . 176, 182

Capped Bust 109

Castorland "Half Dollar". 221

Cent. 58, 215, 224, 227, 233

Central High School
Desegregation 179

Chalmers. 221

Christopher Bechtler 257, 259

Cincinnati Mining and Trading
Company. 245

Cincinnati Music Center 158

Civil War 165, 172, 182

Clark, Gruber & Company 255

Classic Head 133, 139

Classic Head Half Cent 57

Cleveland-Great Lakes
Exposition. 158

Colorado Gold. 255

Colorada Quarter 104

Columbia, S.C.,
Sesquicentennial. 158

Columbian Exposition 153

Columbus Discovery -
500th Anniversary164, 168, 181

Commemorative Coinage. 153

Confederatio 229

Congress Bicentennial. . . . .
. . . . 163, 167, 181

Connecticut Quarter 99

Connecticut Tercentenary 157

Constitution Bicentennial. . . . . . .
. . . . 166, 180

Continental "Dollar". 211

Copper Company of Upper
Canada 222

Coronet Cent 60

Coronet Head 134, 139, 143

D

Daniel Boone Bicentennial . . . 156

DC and Territories Quarter . . . 107

Delaware Quarter 99

Delaware Tercentenary. 158

Dime 79

Disme 234

District of Columbia Quarter . 107

Dollar . . . .
. .120, 160, 166, 186, 241, 242,
258, 259

Dolley Madison 175

Draped Bust Cent 59

Draped Bust Dime 79, 80

Draped Bust Dollar. 120, 121

Draped Bust Half Cent. 56

Draped Bust Half Dime 69

Draped Bust Half Dollar 108

Draped Bust Quarter 89

Dubosq & Company 245

E

Early American Patterns 229
Early American Tokens . . .206, 220
Early Federal Coinage 232
Eisenhower Centennial. 167
Eisenhower Dollar. 128
Elephant. 206
Elgin, Ill., Centennial 158

F

Farthing 205, 207, 208
First Flight Centennial . . . .
. . . . 165, 177, 183
First Spouse Gold Coinage 192
Florida Quarter 103
Flowing Hair Cent. 58
Flowing Hair Dollar 120
Flowing Hair Half Dime. 69
Flowing Hair Half Dollar 108
Flying Eagle Cent. 61
Fort Vancouver Centennial. . . .155
Franklin Delano Roosevelt 182

Franklin Half Dollar 117
Franklin Press. 222
Fugio "Cent". 232

G

George Washington 129
George Washington Death
  Bicentennial. 182
George Washington, 250th Birth
  Anniversary 163
Georgia Gold 257
Georgia Quarter 99
Gloucester. 207
Gobrecht Dollar. 122
Grant Memorial 154, 161
Guam Quarter 107

H

Half Cent 56, 215
Half Dime. 69
Half Disme 234
Half Dollar 108, 153, 163, 228
Half Eagle 250

Halfpenny 205, 214, 222, 226

Hawaii Quarter 106

Hawaiian Sesquicentennial . . . 156

Hibernia 208

Hibernia-Voce Populi 207

Higley or Granby 207

Hudson, N.Y.,
   Sesquicentennial 157

Huguenot-Walloon
   Tercentenary 155

I

Idaho Quarter 105

Illinois Centennial-Lincoln 153

Illinois Quarter 102

Immune Columbia 229

Indian Head Dollar 136

Indian Head 142, 146

Indian Head Cent 61, 62

Indiana Quarter 101

Iowa Quarter 103

Iowa Statehood Centennial . . . 160

Issues of 1792 233

J

J. H. Bowie 245

J. J. Conway 256

J. S. Ormsby 251

Jackie Robinson 174, 182

James Madison Dollar 130

James Madison -
   Bill of Rights 164, 169, 181

James Monroe 130

Jamestown - 400th
   Anniversary 179, 183

Jefferson - Westward Expansion -
   Lewis & Clark Bicentennial
   Nickel 78, 79

Jefferson large facing portrait -
   Enhanced Monticello
   Reverse Nickel 79

Jefferson Nickel 75, 76

John Adams Dollar 130

John Marshall, 250th Birth
   Anniversary 178

John Parsons 257

John Quincy Adams Dollar . . . 130

K

Kansas Quarter 104

Kellogg & Company 248

Kennedy Half Dollar 118-120

Kentucky Quarter 100

Kentucky Token 222

Korean War - 38th
    Anniversary 167

L

La Fayette Dollar 160

Leif Ericson Dollar 176

Lewis and Clark Corps of
    Discovery Bicentennial 177

Lewis and Clark Exposition . . . 161

Lexington-Concord
    Sesquicentennial 155

Liberty 148, 149

Liberty Cap . . . 133, 137, 142, 143

Liberty Cap Cent 58, 59

Liberty Cap Dime 80

Liberty Cap Half Cent 56

Liberty Cap Half Dime 70

Liberty Cap Quarter 90

Liberty Head 147

Liberty Head - Type 1 131

Liberty Nickel 73

Library of Congress 176, 183

Lincoln Bicentennial 67, 180

Lincoln Cent 63

Long Island Tercentenary 158

Lord Baltimore 203

Louis Braille Birth
    Bicentennial 180

Louisiana Purchase
    Exposition 161

Louisiana Quarter 101

Lynchburg, Va.,
    Sesquicentennial 159

M

Machin's Mill 218

Maine Centennial 153

Maine Quarter 102

Martin van Buren Dollar 131

Maryland Quarter 99, 203

Maryland Tercentenary 156

INDEX

Massachusettes and California
    Company 249
Massachusetts Quarter 100
McKinley Memorial. 161
Mercury Dime 85
Michigan Quarter 103
Miners Bank. 249
Minnesota Quarter 104
Mississippi Quarter 101
Missouri Centennial 154
Missouri Quarter 103
Moffat & Company 249
Monroe Doctrine Centennial . .155
Montana Quarter. 105
Morgan Dollar. 125
Mormon Issues 261
Mott Token 222
Mount Rushmore 50th
    Anniversary. 163, 168, 181
Myddelton Token 223

National Prisoner of War
    Museum 170
Nebraska Quarter 105
Nevada Quarter 105
New England 203
New Hampshire Quarter 100
New Jersey Quarter. 99
New Mexico Quarter 107
New Rochelle, N.Y.. 160
New York Quarter. 100
New York Theatre. 223
New Yorke. 208
Nickel 3 Cents. 69
Norfolk, Va., Bicentennial 159
Norris, Greig, & Norris. 250
North American 223
North Carolina Quarter 101
North Dakota Quarter 105
Northern Mariana Islands
    Quarter 107
Nova Constellatio. 230

N

O

National Community Service . .173
National Law Enforcement
    Officers Memorial 174

Oak Tree 203
Ohio Quarter 102

INDEX

Oklahoma Quarter 107
Old Spanish Trail 157
Oregon Exchange Company. . .260
Oregon Quarter. 104
Oregon Trail Memorial. 155

P

Pacific Company. 251
Panama-Pacific Exposition . . . .
. . . . .153, 161
Panama-Pacific Exposition
   Octagonal 162
Panama-Pacific Exposition
   Round 162
Peace Dollar. 127
Pennsylvania Quarter 99
Penny. 209, 214
Penny (Denarium) 203
Pilgrim Tercentenary. 153, 154
Pine Tree 204
Pitt 208
President Dollars. 129
Puerto Rico Quarter 107

Q

Quarter 89, 153, 234

R

Revolutionary Coinage . . 211, 212
Rhode Island Quarter 101
Rhode Island Ship 223
Rhode Island Tercentenary . . . 159
Roanoke Island, N.C.. 159
Robert F. Kennedy 175
Roosevelt Dime 87, 88
Rosa Americana 209
Royal Patent Coinage. 208

S

Sacagawea Dollar. 129
Saint-Gaudens 151
San Diego-Pacific International
   Exposition 157
San Francisco Mint
   Museum. 179, 183

INDEX

San Francisco-Oakland Bay
    Bridge 159

Schultz & Company 252

Seated Liberty Dime 81

Seated Liberty Dollar. 123

Seated Liberty Half Dime 70

Seated Liberty Half Dollar 111

Seated Liberty Quarter 90

Shield Nickel 72

Shilling. 203

Silver 3 Cents. 68

Smithsonian Institution 150th
    Anniversary. 174, 182

South Carolina Quarter 100

South Dakota Quarter. 105

Special Olympics World
    Games 172

St. Patrick or Mark Newby 205

Standing Liberty Quarter 95

Standish Barry 224

State Coinage. 212, 220

Statue of Liberty Centennial . . . . . .
    . . . . 163, 166, 180

Stone Mountain Memorial 155

Susan B. Anthony Dollar 129

T

Talbot, Allum & Lee 224

Templeton Reid 252, 258

Tennessee Quarter 102

Texas Centennial 156

Texas Quarter 103

Thomas A. Edison - Electric Light
    125th Anniversary 178

Thomas Jefferson Dollar 130

Thomas Jefferson 250th Birth
    Anniversary 169

Trade Dollar 124

Turban Head. 133, 138

U

U. S. Capitol Visitor Center . . . 165

U.S. Botanic Gardens 175th
    Anniversary 174

U.S. Capitol Bicentennial. 170

U.S. Marine Corps, 230th
    Anniversary 178

U.S. Military Academy at West
    Point -Bicentennial 177

U.S. Sesquicentennial 156, 161

United States Assay Office of
Gold 252

US Virgin Islands Quarter. 107

USO 50th Anniversary 168

Utah Gold 261

Utah Quarter 106

V

Vermont Quarter. 101

Vermont Sesquicentennial 156

Vietnam Veterans Memorial. . .170

Virginia Halfpenny 211

Virginia Quarter. 100

W

Walking Liberty Half Dollar . . .116

Washington Pieces 224

Washington Quarter 96, 106

Wass, Molitor & Company 253

West Virginia Quarter 104

White House Bicentennial 169

Willow Tree 205

Wisconsin Quarter. 103

Wisconsin Territorial
Centennial. 159

Women in Military Service
Memorial. 171

World War II 50th
Anniversary 164, 169, 181

Wyoming Quarter 106

Y

Yellowstone Quarter 175

York County, Maine,
Tercentenary 159

New in 2010

A new cent design will be the highlight of 2010. A shield symbolizing Abraham Lincoln's preservation of the unity of the United States will be placed on the reverse of the cent, replacing the Lincoln Memorial as the standard reverse design. The obverse will continue to feature Victor David Brenner's portrait of Lincoln.

Five dollar coins will be struck for circulation.

The 2010 Native American dollar will feature five arrows bound together and a Hiawatha Belt on the reverse. The arrows symbolize the five nations of the Iroquois Confederacy, also known as Haudenosaunee. The obverse will be the Sacagawea portrait used since 2000.

2010 Cent reverse

Four 2010 Presidential dollars will be struck. They are Millard Fillmore, Franklin Pierce, James Buchanan and Abraham Lincoln. The reverse common to all four is the Statue of Liberty design used since this series started in 2007.

There will be two .900 fine commemorative silver dollars produced in 2010. One honors disabled veterans. The other marks the centennial of the founding of the Boy Scouts of America.

Also in 2010 will be five new quarters designs to commence the America the Beautiful series honoring National Parks and other sites in the 50 states and six territories. They will be produced at a rate of five per year as was the case with the state quarters.

The first five will be for Arkansas, Wyoming, California, Arizona and Oregon.

2010 Disabled Veteran Commemorative Silver Dollar

2010 Presidential Dollars

2010 Disabled Veteran
Commemorative Silver Dollar

2010 Native American Dollar

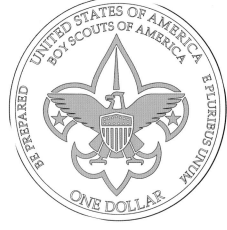

2010 Boy Scouts of America Commemorative Silver Dollar

2010 Presidential Dollars

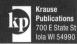